The Role of Aı
in China's Moᴄ

In the waning years of the Cold War, the United States and China began to cautiously engage in cultural, educational, and policy exchanges, which in turn strengthened new security and economic ties. These links have helped shape the most important bilateral relationship in the late twentieth and early twenty-first centuries.

This book explores the dynamics of cultural exchange through an in-depth historical investigation of three organizations at the forefront of US–China non-governmental relations: the Hopkins-Nanjing Center for Chinese and American Studies, the National Committee on United States–China Relations, and The 1990 Institute. Norton Wheeler reveals the impact of American non-governmental organizations (NGOs) on education, environment, fiscal policy, and civil society in contemporary China. In turn, this book illuminates the important role that NGOs play in complementing formal diplomacy and presents a model of society-to-society relations that moves beyond old debates over cultural imperialism. Finally, the book illuminates the increasingly significant role of Chinese Americans as bridges between the two societies.

Based on extensive archival research and interviews with leading American and Chinese figures, this book will be of interest to students and scholars of Chinese politics and history, international relations, and transnational NGOs.

Norton Wheeler is Assistant Professor of US and Asian History in the Social Science Department at Missouri Southern State University, USA.

Asia's Transformations
Edited by Mark Selden,
Cornell University, USA

The books in this series explore the political, social, economic and cultural consequences of Asia's transformations in the twentieth and twenty-first centuries. The series emphasizes the tumultuous interplay of local, national, regional and global forces as Asia bids to become the hub of the world economy. While focusing on the contemporary, it also looks back to analyse the antecedents of Asia's contested rise.

This series comprises several strands:

Asia's Transformations

Titles include:

Asia's Great Cities

Each volume aims to capture the heartbeat of the contemporary city from multiple perspectives emblematic of the authors own deep familiarity with the distinctive faces of the city, its history, society, culture, politics and economics, and its evolving position in national, regional and global frameworks. While most volumes emphasize urban developments since the Second World War, some pay close attention to the legacy of the longue durée in shaping the contemporary. Thematic and comparative volumes address such themes as urbanization, economic and financial linkages, architecture and space, wealth and power, gendered relationships, planning and anarchy, and ethnographies in national and regional perspective. Titles include:

Asia.com is a series which focuses on the ways in which new information and communication technologies are influencing politics, society and culture in Asia. Titles include:

Literature and Society

Literature and Society is a series that seeks to demonstrate the ways in which Asian Literature is influenced by the politics, society and culture in which it is produced. Titles include:

1. **The Body in Postwar Japanese Fiction**
   Douglas N. Slaymaker

2. **Chinese Women Writers and the Feminist Imagination, 1905–1948***
   Haiping Yan

Routledge Studies in Asia's Transformations

Routledge Studies in Asia's Transformations is a forum for innovative new research intended for a high-level specialist readership. Titles include:

1. **The American Occupation of Japan and Okinawa***
   Literature and memory
   Michael Molasky

2. **Koreans in Japan***
   Critical voices from the margin
   Edited by Sonia Ryang

3. **Internationalizing the Pacific**
   The United States, Japan and the Institute of Pacific Relations in war and peace, 1919–1945
   Tomoko Akami

4. **Imperialism in South East Asia***
   'A fleeting, passing phase'
   Nicholas Tarling

5. **Chinese Media, Global Contexts***
   Edited by Chin-Chuan Lee

6. **Remaking Citizenship in Hong Kong***
   Community, nation and the global city
   Edited by Agnes S. Ku and Ngai Pun

7. **Japanese Industrial Governance**
   Protectionism and the licensing state
   Yul Sohn

8. **Developmental Dilemmas***
   Land reform and institutional change in China
   Edited by Peter Ho

9. **Genders, Transgenders and Sexualities in Japan***
   Edited by Mark McLelland and Romit Dasgupta

10. **Fertility, Family Planning and Population Policy in China***
    Edited by Dudley L. Poston, Che-Fu Lee, Chiung-Fang Chang, Sherry L. McKibben and Carol S. Walther

11. **Japanese Diasporas***
    Unsung pasts, conflicting presents and uncertain futures
    Edited by Nobuko Adachi

Critical Asian Scholarship

Critical Asian Scholarship is a series intended to showcase the most important individual contributions to scholarship in Asian Studies. Each of the volumes presents a leading Asian scholar addressing themes that are central to his or her most significant and lasting contribution to Asian studies. The series is committed to the rich variety of research and writing on Asia, and is not restricted to any particular discipline, theoretical approach or geographical expertise.

* Available in paperback

The Role of American NGOs in China's Modernization

Invited influence

Norton Wheeler

To Travis v Karen

Love,
Dad / Norty
August 2015

Routledge
Taylor & Francis Group

LONDON AND NEW YORK

First published 2013
by Routledge
2 Park Square, Milton Park, Abingdon, Oxon OX14 4RN

Simultaneously published in the USA and Canada
by Routledge
711 Third Avenue, New York, NY 10017

Routledge is an imprint of the Taylor & Francis Group, an informa business

First issued in paperback 2014

British Library Cataloguing in Publication Data
A catalogue record for this book is available from the British Library

Library of Congress Cataloging in Publication Data

The role of American NGOs in China's modernization; invited influence / Norton Wheeler.

p. cm. —(Asia's transformations; 38)

Includes bibliographical references and index.

1. Non-governmental organizations–Influence–Case studies. 2. Non-governmental
organizations–United States–Case studies. 3. Non-governmental organizations–China–Case
studies. 4. Cultural relations–Case studies. 5. China–Civilization–American influences.
6. China–Relations–United States. 7. United States–Relations–China, 8. Hopkins-Nanjing
Center. 9. National Committee on United States–China Relations. 10. 1990 Institute
(South San Francisco, Calif.) I. Title.

JZ4841.W54 2012

068'.51–dc23   2012007951

ISBN: 978-0-415-50657-1 (hbk)
ISBN: 978-1-138-02275-1 (pbk)
ISBN: 978-0-203-10001-1 (ebk)

Typeset in Times New Roman
by Cenveo Publisher Services

Dedicated to Morey Wheeler, who introduced me to East Asia at an early age.

.

Contents

Preface

This book began at the fortuitous intersection of a China-oriented business career and belated entry into graduate school. In the 1990s, I made several trips to China on business, and in late 2003, my employer sent me to Nantong, Jiangsu with a three-year mission to establish a factory. During the same period, I enrolled in the American Studies doctoral program at the University of Kansas. My master's thesis explored the motivations and achievements of the Americans, mostly Chinese Americans, who had established The 1990 Institute as a policy research organization that could assist China's modernization. Building on this initial research, my doctoral dissertation looked, additionally, at the Hopkins-Nanjing Center for Chinese and American Studies and the National Committee on United States–China Relations. The dissertation took a broader view, exploring how various Chinese actors viewed and responded to the initiatives of US-based NGOs. Over several more years, I continued my research and expanded discussion of the broader implications of my research for understanding contemporary China, the United States in the world, and transnational relations.

A special challenge of my research was gaining access to the files and principal participants of the three organizations that constituted my case studies. Only the Hopkins-Nanjing Center had formally archived documents at a research library, and only for its first decade. I extend special thanks to John Holden (former president) and Jan Berris (long-time vice-president) of the National Committee, Kathryn Mohrman (former executive director) of the Hopkins-Nanjing Center's Washington Office, and the executive committee of The 1990 Institute for opening the doors of their organizations to me. I am indebted to the dozens of Americans and Chinese who candidly talked with me, providing many of the details that comprise the following narrative. James Stimpert, university archivist at the Johns Hopkins University Sheridan Libraries, was extremely helpful in providing access to the Hopkins-Nanjing archives at the Milton S. Eisenhower Library.

Another research challenge was linguistic. My Chinese was socially but not academically competent. Faced with a choice between delaying research (to focus on language study) and using translators and interpreters, I opted for the latter. I have written elsewhere about some of the interesting byways down which this choice led me.[1]

There is one further point related to my interviews. I follow a common practice of not naming Chinese interviewees who are not otherwise readily identifiable. The reason is to shield these individuals from trouble, should the future political climate become more restrictive than it is as this book is being published.

I am deeply grateful to the following individuals who read and critically commented on the manuscript at various stages – tirelessly and repeatedly in several cases: Robert Antonio, Jan Berris, Steve Cohn, Carla Freeman, J. Megan Greene, Charles Hayford, Jan Kiely, Rosalyn Koo, Richard Schneirov, Mark Selden, Martin Sklar, C. B. Sung, Carolyn Townsley, Terry Wheeler (to whom I am grateful, additionally, for cheerfully enduring my long preoccupation with this project), Theodore Wilson, Norman Yetman, and Xiao-huang Yin. I also thank two anonymous reviewers for helpful suggestions at a late stage. Members of the editorial staff at Routledge – Stephanie Rogers, Leanne Hinves, Ed Needle, and Hannah Mack – flawlessly ushered the book through the publication process. Finally, I thank James Kaplan, Sr, and James Kaplan, Jr, my former employers at Harlan Global Manufacturing, for patiently accommodating my research schedule.

Much of Chapter 1 and passages from Chapter 6 were previously published as 'Educational Exchange in Post-Mao U.S.–China Relations: The Hopkins-Nanjing Center,' *Journal of American–East Asian Relations*, 17: 1 (2010), pp. 56–88. I thank Koninklijke Brill NV for granting permission to republish that material.

Acronyms and abbreviations

ACWF	All-China Women's Federation
ACYF	All-China Youth Federation
ADB	Asian Development Bank
ASHA	American Schools and Hospitals Abroad
BA	Bachelor of Arts
BS	Bachelor of Science
CASS	Chinese Academy of Social Sciences
CCTF	China Children and Teenagers' Fund
CDB	China Development Brief
CECC	Congressional-Executive Commission on China
CEIBS	China Europe International Business School
CEO	chief executive officer
CFO	chief financial officer
CIDE	Center for International Development and Education
CIETC	China International and Economic Trade Arbitration Commission
CNCC	China National Children's Center
CPIFA	Chinese People's Institute of Foreign Affairs
CRF	China Reform Forum
CSCPRC	Committee on Scholarly Communication with the People's Republic of China
CYDF	China Youth Development Foundation
DOE	Department of Education
EPA	Environmental Protection Agency
EPB	Environmental Protection Bureau
ESD	Ecologically Sustainable Development
FPC	Foreign Policy Colloquium
FRBSF	Federal Reserve Bank of San Francisco
GDP	gross domestic product
GEF	Global Environmental Facility
GIS	geographic information system
GONGO	government-organized non-governmental organization
HNC	Hopkins-Nanjing Center for Chinese and American Studies
HUD	Department of Housing and Urban Development

ICF	International Crane Foundation
ICWA	Institute of Current World Affairs
IECLG	Innovations and Excellence in Chinese Local Government
IMF	International Monetary Fund
ISC	Institute for Sustainable Communities
JD	Juris Doctor
JHU	Johns Hopkins University
LCS	Loving Care Supermarket
MA	Master of Arts
MBA	Master of Business Administration
MIT	Massachusetts Institute of Technology
MOCA	Ministry of Civil Affairs
NATO	North Atlantic Treaty Organization
NENU	Northeast Normal University
NGO	non-governmental organization
NPO	non-profit organization
NYU	New York University
OECD	Organization for Economic Cooperation and Development
OYCF	Overseas Young Chinese Forum
PDP	Preventative Defense Project
PhD	Doctor of Philosophy
PIP	Public Intellectuals Program
PRC	People's Republic of China
PUMC	Peking Union Medical College
RBF	Rockefeller Brothers Fund
SAIS	School of Advanced International Studies
SARS	severe acute respiratory syndrome
SASS	Shanghai Academy of Social Sciences
SAT	State Administration of Taxation
SEPA	State Environmental Protection Administration
SLE	Student Leaders Exchange
SOP	Scholar Orientation Program
SUSTC	South University of Science and Technology of China
UCLA	University of California-Los Angeles
UNDP	United Nations Development Programme
USAID	United States Agency for International Development
USIA	United States Information Agency
USTTA	United States Table Tennis Association
VAT	value-added tax
WRSA	Western Returned Scholars Association
WTO	World Trade Organization
YLF	Young Leaders Forum

Figures

Picture credits

5.1 "NOT ONE LESS" © 1999 Columbia Pictures Film Production Asia Limited. All rights reserved. Courtesy of Columbia Pictures. Used with permission.

5.2 *The Story of Xiaoyan*. Used with permission of Shandong Film & TV Production Center.

5.3 *The Story of Xiaoyan*. Used with permission of Shandong Film & TV Production Center.

5.4 "Portraits of the West," CCTV-7 newscast, 12 June 2002.

5.5 "Portraits of the West," CCTV-7 newscast, 12 June 2002.

5.6 *The Story of Xiaoyan*. Used with permission of Shandong Film & TV Production Center.

5.7 "Portraits of the West," CCTV-7 newscast, 12 June 2002.

5.8 "Spring Bud Project," produced for The 1990 Institute by AFEWS & ViewAround, Inc.

5.9 "NOT ONE LESS" © 1999 Columbia Pictures Film Production Asia Limited. All rights reserved. Courtesy of Columbia Pictures. Used with permission.

5.10 *The Story of Xiaoyan*. Used with permission of Shandong Film & TV Production Center.

Introduction

The Role of American NGOs in China's Modernization brings out of the shadows an important group of actors in contemporary US–China relations: non-governmental organizations. Who are the individuals and organizations engaged in non-governmental (a.k.a. transnational) relations between the United States and China? What are their motivations? What have they accomplished? What roles have Chinese actors played? Has the informal diplomacy of exchanges been independent of, subordinate to, complementary to, or antagonistic to formal US diplomacy? Does Beijing's seeming embrace of foreign and domestic NGOs mean that the Communist Party is relinquishing its monopoly on political power? What contributions have Chinese Americans with connections to both societies made to the exchange process? These are some of the questions that this book will attempt to answer. It will do so through an examination of three organizations that have been at the forefront of US–China non-governmental relations: the Hopkins-Nanjing Center for Chinese and American Studies (a joint-venture university in China), the National Committee on United States–China Relations (a public education and exchange organization), and The 1990 Institute (a Chinese American-led think tank and social action organization). Collectively, they are representative of a large and growing body of China-focused American NGOs.

Other social forces have been more visible in US–China relations. No visitor to China in recent decades has missed the proliferation of McDonald's, Kodak, and other familiar logos on storefronts or the popularity of Buick automobiles and Hollywood DVDs (whether legitimate or pirated). Correspondingly, Americans have become increasingly familiar with such Chinese exports as basketball player Yao Ming, the Confucius Institutes, and Haier appliances. News media in both nations routinely cover meetings between leaders, China's large holdings of US Treasury bills, conflict over the yuan–dollar exchange rate, and military build-up in the Pacific by both nations (in part driven by regional disputes over control of the South China Sea). Furthermore, numerous scholarly publications have explored in depth the foregoing diplomatic, business, and popular culture dimensions of contemporary US–China relations.[1] Largely missing from this picture, however, is a clear understanding of the role played by non-governmental organizations.[2]

Conceptual context: the United States and the world

While diplomatic/military and economic power – the latter often intertwined with American popular culture – have, for a century, constituted the core of American global influence, a 1979 article by Akira Iriye ignited sustained consideration by diplomatic historians of the role of cultural exchange. Two subsequent articles by Iriye brought NGO exchanges into the picture.[3] Numerous scholars built on Iriye's programmatic ideas, leading one to introduce a monograph by writing, 'The people who used to be called diplomatic historians increasingly regard their task as the investigation of encounters between peoples of different nations, whether or not these people represent their nations officially.'[4]

This turn to culture has generated two sets of controversies. The first deals with the utility of studying diplomatic history through a cultural lens. Critics argue that the most extreme, postmodernist versions of cultural studies retreat from the study of cause and effect into mere symbolism.[5] Other practitioners of a cultural approach remain focused on historical causation, arguing that cultural factors are one important factor, among many, shaping state policy.[6] This book builds on and expands this moderate cultural approach.

The second controversy – over cultural imperialism – has unfolded largely within the culturalist camp. It is animated by the question: is the United States a civilizational juggernaut, ineluctably shaping the agenda of every society with which it comes into contact? From pre-World War I anxiety over 'Americanization of the world,' to interwar 'awkward dominion,' to the United States' emergence from World War II as the leading superpower, and its survival of the Cold War as sole superpower, scholars, government officials, and the general public world-wide have answered affirmatively.[7] Scholarship on US cultural relations with Europe, the Soviet Bloc, Japan, and South America depict those nations and regions variously adopting, adapting, or rejecting core features of the American societal model – i.e., democracy, individualism, mass consumption, and a self-organized civil society. Organizing themes such as informal empire, cultural imperialism, developmental imperialism, missionary capitalism, and real ambassadors suggest the role of non-state forces in this dynamic.[8] They also highlight the central points of contention within a shared outlook: to what degree has the United States achieved its global influence through compulsion? Has the influence been exploitative or helpful?[9]

The Role of American NGOs in China's Modernization explores the role of cultural exchange in what a former American ambassador to China has called 'the most important bilateral relationship of the twenty-first century.'[10] Moreover, as the subtitle, *Invited Influence*, suggests, the following chapters move beyond controversies over cultural imperialism. They do so by highlighting the considerable agency Chinese actors have exercised in their interactions with Americans since China began opening to the world in the 1970s. Chinese actors have variously tolerated, encouraged, and actively solicited the involvement of American institutions in the modernization of their nation.[11] In many cases, they have substantially shaped the agendas of resulting exchanges.[12]

Historical context: the United States and China

Neither the Chinese desire for American practical knowledge nor the American urge to relate to – and reshape – China was new in the 1970s. Specific historical conditions, however, evoked novel patterns of interaction as well as echoes of earlier patterns.

The most crucial new circumstance was the Cold War, which spurred Chinese and American leaders to perceive a mutual interest in countering threats from the Soviet Union.[13] At the same time, geopolitics was inseparable from international political economy.[14] An important segment of the Chinese leadership saw economic relations with developed countries, particularly the United States, as a way to boost recovery from the chaos of the Great Leap Forward and the Cultural Revolution.[15] Cold War historian Chen Jian argues that Mao's 1974 'three worlds' theory had already indicated a shift in emphasis from class struggle to economic development, a direction closely associated with the US–China opening of the early 1970s.[16] Correspondingly, as a product of a burgeoning US–China relationship, American officials and business leaders reactivated longstanding visions of both short-term financial gain and enduring expansion of a global system of open markets.[17]

As China and the United States cautiously engaged, cultural, educational, and policy exchanges reinforced new security and economic ties. There were initiatives from both sides and exchanges in both directions from the outset, but the Chinese held back from long-term commitments until full normalization at the beginning of 1979.[18] Then, organizations such as the National Committee on US–China Relations and the Committee on Scholarly Communication with the People's Republic of China were able to move forward with exchange programs that they had on the drawing board.[19]

Periodic shocks tested all dimensions of the relationship. The most serious to date has been Beijing's bloody suppression of demonstrators in Tiananmen Square in June 1989. From euphoria about relations during the 1980s, Americans' emotions swung to anger and disillusionment.[20] In some cases, particularly where there were large concentrations of Chinese Americans and visiting Chinese students, these sentiments spilled over into public protest against the Beijing government.[21] Concrete manifestations of this tense climate included the short-term curtailment of business deals, tourism, and society-to-society exchanges, as well as the downgrading of official relations.[22] The crisis also elicited the formation of organizations, like The 1990 Institute, that sought to ameliorate tension in bilateral relations. Another consequence was a one-time permanent residency amnesty for thousands of Chinese students then resident in the United States. Some eventually returned to China, and many entered careers that involved close engagement with both societies, including involvement in transnational NGOs.

Beijing's harsh response to domestic demonstrations reflected, in part, concern over events unfolding within the Soviet Union and Eastern Europe. Determined to avoid the impending fate of the Soviet Union, a centrist bloc of Chinese leaders ultimately chose to crush the protest movement and restrict political reform while pushing ahead with market-oriented, growth-promoting economic reforms. Although – or perhaps because – he was not prepared to relinquish one- (i.e., Communist) party rule, preeminent leader Deng Xiaoping insisted on continuing to prioritize economic growth. As Joseph Fewsmith explains:

> Deng had always coupled 'reform' with 'opening up' not only because he believed that China's economic modernization needed capital, technology, and export markets that only the West could provide, but because he recognized that jettisoning the Maoist emphasis on international class struggle was necessary for dampening domestic … class struggle, [which] would (and did) make the implementation of economic reform more difficult.[23]

The next shock came from an American action. Chinese citizens were outraged over the 1999 wartime bombing of the Chinese Embassy in Belgrade by the US-led North Atlantic Treaty Organization (NATO). Students and other Chinese engaged in widespread protests against the United States and all things American. The threat to bilateral exchanges was short-lived, however. More influential on the Chinese side, in addition to Beijing's strategic priorities, was the near-steady expansion of opportunities for provincial and local government bureaus, quasi-governmental organizations, and independent associations to interact with foreign counterpart organizations.[24]

By the mid-1980s, the Soviet Union had improved relations with both China and the United States, and by 1991, it no longer existed. As the Soviet threat receded, Beijing and Washington gradually recalibrated the foundation for their relationship, with economic ties playing an increasingly prominent role. US–China trade had grown from $5 million in 1971, to $2.3 billion in 1979, and to $26.6 billion in 1991. Trade continued to grow by roughly 20 percent annually during the 1990s, as China went from the tenth to the fourth largest trading partner of the United States.[25] Shock over the 1989 Tiananmen Square events, combined with expanding economic relations, increased the interest of Americans in what was happening inside China, and this growing interest helped spur the proliferation of exchanges. Issues of interest ranged from intellectual property rights, to environmental threats, to unmet social welfare needs, to democracy and human rights.

In addition to the evolution of official relations between the United States and China, changes within the two societies have facilitated or constrained the field of action for non-governmental initiatives. Lester Salamon has highlighted a 'global associational revolution that … may … prove to be as significant a development of the late twentieth and early twenty-first centuries as the rise of the nation-state was of the late nineteenth and early twentieth centuries.' Globalization and neo-liberalism both propelled and were reinforced by the rapid proliferation of NGOs.[26] As the United States participated in this revolution in the 1980s and beyond,[27] many US-based associations formed around China-related issues or added a China agenda to an existing program. Also, liberalization of US immigration law in 1965 had facilitated expansion of the Chinese American population, thus enlarging an important constituency for US–China exchanges. For its part, China dramatically eased restrictions on contact with foreigners and travel abroad and, with occasional interludes, curtailed the demonization of Western influences.

Preview

The first three chapters provide histories of the Hopkins-Nanjing Center for Chinese and American Studies, the National Committee on United States–China Relations, and The 1990 Institute. Chapters 4–6 explore the consequences of the three groups' exchange programs for participants, for China's modernization, and for US–China relations. They do so by studying the effects of exchanges on China's domestic policies, on the development of civil society in China, and on the education of China's youth.

Contemporary Sino-American exchanges reside at the intersection of a complex set of relationships – between China and the United States, between formal and informal diplomacy in the United States, between the Chinese Communist Party's grip on political power and its pursuit of economic growth and social stability. The following study will bring important features of these relationships into sharper focus.

1   The Hopkins-Nanjing Center for Chinese and American Studies

The Hopkins-Nanjing Center for Chinese and American Studies, which occupies the northwest corner of Nanjing University, was founded in 1986 as a joint venture between Nanjing University and the Johns Hopkins University. Its founding program issues a certificate to graduate students who study at the Center for a full academic year, and since 2006 some students have earned a two-year master's degree that both universities recognize. The vision that animated the Center ranges well beyond educating students, however. In a formulation often repeated by Chinese and American faculty, students, and staff, the Center's website proclaims: 'The ultimate vision was that one day, the U.S. Secretary of State and the Chinese Foreign Minister will find that they are both graduates of the Hopkins-Nanjing Center for Chinese and American Studies.'[1] Beyond this mutual interest in improving cultural understanding as a way to mitigate political conflict, the Chinese made a conscious decision to draw on American expertise as they sought to modernize their system of higher education, while many of the Americans involved over the years brought their own visions of a modern society.

Historical background

Both Nanjing and Johns Hopkins Universities have had long histories of involvement in US–China educational exchange. The vicissitudes the Hopkins-Nanjing Center (HNC) withstood during its first two decades were milder versions of the geopolitical turmoil and internal conflict that had doomed earlier experiments. In 1888, American Methodist Episcopal missionaries in Nanjing founded the Huiwen Academy, one of the ancestors of Nanjing University. The nationalist revolution of 1927, however, ended significant foreign participation in the administration of Chinese universities, and the 1949 communist revolution erased most residual Western practices.[2] Johns Hopkins University (JHU), correspondingly, had historical ties to China. Frank Goodnow, President of Johns Hopkins from 1914 to 1929, was a legal scholar who in 1913–14 served as constitutional advisor to Yuan Shikai, President of China. William Henry Welch, Dean of the Hopkins School of Medicine in the early 1900s, helped the Rockefeller Foundation establish the Peking Union Medical College (PUMC), which exchanged students and professors with JHU for 25 years.[3] One historian has described PUMC as 'very obviously an American institution, a Johns Hopkins implanted in China.' The tension over control of PUMC's identity and agenda was an issue which the parties to the Hopkins-Nanjing joint venture have also confronted since the Center's conception.[4]

For three decades after the establishment of the People's Republic of China, there were no opportunities for American academic exchanges with the Chinese mainland.[5] Further inhibiting exchange opportunities, from the onset of the Cultural Revolution in 1966 until the reform period began in 1978, China's university system was effectively suspended, replaced by various forms of mass mobilization of youth.[6]

Reconnecting

In 1963, at the height of a distinguished career as an educator, Kuang Yaming became president of Nanjing University, only to come under attack as the Cultural Revolution gained steam in 1966. Although (or perhaps because) he had been a Communist Party member since 1926 and had held numerous responsible positions in journalism, education, and party publicity work, the radicals branded him a 'capitalist roader' and consigned him to labor reform, restricted to a 'cow's pen.' In 1978, the new reform leadership restored Kuang to the presidency of Nanjing University, and he in turn rehabilitated other professors and educational leaders who had been 'knocked down' during the Cultural Revolution.[7]

The Ministry of Education appointed Kuang to lead a 1979 delegation of Chinese university professors to the United States. According to Chen Yongxiang, the longest-serving Chinese co-director of the Center (1994–2003), Kuang's prestige lent indispensable credibility to his recommendation to move toward an educational joint venture. 'Without Kuang as leader of Nanjing University at that time, it would have been impossible to set up the Chinese–American Center at Nanjing University.' The first American co-director, retired Foreign Service officer Leon Slawecki, described Kuang as 'a far-sighted individual who wanted to aid China in its opening to the world and was not afraid to take a risk at a moment when the U.S.–China relationship, just beginning, was delicate ...' Hopkins president Steven Muller commented in his no-nonsense way that Kuang 'had the imagination and the sort of largeness of mind to see what could come of this and not quibble over little bits of crap that could have destroyed the whole thing.'[8]

Across the Pacific, Muller was contemplating the lessons of a European experience. In 1955, Hopkins' School of Advanced International Studies (SAIS) had established a university campus in Bologna, Italy. In 1971, Milton Eisenhower, Muller's predecessor as Hopkins president, wanted to close the Bologna facility because of financial problems. Muller, then provost, argued against closure. He felt the benefits gained through improved US–European understanding justified the expense. By the 1970s, 'those who had lived together in, say, the late '50s, had risen in positions in their own countries. You had, maybe, somebody who was a high-level person in the State Department dealing with somebody who was a high-level person in the Foreign Ministry of Italy or Germany.' Eisenhower told Muller, 'Well, you can take this over. If you want it, you can have it.'[9] Muller accepted the challenge, and the Bologna campus celebrated its 50th anniversary in 2005. Speaking at the celebration, Under Secretary of State (and SAIS alumnus) Nicholas Burns called SAIS-Bologna 'the greatest European-American educational achievement of the post-war era.'[10]

The SAIS-sponsored entity that ultimately emerged in China differed in two significant respects from the Bologna campus. First, while SAIS-Bologna is an American institution on Italian soil, the Hopkins-Nanjing Center for Chinese and American Studies is a bi-national joint venture. Second, whereas all classes at the Bologna campus are taught in English – to American as well as European students – American and other international students at the Hopkins-Nanjing Center study in Chinese. To Muller, however, it was the extended experience of living and studying together that was special about Bologna. By the late 1970s, he was determined to replicate this experience in Asia. While some suggested Japan, he said, 'No, I really don't want to do it in Japan, because the real challenge [in US–Asia relations] is China.'[11]

Though Kuang and Muller shared an interest in Sino-American educational exchange, Kuang was not fluent in English, Muller spoke no Chinese, and neither was familiar with the other country's higher education system. Thus there was a need for a cultural mediator. That indispensable role was filled by Chih-Yung Chien, a Hopkins physics professor, with whom Muller had developed a friendship and whose reputation had made its way to Kuang.[12] Chien had left the Chinese mainland for Taiwan in 1946 and earned a BS from Taiwan University in 1960. Taiwan had no graduate schools at that time, so in 1961 he went to the United States to study at Yale, where he earned an MS in 1963 and a PhD in 1966, with a specialty in high-energy physics. He taught at UCLA from 1966 through 1969 and at Johns Hopkins University from 1969 until the present.[13]

As he became increasingly integrated into American society, Chien nevertheless maintained a keen interest in China and in relations between the two countries, especially in conflict resolution. 'By early '70 or so,' he says, 'I came to the conclusion that, in the last hundred years or so, the Sino-American relationship had been – and still has been – mostly based on misunderstanding rather than understanding.' Chien's examples include: first, American enthusiasm for Chiang Kai-shek, based largely on his supposed sympathy for Christianity; and second, major misunderstanding by each side of the other's needs and intentions during the Korean War. Chien's phraseology, if not his vision, for what became the Hopkins-Nanjing Center, is less idealistic than Muller's:

> I was a realist. I felt that 20 years later – which is now – there would still be fundamental differences between China and the United States. Their interests would not overlap. Their cultures would still be different. There would be conflicts all the time. But at least, at that time, the people dealing with each other would have a better understanding of how things work on each other's side; don't take things at face value.[14]

In 1979, events drew Kuang, Muller, Chien, and their visions together. Although Nixon's 1972 visit had facilitated direct communication, the United States and the PRC did not establish formal relations until 1 January 1979, and they first exchanged ambassadors in March of that year. By summer, a group of Chinese American scientists, including Chien, felt it was urgent 'to establish personal contact among the leaders on both sides and also give them a worldview of both sides.' The scientists thought the best way to do this was to invite Wan Li, a respected senior party member, to visit the United States. Wan had led successful economic reform efforts in Anhui Province, was known to have an open mind toward the outside world, and was scheduled to become a vice premier. Nobel Laureate C. N. Yang orchestrated the invitation, which was actually issued as a governor-to-governor invitation by Maryland Governor Harry Hughes. Wan visited the United States in September, at which time he and Chien met. Upon his return to China and elevation to vice premier, Wan became the champion of educational exchange programs within the State Council.[15]

Two months later, Kuang Yaming led a delegation of ten university presidents to the United States, the first such delegation ever sent by the People's Republic. A member of the Chinese Embassy, Ms Guo Yixing, knew Chien and was aware of his interest in improving bilateral understanding. 'This may be the kind of thing you're interested in,' she told him and asked whether he would meet with the delegation. The meeting took place on Thanksgiving, the only day the visitors were not booked with various politicians and government officials. Kuang had heard about Chien, possibly through Guo. At the end of the visit, he made it clear he would welcome an invitation to Chien's home, following the afternoon meeting. After several phone calls to his wife, to whom he is 'eternally grateful,' Chien arranged a sit-down dinner for 40: the official Chinese delegation, 10 members of their entourage, and 20 Americans to host the 20 Chinese. That evening, Kuang invited Chien to visit China the following summer to make a fact-finding trip on potential bilateral projects. Muller agreed that the timing was right, and he and Chien spent seven weeks in China the following summer. For linguistic reasons, most of the fact-finding work fell on Chien.[16]

Chien visited the campuses of the ten presidents who had been in the United States, as well as several other universities. Additionally, he gained a perspective on the primary and secondary sectors of China's education system, largely through 'research assistant' work by his wife and three children. His wife visited nursery schools, while his daughter and younger son attended local primary and high schools, respectively. His older son, having just graduated from college, 'roamed around in all the research labs, helping them set up equipment.' Having done this fieldwork, Chien called Muller from Beijing and recommended that Johns Hopkins University create a partnership with Nanjing University.

> Steve only asked two questions. He said, 'Why not Beijing University?' …
> But I said, 'My assessment is that every time Tiananmen sneezes, Beijing University will catch pneumonia.' … And then he asked me, 'Why not Shanghai?' I said, 'Yeah, Shanghai would be a lot more convenient. … On the

other hand, exactly for that reason, I'm afraid within 15 years Shanghai will be very commercialized, everyone will be looking for money. For example, New York is not the best place to found a research university. And Washington is not a good place to have something politically sensitive. So, in the sense that Boston is a good place, Nanjing is a good place.'[17]

Muller had, in fact, already developed his own preference for Nanjing, with its distinguished history and its distance from Beijing. SAIS's experience in Italy guided him: Rome had 'too many bureaucrats, too much stuff, which is why we went to Bologna.'[18]

Neither side could act entirely independently of its own government, however. In the United States, Hopkins needed only the government's pro-forma 'acceptance.'[19] In China, however, such an innovative venture could not proceed without formal approval of the State Council. Following endorsement by Wan Li and three other vice premiers, approval was granted.[20] As has happened in previous periods of Chinese history, the government invited a foreign institution in, hoping it would contribute to China's modernization without undermining the state's political and cultural authority.[21]

The next key challenges were to agree on the Center's mission, define its scope of freedom, and establish a facility. Chien's ability to understand both sides – linguistically and culturally – helped reconcile initially divergent interpretations of the Center's mission. 'The Americans started out saying, "This Center will train the future leaders for both countries." The moment the Chinese saw that, they fainted. Only Deng Xiaoping could choose China's leaders.' So, Chien modified the wording to indicate training future 'talents' for each country.[22]

The partners had to make concessions on substantive issues with symbolic importance to both sides; sovereignty was important to the Chinese, academic freedom to the Americans. The agreement, signed on 28 September 1981, provided for a jointly managed campus on the grounds of Nanjing University. Construction costs would be 'shared equally between NJU and JHU,' but Nanjing University would 'require sovereignty over these facilities.' Each partner would 'arrange funding and tuition according to its own procedures for the expenses of faculty and students from its own nation, including the national co-director.'[23] The use of the word 'sovereignty' in an agreement between two educational institutions, reflected Leon Slawecki, 'obviously expresses deep sensitivity on the part of the Chinese side to any kind of alienation of Chinese land such as occurred in the nineteenth century.'[24]

For the American side, freedom of inquiry, symbolized by an uncensored, open-stack library, was a non-negotiable principle. When Muller said the Center would need its own library, the Chinese asked, 'What kind of books will you have?' Muller replied that the Chinese students would need books typical of an American university. 'Their first response was that they would have to look at each of these books, to see whether they were appropriate. I said, "Look, if you're going to do that, let's forget the whole thing." … Well, "Let's forget the whole thing was not acceptable for them, so they said "ok."'[25] While academic freedom at the Center may not have reached American standards, the library has been noteworthy for its symbolic and practical effects. Scholars outside the Center – Chinese and foreign – can apply for access, and every relevant department at Nanjing University has a library card that its faculty can use.[26]

The founding agreement stipulated that each semester there should be 50 American students, who would study in their target language (Chinese) with Chinese professors and 50 Chinese students, who would study in their target language (English) with American professors. It also specified that the day-to-day operations of the Center be managed by two co-directors, one American and one Chinese. The Chinese side initially said that the Center should have Chinese management, since it was on Chinese soil, but the Americans would not agree. Chien thought there should be rotating directors, but he and the Chinese side ultimately agreed to Muller's proposal for two co-directors.[27]

While not specified in the agreement, an important feature of the Hopkins-Nanjing Center from the outset was the cross-cultural learning that took place in dorm rooms. Realizing Stephen Muller's early vision, each room housed one Chinese and one American student. In most cases, roommates became friends as they learned each other's study habits, family background, career aspirations, etc. One American student reported, 'My roommate had no sense of privacy – that bugged me – but then I realized his asking me questions concerning my personal life was actually a Chinese way of showing friendship.'[28]

What kind of facility would these students, professors, and administrators inhabit? Initially, Nanjing University proposed six or seven unoccupied rooms on its campus. Had the Americans accepted that plan, or negotiated an upgrade, the Center 'could have opened as early as 1982,' recounts Chien. They held out, instead, for a building that would come closer to American standards for university buildings. Another Chinese suggestion involved a new building that would have required tearing down a Sun Yatsen landmark. Chien insisted on not doing that. 'In the long term, people would blame us.'[29]

As an example of the complexities involved, it took six months simply to decide whether the facility would be air-conditioned. (There were no centrally air-conditioned buildings in Nanjing in 1981.) Architectural design could not begin prior to this decision, because ceilings must be higher in un-air-conditioned buildings. While Nanjing University officials initially said, 'no problem,' Chien pointed out that they needed to confirm whether they could actually get access to the required allocation of electricity. The university's meteorology department calculated that an air-conditioned facility would use as much electricity as the entire existing Nanjing University campus. As it turned out, the Center was able to secure adequate commitments from two power stations, thus providing a backup, and also bought a generator as a secondary backup.[30]

Far more complicated was the securing of land rights for a 6,000 square meter building at the corner of Beijing West Road and Shanghai Road. One dimension of the challenge was administrative; there were over 300 chop impressions on the deed by the time it was finalized. The other dimension was practical. Several hundred residents had to be displaced and relocated to short-term, mid-term, and, finally, long-term housing. The burden of relocating these residents caused hesitation among the institutions responsible for them. Chien quickly realized that the key players were the chief of a state-run vegetable company, the principal of a primary school, the head of the district office, the Nanjing mayor, and a provincial official. 'They all had to agree to something before we could clear the land.' Chien wanted to sit them all down for a meeting, but his main contact in the Nanjing Foreign Affairs Department told him that would be impossible, because the individuals were all at different levels in the administrative hierarchy.[31]

After months of ineffective exhortation, Chien was despairing of success. As a last resort, he invited all the key players to an informal lunch. Chien made no speech. He simply toasted the provincial secretary general, Xu Jing'an, with three glasses of strong Chinese *moutai* and sat down. 'He had never seen professors who could drink the white stuff, three glasses. And I didn't bother telling why I invited him, just that I wanted to drink with him.' The two went on to discuss Tang Dynasty poetry, Song Dynasty monks, and Yixing teapots. Finally, Xu stood up and said, 'As you know, this thing is being promoted by Professor Chien, and the Center has been approved for three years by the State Council, but so far it's not going. ... I cannot do it, so I toast three glasses with you guys.' In a closed-door meeting immediately afterwards (without Chien), the attendees made the necessary commitments to relocate hundreds of residents, and the biggest facility problem was solved.[32]

Building a durable institution

Administrative challenges

After seven years of discussion and planning, the Johns Hopkins *Gazette* announced in the fall of 1986:

> On September 10, The Johns Hopkins University will open the Hopkins-Nanjing Center for Chinese and American Studies in the People's Republic of China (PRC), launching an unprecedented international partnership in advanced education. A remarkable achievement in U.S.–China cooperation, the Center will be the first fully equal and jointly administered educational facility on Chinese soil since the U.S. resumed diplomatic relations with Beijing.[33]

Hopkins president Steven Muller highlighted the theme of training future talent that was so important to both sides, though with different emphases and motivations: 'The Center offers the prospect of becoming the single most significant training ground in both countries for future professionals whose careers involve Sino-American relations.' He also accurately anticipated three key challenges the Center would face:

> The risks ... include the dependence of the entire venture on the state of U.S.–China relations; the awkwardness of joint management between two institutions separated by much more than geographic distance; and cost so

high that the ability of Hopkins to live up to its part in the enterprise rests on widespread recognition that the center is a *national* resource for the United States, not simply a program carried out by a single university.[34]

Much of the work of making 'joint management' a viable strategy fell upon the first two co-directors, linguist Wang Zhigang and retired diplomat Leon Slawecki. Wang had taught English at Nanjing University, beginning in 1963. He had been the chief and senior reviser of the Chinese Translation Section at UNESCO in Paris from 1978 to 1983 and a Fulbright scholar at Georgetown University for the 1984–5 academic year. Wang was not happy with his appointment as the Chinese co-director; he was more interested in pursuing linguistic research. In retrospect, though, he has fond memories of the assignment.[35]

Slawecki had pursued both African and Chinese studies at SAIS in the early 1960s. He was working on a PhD in Chinese studies at Yale, when he ran out of money to finish his dissertation on the Chinese of Madagascar. Connecting study with work, he was able to get a diplomatic assignment in Madagascar from 1965 through 1967. Although he completed his dissertation in 1969, he stayed on at the State Department until 1986. After a few years in Sudan and Senegal and a short assignment as Polish desk officer, he worked in Hong Kong. About the time he retired from the Foreign Service, Slawecki heard about the new Hopkins-Nanjing Center and actively sought the position of American co-director. He and Wang became friends as well as colleagues. Although Wang stepped down after eight years and Slawecki after only two, they kept up contact through the years, especially after Wang immigrated to the United States in 1999. As if to foreshadow their future association, they discovered that they had probably been in Korea – on opposite sides of the war – at the same time.[36]

Many of the issues Wang and Slawecki dealt with seemed merely symbolic, but their smooth resolution laid the groundwork for effective collaborative leadership in the future. For example, before the beginning of the Center's first session in 1986, *China Daily* ran an article that referred only to Wang as the Center's 'director.' He and Slawecki jointly wrote a letter to the paper, explaining that there were two co-directors and asking the paper to publish a correction. 'Although it did not do so, the misunderstanding between the two sides was cleared.' The co-directors determined who would work in office A101, understood to be the 'elder brother' office, with a flip of a coin – which Wang won. The placing of names on Center stationery was no less laden with symbolism. Wang and Slawecki established a policy that all stationery printed and used in China (regardless of language) would list Nanjing first, whereas Hopkins would appear first on stationery printed and used in the United States.[37]

Surviving conflict and crisis

Many of the challenges to the durability of the Center as a partnership came in the form of spectacular and unforeseen events, some of which confirmed Muller's concern about the influence of the 'state of U.S.–China relations.' The first major conflict split the student body. It began innocently with a 1988 Christmas party, hosted by African students at nearby Hohai University, an engineering school specializing in water resources and hydraulics. At some point during the evening, a scuffle developed, and several African students injured a Chinese guard. The guard bled from a head wound but was not seriously hurt. Rumors quickly spread through the city, though, that African students had killed a Chinese university guard. Ten nights of angry marches through the university district by hundreds of students followed, even after the news got out that the guard was alive. The fact that police had sent African students back to their dorm rooms but had arrested Chinese students gave the protests momentum – and an anti-foreign, racist edge.[38]

The atmosphere at the Center was tense. One night, marchers demanded to know whether any African students were inside. According to Milo Manley, long-time deputy American co-director who was then a student at the Center, 'We said, "We're Americans, we don't have African students." We did indeed have two African American students here at the time who were pretty concerned.' At that time, there was one joint class on international relations, with mandatory attendance by all students and alternating lectures by Chinese and American professors. By coincidence, Professor Richard Gaulton had just lectured on the Chinese Exclusion Acts. American students had discussed racism in their own society and the need to overcome it. With racism on the agenda, it seemed natural for the Center's Chinese students to critically reflect on the actions of the anti-African protesters. Instead, the Chinese students denied that racism was involved. They maintained they were only protesting favorable treatment for foreigners, such as subsidies and better living conditions. 'But when they were marching down the streets at night,' recalls Manley, 'they weren't chanting "More equal treatment" or "Give us bigger financial aid." They were chanting "Down with blacks."' The Americans were upset by this near-unanimous Chinese attitude – to the extent that five students did not return for the second semester.[39]

Despite the anguish and the violence to which it ultimately led, China's spring 1989 Democracy Movement 'was a very lucky thing' for the academic year at the Hopkins-Nanjing Center. 'If we hadn't had that,' observes Manley, 'our class would have remained very fractured, and relations probably would not have been good all year long.' The common sympathy that Chinese and American students felt toward the Democracy Movement brought them back together. The Chinese students made it clear, however, that their movement was 'a home-grown thing.' The American students agreed to cheer from the sidelines but not try to join demonstrations or meetings, which were occurring in all major Chinese cities from April through the 4 June crackdown.[40]

What may have been healthy for one cohort of students, though, was nearly fatal to the Center as an institution. 'After June 4, 1989,' reported Executive Director (of the Washington Office) Anthony Kane, 'many people thought we would never reopen.' Cancellation of commencement was the only official change.[41] Still, Kane felt that the program 'was under a dark cloud.' The library remained open, but the reinstitution of political training on campuses nationwide was accompanied by a list of banned books. Librarians moved some of the most controversial books to less prominent locations, but they all remained available to any student at the Center.[42]

More so than at any time since its birth, the continued existence of the Hopkins-Nanjing Center was dependent on government goodwill – in both Washington and Beijing. In a sequence that is unclear, Beijing and Washington temporarily suspended Fulbright exchanges, a government-to-government program. The US administration implemented limited sanctions, including travel warnings to Americans, suspension of military sales, postponement of high-level military and diplomatic exchanges, and restrictions on lending by international financial institutions. Nevertheless, Washington encouraged the maintenance of informal channels of communication, such as cultural and educational exchanges. According to one report, a State Department official said, 'The Hopkins program is just the kind of thing the president had in mind.'[43]

Despite sharing most Americans' displeasure with the actions of the Chinese government, Muller hoped to keep the Center operating – as long as there was no compromise in its mission. He wrote to Nanjing University President Qu Qinyue that he was 'profoundly concerned' about reports of new restrictions on foreign television and print materials. He sought reassurance about 'the integrity of the Center's library' as well as visas for American faculty, students, and staff. Qu assured Muller that foreign newspapers were being deposited in the Center library as usual and that there were no visa problems. He stressed his continued support for the Center and urged a corresponding American commitment.[44]

Richard Gaulton, who had become the American co-director, reported that 'officials from Nanjing University approached him and made it clear they wanted the center to stay open.'[45] Chih-Yung Chien had largely stayed in the background since the launch of the enterprise, but the Tiananmen crisis drew him back into the picture. He flew to China to assess whether academic freedom would be impeded at the Center. After talking with a cross-section of educators and officials, including Kuang Yaming, he concluded that it would not. Muller vigorously defended the Center against calls from Hopkins staff and alumni to drop support for it.[46]

The crisis did not fully subside until 1991, when the two sides signed the first five-year renewal of the original joint venture agreement. Negotiations were 'quite contentious.' SAIS Dean George Packard had to steer a course between angry American backers and assertive Chinese partners. Stephen Muller had used some Medical School funds in launching the Center, and post-Tiananmen critics included 'the powerful medical establishment at Hopkins,' which was 'furious' over continued funding. Meanwhile, '[t]he Chinese side entered into negotiations assuming that they now 'owned' the Center and could call all the shots.' A passionate plea by eminent SAIS China scholar A. Doak Barnett helped Muller and Packard overcome American criticism, and the Chinese 'finally yielded the point that we were co-owners and could negotiate as equals.'[47] Thus the Hopkins-Nanjing Center survived a potentially fatal crisis – partly because of the commitment of the two partner universities and partly because the program suited the interests of their respective governments in maintaining informal contact through exchange programs.

Robert Daly, American co-director from 2001 to 2007, quips that 'spring is crisis season in China. ... If the optimism of the Center model is at all justified, then HNC students should shine in times of crisis, especially if crises occur in the spring, when students have a semester of study and interaction under their belts.'[48] The NATO bombing of the Chinese Embassy in Belgrade on 7 May 1999 gave Hopkins-Nanjing students another spring opportunity for conflict resolution. Washington insisted that the bombing was accidental, while most of the Chinese public believed it was intentional. The American co-director at the time, Elizabeth Knup, wrote a series of letters that described the scene at the Center. 'Around mid-day [Sunday, 9 May], we learned about the events at the Chengdu consulate, where students scaled the wall of the compound and burned the consul general's home. ... Later we also learned that a poster went up at Nanjing University encouraging students to protest in front of the center.'[49]

Protest crowds in Nanjing reached a scale of 20,000 to 30,000 people. The Chinese co-director, Professor Chen Yongxiang, forbade the Center's Chinese students from joining the protests, a prohibition which frustrated some of them. The students called a meeting for Monday evening. Though they reached no consensus, their candid airing of emotions relieved a lot of tension.

> What happened at that meeting would not have been possible at any other educational institution in China at this time. For American and Chinese students to sit around a table, admit their feelings, and reach out to comfort each other was what the center was established to create – an atmosphere in which the two cultures would try to find mutual understanding.[50]

Leaders in Beijing called for restraint in the demonstrations. Much like US leaders at the time of the Tiananmen crisis, they did not want a state-to-state conflict to undermine the broader relationship, including China's hoped-for accession to the World Trade Organization (WTO).[51]

A friendship between one pair of Chinese and American alumni suggests the kind of contribution the Center's 'enforced intimacy' can make to mutual understanding on contentious issues. The American student was an advocate of Tibetan independence. His Chinese counterpart was not 'hard-core patriotic, but I really think that Tibet is part of China – or, even if it's not, it's none of the United States' business.' After extensive discussion, the two agreed that each had limited information. Neither had been to Tibet, and the American knew only a few wealthy Tibetan refugees. They agreed that they would both be open to revising their opinions, if they had a chance to visit Tibet and form firsthand impressions of the people there.[52]

Though it was not related to either student or diplomatic conflicts, by the spring 2003, the SARS (Severe Acute Respiratory Syndrome) outbreak of the preceding winter tested the commitments of the two sides as thoroughly as had previous crises. The epidemic took dozens of lives in China and led to the sight of thousands of frightened people wearing facemasks in public.[53] The widespread panic disrupted classes, and HNC officials worried about 'the health of the program for the 2003–2004 academic year,' as well as 'the health of students and faculty at the Center.' In Washington, an emergency response team was formed, including Johns Hopkins' leading epidemiologists and China specialists, as well as representatives of the Center and SAIS.[54]

On April 22, the leadership decided to close the Center, six weeks ahead of schedule – too late according to some parents, an overreaction according to others. By 18 May, with dozens of Chinese and foreign students uncertain whether they could attend the institution to which they had been accepted for the fall 2003 semester, the Center announced a bold and creative plan. For the first half of the following academic year, the entire campus – administration, faculty, students, and classes – would temporarily relocate to the East-West Center of the University of Hawaii in Honolulu.[55] Despite the inconvenience for all and the American students' missing a semester of daily life in China, there were some bright spots in the temporary arrangement. The Chinese students were able to experience an American social and civic environment firsthand. Hawaii Governor Linda Lingle welcomed the Center's students upon arrival, and American and Chinese students later had an opportunity to pose questions to two US senators and two members of the House of Representatives, who were visiting Hawaii as part of an Aspen Institute delegation.[56] Additionally, Chinese professors – who usually live apart from the Center campus and have a heavy teaching load at Nanjing University in addition to the courses they teach at the Center – lived on campus with everyone else and had ample time for extra-curricular interaction.[57]

Financial challenges

Like most non-profit institutions, the Center faced significant ongoing fundraising challenges.[58] This was especially true on the American side, since tuition did not fully cover the cost of American professors' salaries. To sustain the institution beyond start-up, the SAIS Development Council spent two years, from mid-1984 through mid-1986, trying to raise money from foundations and various agencies of the United States government. When these early efforts met with only minimal success – such as a $10,000 check from David Rockefeller – Muller decided there should be a professional fundraiser specifically devoted to American responsibilities for the Hopkins-Nanjing Center. In June 1986, SAIS hired Patricia Lloyd, whose background was political fundraising and who remained the American director of development for the Center until the end of 2002.

Three factors ultimately led to financial stability on the American side: sustained US government funding, increased emphasis on raising money from corporations and individuals, and energetic support from a retired diplomat. The logical government agency to approach for long-term financial support was the

Department of Education (DOE). Hopkins President Muller personally forwarded a request for an initial $115,000 grant. Although the acting assistant director of the DOE believed 'the Center is providing a unique service that the department should fund,' the official in charge of funding decisions at the DOE's Center for International Education used a 'Dear Colleague' form letter to convey rejection of Muller's request. The sympathetic acting assistant director confided that the Center's uniqueness might have hampered efforts to fit it into the DOE's standard grantee categories.[59]

The Center was more successful with the United States Information Agency (USIA), Washington's leading player in the public diplomacy arena in the 1980s and early 1990s. USIA granted the Center $59,000 for fiscal year 1988 and $136,000 for both 1994 and 1995. This modest funding was the fruit of considerable lobbying on the Center's behalf, by Ambassador Stapleton Roy as well as by its own staff. The money, however, came from a China-specific budget pool that dried up after the grants for 1994 and 1995.[60]

Lloyd's most enduring success in raising government funds came at American Schools and Hospitals Abroad (ASHA), a division of the United States Agency for International Development (USAID), a bilateral development institution of the US government. According to its website, 'The goal of the ASHA program reflects the intent of its enabling legislation: "to assist schools, libraries, and medical centers outside the United States founded or sponsored by U.S. citizens serving as study and demonstration centers for ideas and practices of the United States."'[61] Beginning with an initial $700,000 grant in 1987, through 2005 ASHA consistently provided 20 to 30 percent of the Center's annual budget.[62] ASHA's decision to provide financial support to the Center was somewhat exceptional in terms of USAID's posture toward China. The US Congress provides funding for all USAID projects. Partly because Congress tends to be confrontational toward China over issues ranging from trade to human rights and partly because China itself has gradually become a donor nation, Congress has limited assistance to modest grants related to infectious diseases, Tibetan development, and governance. Lloyd, however, found creative and flexible USAID supporters, who were able to win Congressional approval.[63]

Foundation funding has been important to the Center, as to most non-governmental, non-profit initiatives with a large US component. In the case of the Hopkins-Nanjing Center, it has accounted for roughly 20 percent of total US funding. The Asia Foundation made large contributions in the early years, and the Henry Luce Foundation and the Ford Foundation have made substantial ongoing contributions. A drawback of foundation funding is that it is typically project-specific and, thus, cannot be predictably budgeted for. The Starr Foundation and the Freeman Foundation have, happily, diverged from this pattern by making annual grants.[64]

Lloyd attributes much of her success with individuals and corporations to unflagging support from Arthur Hummel, Jr, a career diplomat and US Ambassador to China from 1981 to 1985. Hummel was born in China to missionary parents, helped both Nationalists and Communists during World War II, was imprisoned by the Japanese, and participated in postwar relief efforts. After retiring from the Foreign Service in 1985, he became chairman of the Hopkins-Nanjing Council, a key advisory and fundraising group. Over a period of seven years, Hummel opened dozens of doors for Lloyd and twice a year accompanied her to meetings with business people, foundation representatives, scholars, and officials throughout Hong Kong and mainland China. 'There was respect for Johns Hopkins and the Hopkins-Nanjing Center, but it was really Art. His reputation got us into many doors.'

Lloyd targeted corporations and individuals more aggressively than had her predecessors at SAIS, and the effort paid off. By the early twenty-first century, each category accounted for 28 percent of the Center's funding.[65] The typical corporate or individual contribution was more modest than what ASHA or foundations contributed. Still, $100,000 from Exxon or $250,000 from Hopkins alumnus Clyde Wu, and $5,000 to $20,000 a year from other corporations and individuals added up. In addition to American businessmen operating in China, Lloyd was particularly successful among Hong Kong businessmen, professionals, and philanthropists. Lloyd and Hummel, for example, solicited Hong Kong lawyer Benjamin Yeung, following an introduction by the future US Ambassador to China, Clark Randt. Yeung made regular personal contributions of $50,000 and then $100,000.

A million-dollar donation in 1990 by the Hong Kong-based Fei Yi-Ming Journalism Foundation illustrated the finesse that transnational fundraising can require. The foundation asked, in exchange for the contribution, that a life-size bust of Mr Fei be commissioned and prominently displayed at the Center. SAIS Dean Packard began celebrating, but Nanjing University's Administrative Council balked at the notion of a bust, arguing that there were few precedents in China. Since the contribution would be given to Johns Hopkins, perhaps a bust could be housed at the Hopkins campus in Baltimore. After three months of negotiations, the two sides arrived at a compromise. Johns Hopkins affirmed that the contribution to the Center's $25 million dollar endowment fund was exclusively for use by the Center; if the Center were ever to close, that portion of the endowment would be returned to the Fei Yi-ming Journalism Foundation. Further, and most importantly, the two sides agreed that a life-size bas-relief of Mr Fei would be prominently displayed on an interior wall at the Center campus.[66]

One disappointment for Lloyd – and for Alice Huang, Dean of Science at New York University, who assisted Lloyd – was the failure to consistently raise substantial sums of money from Chinese Americans. There were some contributions from the beginning. The 1990 Institute's co-founder C. B. Sung and his wife, Beulah Kwok-Sung, for example, contributed in the 1980s and early 1990s. In 1992, they hosted a dinner in the Bay Area to honor Hummel for his role in supporting the Center.[67] More recently, a growing number of HNC alumni of Chinese ancestry, as well as the US-based J. T. Tai Foundation, have become regular contributors. Various barriers have limited support from this potential constituency, however. Some lacked enthusiasm for the Center's mission, while others were simply over-committed to other causes. The most immediate frustration for Lloyd and Huang, however, was the highly restrictive solicitation policies of Johns Hopkins University and its SAIS program. JHU and SAIS prohibited the Center from soliciting any alumni who had previously contributed to either the university or its SAIS program. In other words, a prime donor community (including its Chinese American sub-population) was off limits.

In two cases, spring crises at the Center carried over into financial challenges. Most serious was the fallout from the Tiananmen Square events of June 1989. As the *New York Times* reported in November 1991, the actions of the Chinese government had significantly alienated American donors to bilateral exchanges. The Center had 'enough money to make it through this year, but may not be able to operate next academic year.' The Commerce Department had just cancelled its annual $400,000 contribution to an American co-sponsored business school in Dalian, resulting in the program's closure, and foundation money was gravitating away from China and toward Eastern Europe and the former Soviet Union.[68] Less mission-threatening, the 2003 SARS epidemic created a short-term but manageable cash flow problem. In addition to meeting all the logistical challenges, the Center had to fund Hawaiian-level living expenses for the Chinese students and faculty. A few large contributions from the New York-based Asia Society and from several Hong Kong Chinese made this 'remarkable' undertaking possible.[69]

Linguistic challenges

The idea that language would be a medium of study, not a goal in itself, was 'the greatest miscalculation of the Center's founders,' according to Robert Daly.[70] Construction problems served as a premonition of the fragility of this premise. The Chinese characters for 'solder' and 'braze' differ by only one stroke, and an American translation error resulted in leaky water pipes and lack of heat during the first year.[71]

During the first academic year, it became clear that many of the Chinese and American students could not study successfully at the graduate level in their target languages. According to Leon Slawecki, the first-year skill distribution was similar for the two student bodies – 'about one-third were qualified enough in the target language to benefit from substantive classes in that language. Another third could succeed if they worked diligently. A final third should not have been admitted to the center's program.' Even with lenient standards, only 24 American students and 43 Chinese students were admitted the first year. By the second year, although there was little improvement in the skill distribution among American students, Chinese recruitment efforts had significantly mitigated the language problem on their side. Associate Dean George Crowell (of JHU) reported a similar scenario, following a spring 1991 visit to the Nanjing campus. While most American students told him that they did not have sufficient language ability to work up to US graduate standards, American faculty reported that by their second semester most Chinese students were doing graduate-level work.[72]

On the US side, the language problem was addressed, in part, by adjusting the awarding of academic credit. For the relatively small number of American SAIS students who enter the Hopkins-Nanjing certificate program, SAIS accepted two semesters (five to six courses) at the Center for one semester of SAIS credit. The concerns were that the students were not taking the full four-course load per semester and that the SAIS faculty had no control or say about the faculty Nanjing University chose to teach the American students. Nanjing University, by contrast, has granted full credit to Chinese students studying in their target language.[73] Nanjing administrators apparently have felt that the benefits of studying with American professors compensate for the reduced volume of reading.

There were reasons to hope for an increase in the number of American applicants. At the time of the Center's tenth anniversary, Anthony Kane noted that China's continuing economic reform and liberalization attracted American students to the prospect of careers with foreign companies doing business in China.[74] Still, progress was slow and uneven. It was not until the 2002–3 academic year that the Center could 'fill the dormitory built seventeen years earlier.'[75]

Even that success depended on two compensatory strategies on the American side. First, five years into the joint venture, the Center established an 'intermediate' track for American students who needed additional preparation for coursework, especially in terms of language skills. These students took special academic courses as well as studying Chinese. The program was limited to ten students, who were mainstreamed the second semester, and remained active through the 2005–6 academic year. Additionally, the second five-year agreement allowed the 'American' side to recruit up to 25 percent third-country students, as long as their English skills were equivalent to 'native' competence. The native-English-speaking contingent was renamed 'international' students.[76]

Growth and change

Sharon Newman served as assistant director of the Center's SAIS-based administrative office in Washington from 1984, two years before the first students walked into their classrooms, until she retired in 2006. Her succinct characterization of the Center's achievement as 'maturity' captures the quality of institutional change. The Center has matured 'in terms of solvency, in terms of having a reputable faculty, in terms of attracting good students.' Another dimension of maturation was the development of Nanjing as an urban center. 'In 1986,' recalls Newman, 'I went to our opening ceremony, and I can remember you just couldn't catch a cab. You had to get one at a hotel.'[77] In the twenty-first century, paying passengers and, thus, taxis are plentiful in Nanjing.

China's growing prosperity has made cross-cultural social interaction more convenient. Ren Donglai was a Chinese student during the Center's inaugural year and went on to become one of its professors. 'Twenty years ago,' he recalls, 'it was difficult to find even a small restaurant.' Further, most of the Chinese students had to survive on an allowance of 100–200 RMB ($27–54 at the 1986 exchange rate) per month, while the American students had a much higher living standard. Today, China's economic progress is reflected in the wider availability of recreational venues as well as more prosperous Chinese students. The latter, thus, 'can spend more time with their American classmates in bars and restaurants.' They are also able to pay for things like the training, clothing, and equipment needed to participate, on the Center's team, in Nanjing's annual Dragon Boat Race.[78]

Faculty members have contributed to the maturation of the Hopkins-Nanjing Center by shoring up institutional continuity. Chinese faculty are simultaneously affiliated with Nanjing University, and there has been no significant turnover among them. On the international side, however, it was only in the late 1990s that professors began teaching consecutive terms or returning to Nanjing after a hiatus. Five of the six 2005–6 international faculty, for example, had previously taught at the Center.[79]

Significant and related changes in curriculum and student motivation occurred during the 1990s. Robert Daly, who had been a Foreign Service officer before becoming the Center's American co-director in 2001, observes that students from both countries have become more career-oriented.[80]

> In the 80s, working to improve U.S.–China relations was the obsession of small bands of pioneer students in both countries, and the Center was a fine place for them to meet. The opportunity to live together as roommates was rare and welcome for American and Chinese students alike. The generalist model, furthermore, was well suited to the job market of the day … Center students of 2004 are not so much academically curious as professionally ambitious. When I was a Chinese language student in the late 1980s, I struggled with Du Mu's poetry in spare moments. Center international students of recent years are more likely to read the annual reports of Chinese multinational corporations or NGOs in their leisure time.[81]

For Chinese students in the late 1980s, a greater interest in humanities and getting to know Americans, as opposed to more 'practical' courses of study, likely grew from the relative intellectual openness of the reform era. In its more radical Maoist phase, the Chinese Communist Party had largely eliminated social sciences from the university curriculum. As Professor Ren Donglai observed, 'The reason is very simple. Because [in the view of the Communist Party at that time] Marxism itself is social science, we don't need sociology, political science, economics, psychology. So, in Nanjing University, we had only Foreign Language and Literature, a Chinese Language Department, and a History Department.'[82]

American students, like their Chinese counterparts, were increasingly career-minded from the mid-1990s onward. Some looked forward to opportunities in international business, others to working with NGOs or the Foreign Service. Among them were a growing number of Chinese Americans. To the extent that the latter grew up in bilingual, bicultural homes, they had a head start on a trans-Pacific career.[83] Small in number in the early years, by the end of the 1990s, they and other Asian Americans accounted for about 20–25 percent of the international student body.[84] The day is not far off, says Daly, when a particular kind of

Chinese American student – one who is culturally and linguistically American but for family reasons has a Taiwan passport – will occasion a political challenge. 'But that's ok. We'll figure it out when it happens.'[85]

In response to changing student motivations, beginning in the 1990s the curriculum for both Chinese and international students de-emphasized history and area studies while expanding course offerings in law, economics, and international relations.[86] This evolution was still in process in the early twenty-first century, with course offerings reflecting 'a growing interest in law, economics, and non-governmental organizations among our students.' Chinese students, in particular, 'want to develop their understanding of multi-national forces, such as the International Monetary Fund, the World Trade Organization, and the United Nations.'[87]

During the 2006–7 academic year, the Hopkins-Nanjing Center expanded the scope and scale of its activities by offering the first Sino-US joint master's degree – in International Studies (International Relations in the Chinese-language version). A Memorandum of Understanding between Johns Hopkins University and Nanjing University listed four reasons for the new departure: (1) there was a greater need by both nations 'to train professionals who could shape bilateral relations based on deep understanding of Chinese and American institutions, language, history, and culture'; (2) both universities had sought to continue to 'internationalize their programs'; (3) the Center faced 'increased competition'; and (4) prospective students were better prepared and had clearer educational and professional goals.[88]

The master's program is administered by a Joint Academic Committee, consisting of representatives of the two parent universities and of the Center itself. The Memorandum recommits the Center to the principle of academic freedom: 'All scholars working at the HNC – students, faculty, and researchers – have, and under the master's program will continue to have, unlimited freedoms of expression and inquiry.'[89] Like the initial one-year certificate program, the new MA program involved architecture and construction. The new Samuel Pollard Building added 200,000 square feet to the Center at a cost of $21 million. The building houses high-tech classrooms, the library, an auditorium, and foreign faculty apartments. It also earned one of 11 design awards for educational and cultural facilities issued by the American Institute of Architects in 2008.[90]

The new degree program had a long gestation period. In 1986, China's then Vice Premier Li Peng, in a meeting with Chih-Yung Chien, endorsed the idea of a joint two-year MA program, but Chien suggested waiting a few years, until the one-year certificate program was running smoothly.[91] The following year, Chinese students expressed an interest in such a program. Executive Director (of the Washington Office) Daniel Wright promoted the idea during his 1999–2004 tenure. Huang Chengfeng, Chinese co-director since 2003, observed that adding a research-oriented program would both satisfy the needs of increasingly career-oriented students and keep the Center competitive as an institution. The support of university presidents William Brody and Jiang Shusheng led to the 2005 Memorandum of Understanding.[92]

During its first year, the master's program accepted ten Chinese and ten international students. For the 2011–12 academic year, there were 42 first-year and 33 second-year master's students.[93] Compared to certificate students, the master's students have stronger academic and linguistic credentials. Also, the cross-cultural dynamic among master's students has a more academic texture. On the one hand, they are not required to have an opposite-nationality roommate, although at least half choose to do so. On the other hand, the MA program provides more opportunities for native-language coursework, which means that there is more interaction of a scholarly nature between Chinese and international students.[94] With the move into research – each MA candidate writes and defends a thesis in his or her target language – new issues arose. Chinese advising norms, for example, entailed far greater direction by advisors and correspondingly less initiative from students compared to American advisor–student interactions. Students and faculty from both cultures had to make adjustments over time.[95]

In early 2011, the Joint Academic Committee commissioned an external review, conducted by Ralph Litzinger, professor of anthropology at Duke University, and Shen Dingli, professor of international relations at Fudan University. Both reviewers noted some clash between Chinese and international students' expectations and their respective research advisors' practices. Shen mentioned Chinese concerns about Hopkins' long-term commitment, driven in part by 'the frequent change in the position of American Co-Director in recent years' and associated gaps in communication. (Although Robert Daly's successor, Jan Kiely, served for three years, his term was followed by two interim co-directors, each serving for one semester.) Shen also suggested better assuring Chinese students' understanding of the United States by facilitating short-term research opportunities for them in the US, at Hopkins and elsewhere. Litzinger noted concerns by some students that their joint master's degree might not be 'as highly valued,' at least in the United States, as would a SAIS degree. While making recommendations – often for better communication – to smooth out these and other rough spots, both reviewers congratulated the Center on making steady progress. Litzinger described the Center's entire program as 'world class,' and Shen said its master's program 'provides a model and a standard from which similar joint undertakings can benefit.'[96]

With a strong record of cross-cultural and academic success and a relatively stable international climate, the most significant challenge facing the Hopkins-Nanjing Center in its third decade may be financial. The 2008–9 global financial crisis hit universities and non-profits hard, including the Center. One effort to improve the situation may have made things worse. In 2009, SAIS scaled down the Center's six-person Washington office – which recruited American and international students and faculty, raised money, and kept in touch with alumni – to one.[97]

One premise of this downsizing was that most of the positions were redundant and that SAIS personnel could recruit, raise money, etc. for the Center. Another was that significant administrative responsibilities – such as fundraising – could be shifted to the American co-director in China, with US-based staff providing support. As part of this change, what had been known as the 'Washington Office' became the 'Washington Support Office,' and the Executive Director title was replaced by Director of the Washington Support Office. In addition to economies achieved, the name changes had the additional benefit of reassuring SAIS's Chinese partners that the Americans upheld the joint-venture spirit and were not asserting primacy in the relationship.

Some flaws appeared in the logic of the first premise. In actuality, the students the Hopkins-Nanjing Center attracts are different from those who apply to SAIS; Chinese language skill is more important than a prestigious undergraduate degree. Also, as had been the case in the early years, subsuming Center fundraising under SAIS fundraising did not yield strong results. After eight months, SAIS administration adjusted course, returning admissions and development functions to a re-staffed Washington Support Office, only this time with a development officer, Center alumnus Patrick Cranley, based in Shanghai.

One indication of concern over finances is the fact that in April 2011, SAIS for the first time presented testimony to the Congressional subcommittee that was evaluating the annual ASHA budget request. SAIS did so as part of an organized effort. About two dozen NGOs had formed an ASHA Coalition to advocate against government funding reductions at a time when they already faced challenges in private fundraising. ASHA has continued to provide $600,000 per year to the Center, which comprises nearly half of total grants and about 14 percent of total funds.[98]

Emulators

There are currently hundreds of academic programs throughout China involving some level of professor and student exchange. Dozens of 'boutique-style' language programs instruct American students in the Chinese language and often include a cultural component. Several American and European universities have established English-language MBA programs in collaboration with Chinese partner universities.[99] Under new Chinese regulations that encourage Western universities to establish world-class research campuses in China, two British universities opened 'foreign cooperative' universities early in the twenty-first century, with several American universities set to follow.[100]

While the aforementioned programs entail all-English instruction to predominantly Chinese students, other exchanges have replicated some of the cross-cultural and cross-lingual features of the Hopkins-Nanjing Center. In fall 2006, for example, Yale College and Peking University launched a joint undergraduate program in which 20 students from each institution study and live together on the campus in Beijing. All classes are in English, though the Americans study Chinese. The Yale students earn Yale credits for their classes.[101] At SIAS University in Xinzheng, Henan Province, Americans comprise about 15 percent of the faculty, one-third of the textbooks are in English, and Chinese students have the option of taking online and video classes at Fort Hays State University in Kansas to earn one of several American degrees.[102]

The Hopkins-Nanjing Center emerged at the intersection of China's post-Mao leaders' turn to the West for support for their nation's modernization and American educators' perennial desire to reform China and promote cultural understanding between the two societies. In contrast to American educational initiatives in China during the late Qing and Republican periods, the Center materialized amid a more equal power relationship between China and the United States. It would not have come into being without genuine Chinese desire for and substantial financial and other contributions to the joint venture. As symbolized by the reference in the initial five-year agreement to Chinese 'sovereignty' over the physical campus, the Center realized the principle of equality between partners to a far greater degree than had earlier bilateral programs. As the first Sino-foreign university partnership since the establishment of the People's Republic, the Center paved the way for and often served as a model for other international partnerships.

2 The National Committee on United States–China Relations

Since its founding in 1966, the National Committee on United States–China Relations has been at the forefront of promoting mutual understanding between the two nations. The programmatic implementation of this unchanging mission has ranged widely over the decades, encompassing varying emphases on public education (at first in the United States only, more recently in China as well), dialogue, and exchanges in cultural, educational, and policy spheres. Henry Kissinger recently said, 'The National Committee is an indispensable part of any long-range approach to China.'[1]

Relations restored

In 1964, McCarthy-era accusations against officials who had allegedly 'lost' China were still fresh in American public memory. Thus it took courage that year for Democratic Senator J. William Fulbright and Clare Boothe Luce, a prominent Republican, to publicly call for open discussion of US policy toward the People's Republic and efforts to improve relations. Fulbright received around 12,000 letters in response to a speech on the Senate floor, and the sentiment was overwhelming favorable.[2] Luce, former Ambassador to Italy, along with her husband, magazine publisher Henry R. Luce, was a prominent supporter of the Republic of China in Taiwan and opponent of the communist government on the mainland. In a commencement speech at St John's University, though, she called for finding ways to coexist with China, 'or your generation will know nothing but endless war in the Orient.' A July 1964 *Saturday Evening Post* editorial endorsed Luce's message, giving it added momentum.[3]

Over the next two years, an alliance of Quaker peace activists, businessmen, China scholars, and philanthropists gave institutional form to this public dialogue. In December 1964, the American Friends Service Committee, the San Francisco World Trade Association, and the University of California Political Science Department convened a conference, 'An Institute on China Today,' in San Francisco. China scholar Robert Scalapino, Friends leader Cecil Thomas, and businessman Jack Gomperts were among the leading organizers. Sensing that without an East Coast presence they could not achieve respectability in the eyes of Washington policy-makers, Thomas and Scalapino organized a three-day

follow-up conference in New York in late April 1965, which drew 800 participants. Interest built, with the U.S. Chamber of Commerce voting 'to explore steps
designed to more effectively open channels of communication with the people of
mainland China' and the League of Women Voters selecting China as its study
issue for 1966.[4]

On 9 June 1966, the first meeting of the National Committee on US–China
Relations was held. The new organization chose Robert Scalapino as chairman,
Cecil Thomas as executive director, Robert Mang as program director, and
Pamela Mang as information officer. The founding was largely an act of faith,
with no funding yet committed. A few weeks later, two Bay Area businessmen
and two foundations pledged a total of $25,000. The Rockefeller and Ford
Foundations eventually made three-year commitments of $450,000 and $350,000,
respectively, but without an immediate personal donation of $20,000 by John D.
Rockefeller III, the newly formed organization would have faced a choice
between paying staff and putting on programs.[5]

Between 1966 and 1972, the National Committee organized 180 forums, seminars, and other programs about American China policy.[6] 'But its original mission
of public education was altered dramatically by the events of April 1971,' writes
Jan Berris, who joined the National Committee as a program officer in September
1971 and has been its vice president since 1980. Berris refers to an invitation to
American table tennis players to visit China, following an international tourna-
ment in Japan. This artful Chinese initiative would soon be immortalized in the
expression 'ping-pong diplomacy.' The Americans wanted to reciprocate, but
'the U.S. Table Tennis Association (USTTA), a small, loosely knit organization
of ping-pong enthusiasts, lacked the administrative and financial resources and
the knowledge of China necessary for undertaking such a project.' The National
Committee offered to provide the needed administrative support, thus shifting the
group's mission in a new direction. While in Beijing, the team proffered a joint
National Committee/USTTA invitation for Chinese players to go to the United
States.[7]

A few months after the Chinese table tennis team's successful April 1972 visit,
China's United Nations Mission, which housed the PRC's only representatives in
the United States, expressed an interest in sending an acrobatic team to the United
States and asked whether the National Committee would be willing to sponsor
such an event. The National Committee answered affirmatively, and an American
tour by the Shenyang Acrobatic Troupe followed. So did a decade of athletic
and cultural exchanges, with more substantive exchanges slowly but gradually
interspersed.

From 1971 through 1979, the National Committee, along with the Committee
on Scholarly Communication with the People's Republic of China, functioned as
a kind of surrogate State Department.[8] As former National Committee President
David M. Lampton explained:

> Before normalization, Chinese leaders would come to the United States, but
> they couldn't meet with the President, because we had Taiwan here, right?

They had to be treated with dignity, yet they couldn't be the guests of the government. So, that meant that we had to, in effect, kind of play a government role.[9]

After normalization, of course, the US government did not need a surrogate to host Chinese officials – or to conduct exchanges – but found it beneficial to keep the society-to-society channel active. For its part, the National Committee was eager to stay involved and, with the backdrop of closer official ties, exchanges increasingly trended from symbolic to more substantive content.[10] According to Berris, though, gains in mutual understanding were initially limited and sometimes superficial. Visiting Chinese city officials, for example, 'spent most of their time in the United States lifting up manhole covers to look at underground cables instead of exploring the human aspects of city administration.' Similarly, a delegation of American political leaders were more interested in shopping for saddles in Inner Mongolia than in learning about the political dynamics of the autonomous region.[11]

An expanding agenda of exchanges necessitated expanded funding. The founding scholars, Quakers, and philanthropists had eschewed government funding – as a way of staying non-partisan and avoiding outside influence. Beginning in mid-1972, the board of directors agreed to accept some US government funding, primarily to cover unanticipated costs related to the security of the visiting Chinese table tennis delegation. However, a cap was put on the percentage it would take.[12] With Washington viewing unofficial contacts as a useful complement to official relations, US government financial support for the National Committee grew throughout the 1980s. Until the late 1990s, when funding from other sources dramatically increased, government grants – mainly from the United States Information Agency and the Department of Health and Human Services – accounted for 25–30 percent of the National Committee budget.[13]

In addition to the state of official relations, China's internal political dynamics also shaped the evolution of exchanges. China increasingly looked abroad for ideas and models that it could selectively incorporate into its development strategy. As Berris observed in 1985, 'The "Four Modernizations" course on which China has embarked has made it possible for both sides to engage in broad discussion and cooperative programs on issues related to China's social agenda.'[14]

Promoting mutual understanding through exchanges

The National Committee took a hiatus from its original public education mission from 1974 until 1987, when a new president, David M. Lampton, restored those activities.[15] Meanwhile, policy exchanges grew in number and importance and by 1984 fell into six categories: governance, international relations, economic development, education, and communications, with transnational issues such as public health and the environment being added in 1990. In dozens of events per year, delegations of teachers, mayors, journalists, legislators, and policy advisors from one country visited the other.[16] In many cases, particularly in the mid-1990s, the Chinese indicated what they wanted to learn about American society or polity and asked the National Committee to organize a tour for a Chinese delegation that would meet that goal.[17]

The National Committee's most durable exchange effort has been in the field of education, specifically its administration of one component of the multi-faceted Fulbright-Hayes educational exchange program between the two countries. In late 1979, the US Office of Education signed a Memorandum of Understanding with its Chinese counterpart, and exchanges began the following year. In an exemplary instance of public–private cooperation, the US government delegated administration and programming functions to private organizations.[18]

While the Committee on Scholarly Communication with the People's Republic of China managed long-term exchanges of students, teachers, and scholars, the National Committee administered shorter-term Fulbright programs. Due to its experience in handling education-focused exchanges (e.g. sending five groups of American educators to China and bringing five delegations of Chinese educators to the United States between 1973 and 1979), the National Committee was asked by the US Office of Education in 1980 to handle logistics and program development for delegations of educators from each country. Each summer – with the exceptions of 1989 (Tiananmen crisis) and 2003 (SARS crisis) – the National Committee has sent 16 to 20 teachers to China for four to six weeks. Varying from year to year, the group has included primary, secondary and post-secondary instructors. The American visitors attend lectures by Chinese scholars, supplemented by relevant historic and cultural site visits, interact with officials and ordinary Chinese, and gather material for required curriculum projects.[19] 'Information and impressions are in turn brought back to the classroom [in the United States], broadening the perspectives of students and piquing the interest of future China hands.'[20]

For the matching side of the Fulbright-Hayes exchanges, each spring and fall the National Committee hosts a delegation of 12 Chinese educators. In this case, the programs are more topically focused, with the visitors setting the agenda. In the early years, Chinese educators were interested in basic issues like teacher training. In later years, programs encompassed more sophisticated themes, such as special needs education and the integration of a university with its local community.[21]

Rule of law issues have long been another strong component of the National Committee's activities. Some early legal exchanges manifested irony as well as substance. In the summer of 1990, a delegation from the China Press Law Research Center traveled to the United States

> seeking to understand what aspects of the American press law might be useful to China. To their surprise, they found no American press law, just a 14-word prohibition against one: 'Congress shall make no law … abridging the freedom of speech, or of the press …'

During the same year, a six-member Chinese delegation investigated American and Canadian laws on non-profit organizations.

> Although they were told many times that the only federal agencies that really have any authority over nonprofit entities are those that are responsible for taxes (i.e., the IRS and Revenue Canada) and that the only state/provincial authority comes in the registration process, they kept searching for additional controls.[22]

Subsequent exchanges involving legal issues brought Chinese academics and legislators to the United States to explore laws on economic crimes (1991), legislative researchers to the United States to study administrative law (1992), American specialists to China to present workshops on legal training and court administration (1998), American judges and legal scholars to China to present workshops on American civil trial procedures (2000), and a return visit by Chinese judges to the United States to get a firsthand view of American civil trials (2000), among others.[23] The National Committee also sponsored high-profile visits to China by US Supreme Court Justice Anthony Kennedy in 1995 and by several senior judges and officials from the Supreme People's Court of China in 2001.[24]

From the beginning of the reform period in 1978, the Chinese government and the Communist Party gave increasing priority to establishing a predictable legal structure. Like 'modernization' and (to a lesser extent) 'human rights,' 'rule of law' has come to constitute a discourse in which leaders and members of nations with diverse social systems and political cultures can conduct dialogues, using a common vocabulary. Thomas Carothers, Director of the Democracy and Rule of Law Project at the Carnegie Endowment for International Peace, defines the rule of law as 'a system in which the laws are public knowledge, are clear in meaning, and apply equally to everyone. ... Despite the close ties of the rule of law to democracy and capitalism, [however,] it stands apart as a non-ideological, even technical, solution [to the problems developing nations face].'[25]

Various Chinese actors have different, often overlapping, motivations in promoting the rule of law. For ordinary Chinese – from factory workers to the growing middle class – insulation from official capriciousness is an attractive goal. For the state, creation of a transparent legal environment is a means of promoting economic growth and global integration.[26] With a delicate balancing act, it can also be a way to maintain the legitimacy of the Communist Party, which is no longer able to command broad allegiance on the basis of Maoist ideology or direct control over citizens' livelihoods.[27] President Jiang Zemin told the Party's 16th Congress in 2002, for example, 'If we do not crack down on corruption ... the party will be in danger of losing its ruling position, or possibly heading for self-destruction.'[28] Individual leaders may also see the rule of law as a path toward incremental democratic reform.[29] For all Chinese, the rule of law holds out the promise of avoiding a recurrence of the chaos that engulfed the country during the Cultural Revolution.

For the most part, it is difficult to quantify the degree to which the National Committee's legal exchange programs have promoted the rule of law within

China. Judge Margaret McKeown found '[t]he curiosity of the Chinese judges [who attended workshops in Shanghai and Jinan in 2000] as to how we process and litigate civil cases ... both genuine and extensive,' but she ventured no conclusion about where that curiosity might lead. Justice Michael Mihm, who participated in both civil trial exchanges, was confident that the National Committee's activity 'has and will have an incremental impact on the course of history.' As restraining factors, however, he noted 'substantial differences in culture [between the two societies] and the reality of the control of the communist party over all legal processes.'[30]

Most participants in education, legal, and other exchanges were not widely known in their host countries, but celebrities occasionally made the news. In 1987, for example, Deng Xiaoping's son, Deng Pufang, led a delegation that visited the United States at the invitation of the National Committee. The younger Deng had become paralyzed from the waist down when a group of Red Guards threw him from a fourth-story window during the Cultural Revolution. At a 1985 dinner honoring two Chinese diplomats in Beijing, Deng happened to be seated next to National Committee Vice Chairman Caroline Ahmanson. He mentioned to Ahmanson his interest in helping China's disabled population and in learning how the United States handled disability policy issues. A National Committee-sponsored trip resulted from this dinner conversation, including a meeting at the White House between Deng and President Reagan and an article in the *New York Times* that featured Deng's views on improving society's treatment of the disabled.[31]

Maturing relationship and programs

As US–China state and economic relations matured during the 1990s, so did the exchange relationship. Gone were 'the days ... when Americans were stared at and followed by large numbers of people and Chinese were a curiosity in the United States.' As novelty wore off, the interests of visitors grew increasingly substantive, like Deng Pufang's. Also like Deng's visit, most of the exchanges were one-time events. There was some thematic continuity from one exchange to the next within the same category, but little or no organized follow-up on the connections made or the insights gained.[32]

The Tiananmen crisis of 1989 threatened to disrupt the National Committee's exchange programs, as it did every other aspect of the bilateral relationship – official and unofficial, economic and cultural. 'Nineteen Hundred Eighty Nine will go down as the most painful year in US–PRC relations in two decades,' wrote National Committee Chairman Raymond Shafer and President David M. Lampton. The board's response was a combined commitment to 'speak the truth about the events in China and their consequences for US–PRC relations,' but also to 'stay engaged, for it has been engagement that has contributed to the change which the Chinese people themselves have demonstrated they desire and which Americans applaud.'[33] For five months after the crisis, however, neither side pushed ahead with new exchanges. During those months, the National Committee diverted exchange funds to public education activities and its Scholar Orientation Program.[34]

Scholar Orientation Program

In 1980, National Committee President Arthur Rosen launched the Scholar Orientation Program (SOP). Rosen was responding to the coincident phenomena of the Iranian hostage crisis and the arrival of the first post-normalization cohort of Chinese students in the United States. Seeing anti-American Iranian students protesting outside the State Department, Rosen 'thought that here were students in this country who really didn't understand American foreign policy and how it worked.' He worried that visiting Chinese students would remain equally isolated from and ignorant of their host country. To forestall that outcome, the National Committee began, several times a year, inviting groups of 13 Chinese students and visiting scholars already present in the United States to participate in a two-week tour of American civic institutions.[35] The program varied somewhat, depending upon the background of the participants (teachers, journalists, lawyers, etc.). Participants typically visited 'Civil War battlefields, farms, factories, think tanks, police departments, jails, newsrooms, and soup kitchens,' meeting 'justices of the Supreme Court, cabinet members, state governors, Congressional representatives, welfare recipients, and street gang members.'[36]

The SOP format remained remarkably consistent over two decades, and most participants felt they gained deeper insights into American society. By the early twenty-first century, however, diminishing funding, a declining applicant pool, and the fact that Chinese students were less isolated than they had once been on American campuses led to the program's demise. '[T]hey began getting cars, they began to travel, they began going to some of these places on their own.' Thus, 2002 was the last year for the Scholar Orientation Program.[37]

In a sense, however, the program was reincarnated in 2007. While the SOP had been aimed primarily at scholars, a companion Consular Orientation Program had treated a smaller number of Chinese diplomats to the same two-week tour during their assignment in the United States. In 2007, the National Committee launched the Policy Leaders Orientation Program, which uses the earlier program model to provide direct access to American institutions, both to Chinese diplomats and, in separate sessions, to visiting mid-career officials from the Ministry of Defense, the People's Bank of China, the State Environmental Protection Administration, and other branches of government. Unlike twenty-first century visiting scholars, such officials often find it difficult to connect to their host society. Homestays with American families during the two-week itinerary have been particularly popular.[38]

U.S.–China Dialogue

Another long-running program, the almost annual U.S.–China Dialogue, began in 1984 and continued through 2002 as a joint project of the National Committee and its counterpart organization, the Chinese People's Institute of Foreign Affairs. This was the National Committee's first Track II dialogue – i.e., discussions between influential but unofficial representatives of two nations. Rather than seeking immediate outcomes on the wide range of bilateral issues they discussed, both sides believed that 'the value of the forum would not be fully evident until personal relationships of candor and trust had been developed and until the bilateral relationship was in trouble.'[39]

Trouble set the stage for the fourth Dialogue, which convened in Beijing just nine months after the Tiananmen Square tragedy. Despite grave challenges to the relationship, Dialogue participants were united in a belief that 'in the long run, healthy U.S.–China relations are in the interest of both countries.' By the 11th Dialogue in Tarrytown, New York in June 2002, the National Committee's assessment was that the 'conversations have gained depth, partially due to the range of representatives on both sides.' That year's participants, for example, included Henry Kissinger (Secretary of State under Presidents Nixon and Ford), Carla Hills (business executive, trade official under President George H. W. Bush, and National Committee Chair), Kenneth Roth (Director of Human Rights Watch), Andrew Kohut (Director of the Pew Research Center for the People and the Press), Tang Shubei (President of the Research Center for Relations Across the Taiwan Straits), Fan Guoxiang (of the China Society for Human Rights Studies), Ni Shixiong (Dean, School of International Relations and Public Affairs, Fudan University), and Qiu Shengyun (Ministry of Foreign Affairs).[40]

Tiananmen was not the last intrusion of geopolitical reality into the calmer realm of cultural exchange. After U.S.-led NATO forces bombed the Chinese Embassy in Belgrade in May of 1999, the hosting Chinese People's Institute of Foreign Affairs (CPIFA) 'felt that the timing was too early' for the 10th Dialogue, which had been scheduled in Beijing for 1–3 June, and postponed it.[41] Feeling that informal dialogue was all the more urgent when official relations became frayed, the National Committee's president, John Holden, reports:

> I wrote to CPIFA in Beijing and said, 'I'd like to come for meetings. This is an important time in U.S.–China relations.' I got no response. And then I wrote back and said, 'I'm coming anyway. I have to be in the region, and I'm going to drop in. I don't need a visa invitation. If I come, will you see me?' And they said, 'Yes.'

The 10th Dialogue was postponed until January 2000, but shortly after his solo trip, Holden organized a delegation for a follow-up visit, and the Chinese agreed to meet with them as well. This group of friends and colleagues included prominent China specialists, such as Ezra Vogel, Harry Harding, and Mary Bullock.[42]

Sustained programming reinforced

On 13 December 1987, Arthur Rosen stepped down after 13 years as president of the National Committee. David M. Lampton, who had spent two decades alternating between China studies and hands-on involvement in policy (e.g. at the American Enterprise Institute), took the helm. 'If the 1980s was the decade of "normalization,"' said the board of directors, 'the 1990s ought to be the decade of "maturity." Future exchanges should promote 'deepening mutual understanding of each other's basic institutions' and 'broadening participation in the U.S.–China relationship by leadership echelons beyond [i.e., below] the national level.' Additionally, the board urged incorporation into the National Committee's programming of a 'multilateral' dimension.[43]

Several factors converged to lead the board to target exchange partners 'beyond the national level' and Lampton to extend this policy to the non-governmental sphere, where possible. One is that the high-visibility exchanges the National Committee had coordinated with Beijing officials prior to normalization now flowed through official government-to-government channels; additionally, other private sector organizations had developed the administrative capacity for working with Chinese partners in their fields of interest. These changes drove the National Committee to seek partners at various levels other than the apex of the Chinese government.[44] Another factor was that in China national leaders spend many years working at the local level before being elevated to positions in the central government. The National Committee thought it would be beneficial to get to know these future leaders at a younger age.[45] Finally, the appearance of a number of new Chinese NGOs and GONGOs (government-organized non-governmental organizations) in the 1990s provided a host of natural exchange partners.[46]

As the National Committee analyzed the emerging situation in 1993, 'Resources in China are being decentralized, a middle class is rising, social problems and new opportunities are developing far faster than the central government can address them, and there is a need for social organizations to meet these needs and seize these opportunities.'[47] The growing influence of these new, or newly empowered, institutions raised a number of questions. While most Americans hoped that these changes were harbingers of liberalization, the Chinese leadership wondered how to unleash new social forces on behalf of modernization without letting them usurp the authority of the Communist Party. The new institutions themselves had many practical questions and hoped that foreign experience could provide some of the answers.[48]

In 1995, the United Nations-sponsored International Women's Forum in Beijing amplified trends that were already orienting the National Committee toward China's civil society. By tradition, the main forum is supplemented by an auxiliary NGO forum, through which non-governmental organizations have an opportunity to inject their ideas into the agenda of the main forum. Chinese authorities, fearful of influences they could not control, housed the NGO forum in Huairou, 25 km from central Beijing. Future National Committee official Elizabeth Knup recalls the scene:

> [T]he NGOs … were used to having access, and they were totally furious that they were really far away. But two things happened. One was a lot of Chinese NGOs, nascent NGOs, or individuals that had that inclination were kind of empowered by all these other NGOs; they hung out with them in Huairou, and they learned from them. … And, secondly, the Chinese government learned that, in fact, NGOs aren't all bad. … Not all NGOs are

confrontational like Greenpeace. In fact, they provide things that the government can't provide in society. So, from that period forward, China slowly began to be more accepting of NGOs in general.[49]

Though acceptance of NGOs has been a gradual and incomplete process, as early as the late 1980s China had begun sending delegations abroad, especially to the United States, to gather ideas about how to establish and support an NGO sector. Visitors asked:

> What is a non-governmental organization? How do they run? How do they get money? What relationship do they have with the government? What relationship do they have with their members? What is the difference between a lobbying and a non-lobbying organization?[50]

The Chinese Ministry of Civil Affairs assumed jurisdiction over NGOs in 1988 and issued preliminary regulations in October 1989. The June 1989 Tiananmen crisis slowed, but did not halt, the process. To glean ideas for permanent regulatory legislation, in April 1990, the Ministry sent a six-person study group on a tour of the United States and Canada. The trip was sponsored by the National Committee and funded by the Ford Foundation. Its purpose was 'to carry out comparative research on non-profit laws and customs in pluralistic societies.'[51] In 1993, the National Committee sponsored a delegation of American foundation leaders, whose tour of China resulted in a report entitled 'The Rise of Non-Governmental Organizations in China: The Implications for Americans.' Correspondingly, in 1995, a group of Chinese foundation leaders visited the United States under National Committee sponsorship.[52]

The following year, another US delegation went to China, where the participants organized workshops on NGOs. At a workshop in Kunming, there was evidence of grassroots involvement in addressing problems such as AIDS, drug abuse, poverty, and minority rights. In Shanghai, the visitors noticed growing professionalism and 'a continuity with groups that had existed before 1949, such as the YMCA.'[53]

Saving Northeast China's wetlands

The Ussuri Watershed Project was the first to fully embody the National Committee's new vision. It was a medium-term project, it involved participants beyond the upper levels of government in Beijing and Shanghai, and it was multilateral. The substantive goal of the three-year project was to make detailed land use recommendations that would support both environmental preservation and economic development on the Russian and Chinese sides of the Ussuri River. One impulse for the choice of an environmental project was acceptability to the Chinese government. The earliest Chinese environmental NGOs were non-threatening, since they generally supported Beijing's policies.[54] Furthermore, environmental policy was becoming a laboratory for the decentralization of authority. Heilongjiang Planning Commission leader and key project participant

Du Youlin told Peter Riggs of Rockefeller Brothers Fund, the primary project funder, that HPC did not need Beijing's approval for 'sub-agreements,' only for the global agreement.[55]

A second impulse for the project was the personal interest in environmentalism of a National Committee board member. Douglas Murray joined the National Committee as a program director in 1970. He served as vice president from 1971 through 1974, interim president between the terms of David M. Lampton and John Holden (1997–8), and board member almost continuously from 1975 through 2007. As early as 1990, Murray became a self-described 'thorn in the side' of the organization on environmental issues. When an environmental organization that had done work in New York State and in Russia approached the National Committee in 1993 about a joint project, he became the project's champion.[56]

There were four parties to the Ussuri Project, each with its own personnel profile and interests. The National Committee, in line with its new direction, wanted to facilitate more international dialogue, to have more extended projects (as opposed to one-off exchanges), and to connect with Chinese actors outside of Beijing. A second American participant was Ecologically Sustainable Development (ESD), the group that had solicited Murray for National Committee assistance. ESD's leader, George Davis, had won a MacArthur Award for a planning model he implemented for Adirondack State Park in New York, and he wanted to see whether the same model could be applied to northern China and the Russian Far East.[57]

On the Russian side of the river, there was much land but few people. The Russian team consisted of environmental scientists, some of whom reflected, in Murray's words, the 'great romanticism about the land and nature' that permeates Russian culture. These specialists had a detailed understanding of the local flora, fauna, animals, and water resources, which they sought to protect.[58]

On the Chinese side of the river, by contrast, there were many people and less land. Officials from the Heilongjiang Province Planning Commission led the Chinese team. They and the scientists they recruited were interested mainly in promoting economic development, which they hoped to do in a 'sustainable' way that would accord with new national priorities.[59] A National Committee investigation found:

> The Chinese interest lies in getting American agreement to a land use plan which will 1) ward off some of the pressure from the international 'greenies,' 2) put them on record as being serious about biodiversity …, and most of all 3) help them attract foreign investors and foreign trade to Heilongjiang.[60]

By the end of 1992, George Davis and ESD had Russian environmentalists lined up for a cross-border project. Murray then secured funding from the Rockefeller Brothers Fund and Chinese commitment to the project. According to a memorandum of understanding signed in Beijing on 18 June 1993, 'the Chinese and American sides agree to undertake a cooperative project for planning of economic growth and ecological protection in the Ussuri River watershed.' The Chinese would organize government officials from Heilongjiang Province to provide data and maps; the Americans would publish a final report and organize press conferences in the United States, Japan, and Korea.[61]

Early in the project, American participants expressed frustration with Chinese cooperation. Team members had brought hiking boots and insect repellent, expecting to engage in field work. 'Instead, every step of the way we were briefed to a fare-thee-well by our solicitous hosts, sitting around day after day in the usual stiff and stuffy Chinese fashion in conference rooms.' The failure of Chinese team leader Du Youlin or his colleagues to produce good maps of the watershed area was especially frustrating, even though their failure reflected the fragmentation of Chinese bureaucracy rather than their own unwillingness. To the surprise of the Chinese, the best map available for a helicopter tour came from the American Defense Mapping Agency, where it could be purchased for $4.00.[62]

The Chinese had concerns as well, particularly regarding control of the project. They complained that the Americans were more interested in Chinese maps and data than in Chinese participation and seemed uninterested in gathering new data. Initially, Davis defended the American position on grounds of urgency and cost. Ultimately, though, the Americans accepted a Chinese proposal to set up a board of ten persons (three each Chinese and Russian and four American, including the chair), with 8–10 specialist groups reporting to it.[63]

During an August 1994 visit to the United States, Russian and Chinese participants paused for dinner with their hosts at a Russian restaurant in New York. A recap of their experiences highlighted the ability of the Americans to provide useful practical examples. The first stop, for example, had been Lake Tahoe, where the delegates learned that not only can 'economic development … occur while maintaining a comparatively pristine environment,' but that 'Lake Tahoe's major tourism industry *depends* on the maintenance of such an environment [emphasis in original].'[64]

Frustrations notwithstanding, field exploration moved forward. As a steering committee meeting convened in Vladivostok in April 1996, a final report was nearing completion.[65] When the four parties to the Ussuri Project published their final report in November 1996, Murray remarked, 'Seeing the report was quite an epiphany – four years between two handsome covers, illustrated, in three languages!' The Americans held several press conferences, fulfilling one of their commitments. Still, Murray had 'one overriding concern: what is our level of confidence about official support for the report's recommendations?' He was more confident about support in China, where he felt Du and his colleagues had been 'reading the official tea leaves very carefully,' but less so in Russia, where he felt official support was 'fluid and fickle.' ESD, conversely, was upbeat about George Davis's upcoming pre-press conference meetings with Russia's krai (province) and Duma (state legislature) officials and hoped the National Committee would not delay press conferences in Harbin and Beijing. Uncertainty about the likelihood of implementation led the National Committee to opine in its newsletter, 'In some ways, the easy work is now complete and the difficult work of implementation of the recommendations remains.'[66] (For the project's aftermath, see Chapter 4.)

Civil society project

In 1997, the Henry Luce Foundation solicited proposals for a multi-year civil society project as a way to 'enrich the U.S.–China relationship,' though not necessarily 'to change China.'[67]

The Luce call for proposals closely correlated with the National Committee's own growing interests in China's civil society and in multi-year exchange programs. In October 1997, National Committee President David M. Lampton submitted a project proposal which stated:

> [T]he National Committee proposes a three-year (1998–2000) exchange project designed to accomplish the following objectives: 1) to move Sino-American exchanges more aggressively beyond China's eastern seaboard ...; 2) to increase American (and National Committee) capacity to deal directly with Chinese citizens throughout the country with minimal mediation of government foreign affairs offices that often monopolize the choice of participants; 3) to encourage Chinese citizens to increase their capacities for decentralization, privatization, and the development of civic organizations; 4) to involve Chinese citizens in a joint process of developing ... programs, rather than simply expecting the Chinese to favorably react to American-generated initiatives; and 5) to help educate influential Americans about emerging trends in the PRC ...[68]

The National Committee received the Luce grant and recruited Marilyn Beach as the program associate to be in charge of the project. Beach had a degree in Chinese Studies and a background in social and environmental policy issues. Her key initial task was to identify individuals, topics, and localities which ought to be involved in the project and establish joint working groups around two issue areas. (Given the relatively relaxed climate of the times, Beach was able to do this on her own to a much greater extent than had been possible in the past.) Building on two existing National Committee program emphases, one group would deal with the environment and the 'decentralization revolution,' another with education and the 'privatization revolution,' and both would attempt to connect with civil society forces.[69]

In May 1998, Beach went to northeast China with Elizabeth Knup to develop a strategy and to look for partners for the environmental component of the project. Knup, her outgoing predecessor, had just accepted a new position as American co-director of the Hopkins-Nanjing Center.[70] Although the new environmental project was in the same area of northern China as the just completed Ussuri Project, there was minimal 'head start' effect. Knup introduced Beach to Du Youlin, but Beach ultimately chose partners other than the provincial Planning Commission he headed. In contrast to the Ussuri Project, the new project's emphasis was more on building civil society linkages than on exchange per se or on policy outcomes. Further, the most enthusiastic of potential Chinese Working Group members were interested in water, as opposed to land use, issues.[71]

China had lost 50 percent of its wetlands since 1950, and the government in Beijing had just spent three years formulating a national preservation policy.[72]

Prior to the May 1999 Working Group meeting, Beach and the National Committee chose as their institutional partners the Environmental Protection Bureau in Heilongjiang Province and the Changchun-based Institute of Geography of the Chinese Academy of Sciences in Jilin. The Chinese team consisted of Chen Wanfeng, professor at the Heilongjiang Environmental Science Research Institute; Deng Wei, professor and deputy director of the Changchun Institute of Geography; Guo Yuan, division chief at Heilongjiang Provincial Environmental Protection Bureau; Li Tingzhang, engineer at Mudanjiang Environmental Protection Bureau with jurisdiction over Jingbo Lake; Ma Yongcai, engineer at Jilin City Environmental Monitoring Station with jurisdiction over Songhua Reservoir; Zhang Hongyan and Shang Jincheng, environmental professors at Northeast Normal University in Changchun; and Wen Li, official at Suihua Eco-Pilot Zone. The four water sites they selected were the Suihua Eco-Pilot Zone and Jingbo Lake in Heilongjiang Province and Songhua Lake and Xianghai wetland in neighboring Jilin Province.[73]

Beach next recruited American Working Group members, based on the types of people the Chinese wanted to work with. The initial American team consisted of: William Chang, former professor and water issue specialist at the National Science Foundation, who worked on the project on his own time; Jim Harris of the International Crane Foundation (ICF), who had participated in a limited way in the Ussuri Project; Francesca DiCosmo of the US Environmental Protection Agency; Don Woodward, hydrologist with the US Department of Agriculture; and Sheree Willis, initially an interpreter who, because of both her interest and her technical background in Chinese environmental issues, eventually became a team member.[74]

The first Joint US–China Working Group meeting convened in Harbin from 19 to 25 May 1999. Members got acquainted, visited the Xianghai Nature Reserve in Jilin, and began discussion of long-term projects that could follow the completion of this limited, three-year endeavor.[75] Two events, however, made May a busier and more intense month than the National Committee had originally anticipated. The first was serious flooding that had occurred in northeastern China during the summer of 1998 and a resulting request to the National Committee for help garnering American technical support. Li Weixiang, chief of the Heilongjiang Environmental Protection Bureau, and Guo Yuan, head of its Foreign Affairs section, had gotten to know the National Committee and Marilyn Beach through the Civil Society Project. As they coped with the technical and human consequences of the flooding, they asked the National Committee for assistance in organizing a workshop in Harbin to develop long-term preventive strategies. The workshop yielded a list of detailed recommendations on forest restoration, establishment of waterbird reserves, water storage, soil conservation, and study of American 'no-till' agricultural technology.[76] Though not part of the initial project plan, the workshop dovetailed nicely with the National Committee's agenda.

'One of the special features of this workshop,' wrote Beach, 'is that it has genuine grassroots origins and reflects needs as defined by the Chinese themselves.'[77]

The other intrusion into the Working Group's plans was the NATO bombing of China's Belgrade embassy. 'I'm sure there is no threat,' Beach wrote to Jan Berris, 'but I am definitely picking up on tensions.' A section of Beach's report during this tense period nicely summarizes the cluster of problems that American exchange organizations face in China:

> [T]he meetings we were to have had in Baicheng today were cancelled for one or all of the following reasons: our five hour trip from Harbin turned into a ten hour one; the local EPB is poor and they are ashamed that they cannot afford to invite us to a meal on our first meeting, as they feel is the right thing to do; political tensions stemming from the bombing are putting up road-blocks; or the reason they have given us: the local EPB chief had to go to Changchun to meet an important visitor.[78]

The second Working Group convened as a November 1999 trip to the United States by the eight Chinese members. The group visited an EPA regional office, a water treatment plant, two Lake Tahoe nature sites, and several other locations. Through its connection with Harris, the National Committee was able to bring the Chinese team members to ICF's headquarters in Baraboo, Wisconsin. During the visit, the Americans not only exposed their visitors to local methods of water management but also emphasized, to an initially skeptical audience, the roles played by civil society forces in America.[79]

During the US tour, the realization by both sides that 'Northeast China was not yet fertile ground for NGO development' led to an adjustment in the project's original goal. The working group 'shifted its focus slightly' from developing civil society to 'ways to structure public-private partnerships that can effectively address local water quality management issues.'[80] Before the November 1999 Working Group meeting was over, the Chinese had invited their American colleagues to bring two or three experts in public-private wetlands management partnerships to the third Working Group, scheduled for July 2000 in China. Several American scientists in the Working Group 'were pleased with the invitation since it gave American specialists access to two environmentally sensitive sites in China's interior that are very seldom frequented by foreign specialists.'[81]

The National Committee hoped that its three-year environmental project would serve as a 'seed grant' that would lead to follow-up projects. 'So, in the course of our discussions,' Beach recalls, 'we reserved a certain amount of time at the end to talk about, "Where could we go from here?"' In its final report to the Henry Luce Foundation, the National Committee identified four areas of potential follow-up bilateral cooperation.[82] (See discussion in Chapter 5.)

Beach started work on the civil society education track a half year later than the environment track. Prior to her September 1998 exploratory trip, she contacted Daniel Wright, who she had heard was living in Guizhou Province in China's southwest interior. Wright had a two-year grant from the Institute of Current

World Affairs (ICWA) to study education in the Chinese interior. With a Chinese wife, two children, and good language skills, he was an ideal resource.[83] Wright responded enthusiastically to Beach's e-mail: '[I]f we are going to understand, much less build an increasingly healthy relationship with China, the U.S. must better understand the country's vast interior, and where possible, do what we can to assist its development.' He agreed to meet with her and to help her make local contacts.[84]

Wright arranged for Beach to meet with about twenty 'teachers, private school entrepreneurs, vocational training specialists, university professors, Project Hope [a Chinese education-oriented charity] representatives, and government bureaucrats.'[85] The diverse definitions of 'private school' and 'civil society' began to make sense. The Chinese term that Americans often translate as 'private schools' – *shehui liliang banxue* – for example, can also be rendered as 'socially strengthened schools.' It implies 'not for profit' and at least some degree of administrative and pedagogical independence from the standard state-run school system.[86]

By the time she returned to China in June 1999, Beach had a working group of vocational high-school educators. Wright, with the help of Qiannan Computer Vocational School Principal Bi Jiangang, had selected three additional schools whose principals would join the Working Group. The participants reflected geographic diversity: a suburb of Guiyang, the most developed city; Zunyi, a relatively developed city; Liupanshui, an industrial city; and Duyun, a less developed city in Southern Guizhou. They also represented the range of institutional forms in China's vocational school sector: '1) owned by the state, 2) owned by the state but run by private individuals, 3) run by the state and subsidized by private individuals, and 4) private schools.'[87]

One important thing was lacking, though: an official Chinese institutional sponsor. Wright counseled that having an enthusiastic 'champion' was more important than the identity of the sponsoring organization.[88] In March 1999, Wright jubilantly reported that Guizhou's provincial vice governor, Guo Shuqing, was that champion. Guo suggested a couple of candidates for a sponsoring organization, including the one that ultimately played that role, the Guizhou Economic System Reform Commission.[89]

The next step would be a formal project kick-off. While Beach had intentionally kept a low profile on her first visit, Wright encouraged her to bring prominent National Committee leaders for this June 1999 event. Dignitaries would provide important credibility with local leaders and would justify media coverage, which would in turn promote broad public support.[90] During the June visit, Beach and Wright signed up the six Chinese Working Group members: Wang Liquan, Deputy Director of the provincial Development Research Center and the highest-ranking Chinese member; Wang Lanshan, a division director within the sponsoring Economic System Reform Commission; Zhu Weide, principal of the provincial Tourism School; Bi Jiangang, principal of the Computer Vocational/ Technical School in Qiannan; Huang Weican, principal of the Secondary Vocational School in Zunyi Development Zone; and Wang Dilun, principal of the

Secondary Vocational/Technical School in Liupanshui. Later in the summer, two school administrators from Appalachia (Dan Branham of the Appalachian Educational Laboratory and Frank Kincaid of Lee County Area Technology Center) and an international education professor (Robert Nelsen of the University of Illinois) joined Wright to round out the American team.[91] The program was to last three years, from 1999 through 2001. Each year there would be at least one international exchange, and 'The Chinese side undertakes to organize one to three inter-province and several intra-province exchanges each year.'[92]

Wasting little time, Beach and Wright organized the first Working Group meeting in Guizhou in August 1999. An American participant was struck by the dearth of infrastructural resources that American educators take for granted. 'Every one of our schools has computer labs, air conditioning, water and sewer, a traffic system. A lot of those schools did not.' On the other hand, he was also impressed by one abundant resource: 'the thirst for education.'[93]

One highlight of the first Working Group was a visit by Pennsylvania Congressional Representative and acquaintance of Wright, Joseph Pitts. After spending two days in the capital city of Guiyang and two hours visiting with the Chinese Working Group members 'in a villa ... built for and used by Zhou Enlai and his wife in 1961,' Pitts felt that he and his wife Ginny had 'experienced the real China.'[94] The desired publicity resulted, with the *Guizhou Ribao* (*Guizhou Daily*) reporting, 'Pitts's visit to Guizhou, on which he was accompanied by his wife and his assistant, aimed to find out the situation of economic development of our province and to investigate the education programs implemented in Guiyang by the National Committee on United States–China Relations.'[95]

China's experimentation with various forms of private education garnered media attention in the United States, as well as at home. In May 2000, Beach informed Henry Luce Foundation Chairman Henry Luce III about a *Wall Street Journal* article that was 'based on a series of conversations with our six Guizhou-based team members.' The article's author observed that 'while private schools in the West are often bastions of the elite, China's serve a generation of have-nots who would otherwise lack opportunities for further studies.'[96]

Though the *Wall Street Journal* article did not mention it, later that month the Chinese members of the Working Group would arrive in the United States for a look at several different styles of vocational education. The National Committee focused the tour on Appalachia, because of its similarities to Guizhou in 'relative poverty, the importance of coal mining, and their mountainous topography.' The Chinese delegation visited the non-profit Appalachian Educational Laboratory in Arlington, West Virginia; the Lee County Area Technology Center in Beattyville, Kentucky; the Kentucky Department of Education in Frankfort; Sullivan College's National Center for Hospitality Studies in Louisville; Mercy Academy, a private, parochial, all-girls high school in Louisville; and several NGO, development, and policy organizations.[97] The visitors took many ideas back to China (see Chapter 5). Additionally, the Americans increased their understanding of the obstacles that their Chinese counterparts faced. For example, although private schools have government moral support, their efforts are constrained by their inability to get bank loans or grant state-recognized diplomas.[98]

Growing emphasis on dialogue and public education

In the early years of the twenty-first century, the National Committee adjusted and reconceptualized its programming. Fulbright education exchanges went on as before. As other organizations entered the arena of policy exchanges, their frequency under National Committee sponsorship declined to fewer than ten per year, roughly half the number typical of the 1980s and 1990s. At the same time, there was increased activity in public education for Chinese and American policy-makers, in programs that reach the next generation of leaders in both countries, and in ongoing dialogues between specialists from China and the United States. As these ascendant programs built on previous experience, the National Committee came to compartmentalize all its activities under four headings, which replaced the earlier six (and then eight): Policy-Makers (mainly one-time educational events for leaders and advisors from both countries); Next Generation (multi-year programs); Dialogue & Cooperation (including policy exchanges but emphasizing ongoing Track II dialogues focused on key issues in the relationship); and Education (the Fulbright exchanges as well as periodic educational events for the general public in both countries).[99]

Policy-makers

The Policy Leaders Orientation Program, discussed above, fits under this heading. So do periodic briefings for members of Congress and senior US military officers. In a new departure, since 2005, the National Committee has expanded its public education to China. An annual Barnett-Oksenberg Lecture on Sino-American Relations provides an opportunity for prominent American officials and academics to engage with about 300–400 Chinese on issues of importance to the relationship. Organized in collaboration with the Shanghai Association for American Studies and the U.S. Chamber of Commerce in Shanghai, it is the only ongoing Sino-American lecture series in mainland China. Speakers have included scholar Kenneth Lieberthal (2006), former Deputy Secretary of State Robert Zoellick (2007), and then Ambassador to China Jon Huntsman (2011).[100]

The next generation

Even before the Scholar Orientation Program ended in 2002, the National Committee had begun to create an array of new, long-term exchanges intended to reach future Chinese – and American – leaders. The first was the Time Warner Intern program, which was initiated by Gerald Levin, Chairman and CEO of Time Warner. When Levin and his assistant Peter Wolff visited Fudan

University's Graduate School of Journalism in Shanghai in 1998, they were so impressed by the quality of students that they decided to invite some of them to work in their company as interns. Their purpose was simultaneously to give the interns practical business experience and to expose them to American life. Wolff, a board member, approached the National Committee about managing the program and got a favorable response. Each spring, for nine years, Jan Berris went to Shanghai to choose three to six interns from the several dozen who applied. The selected students then spent three months the following autumn working in one of Timer Warner's divisions. The first three interns arrived in September 1998 and the program continued through 2006.[101]

Each annual program began with 'a two-week orientation [that is] very similar to the SOP, where we try to expose them more broadly to American society.' Though the program was 'a little unusual [for the National Committee] in that it serves a particular corporate interest,' the National Committee 'was happy to do it,' according to former National Committee President John Holden, 'because it also clearly serves the broader interests in U.S.–China cross-cultural exchange and dialogue.'[102] (See Chapter 6 for participant reactions.)

The Young Leaders Forum (YLF) had its origins in Holden's informal diplomacy trip to China during the Belgrade bombing crisis. While in China, his delegation visited Peking University, where they spent several hours talking with students. 'They were in good form and attacked America pretty steadily, steadfastly and seemed convinced that we had bombed the embassy deliberately.' China Studies professor and National Committee board member Ezra Vogel, who was with the delegation, told Holden that he had heard similar criticism from visiting Chinese students at Harvard. Vogel's comments were 'really a revelation' to Holden, who came to the realization that the problem was more than one of 'access to information.'[103]

With encouragement and suggestions from Joshua Ramo, *Time* magazine's international editor, the National Committee launched the Young Leaders Forum as an exchange between future leaders of the United States and China. Since 2002, each year the YLF has brought together an eclectic group of young (under 40) leaders in their fields (business, the arts, the military, science and technology, government, education, etc.), half American and half Chinese, for a four- to five-day retreat. The program is conducted in English, and the venue alternates between the United States and China.[104]

Among the attendees at the 2003 forum, for example, were the following future leaders: Du Changping, vice mayor of Fuyang City in Anhui Province; Fang Xinghai, deputy CEO of the Shanghai Stock Exchange; Shao Yibo, founder of Chinese e-commerce giant Eachnet; Gabrielle Giffords, the youngest woman elected to the Arizona State Senate and later to become a Congresswoman; Steve Okum, Vice President of Public Affairs for UPS Asia-Pacific Group; Mark Kelly, astronaut and Giffords's future husband; and Philip Reeker, spokesman-at-large for the US State Department.[105] Alumni of YLF tend to maintain long-term contacts. It is too soon to say, however, whether Holden's vision – which uncannily echoes a recurring refrain at the Hopkins-Nanjing Center – will be fulfilled: 'One of them might end up as the Chinese Foreign Minister, the other as the American Secretary of State. In the next crisis, should there be one, they might be able to pick up the phone and say, "Hey, Lao Wang" or "Hey, buddy, here's what's really going on."'[106]

A second programmatic offspring of the 1999 Belgrade bombing was the Foreign Policy Colloquium (FPC). In addition to the broader goal of improved mutual understanding, Holden saw a specific need to correct Chinese 'misunderstandings [about] the nature of American power and intentionality.' With their history of five-year plans, Holden felt that many Chinese overestimated the degree of planning that went into American foreign policy. Further, as Program Officer Kathryn Gonnerman observed, 'So many [Chinese] students come here and don't learn anything about American government, American policies. They just focus on whatever small field they are studying and don't really get to see the bigger picture.' Holden thought it would be helpful to educate young Chinese about the processes by which American foreign policy is actually formulated.[107]

The first FPC took place in 2003 at George Washington University's Elliott School of International Affairs, the National Committee's partner in the project. The annual event draws 150 to 200 visiting Chinese graduate students and takes place over a three-day period. Authoritative foreign policy figures such as former Secretary of State Madeline Albright and former Senator Chuck Hagel speak and field 'an awful lot' of questions from the audience.[108] One participant observed, 'These seminars and lectures help us reopen our eyes to look at many problems from different perspectives. This approach is much more important than the detailed knowledge itself, which can be found in any college textbook.'[109]

In addition to the foregoing programs, which are aimed in part or solely at Chinese youth, in the early twenty-first century, the National Committee developed two exchanges to educate American youth about China. The first came about as a response to a Chinese invitation. 'In March 2004, Chinese Embassy education officials approached the National Committee with a special request: to develop a new program that would send top-notch American students to China.' The resulting U.S.–China Student Leaders Exchange (SLE), which began later that year, sends 12 Presidential Scholars (from the U.S. Department of Education program by that name) to China for two weeks.[110] The American teenagers tour historical sites in places like Xi'an and Luoyang and stay with Chinese families, where they are paired with 'host siblings.' The 2008 SLE cohort was featured on the popular Chinese television program 'Us.'[111]

The second, the Public Intellectuals Program (PIP), was the National Committee's idea and targets the younger generation of American China specialists. Funded by the Henry Luce Foundation and the Starr Foundation, 'PIP identifies outstanding members of the next generation of American China scholars, enriches their understanding of policy-making processes in both the United States and China, helps them establish relationships with their academic colleagues and with policy practitioners, and nurtures their ability to engage in public policy debates.' Fellows gain these experiences by participating, over a two-year period, in policy seminars in Washington and San Francisco and in study tours to China, where they serve as scholar-escorts for National Committee delegations and organize public education events.[112]

Dialogue and cooperation

In addition to continuing to organize short-term policy exchanges, the National Committee has built on the success of the U.S.–China Dialogue by developing several other Track II dialogues. The longest-running Track II program is in the realm of security. In 1994, trying to assist recovery from the break in military-to-military ties between the two countries in the aftermath of Tiananmen, the National Committee organized a group of four retired four-star generals, led by former Secretary of Defense Robert McNamara, to visit China for talks with their counterparts. Building on the success of that meeting, in 1996 the organization sent five retired four-star generals to China, this time under the leadership of former Secretary of Defense James Schlesinger. Not long after, National Committee leaders heard that just-retired Secretary of Defense William Perry, founder of the Preventive Defense Project (PDP),[113] was interested in engaging with China. (Up to that point, PDP had been involved with Russia and former Soviet satellite countries.) The two organizations teamed up and have run almost annual programs since 1999, primarily focusing on cross-Strait relations and Northeast Asia security issues.[114]

In 2009, in partnership with the China Foundation for Human Rights Development, the National Committee launched an annual Sino-American Dialogue on the Rule of Law & Human Rights. The formal balance in a report on the second meeting (in Xi'an, December 2010) reflects the reality that such dialogues can succeed only when each side displays respect for the concerns and positions of the other

> The discussions were lively, candid and wide-ranging. Topics included … the role of lawyers in the legal systems of China and the United States, … China's recent open government regulations, the Obama Administration's open government directive, reeducation through labor in China, immigration detentions in the United States, legal ethics, and habeas corpus.[115]

The Track II Economic Dialogue, launched in 2010, brings leading Chinese and American economists and former government officials together. Participants develop a set of policy recommendations, which they give to senior officials in both governments. The third meeting took place in New York in January 2011. Delegates exchanged views on short-term (monetary), medium-term (e.g. debt levels in the two countries), and broader global issues (e.g. international financial regulation).[116]

In addition to such multi-year Track II programs, the National Committee has continued, on a reduced scale, to organize short-term policy exchanges. In March 2001, for example, the organization brought government officials and NGO representatives from Taiwan, Hong Kong, and mainland China to the United

States to share experiences with the Americans and each other about disaster relief.[117] In 2010, with China's NGO sector more developed, US and Chinese delegations visited each other and exchanged lessons in recovering from Hurricane Katrina (2005) and the Sichuan Earthquake (2008).[118] And in 2011, the National Committee organized an exchange of environmental lawyers that included fellowships in both countries.[119]

One of the more creative short-term programs developed on the spur of the moment as a response to China's 2003 SARS crisis. On 18 June, 150 academic and business specialists convened in New York for a half-day SARS conference. 'As SARS-related travel advisories forced postponement of exchange programs, the National Committee turned to videoconferencing as a means of bringing American and Chinese citizens together to discuss issues of mutual concern.' The June conference linked participants in New York with their counterparts in Beijing. Based on its success, a follow-up conference in November linked New York attendees with colleagues in Shanghai.[120]

Over four and a half decades, the National Committee has creatively adjusted its programming mix. Former National Committee President David M. Lampton sees the organization's role as a 'counter-cyclical' one:

> When optimism about China and U.S.–China relations soars beyond any sustainable level, I think the Committee finds itself trying to introduce a certain amount of realism … And when the relationship plunges to the depths of despair, it then becomes counter-cyclical in the opposite direction, saying that it hasn't all gone to hell.[121]

If Lampton's assessment is valid, given the complex nature of Sino-American relations, the National Committee is likely to continue to fill a vital, unofficial niche in relations between the two nations.

3　The 1990 Institute

Chinese Americans bridge the Pacific

Chinese Americans often bring special resources to bilateral exchanges: trans-Pacific personal and family ties and bicultural skills that lubricate their navigation within two societies. Ethnic Chinese have, on occasion, played important roles in the National Committee on US–China Relations and the Hopkins-Nanjing Center. In the case of The 1990 Institute, Chinese Americans have been indispensable from its inception, initiating the organization and constituting at least two-thirds of its leadership and membership. The Institute's original mission was to provide research support for China's economic reforms, as a way both to help the Chinese people and to improve US–China relations. Later, direct-action social reform projects were added to the agenda. Like other promoters of non-governmental exchanges, The 1990 Institute has at times run up against competing agendas, not least those of the Chinese state, which continues to exert significant control over the nation's expanding civil society.

Initially, most Institute leaders and supporters were older Chinese Americans who had come from mainland professional or business families and had been exposed to American education. Arriving in the United States in the 1940s to study, they remained because of the turmoil and uncertainty of China's civil war, which ended in 1949. As individuals with a common background, the Institute's founders can be considered as a cohort. Culturally and structurally assimilated to American society, they share a worldview that includes loyalty to their adopted country, a desire to help their ancestral country, and a disposition to work toward gradual rather than abrupt social change in China. Over time, this initial leadership group assured institutional stability by attracting second-generation Chinese Americans as well as non-Chinese Americans to the organization.

Who are The 1990 Institute?

The immediate catalyst for the birth of The 1990 Institute was the conjunction of a prominent Chinese American professional fraternity's search for a service project with attempts by individual Bay Area Chinese Americans to fashion a constructive response to the tragic events of June 1989 at Tiananmen Square. In an important sense, an organization is the sum of its members, particularly its leadership. Biographical profiles of The 1990 Institute's first generation of leaders can help us understand the nature and depth of commitments that shaped the organization's goals and sustained it through its first two decades.

C. B. Sung

Son of a Shanghai textile engineer, C. B. Sung[1] came to the United States in 1947 for graduate study. Though he had a good job offer with China's Railroad Commission, his father pushed him to go to the United States for further study. 'He didn't say why, but I think he had a sense that something was going to happen.' Sung earned a graduate engineering degree at MIT and an MBA at Harvard. While in the United States, he also met and married his wife, Beulah Kwok-Sung, and in 1967 became the first Asian American corporate vice president of a Fortune 500 company, Bendix. Beginning in 1974, he struck out on his own and built numerous successful companies. When business opportunities emerged in China with the initiation of economic reforms in 1978 and formalization of Sino-US relations in 1979, Sung analyzed the situation strategically: 'Our principle is not [the interests of] China. I believe the U.S. must have a partner in Asia. ... So, when China opened up, I said, how does the U.S. compete against Japan? You must have a manufacturing foothold somewhere in Asia.'[2]

For 26 years, the Sungs maintained limited contact with their families in China by mail and met with them once in Hong Kong. President Nixon's 1972 opening to China made it possible for them to visit their parents on the mainland in 1973. Both sets of parents had suffered under Mao as despised 'capitalists.' Beulah's father had been the head of the large Wing On Department Store. C. B.'s father, an engineer, received somewhat milder treatment, since he could argue that he was a 'professional' rather than a 'capitalist.' Still, the family's stress over the abuse he received led to Sung's mother suffering a stroke. Thus the Sungs were surprised to hear from their parents 'not just encouragement, almost demanding: "You must come back to help China."'[3]

The Sungs eventually found a variety of ways to respond to their parents' plea. In 1979, they facilitated the first post-1949 American lectures in China on management. As C. B. Sung recalled two decades later:

> Because of my position as the Bendix Corporate Vice President and Group Executive in charge of its Advanced Technology Group, [after 1973] I gave lectures in China (at the invitation of the Chinese) on science and technology, which was a favorite topic of the Chinese in those days. But I was never invited to lecture on management, which was badly needed in China. I attempted many times to convince various leading Chinese organizations they needed to learn more about management. They always pointed to Chairman Mao's little red book indicating that this was all the management education they needed, but they insisted they needed to learn science and technology from the developed countries. Just after the collapse of the 'Gang of Four,' in October 1976, their attitude started to change. They invited me to give lectures on management.[4]

Instead, Sung arranged for professors from the Harvard Business School to give a two-week series of lectures during the summers of 1979 and 1980 in Beijing, Shanghai, and Harbin.[5] Beginning in 1984, at the invitation of the China Enterprise Management Association, Sung's company, Unison, joined with the Xerox Foundation to organize a three-year program of one-month lecture tours, similar to the Harvard program of 1979–80.[6]

In 1979, as a creative response to a request from Chinese officials to help China quickly equalize its foreign exchange account, one of the Sungs' companies contracted to build the Great Wall Sheraton Hotel in Beijing. The hotel was one of the first three reform-era foreign-invested joint ventures that, as a group, received Beijing's approval. The Sungs subsequently made several investments in Chinese industries, and their China umbrella company, Unison International, brokered dozens of joint ventures, including Beijing Jeep, the first Western-invested automobile manufacturer in China.[7] In Sung's view, a joint venture would be 'an educational institute of sorts,' a vehicle for China to gain practical and managerial experience, as well as financial benefits.[8]

In 1984, the Sungs made their first commitment to an ongoing organization involved with Sino-American relations. Friends encouraged them to attend the annual conference of the Pacific Forum in Honolulu. Retired Admiral L. R. ('Joe') Vasey had initiated the Forum in 1975 as a way to 'keep the US engaged in Asia' and 'inform the policymaking process' by 'bringing into focus diverse national views.' The Sungs liked the organized exchange of views and were particularly impressed by the Forum's low-budget operation. They were more interested in economic issues, however, than in the Forum's security focus. They proposed and offered to fund a three-year dialogue on US–China economic relations, and Vasey accepted. For C. B. Sung, the exchange provided an opportunity to get to know invited Chinese officials, such as economic reformer and future Premier Zhu Rongji.[9]

Sung was an early contributor to and Advisory Council member of the Hopkins-Nanjing Center.[10] He was also a founding leader of the Committee of 100, an organization of elite Chinese Americans that has a dual agenda of improving the domestic image of Asian Americans and building bridges between the United States and China.[11] His deepest associational commitment to US–China relations, however, would commence with the founding of The 1990 Institute.

Hang-Sheng Cheng

In 1948, with China in turmoil, Cheng completed his BA in history at Tsinghua University in Beijing and accepted a high school teaching position in Taiwan. The following year, as the Communists emerged victorious on the mainland and the Guomindang retreated to Taiwan, he had an offer to stay where he was, another to return to Beijing as a professor, and a third to pursue further study in the United States. The last, which included funding and which he accepted, came from his brother, a mid-level official of the Republic of China (Taiwan) government, who was stationed in Washington. Cheng earned an MA in international relations at George Washington University in 1953, worked for a decade as a research economist at the International Monetary Fund, earned a PhD in economics at Princeton in 1963, and taught economics at Iowa State University from 1963 through 1971. That year, the Center for Pacific Basin Studies of the Federal Reserve Bank of San Francisco (FRBSF) recruited Cheng as a researcher, and he became the Center's director and a vice president of the bank in 1973, positions he held until retiring in 1992.[12]

Throughout the 1970s and 1980s, Cheng's career kept him engaged, at the level of scholarship, with China as well as the other Pacific Rim countries. He edited books on monetary policy in those countries, participated in panel discussions on Confucianism and economic development, and wrote several long articles for the bank's journal, *Economic Review*, as well as dozens of shorter articles for the *FRBSF Weekly Letter*.[13] After China's reform period began in 1978, Cheng wrote about developments there with increasing animation, alternately enthusiastic and apprehensive. A sampling of articles from his *Weekly Letter* illustrates Cheng's evolving understanding of events unfolding in his homeland.

[January 1979] China has thrown open its door to the West in a sudden flurry of modernization. ... Modernization is the key word that captures the spirit of China's current policy. ... [M]odernization means importing more goods *and more knowledge* from the outside world. [Emphasis added][14]

[October 1980] A great experiment is in progress to determine what the market mechanism can do to improve the performance of a socialist economy. On the outcome of that experiment depend not only the livelihood of one-quarter of mankind, but also the peace and prosperity of a vitally important region of the world.[15]

[January 1985] [My] 1984 visit left little doubt that the great majority of the people, especially those in the countryside, are living much better today than they did a mere four years ago. ... Yet, to applaud the progress is not to say that China's Modernization is no longer fraught with difficult unresolved problems.[16]

[November 1988] Reform has exacerbated several existing economic and social problems, the most serious of which is inflation. ... Actually, inflation is nothing new in China. The hyper-inflation of 1948–49 was a major factor contributing to the downfall of the Nationalist government and the Communists' rise to power in 1949.[17]

[June 1989] Although not all political upheavals have economic roots, in this case, economic factors seem to have played a central role. ... No matter how the current political turmoil is settled, China will have to face up to the fundamental defects of the economic reform that lie at the root of the turmoil.[18]

Rosalyn Koo

Rosalyn Koo's father went to the United States in 1919 as a Boxer Indemnity scholar, earned an MBA at Harvard, and returned to China in 1923 to begin a career in banking.[19] In the late 1930s, her older brother went to the United States to attend Mt Herman Boys School, a prep school in Massachusetts. He went on to earn a BS degree from Harvard in 1949, then briefly returned to Shanghai that year before relocating to Taiwan, where he became an industrialist. Her father also moved to Taiwan before the Communists' victory in 1949 on the mainland. Koo's mother 'always believed in women's rights' and sent her to McTyeire, an all-girls high school in Shanghai that was operated by American Methodist missionaries. These family experiences made it a plausible decision for Koo to go to the United States in 1947 to attend all-female Mills College. As with C. B. Sung and Hang-Sheng Cheng, the chaos and uncertainty following the 1949 revolution led her to remain in the United States and ultimately to become an American citizen.[20]

In November 1978, Koo returned to China for the first time in three decades, hoping to find relatives with whom she had lost contact. Reconnecting took another year and the help of Xue Zheng, the retired principal of McTyeire. McTyeire had become a co-ed school, was overcrowded and dilapidated, and was now named Shanghai Public High School III. In 1979, Koo told Xue, 'You go tell the government that *if* you are allowed to return to a girls' school, then all the alumnae from abroad will come in to support you.' Xue persuaded the government to restore the high school to its former status, and Koo began networking with other overseas alumnae. By 1984, they had established a formal alumnae association and were donating money for new science laboratories.[21]

In the meantime, an episode in international hospitality illustrated the intersection between formal and informal diplomacy that Sino-American relations have frequently manifested. The two nations formalized relations on 1 January 1979, and by the end of the month, Deng Xiaoping was kicking off a grand tour of the United States. The National Committee on US–China Relations helped organize a reception for Deng and his entourage at the National Gallery in Washington, DC – 'a grand gathering of American China specialists from government, academia, the media, and the business world.' Among the invitees was Koo, who had come to the organizers' attention through her role as president of the Chinese Culture Foundation of San Francisco.[22]

By 1992, Koo was handling administrative affairs for The 1990 Institute. Though she did not know it at the time, a request from Xue, her former principal, helped her create a model for programs she would later organize on a larger scale under Institute auspices. Xue asked Koo whether the McTyeire alumnae would assist several poor students by donating money to Project Hope, a charity established for that purpose in 1989 by the All-China Youth Federation, one of China's government-sponsored 'mass organizations.'[23] Koo preferred more personalized contact with students, and further networking led her and the McTyeire alumnae to a relationship with a high school in impoverished rural Jiangxi Province, where $12,000 they raised kept 40 girls in school for two years.[24]

William Ming-Sing Lee

Having grown up in Shanghai, William Lee came to the United States in 1947 to attend Phillips Academy, a prep school in Andover, Massachusetts. Like Koo, he was following the precedent of his father, who had attended Phillips and had subsequently graduated from Amherst College. The decision that Lee would also attend Philips was his father's: 'He arranged it, and I just followed his direction.' While at Phillips, Lee met C. B. Sung, who was attending nearby Harvard. Sung later recruited Lee into F.F., a Chinese American professional fraternity that had provided a career-oriented social networking venue for upwardly mobile Chinese Americans since the early 1920s.[25]

Lee went on to earn BA and MA degrees in architecture at Yale. In the mid-1970s, Sung arranged for Lee to visit Tsinghua University, as part of a lecture delegation of American architects. By the early 1980s, the Chinese government had begun a process of paying emigrated former citizens for assets seized by the govern- ment after the 1949 revolution. The catch was that the money could not be taken out of the country. Lee and his three siblings received the equivalent of $20,000, and he decided to use his share to create a scholarship fund for young Chinese architects. Partly in connection with the scholarships, Lee continued to receive invitations from Chinese universities throughout the 1980s and 1990s. He lectured on architecture at Tsinghua, Tongji, Guangdong, Shenzhen, and Ningbo Universities.[26]

James Luce

James Luce's grandfather, Henry Winters Luce, spent most of his adult life (1897–1925) in China as a Presbyterian missionary. Among other activities, he helped found Yenching University (now Peking University) and served as its first vice president. His four children were born in China. The firstborn, Henry R. Luce (b. 1898), became a titan of journalism and a passionate advocate on China- related issues. He also founded the Henry Luce Foundation, which has provided millions of dollars to educational projects that better inform Americans about China. The youngest of Henry W.'s children, James Luce's father, Sheldon (Xiao Ling, or Little Bell, in Chinese), was born in 1909.[27] 'Because my father spent most of his early years with his Chinese nanny,' says Luce, 'he spoke Chinese before he spoke English.'[28]

Though he grew up 'on a sheep farm in California,' Luce heard family lore from his father, as well as from other relatives during visits to the eastern United States. 'China has been part of my memories going back to when I was three or four years old.' After graduating from law school in 1974, Luce established a commercial litigation practice in California. Though he never learned to speak Chinese, he 'spent a lot of time studying Chinese history and culture in college and after- wards and visited China in 1984.' He once suggested to fellow 1990 Institute executive committee member William Lee (who had contrasted his own Chinese perspective with Luce's American outlook), 'I think I bring, very definitely, a Sino-oriented view to this whole process, rather than an American one.'[29]

Matilda Young

As the 1949 revolution unfolded on the mainland, Matilda Young's family left Shanghai for Hong Kong. She jokes that she does not have as 'illustrious' a background as some of her friends in The 1990 Institute. She had family exposure to the United States through her father's employment by a New York stock brokerage firm. In 1949, her father moved the family, including Matilda, to Hong Kong. In the same year, her older brother went to UC Berkeley to study, and he remained in the United States. 'The whole generation of kids my age just sort of followed suit' by going to the United States to study. In 1958, Young left Hong Kong to enroll as an undergraduate at Wellesley College. After earning a BA in mathematics, she worked as an editor of mathematics textbooks, first at D. C. Heath in Boston, then for a series of New York publishers. In 1972, she moved to California, where she devoted herself to raising her children through most of the 1980s. 'I was planning, or hoping, as soon as my kids went to college, that I could spend more time in China. I was trying to find some volunteer work to get involved in. I just didn't have any vehicle of working this out.'[30]

Wei-Tai Kwok

A younger, second-generation Chinese American, Kwok was born in Washington, DC, in 1964 and grew up speaking only English. His parents came from educated families that were involved with banking in China. Kwok's father was originally from Hong Kong but grew up in Shanghai. His mother was from Shanghai, where both parents were friendly with William Lee. Kwok's father became fluent in English at missionary-founded St John's University in Shanghai, where he earned an undergraduate degree in 1946. That same year, he went to the United States to earn a graduate engineering degree at the Case Institute of Technology. Around 1950, Kwok's mother initially went to the Philippines, where her parents had fled in 1949. She studied at an American missionary school. Several years later, with missionary sponsorship, she went to the United States to study biology at Temple University.[31]

In 1983, Kwok's father returned to China for the first time and took Wei-Tai with him. 'It was very interesting for me, as a son, to see my dad recall his childhood memories of Shanghai.' The experience motivated Kwok to learn more about China. In 1981, he entered Yale as an undergraduate, majoring in economics and political science. His focus in both fields was China, and he also studied Mandarin for four years. He took every opportunity to engage with China, spending two summers there as an escort for American tour groups and working as a volunteer interpreter for the Chinese fencing team at the 1984 Olympics in Los Angeles. Still not satisfied with his *Hanyu shuiping* (Chinese language ability), in 1985 Kwok enrolled at Fudan University in Shanghai for a year of further language study. 'With China someday to be a world force and me being Chinese American, I wanted to do something and be involved. And the first step had to be to learn the language.' After his year at Fudan, Kwok worked in Shanghai for a year as legal translator for a New York law firm. He returned to San Francisco in 1989, where he helped start an Asian language advertising business.[32]

Charles McClain

Until the 1980s, American scholarship on Chinese Americans and on US–China relations was largely compartmentalized. Whether Chinese immigrants were portrayed as sojourners, unassimilable aliens, or a model minority, the scholars who studied them were generally uninterested in international relations. Correspondingly, few diplomatic historians with a focus on US–China relations displayed an interest in Chinese Americans. The scholarly landscape became more complicated and intertwined with the work of immigration scholars like Sucheng Chan and diplomatic historians like Michael Hunt. While not formally a part of the 'transnationalist' current of scholarship that integrates immigration and diplomatic history approaches, Charles McClain embodies this convergence through the combination of his scholarship, family history, and civic activities.[33]

McClain earned MA and PhD degrees in history, at Columbia and Stanford Universities, before earning a JD from UC Hastings in 1974. He represented the Western Regional Office of the American Association of University Professors from 1974 to 1977, then became lecturer in residence and vice chairman of UC Berkeley Law School's Jurisprudence and Social Policy Program. McClain has written extensively on the legal dimensions of Chinese American resistance to discrimination. His wife and occasional co-author, Laurene Wu McClain, is a third-generation Chinese American. McClain has 'always been interested in international and foreign affairs, and that predates my interest in China.' For example, during the 1980s, he and his wife regularly attended annual conferences of the World Affairs Council of Northern California. During the mid-1970s, they traveled to Hong Kong and Taiwan, and in the late 1970s, Laurene joined one of the earliest groups of Americans to visit the mainland.[34]

Response to Tiananmen

As reported in its third newsletter, 'The 1990 Institute was the brainchild of Hang-Sheng Cheng.' Shocked by the events of June 1989 and subsequent turmoil, he brainstormed with Teh-Wei Hu, Professor of Economics and Health Policy for UC Berkeley, and Fan Di, a Chinese visiting scholar at UC Berkeley. The three shared the conviction that the Tiananmen crisis revealed problems whose cause ran far deeper than the immediate clash between student demonstrators and an authoritarian government. They believed that the tragedy highlighted problems that are common to modernizing societies on the one hand, but that were also shaped by China's unique history on the other. As scholars, they felt they could best contribute to the amelioration of those underlying problems by promoting research on the economic reforms with which China had been experimenting since 1978.[35]

In the summer of 1989, Cheng, Hu, and Fan came up with the then-novel idea of teaming American and Chinese economists to conduct a series of research projects, with the hope that the results would be beneficial both to Chinese policy-makers and to Americans trying to understand developments in China.

They solicited funding from several foundations, but, lacking a track record, they failed to find donors. They were at a standstill in December, when a group of regular dining friends encouraged Cheng to form an organization to solicit donations. Between that discussion and an organizing meeting on 16 December, Cheng met C. B. Sung at a luncheon meeting of the Business Council for International Understanding.[36]

Sung, who was already thinking about ways to expand his own contribution to China's reform process, liked the idea of a joint research project. Additionally, his professional fraternity, F.F., was looking for a service project with which to commemorate its hundredth anniversary. From his F.F. circle of friends, Sung recruited other supporters for the embryonic research organization. Among them were William Lee, Wei-Tai Kwok, and (through her husband's membership) Rosalyn Koo. F.F. adopted The 1990 Institute as its anniversary service project, and the fraternity played a critical role in providing the manpower and money that got the Institute off the ground. Another key source of support was Cheng's boss, Robert Parry, President of the Federal Reserve Bank of San Francisco. Parry lent both his personal prestige and that of the bank, which provided rooms for the Institute's early meetings and its founding press conference on 4 April 1990. Sung was the organization's founding chairman, Cheng its president.[37]

The distinctiveness of The 1990 Institute

Three characteristics defined The 1990 Institute at the outset and continued, subsequently, to shape its strategy: the prominent role of Chinese Americans, a posture of constructive engagement with China, and a balanced approach toward 'the forest and the trees' of Chinese reform and modernization. Long-resident Americans of Chinese ancestry founded the Institute, and their personal ties and cross-cultural competence often smoothed the way toward implementing programs. Cheng, Sung, and the others, however, quickly and intentionally attracted non-Chinese Americans. In doing so, they distinguished the Institute from exchange organizations like the National Committee on US–China Relations (in which Chinese Americans have participated but not prominently) and the Committee of 100 (which is comprised exclusively of Chinese Americans).

Non-Chinese American founding honorary co-chairs included: Robert Parry; Philip Habib, former Undersecretary of State; Steven Muller, President of Johns Hopkins University and co-initiator of the Hopkins-Nanjing Center; Robert Scalapino, Director of UC Berkeley's Institute of East Asian Studies and key figure during the early years of the National Committee; and Harold T. Shapiro, President of Princeton University. Donald Kennedy, President of Stanford University, was added to the list within the first year, as was former Senator Adlai Stevenson III (D-Illinois) in 1993. Stevenson, Parry, and Scalapino spoke at annual dinners and otherwise remained active supporters of the Institute.[38]

Two non-Chinese Americans, James Luce and Charles McClain, became part of The 1990 Institute's core leadership at an early stage. After reading in the *San Francisco Chronicle* about the Institute's founding press conference,

Luce contacted C. B. Sung. When the two met, Luce affirmed that Sung's vision of a 'non-political' association was the same as his own and offered his support. He quickly helped secure a $25,000 grant from the Henry Luce Foundation to fund research by one of the visiting Chinese scholars. Over the years, Luce actively contributed to strategy deliberations and provided legal advice.[39] In May 1993, Charles McClain and Hang-Sheng Cheng met at a two-day annual conference of the World Affairs Council of Northern California. Expressing interest in a forthcoming Institute monograph on Chinese legal reform, McClain promptly joined, became a board member in 1994, co-organized (with Cheng) a bi-national pair of law conferences in 1995, and joined the executive committee in 1999.[40]

Like most other Americans, the founders of The 1990 Institute were dismayed and angered by the Chinese government's response to pro-democracy demonstrations in the spring of 1989. Sympathizing with the demonstrators and being appalled by the government's violent reaction, however, did not translate into belief that the demonstrators had a viable program or strategy for achieving it. Several Institute leaders thought the more extreme calls for immediate, Western-style democracy were unrealistic and that the students probably lacked a clear understanding of the institutional basis for democracy.[41]

For Kwok, 'the crackdown in the end was very disheartening.' Cheng was 'moved to tears' when he saw students being 'massacred.' 'It was clear,' says Koo, 'all of us thought the government was atrocious.'[42] Similar reactions inspired dozens of new and existing organizations in the United States and worldwide to pursue a confrontational strategy toward the post-Tiananmen Chinese government, hoping that the pressure of sanctions and public opinion would cause the government to mitigate its repressive policies. In the Bay Area alone, a dozen new Chinese American protest organizations sprang up.[43] Combining a sense of the practical limits to outside pressure with a perception that China's societal fault lines were more complex than a clash between good students and bad dictators, the Institute's founders charted a lower-key, longer-term strategy. The reforms with which The 1990 Institute could realistically help China were, in Koo's words, 'not so much political as social and economic.' While personally hoping for political democratization in China, McClain similarly emphasized the incremental contributions the Institute could make to helping China develop 'a modern, functioning legal system, ... a tax system and a social security system, a modern economy.'[44]

Policy research

In line with Cheng's original plan for joint research, the Institute's initial project was an edited book that reviewed and evaluated the experiences of China's first decade of economic reform.[45] Retired economist Walter Galenson agreed to serve as editor and research director, enhancing the book's credibility by virtue of his background. Galenson had been the founding director of UC Berkeley's Center for Chinese Studies, professor of economics at Cornell University, and director of research for the US Committee on the Economy of China. Ten American scholars (including six Chinese Americans) teamed up with nine Chinese visiting scholars who had been stranded in the United States because of the turmoil in China. 'The seven teams – covering macroeconomy, agriculture, enterprises, foreign trade, prices, labor, and decentralization – completed their first drafts in the fall of 1991 ...'[46] Following a forum-style review at an Institute-organized conference at the Federal Reserve Bank of San Francisco in December 1991, the authors revised their chapters for publication. With her background in publishing, Matilda Young volunteered to manage publications for the Institute. She arranged for the University of Michigan to distribute the book, with The 1990 Institute as the publisher and copyright holder.[47]

In terms of research conducted within the United States, the project went relatively smoothly, especially considering its management by a start-up, all-volunteer organization. Interaction with would-be partners in China, however, was more complicated. 'As we all expected,' Cheng reminded the executive committee in December 1990, 'the greatest obstacle to our effort lay in official suspicion of our Institute's motives.'[48] What had seemed a boon to the Institute's first book, participation by Chinese scholars stranded in the United States, heightened official Chinese reservations about collaboration with The 1990 Institute. It took two years of travel, meetings, and networking by Sung and Cheng to allay these suspicions. Without top-level 'clearance' to collaborate with such quasi-governmental policy think tanks as the Chinese Academy of Social Sciences, the Development Research Center, and the Economic Research Center (a division of the powerful State Planning Commission), Institute-sponsored scholars could not gain access to either the latest economic data or the ears of policy advisors. It was not until May 1992 that Cheng could send Sung a fax reporting, 'After two days of intensive meeting, I can now report that already the visit to pave the way for our Phase II research projects has been a success.'[49]

In December 1992, five of the American researchers joined C. B. and Beulah Sung in presenting summary results at conferences the Institute co-sponsored for that purpose in Shanghai and Beijing. In 1993, *China's Economic Reform* was published in both English and Chinese editions. In December of that year, in a scene captured on Chinese national television, C. B. Sung presented a copy to Chinese President Jiang Zemin at the 80th anniversary dinner of the Western Returned Scholars Association (WRSA).[50] The WRSA had been founded in 1913 as the European and American Returned Students by American-educated Chinese diplomat Wellington Koo, Tsinghua University President Zhou Yichun, and American Minister to China Paul Reinsch. From its inception, the organization was controversial in China – because the strategy of seeking Western help and ideas for China's modernization was contentious – until the government closed it during the Cultural Revolution (1966–76). Beijing re-established the organization in 1982 as the Western Returned Scholars Association, retooling it in an era of transnationalism to solicit support from overseas Chinese for China's modernization.[51]

By April 1991, with work on *China's Economic Reform* well underway, the Institute began referring to that research project as Phase I and started planning a follow-up group of projects under the heading Phase II. The new projects would focus on specific sectors of China's economy.[52] By June 1992, the Institute had identified the six 'critical' subject areas on which it would focus: taxation, finance, agriculture, enterprise, labor, and law (with an emphasis on foreign economic relations).[53] In addition to being more in-depth, the new studies would be based on a modified research strategy. While input on *China's Economic Reform* from the visiting Chinese scholars had been helpful, their contributions, overall, did not meet Cheng's expectations – partly because their data and insights became progressively outdated as they remained in the United States, partly because career priorities competed for their attention.[54] Instead, the Institute decided to produce its Phase II studies by relying exclusively on American scholars and establishing relationships with Chinese think tanks and policy institutions.

There were some frustrating delays and personnel changes in the Phase II projects, but in each case one or more reputable scholars ultimately produced a competent piece of work. Each author initially committed to producing a 'policy paper,' but several expanded their research into book-length works. The first completed was Pitman Potter's *Foreign Business Law in China: Past Progress and Future Challenges*, published as a monograph in English and Chinese in 1993. While there is no direct evidence of the book's influence in China, 'a number of high-ranking Chinese officials' told Potter that they found it useful. Contribution to Western scholarship on Chinese legal reform is more tangible. One expert called Potter's book a 'landmark study of a very timely topic,' and several others have cited it favorably.[55] The book served as the primary background document for law conferences the Institute organized in San Francisco and Beijing in March and April 1995. Cheng organized the conference in Beijing while McClain organized the one in San Francisco, where he reports the discussion was livelier.[56]

Cheng had originally planned to do the financial reform study, but by late 1993 he realized that he was too busy. Further, it turned out that Chinese economists had already done much of the research Cheng had planned. Instead, he co-opted a timely paper by UC Davis economist Thomas Mayer, entitled 'Should China Tolerate High Inflation?'[57] In 1993, just after the WRSA 80th anniversary dinner, Mayer had accompanied Cheng to meet with policy advisors in Shanghai and Beijing. Several of their counterparts asked whether The 1990 Institute could prepare specific policy papers for them, and Mayer's paper on inflation followed.[58] The Institute first published it as an Issue Paper, then translated it into Chinese and circulated it in China. One of China's senior reform economists, Wu Jinglian, reported to the Institute that the journal *Reform*, which he edited, would publish the paper and that Vice Premier Zhu Rongji had read it and found it 'very helpful.'[59]

Next off the press was *China's Ongoing Agricultural Reform*, a 1996 monograph with UC Davis professor of agricultural economics Colin Carter as lead author. In an exception to its policy of not using Chinese scholars in Phase II, the Institute agreed to Carter's request to involve two Chinese co-authors and a Chinese research assistant, all of whom Carter had recruited. One of the authors' central arguments was: 'The central government should discontinue the disproportionate emphasis that it places on the economic well-being of urban residents compared to rural residents.'[60] This perspective proved prescient. The urban–rural income disparity continued to worsen, and in the early 2000s the Chinese government made narrowing the gap a policy priority.

The Institute's Phase II publication on tax reform had the most tangible impact on China's policy deliberations. Roy Bahl had begun doing research in China for the World Bank in the early 1980s. By the time Cheng first contacted him in 1991, he had already established a substantial network in China.[61] Still, without Chinese language skills, he found himself dependent on bilingual intermediaries. Thus he saw an opportunity in the Institute's overture and provided Cheng with a detailed list of data he sought help in gathering. Cheng enlisted Julia Xue, a Chinese friend of C. B. Sung and the Institute, to arrange a research itinerary for Bahl in September 1992.[62] Largely because a major reform of the Chinese tax system in 1994 made his subject a 'moving target,' *Fiscal Policy in China: Taxation and Intergovernmental Fiscal Relations* was not published until 1998.[63] The deputy director of the State Administration of Taxation (SAT), Xu Shanda, thought enough of Bahl's book to ask the Institute for permission to translate it into Chinese and distribute it within China.[64]

The labor market reform project was a source of ongoing frustration for Cheng and the Institute. In April 1992, prominent labor economist Richard Freeman contracted to write a 40-page policy paper by the end of June 1994. Like Bahl's research, Freeman's allowed The 1990 Institute to piggyback on a larger-scale basic research project that the author had undertaken for the Ford Foundation. The Institute obtained a $50,000 grant from the Henry Luce Foundation to enable Freeman to explore the policy implications of his analysis.[65] By 2003, after years of correspondence and having received 'a few chapters, which were not up to par,' Cheng obtained the approval of the board of directors to terminate the project. It was an awkward ending for the Institute, which had received and disbursed the first half of the Henry Luce Foundation's funding. There were apparently no hard feelings, though, as the foundation subsequently sent The 1990 Institute an unsolicited $20,000 contribution toward a banking reform project.[66] As a practical matter, the Institute did ultimately produce a competent piece of scholarship on an important aspect of labor market reform. In 2002, Cheng and Institute director Michael Keran wrote an Issue Paper on the development of China's social pension system.[67]

Like labor market reform, the enterprise reform project took an indirect route. Economists Anthony Koo of the University of Michigan and Kung-Chia Yeh of RAND signed up for this project in 1993. It took considerable effort by Cheng to persuade his two friends initially to accept the assignment and later to stick with it. As of July 2000, 'the project [was] near completion,' with a rough draft due by summer's end. Two years later, though, one researcher was ill and the other had dropped out.[68] An opportunity to recover presented itself in March 2004 when The 1990 Institute, in partnership with the Shanghai Academy of Social Sciences, organized a two-day conference on 'State-Owned Enterprise Reform' in Shanghai. Mainland Chinese scholars were joined by counterparts from Taiwan,

Hong Kong, Singapore, France, Poland, Russia, and the United States, who provided international perspectives on China's attempt to define 'the role of the government in a socialist market economy.' A combined Chinese-foreign group summarized the conference findings in a 'confidential report to government leaders,' though there was no feedback channel to ascertain substantive official reaction.[69]

Windows, fresh air, and flies

Whereas Phase II was a refinement of the policy research program of Phase I, The 1990 Institute expanded its work in new directions with Phase III. By the mid-1990s, two things were becoming increasingly clear to the Institute's leaders. First, as China's own reform-oriented research capacity matured, interest in foreign ideas about macroeconomic policy waned. On the other hand, Institute leaders increasingly saw the Chinese people suffering from the *consequences* of reform – such as corruption, environmental degradation, and gendered rural poverty.[70] Second, 'A lot of people [in our US constituency] recommended we branch out, not just focus on economic reform, because very few people could participate in the economic reform projects.' William Lee recalls that board meeting attendance was dropping, 'because most of the board members are not economists. There was a report from C. B. and Hang-Sheng about what was happening, but you don't need to attend a board meeting to learn that.'[71]

The Institute responded to these twin challenges by creating organizational space for individual leaders to propose new projects that would not require expert knowledge of economics or policy issues but, rather, would entail practical participation in some of China's reforms. Calling the new type of activity 'direct action projects,' the executive committee tasked volunteers with raising funds for and managing to completion the projects they proposed. Sung would later characterize this organizational spirit as 'ultimate volunteerism.'[72]

Though the Institute formally adopted its Phase III program at its board of directors meeting in September 1996, two preceding activities suggested a template for the new strategy. One was the paired law conferences that Cheng and McClain had organized in Beijing and San Francisco in 1995. Managing the San Francisco conference largely on his own drew McClain into a more active – and 'gratifying' – role.[73]

Second, Stephen Lee wrote an article for a 1994 issue of the *Newsletter* entitled 'Social Ethics, Law and Free Market Economy.' Deng Xiaoping had famously urged his fellow citizens to accept the risk of 'flies' (undesirable influences of foreign and domestic origin) coming in when China opened the 'window' (of reform).[74] Lee proposed that The 1990 Institute help swat some flies by addressing China's growing corruption problem. Initially, the Institute sponsored and Lee organized a serious of three forums in the Bay Area. The first featured American China scholar Orville Schell and Chinese environmental activist Liang Congjie.[75]

For the first official Phase III project, Stephen Lee and the Institute, in partnership with the Shanghai Academy of Social Sciences (SASS), organized a Social Ethics essay contest for Chinese college students and professors. Over 90 scholars from throughout China submitted essays. The Institute and SASS held a conference in Shanghai on 10 December 1996 to honor the authors of the winning essays. SASS published the best 25 essays, and the Institute published the top three as an Issue Paper. The number one essay was entitled, 'Professional Ethics and China's Economic Reform.'[76]

William Lee liked the people-to-people aspect of the Social Ethics Contest and wanted to do something related to the environment. He nearly accomplished much more. In February 1997, he made an exploratory trip to Ningbo, his family's ancestral home, where relatives helped him connect with local officials. He hoped to set up a 'model urban plan for simultaneous achievement of both the city's economic development and environment protection.'[77] By July, Lee had recruited a team of five environmental scientists from UC Berkeley's College of Environmental Design. He accompanied them to Ningbo, where the Institute, UC Berkeley, and Ningbo University signed a letter of intent for a research project.[78] After two years of futile effort to get the local government's approval, though, the Institute had to terminate the project.

The story of the project's failure illustrates some of the pitfalls that await foreign organizations operating in China. The Institute's target funder was the Asian Development Bank (ADB), where former Institute director Linda Tsao Yang was the US Ambassador and executive director on the board of directors. Yang predicted approval of a grant for one million dollars for the Institute's proposed basic research project, if a partner Chinese local government would borrow $250,000 to be bundled into the project. The city of Ningbo initially indicated its agreement to this plan. Three obstacles emerged, however. First, the ADB changed its policy. It now required $400,000 in local participation and, conforming to World Bank policies, required an implementation project as a follow-on to the pure research. Second, the Institute learned that the People's Bank of China, which would provide Ningbo's funding and where C. B. Sung and Hang-Sheng Cheng had good connections, was not the real decision-maker. The Environmental Department of the State Planning Commission played that role, and the Institute's proposal was just one of many before it for consideration. Finally, the Ningbo officials were less than completely candid with their Institute counterparts, who eventually learned that Ningbo had already borrowed $400,000 from the World Bank for the project. They were hoping to add ADB money to this sum, but ADB would not fund an environmental project in the same city as the World Bank.[79]

Given the project's 'vision and promise,' Cheng, speaking at the Institute's 9th Annual Dinner, called its failure a 'major disappointment.' The lesson: 'We are a small research organization. … For such a small, all-volunteer organization, there is a limit to what we can do. In the future, we shall think twice before taking on any projects that would require large funding.'[80] The project's demise also illustrates the limits to *guanxi* (relationship) and the vulnerability of American initiatives to conflicting Chinese agendas.

Key to two projects that became successful multi-year endeavors was a connection The 1990 Institute was able to establish with the All-China Women's Federation. The ACWF is a 'mass organization,' sharing that category with a handful of other organizations such as the All-China Federation of Trade Unions and the All-China Youth Federation. Their role is elaborated in Chapter 5.

In 1995, the ACWF's Feng Cui was working in China's United Nations office. From New York, she coordinated that year's historic International Women's Forum in Beijing. The following year, she was put in charge of the ACWF's International Liaison Department. Shortly after that new appointment, she and her husband sought the advice of their friend William Lee on remodeling their Beijing apartment. Over a casual dinner, the three also explored the possibility of collaboration between the ACWF and The 1990 Institute. Back in the United States, Lee and several women from the Institute formed an exploratory committee. In the meantime, in 1998 C. B. Sung paid a visit in Beijing to Gu Xiulian, friend and former governor of Jiangsu Province, who had recently become national president of the ACWF. Ultimately, the Institute's exploratory committee proposed launching several environment-related projects, and the ACWF counter-proposed starting with a forum. The Institute agreed and planning began.[81]

Two years before the resulting April 2000 Forum was held in San Francisco, the ACWF had adopted a five-year plan with three main goals: improve the environment (as a way to protect women and children), extend women's rights in all spheres of society, and expand women's competence.[82] These goals are evident in the theme of the San Francisco Forum: 'Women, Leadership, and Sustainability.' The ACWF sent a ten-woman delegation representing government, academic, and private sectors, and 65 similarly representative Americans participated. In addition to attending two days of meetings and The 1990 Institute's 10th Anniversary Dinner, the Chinese delegates and some of the Americans took environmental tours of UC Davis, Lake Tahoe, and Honolulu's Nature Conservancy.[83] Linda Tsao Yang modeled the difference women activists can make. 'Because she was there, one half of 6 million scholarships for children were allotted to girls as a condition of an Asian Development Bank Loan.'[84]

One outgrowth of the Institute–ACWF relationship was a series of exchanges involving children's environmental art. At the time of William Lee's 1997 home design consultation in Beijing, the ACWF was trying to develop programs on environmental awareness. Gu Xiulin, who would head the Chinese delegation to the April 2000 Forum in San Francisco, introduced Lee to an ACWF affiliate, the China National Children's Center (CNCC).[85] According to Chen Ying, head of CNCC's Foreign Affairs Office, the Center's mission of fostering child development and protecting the rights of children led it to become concerned about environmental degradation. 'If children cannot get clean water and fresh air, how can they grow healthily?' From the US side, Lee envisioned a program that would educate American and Chinese children both about the environment and about each other. He envisioned 'thousands of school children going there, thousands of school children coming here.'[86]

The first phase began in May 2002. About one million school children from 1,000 communities throughout China created environment-themed works of art. Their schools submitted 606 drawings and paintings to a bi-national committee of judges, who selected 100 to be displayed for a month at CNCC, then sent on tour throughout the United States. The prestigious project co-chairs – Minster Xie Zhenhua of China's State Environmental Protection Administration and Sarah Randt, wife of US Ambassador Clark T. Randt – passed out awards at an October dinner in Beijing.[87]

The next activities – under the new project name C2C-C2C (Children to China and Connecting Two Countries) – involved bringing Chinese and American children together, face to face. In April 2004, Hillview Middle School of Menlo Park, California, sent 15 students to Shanghai, Xi'an, and Beijing, where they learned about life in contemporary China. (Lee got the idea when he saw a photo of a flower garden painted by Hillview students for one of their annual mural projects. School art instructor Terry McMahon responded favorably to Lee's proposal.) The highlight was two days in Beijing, during which the American children paired up with Chinese children to paint a mural – a scene of wild animals – outside the China National Children's Center.[88]

In August 2005, 20 Chinese art students, ranging in age from eight to 17, traveled to California for a 'Paint California Environment' exchange. The students made sketches and took photos in San Francisco, Lake Tahoe, Napa Valley and other parts of the state, with the goal of publishing a booklet entitled, 'California's Environment Seen through Chinese Children's Eyes.' Similar to the Hillside students in Beijing, the Chinese students visiting California spent two days with American students. Most could communicate to some degree in English. Chen Ying, one of four adults accompanying them, observed that the American and Chinese students got along well socially, an indication that the exchange was achieving one of its goals.[89]

The second Institute program facilitated by its ACWF relationship consisted of a series of projects supporting education for girls in China's impoverished countryside. Two pre-existing factors facilitated this Institute–ACWF joint effort. The first was Rosalyn Koo's long-standing interest in the education of girls in China. The second was the recognition among China's leaders, mass organizations, NGOs, and public intellectuals of a growing problem of rural poverty. While agricultural reforms of the 1980s benefited most of the population by releasing farmers' energy, complications proliferated in the 1990s, often confronting policy-makers and foreign reformers alike with zero-sum problems. Industrial reforms polluted farm land, siphoned migrant workers to the cities, led to confiscation of farmland for commercial development – and corruption heightened the effects of all these phenomena.[90] In Phase III, The 1990 Institute responded to this set of problems with small-scale demonstration programs rather than comprehensive policy solutions.

Koo met Gu Xiulian for the first time at the April 2000 Women, Leadership and Sustainability Forum in San Francisco. At one point, after they had become acquainted, Gu said, 'Look, if you want to continue your work on educating girls, you should support *Xibu da kaifa* [the government's 'Open Up the West' campaign].' Koo 'had no idea what that was,' but Gu invited her to come to China and find out. In October 2000, Koo made a two-week tour of Gansu, Shanxi, and Shaanxi Provinces in western China. Matilda Young and Elisabeth Tsai of the Institute, Women's Foundation President Patti Chang, and former Chinese diplomat Xie Heng accompanied her. Determined to have accountability for what happened to any funds the Institute raised, the Institute delegates evaluated local ACWF representatives as well as potential projects in several areas. In addition to selecting two short-term projects, they chose Wang Hong of Shaanxi Province as their partner for a longer-term scholarship program.[91]

At the Institute's 11th Annual Dinner in April 2001, Koo and Chang announced the start of the Dragon Fund, whose mission was to help educate girls in China's poor rural areas and whose name derived from 2001 being the Year of the Dragon in the Chinese lunar calendar. After Koo provided background information, Chang, whose San Francisco-based Women's Foundation had agreed to provide start-up funding, outlined the initial three projects: provide the final 25 percent funding ($25,000) for a Women's and Children's Training Center in Zhang Xian, Gansu; build a new greenhouse in Zhang Xian, in which women could learn new techniques in cultivation, marketing, distribution, and management; and, under the ACWF-initiated Spring Bud scholarship program, help 1,000 girls in several of Shaanxi Province's villages enroll in fourth grade and graduate from sixth grade.[92]

A year later, in October 2001, C. B. and Beulah Sung led an Institute delegation that, accompanied by Cui Linlin of ACWF's Beijing national office, visited Gansu and Shaanxi Provinces to assess the Institute-funded projects. They were gratified by the progress they saw, including Institute-sponsored initiatives, but the experience also reinforced in their minds the need for what they were doing. The trip report noted:

> What sometimes happens is the family sends the children to school for a day or two – long enough for official census figures to be recorded – and then insists the child help out at home. All too often, young girls are the losers in this scenario.[93]

Speaking to girls in Ankang, a village near Xi'an, Koo said, 'I hope you will be successful and become women leaders in the future. ... I will come back and see you every year.'[94] Koo did return each year, including attending the girls' graduation ceremonies in the spring of 2004.[95] Pleased with the success of the three-year project, she decided the Dragon Fund should continue supporting the 1,000 girls through middle school. Additionally, the top 299 girls entered four 'key' schools, from which they were likely to go on to senior high school and college or university.[96]

In the meantime, the Institute experimented with other formats for supporting girls' education in rural China. In 2001, the Shandan Bailie School in Lanzhou, capital of Gansu Province, asked the Dragon Fund for money to buy computers.

(Rewi Alley, a New Zealand supporter of the Chinese revolution, had founded the school in 1944.) Institute supporters John and Elizabeth Pan donated a third of the money needed for computers. In September 2002, Matilda Young led a delegation that visited the school and saw students, two-thirds of them girls, who had mastered all the latest Microsoft software.[97] In 2005, Young initiated a different approach to participating in ACWF's Spring Bud program. Instead of pledging to support a certain number of girls, she first recruited financial supporters, the level of whose commitment determined the number of girls they would fund. Under Young's model, supporters would be more actively involved in monitoring and encouraging the students, whether by corresponding or visiting. By the end of the first year, they were supporting several dozen girls in five schools.[98]

In late 2007, former investment banker Dan Chao proposed a micro-finance program. The Institute's leadership enthusiastically agreed, and Chao began raising funds, establishing local contacts in China, and initiating a project in Pucheng County, Shaanxi Province. The Institute partnered with an existing local project that Chao determined to have greater management skills and, especially, accountability than other micro-finance projects in China. The Institute set an aggressive goal of raising $500,000 in the United States by the end of 2011 and leveraging that money to borrow $1 million from local banks in China. The actual amount raised was just over $450,000.[99] The Institute wants to use the Pucheng project as 'a model for a sustainable, scalable, and well-managed microfinance institution ... that can be emulated throughout China.'[100] If successful, the micro-finance program could turn out to be the Institute's most influential.

And more policy research

With Phase II as complete as it was going to get and eyes on retirement, Cheng made a final effort in 2000 to institutionalize the Institute's policy research in a way that could survive his own active involvement. On 30 October, he convened a meeting of ten prospective members of a new Research Advisory Committee. He proposed applying to policy research the same model of 'director involvement' that had yielded successful direct action projects in the fields of social ethics, women, and the environment. Although the research committee did not reconvene, its sole session led to two projects. Michael Keran and Cheng eventually produced their previously discussed paper on pension reform. Also, a scholar who had been unable to attend, Richard Holton, proposed a study on the effects on bilateral trade of China's accession to the WTO. Rather than a study, Holton's proposal evolved into a half-day conference for an American business, policy and academic audience at the Federal Reserve Bank of San Francisco.[101]

As the twentieth century gave way to the twenty-first, it became clear to all that the Institute as a whole, and particularly its policy research program, had become overly dependent on an aging leadership. Cheng was candid in assessing the problem:

> The core people are getting old. I am a prime example of that. ... Who is going to be a fool like we are, to volunteer our time and effort? We cannot

find anybody else to do that. Younger people, they have their own careers to pursue. ... And older people, you cannot find people like us.[102]

In fact, the Institute did find a younger leader willing to shoulder the administrative burden. On the first day of 2008, Wei-Tai Kwok became the second president of The 1990 Institute, allowing Cheng to retire.[103] In early 2011, C. B. Sung resigned from the chairmanship, Kwok replaced him, Rosalyn Koo became president, and Rick Chong (another member of the younger generation) was chosen as executive vice president, with the understanding that he would assume the presidency in 2012.[104]

While the succession of Kwok to the Institute's presidency resolved the problem of administrative continuity, the challenge of perpetuating the Institute's role in policy research remained. A possible solution to the latter began to emerge in 1999 with the formation of the Overseas Young Chinese Forum and its subsequent deepening relationship with The 1990 Institute.[105] According to its official brochure, the 'Overseas Young Chinese Forum (OYCF) was established in 1999 to provide a forum for young Chinese scholars, graduate students and professionals to exchange views on issues concerning China and to develop common aspirations.'[106]

Initially, the OYCF's members were all based in the United States, with the center of activity migrating from the East to the West Coast. The organization's genesis was in a series of discussions on political liberalism and its relevance for contemporary China, organized by Bo Li and fellow students at Harvard.[107] An annual themed retreat of approximately 70 members is the glue that holds the group together. Themes have ranged from civil society to China's rural problems to women's issues. The OYCF's three other major activities are: a bimonthly online, bilingual journal; short-term university teaching in China; and sponsorship of policy research. By 2005, as many as 20 percent of OYCF members had returned to China to work, but many of them stayed involved with the organization by e-mail.[108]

In 2000, as part of his fundraising efforts, OYCF co-founder Bo Li contacted C. B. Sung and other members of The 1990 Institute. Despite obvious demographic and agenda differences between the two organizations, a common interest in China-related policy research constituted an important overlap in missions. Over time, leaders of each organization joined the other's board. The OYCF invited C. B. Sung and Hang-Sheng Cheng to join its advisory board, and its president, Lei Guang, was a keynote speaker at the Institute's 2006 annual dinner.[109] This pattern of connections led Hao Zou, an OYCF member who joined the Institute's board, to describe the evolving relationship as a 'strategic partnership.'[110] In 2001, Li wrote to Hang-Sheng Cheng, suggesting that the Institute consider funding OYCF teaching and research fellowships. The Institute declined to fund the teaching program but agreed to fund research.

The Institute's executive committee segued from noting its own 'shortage of research personnel' to focusing on the OYCF as a surrogate. Cheng saw the OYCF as sharing the Institute's objective of using policy research to 'contribute to China's modernization.' For William Lee, the new partnership was a way to 'pass the baton' to 'a group of very, very talented young people.'[111] In October 2002, the two organizations announced the creation of Joint OYCF – The 1990 Institute Fellowships. Although OYCF members discuss and advocate gradualist political reforms for China, the fellowship guidelines adhere to the Institute's strictly 'non-political posture.'[112] The Institute initially funded the program with $10,000 for one year, 2003, with an option – which the Institute and the OYCF have continued to exercise (as of 2011) – of annual renewal.[113] Fellowships have sponsored research on such topics as rural taxation, rural long-term healthcare, village elections and taxation, and labor training for poverty alleviation.[114]

In his speech to The 1990 Institute's 15th Anniversary Dinner in April 2005, Chairman C. B. Sung summarized the Institute's organizational challenges as 'three-dimensional (3D) growth ... (1) adding action-oriented projects to policy research projects, (2) adding youth to the aging core group, and (3) adding research capabilities in China to the expertise in the U.S.'[115] Sung was acknowledging two kinds of challenges. First, like the Hopkins-Nanjing Center and the National Committee, the Institute had to adapt its agenda to evolving Chinese interests. By the early twenty-first century, Chinese economists had achieved a considerable degree of sophistication. Thus, seeking foreign advice on structural reforms became a lower priority for the government and various think tanks. Second, unlike the other two organizations, the Institute had to assure its own continuity as a volunteer association by managing a generational transfer of leadership. By initiating direct action projects that meet China's new priority of coping with the negative consequences of its reform policies, while staying connected to research through its ties to the OYCF, the Institute has successfully navigated the first challenge. The second, generational, challenge is no small one. An aging leadership was a key factor in the demise of the American Asiatic Association, a business group with a broader Sino-US relations agenda in the first decades of the twentieth century.[116] While the assumption of the presidency by Wei-Tai Kwok is an important transitional step, a fuller assessment must await future developments.

4 Invited influence in the policy sphere

How do foreigners influence China's policy process? Or, alternatively, how do Chinese policy-makers and institutions incorporate foreign models and expert knowledge into their own agendas? This chapter will provide answers to these questions by contextualizing and describing representative activities of the three associations under investigation here.

Prologue: a policy advisor's story

In the summer of 1993, a friend from the United Nations Development Programme (UNDP) told American economist James Galbraith that China's State Planning Commission (SPC) had asked the UNDP to help it recruit a chief technical advisor for a macroeconomic reform project. Would he be interested in the position? Galbraith's wife and friends told him that he 'couldn't do any harm,' so he flew to Beijing for an interview. After listening, over a two-day period, to eight hours of presentations, mainly on American economic policy and policy institutions, the SPC offered him the job for three years. For eight subject areas – such as industrial policy, human resources, and international economic policy – Galbraith's assignment was to marshal the best available expert American advice in the form of conferences, papers, and training missions.

In late 1995, for example, Galbraith organized a conference in Huairou, a suburb of Beijing, on international monetary policy. He approached Robert Eisner, a prominent Keynesian economist, about speaking on the topic. When Eisner expressed interest, Galbraith 'told him the price: "You've got to stop them from liberalizing their capital account."' Eisner agreed with Galbraith and made their mutual case in Huairou. Joseph Stiglitz, former chief economist and senior vice president at the World Bank and former member of President Clinton's Council of Economic Advisors, later credited China's maintenance of controls over foreign capital as a major factor in shielding China from the 1997 Asian financial crisis. 'You never know,' says Galbraith, 'what substantive influence any particular person might have had, but I felt that I was in an excellent position to bring over [to China] people who were open-minded – to give, you know, a very different, a much broader range of views than, for example, the Russians got.' Galbraith viewed his role much as did his Chinese hosts and collaborators – to provide some 'outside perspective' as opposed to detailed plans. 'There is very little transferability of institutions and models from one place to the next. You have to build on the institutions you have.'[1]

Galbraith's story has been told by numerous scholars and policy advisors, though with different nuances in the plot. Nearly a decade before he began his research in 1992 on a tax reform book for The 1990 Institute, for example, Roy Bahl had provided advice on China's fiscal policy – sometimes through the World Bank, sometimes directly to the Chinese government.

> I'd get calls. 'Professor Bahl, come to China.' 'When?' 'February 12, Hangzhou. All will be taken care of. Stay two days.' Unlike other countries, the Chinese always sort of picked your brain about things. But it was clear from the get-go that you were never going to be on the inside in policy-making. You weren't going to sit with the minister and work out the details of it. You were like a plumber.[2]

With respect to public administration, Caroline Haiyan Tong and Hongying Wang tracked Chinese adoption of Western (particularly American) practices, as a way of gauging influence. They concluded, 'The correlation between China's adoption of American models and norms and Sino-American education exchanges makes a highly plausible, though not definitive, case of an important impact of the latter on the former.'[3]

These anecdotes suggest the essential features of 'invited influence' in the policy sphere of contemporary US–China transnational relations: Chinese official and semi-official policy bodies actively seek out information on American practices and advice from Americans; a variety of Americans, often with their own agendas, establish advisory or exchange relationships with Chinese institutions; the Chinese maintain substantial control over the agenda and adapt foreign ideas to their own conditions and needs; and, finally, evidence of American influence is typically more suggestive than definitive. Within this common framework, specific exchanges and their influence on policy can follow diverse paths. Policy influence may be a precondition of an exchange, a byproduct of a different agenda, or a planned outcome. The experiences of the Hopkins-Nanjing Center, the National Committee on US–China Relations, and The 1990 Institute yield illustrations of each scenario.

Policy influence as precondition: the Hopkins-Nanjing Center and university autonomy

Nothing in the documentary record or participants' reflections suggests that former Johns Hopkins University President Stephen Muller, Chinese American physicist Chih-Yung Chien, or others on the American side saw a joint-venture institution of higher education as a means of changing China's higher education system. They sought, rather, to better educate young Chinese and Americans about each other's culture and institutions, in the hope that deeper and more personal knowledge between the two peoples would improve international understanding. The Americans did, however, bring to the collaborative venture educational values and practices that were, in effect, minimum conditions for their participation.

In the American tradition of higher education, universities have a high degree of autonomy from government authorities on questions of student selection, finance, curriculum development, and access to information. Neither Muller, nor the American administrators and faculty, nor the individuals and institutions that provided funding from the United States would have accepted significant limits on these customary prerogatives. Muller was prepared to end preliminary discussions if the Chinese side had resisted an open-stack library or insisted on the right to censor the selection of books. The freedom of each side to select its own students has not yet arisen as a point of contention, although former American Co-Director Robert Daly speculated that the selection of a US-resident student with a Taiwan passport would be controversial.

For most of Chinese history, on the other hand, universities and the Confucian academies that preceded them have served the state. There was limited progress toward autonomy during the Republican period (1912–49), followed by a dramatic decline when the new communist government imposed the Soviet model of comprehensive state control in 1952.[4] During the Cultural Revolution (1966–76), the question of autonomy became moot, as Mao's supporters closed most universities and sent students to 'learn' from the peasants.

The idea of Sino-foreign educational joint ventures could not have gained traction on the Chinese side from the late 1970s onward outside the broader context of vigorous domestic debate and policy change in China regarding the question of university autonomy. The establishment, survival, and maturation of the Hopkins-Nanjing Center for Chinese and American Studies constitutes an important foreign contribution to the emergence of limited university autonomy in China during the post-Mao reform period. At times, the Center has tested the limits of reform.

As Chinese leaders prioritized economic reform and prosperity in the late 1970s, they focused on a critical role that universities needed to play: training experts. They also increasingly realized that a less restrictive intellectual environment was more conducive to training innovative experts.[5] A series of official policy statements and laws guided the relaxation of state control. In 1985, the Communist Party Central Committee issued a Decision on Educational Reform, which it expanded in 1993 with a Mission Outline of the Reform and Development of China's Education. Formalizing these statements of policy, the National People's Congress passed the 1995 Education Law and the 1998 Higher Education Law, which were designed officially to enhance university autonomy.[6]

As a result of these reforms, universities have gained considerable control over internal matters, such as personnel, student selection, and curriculum development. They also have far greater budgetary authority, although this new 'freedom' is largely the result of the state's reduction in financial support for higher education since 1978 from close to 100 percent to about half by the end of the twentieth century. Institutions must make up the balance from tuition, local government funding, philanthropy, and establishing their own businesses. At the leading edge of all these trends are *minban*, or private, universities, which have proliferated since the first experimental institution, Zhonghua Shehui Daxue (Chinese Social University), was established in 1982.[7] In concert with all this progress, however, in the wake of the Tiananmen Square rebellion, the Communist Party deployed a new presidential responsibility system to strengthen its position within public universities and in the early twenty-first century expanded its influence on private campuses as well.[8]

Western experience has been a significant input in China's deliberation and practices with respect to university autonomy. One channel for acquiring foreign expertise in higher education has been the large number of Chinese students who have studied abroad – over 1.4 million from 1978 through 2011.[9] A 2003 country survey found that more than half of China's university presidents and vice presidents had studied abroad.[10] China simultaneously pursued the more direct route of formally investigating foreign models of higher education. With encouragement and funding from the World Bank, sending experts abroad to study systems of higher education was one of the earliest initiatives of Deng Xiaoping and his allies, even before they solidified political power in 1978.[11] Since then, thousands of experts and delegations have traveled to the West to learn and to China to teach.[12]

China officially accepted foreign educational institutions on its soil in 1995, when the State Council issued Provisional Regulations on Chinese–Foreign Cooperation in Running Schools. Beijing formalized this acceptance in 2003 with a set of Regulations on Chinese–Foreign Cooperation in Running Schools.[13] The Hopkins-Nanjing Center had established a foreign presence in China well before the State Council's new policies, however, and its success was likely a key consideration in the promulgation of those policies and the expanded university autonomy they entailed. Knowledge of the Center's freedom to design its curriculum, the latitude of students in choosing classes, and the uncensored library circulated widely in China. For one thing, the Center broke the ice on the issue of sovereignty. Prior to its establishment, no foreign university – not even a Soviet one, during the height of Sino-Soviet friendship in the 1950s – had been allowed a legal presence on mainland Chinese soil since the People's Republic was founded in 1949. The decision to approve the Center was a momentous one.

It is likely that the Center's ability to survive the Tiananmen crisis – the most serious flare-up between China and the United States since the normalization of relations in 1979 – convinced Chinese leaders that it was safe to grant additional foreign universities a legal presence in China. There was uncertainty – and, ultimately, reassurance – on the American side, as well. Recalling his discussions at the time with Hopkins President Muller, Chih-Yung Chien says the trustees were prepared to 'shut it down and solve a long-term financial burden,' if they did not feel assured that the Center could maintain its academic freedom.[14]

A pattern of events suggests that the Center's experience has provided a model, various elements of which other foreign institutions have replicated or arrived at independently. One other Sino-foreign university won approval prior to the 1995 Provisional Regulations. In 1994, the European Commission (later to become the European Union) and the Chinese government signed a memorandum of understanding to establish the China Europe International Business School (CEIBS), while Shanghai Jiaotong University and the European Foundation for Management Development signed an operational agreement. CEIBS began operations on Shanghai Jiaotong's campus in 1995 and opened its own world-class campus in 1999.[15] CEIBS is cross-cultural mainly in that it exposes Chinese students to Western management knowledge. The student body is Chinese, 95 percent of the faculty members are non-Chinese, and all classes are in English. A Chinese president and vice president share day-to-day administrative responsibility with a European president and vice president. According to Vice Dean Zhang Weijiong, the university's special legal status gives it 'a high level of self-regulation which makes it unusual in China's management education system.'[16] As a 'non-profit educational institution with a fully licensed legal person status,' it has considerably more autonomy – with respect to curriculum, admissions standards, and hiring – than do Chinese business schools.[17]

In 1998, Chinese American businessman Shawn Chen funded and established a Western-style university in impoverished Henan Province. SIAS University derives its name from Chen's company, the SIAS Group. A native of Chongqing, Chen attended college in the United States, took US citizenship, and became wealthy importing Chinese products. He leveraged some of his own money to secure a $12 million loan from the Bank of China and established SIAS with this combined funding. The curriculum includes liberal arts, business, and technical programs.[18]

Chen set SIAS on a unique path to university autonomy by gaining approval for it as a non-profit enterprise, rather than as a university. It appears that political connections, driven more by short-term economic incentive than long-term human capital needs, were helpful. The *Los Angeles Times* reported:

> Henan officials were hungry for investment, and Chen knew things looked good when, after a meeting with Communist Party leaders in the provincial capital, Zhengzhou, they called the airport and ordered the plane to wait for a tardy Chen. 'My impression is that [Chen] is a clever and a shrewd person,' said Zheng Haodong, vice mayor of Xinzheng City.[19]

Since the promulgation of the 2003 regulations, several additional foreign universities have established, or contracted to establish, campuses in China. In the fall of 2004, the University of Nottingham welcomed students at the Ningbo campus of its partner, Zhejiang Wanli University, and a year later opened its own campus in Ningbo. The University of Nottingham-Ningbo (UN-Ningbo) was the first Sino-foreign university to gain Chinese Ministry of Education approval under the 2003 regulations. It offers degrees in international studies, computer science, international business management, and other business fields. All students are Chinese, all classes are taught in English, and degrees have the same status as degrees earned at Nottingham's UK campus. The Xi'an Jiaotong-Liverpool University opened its campus in Suzhou on 29 May 2006, and classes began with the fall 2006 semester. Its program is similar to UN-Ningbo's, though more oriented toward technology. Like UN-Ningbo, Xi'an Jiaotong-Liverpool teaches Chinese students exclusively in English. Both British institutions have the kind of independent control over pedagogy for which the Hopkins-Nanjing Center established a precedent.[20]

Several American universities have announced agreements for new degree-granting campuses in China. All affirm that they will be able to protect academic freedom. New Jersey-based Kean University, for example, announced in May 2006 that the next year it would 'open the first American university in China.' (The statement apparently meant the first under the new 2003 regulations.) Kean's partner is Wenzhou University, located in economically booming south-eastern Zhejiang Province. Kean spokesman Daniel Higgins stated that the campus would not compromise on academic freedom: 'It's total access, complete freedom of speech. That was crucial to the deal.'[21] The new campus did not open on schedule in 2007, but the Ministry of Education finally approved the project in December 2011.[22]

Duke University has encountered a series of obstacles that are better documented. In early 2010, Durham's *Herald-Sun* reported, 'After two years of planning, Duke University officially committed Friday to a significant presence in China.' At a groundbreaking ceremony in Kunshan, an industrial hub between Shanghai and Suzhou, Duke President Richard Broadhead hailed an agreement with its partner, Shanghai Jiaotong University, as 'a new model of international educational collaboration.' By the end of the year, the planned opening of the business school had been delayed from fall 2011 to fall 2012, and Shanghai Jiaotong had reversed a commitment to sponsor the university to the Ministry of Education. Although Kunshan is providing the land and paying for construction, estimates of Duke's financial commitment for the first ten years have risen from 'limited' to $11 million to $42.5 million. As of September 2011, Duke was still awaiting Ministry approval of a new partnership with Wuhan University, and Duke faculty members were voicing concerns about cost and academic freedom.[23]

More recently, and apparently with fewer hitches, New York University embarked on the path to a campus in China. In March 2011, NYU's president signed an agreement to build a campus in Shanghai's booming Pudong district that would eventually accommodate 3,000 students. According to a *New York Times* report, President John Sexton 'compared the more cosmopolitan horizons of today's students and professors to the Italian Renaissance, when talented artists moved from their homes to cities like Florence, Milan and Venice to pursue their work.'[24] NYU Shanghai, a partnership with East China Normal University, will reach beyond the business and technical emphasis of most foreign campuses (other than Hopkins-Nanjing). It will be 'a comprehensive research university with a liberal arts and science college.' Classes will be conducted in English.[25] Most of the students will be Chinese, but some US-enrolled students will be able to spend time at the Shanghai campus as part of NYU's Study Away program.[26] As of late 2011, NYU Shanghai was on schedule to begin classes on the campus of East China Normal University in the fall of 2013 and at its own new campus a year later.[27]

While the successful example of the Hopkins-Nanjing Center seems to have inspired both domestic legislation and emulation by other foreign universities, it is clear from Chinese and foreign discourses and from events on the ground that university autonomy remains fragile and contested. In the wake of the establishment of the University of Nottingham-Ningbo, founding provost Ian Gow believed it

> unlikely that any other institution will negotiate the sort of freedom that the University of Nottingham and the University of Liverpool achieved. It is much more likely that institutions will come in and teach and research what the Chinese want them to teach (science and technology) and where they want them to teach it.[28]

According to one report, Stanford University and Columbia University have avoided major commitments in China largely out of concern about academic freedom, instead limiting their presence to light-footprint academic centers.[29] To Peggy Blumenthal, Executive Vice President of the Institute of International Education, such critiques as one-sided. 'If China does not succeed economically, educationally, financially, we are all in trouble. ... We should be doing everything we can around the world to make sure that China's higher education system is benefitting from all our institutions.'[30]

Chinese observers are no less conflicted than foreigners. In May 2010, Beijing issued a new set of guidelines that explicitly address university autonomy. According to one expert, the guidelines constitute 'one of the most important educational-reform documents of the last 30 years.' In particular, they expand universities' autonomy in teaching, research, enrollment, and international exchanges. There was contention over some of the new provisions within the National People's Congress, however, and not all supporters of university autonomy are satisfied with the outcome. Professor Zhang Ming of Renmin University complained that there is still too much government control. 'The transformation of the system from Soviet-style to American-style is far from complete.'[31]

One visiting Chinese scholar who contributed to an Organization for Economic Cooperation and Development (OECD) forum was defensive in urging the Chinese government to allow more autonomy: 'Freedom and autonomy are not anti-government concepts to gain political rights.' Another, who helped conduct a 1998 survey of 20 universities for the Ministry of Education, more hopefully reported that most 'university leaders' felt their institutions had more autonomy than in the 1970s. His conclusion – 'As an administrative concept in higher education, university autonomy is an inevitable result of political reform and opening to the world' – was more guarded than it might appear upon an initial reading. Note the narrow emphasis on autonomy as an *administrative* concept.[32]

A recent survey of Chinese professors found that most saw a significant expansion of autonomy over the past three decades, but they also understood the continuing political limits. One said, 'There is freedom in research except around political issues …' Another was more specific: 'You cannot do research on the June 4 Incident – its merits, demerits, historical position – or on the Four Basic Principles [of communist rule].' Others noted the continued presence on campuses of party officials responsible for 'political education' and the importance of personal connections (*guanxi*) for attaining research funding, career mobility, and other tokens of autonomy.[33]

Academic freedom – the open exchange of ideas and information within a university environment – is a central dimension of university autonomy. A 2009–10 episode at the Hopkins-Nanjing Center served both to clarify the boundary between academic freedom and political freedom and, again, to put the Center at the forefront of Western contributions to discourse and policy affecting university autonomy in China. A *Bloomberg News* article reports that in late 2009, an American student at the Center published an academic journal that included an article on Chinese protest movements and that the Center's administration would not fund the journal or permit its distribution outside the Center. While the emphasis of the Bloomberg article is on restriction of expression beyond the campus, the other half of the story is that there were no restrictions on publication or on circulation within the confines of the Center. A copy was even placed in the library. Hopkins President Ronald Daniels acknowledged the limits on the rights of Center students beyond the walls of the campus but affirmed the value of the intellectual exchange that occurs within those walls. The presidents of two universities whose campuses will soon open in China have followed suit. President John Sexton of NYU says, 'I have no trouble distinguishing between rights of academic freedom and rights of political expression.' Similarly, President Richard Brodhead of Duke, referencing 'pretty good discussions with people at Hopkins,' is comfortable distinguishing between 'intra-campus discussion and what you do at large.'[34]

Policy influence as byproduct: the Ussuri River project

As with the Hopkins-Nanjing Center, contributing to China's policy formation process was not the primary focus of the National Committee's involvement in the Ussuri River project. Like the Center, the National Committee sought to improve international understanding. As the National Committee's Ussuri project director, Elizabeth Knup, says, the organization's 'motivation has always been – and was particularly in this case – the interest of bringing together different groups of people that had a common objective.'[35]

The Ussuri project did, however, produce a detailed report – *A Sustainable Land Use and Allocation Program for the Ussuri/Wusuli River Watershed and*

Adjacent Territories – complete with maps, charts, and policy recommendations. The National Committee realized that promoting implementation of the report's recommendations was beyond the scope (and financial resources) of its project and without precedent in its own history as a public education and exchange organization. Project participants, nevertheless, hoped that their Russian and Chinese partners, with support from international funding institutions, would ultimately make constructive use of some of the data and recommendations in the published report.

Wetland degradation in reform China

The development policies that China has pursued since the 1950s have been resource-intensive and have placed considerable strain on every aspect of the nation's environment, including wetlands that have been converted to agriculture. The post-1978 rural reforms and the added the stress of urbanization have accelerated the depletion of wetland natural resources.[36] The 19 million-hectare Sanjiang Plain is China's largest wetland area, including 2 million hectares of wetland, 37 ecosystems, over 1,400 species of flora, and more than 1,000 species of fauna. The Chinese word Sanjiang means 'three rivers' and refers to the area in northeastern China surrounding the Heilong, Ussuri, and Songhua Rivers. The first two run along the Chinese–Russian border, while the Songhua flows through the plain within China.[37]

Over the past two decades, both domestic environmentalists and international institutions have raised consciousness within Russia and China about the long-term social and economic costs of wetland degradation, and policy-makers have often responded positively. China, for example, enacted a Wild Animal Protection Law in 1988 and issued a Biodiversity Conservation Action Plan in 1994. In 1996, Heilongjiang Province issued a Regulation of Nature Reserves, and in 1998, it suspended the conversion of wetlands to farmland. As of 2005, Heilongjiang had established 28 nature reserves in the Sanjiang Plain wetlands.[38]

Increasingly pro-conservation government attitudes and laws, however, have not assured the implementation of conservation policies. Among the limiting factors are: lack of alternative livelihood enterprises for farmers; weak technical capacity; inadequate financing for research and implementation; and, especially, fragmentation of authority among different government agencies.[39] Two Chinese environmental scientists illustrated the latter problem, as they surveyed a series of transnational conservation initiatives (including the National Committee's Ussuri Project) targeting Lake Xingkai/Khanka along the Sino-Russian border. The first level of fragmentation is national: Chinese and Russian scientists typically compile separate statistics, use different methods to calculate oxygen demand, and use partial maps that cut the lake down the middle. The second level is fragmentation within each country: Four administrative units on the Chinese side and six on the Russian side have authority over the lake.[40]

Early in the National Committee's Ussuri Project, Elizabeth Knup encountered the fragmentation of environmental policy authority in China:

> The HLJ [Heilongjiang Province] Forest Bureau is in charge of most nature reserves in HLJ. The land, however, is owned by the Farm Bureau. Hence, there is a great deal of conflict and lack of cooperation between the two *danwei* (work/administrative units). … [Further,] Beijing has retained authority over planning largely because the money still comes from Beijing.[41]

Compounding the dispersion of administrative authority, there is often a divergence of economic interests, with pro-growth local governments resisting environmental controls.[42]

Ussuri project report: environmental policy guidance

On 7 February 1997, National Committee President David M. Lampton reported the project's completion to its major funder, the Rockefeller Brothers Fund (RBF):

> We have distributed 500 copies of the report to each of our Chinese and Russian counterpart organizations. In addition, the National Committee and Ecologically Sustainable Development have begun a coordinated effort to distribute the report to interested parties, including potential investors – both public (for the conservation aspects) and private (for the economic development dimension).[43]

Within four months of the report's publication, the prestigious journal *Science* took note of its potential as a policy guide, calling it 'a road map for preserving a unique biological milieu in the 25-million-hectare watershed.'[44] In a congratulatory letter to the National Committee, Peter Riggs of RBF exuded optimism: 'The report is a springboard, because this is merely the completion of Phase I. Now comes the implementation phase.' Riggs highlighted the need for 'major' (i.e., larger scale than RBF could provide) funding and offered to help solicit financial support from such institutions as the World Bank and the Asia Foundation.[45]

In October 1997, a group of Chinese, Russian, and American environmental scholars analyzed the National Committee's Ussuri project in *The Forestry Chronicle*. Although their purpose was to 'draw some lessons for forest biodiversity planning in North America,' their discussion also suggested the project's policy implications for Russia and China. The article called for 'establish[ing] new laws in each country at the krai and province level that will enact the Ussuri Basin Plan.'[46] In 1997, Russian, Chinese, and American representatives signed a memorandum of understanding to establish a tri-national Secretariat, with the National Committee representing the American side of the project. They would 'continue to work together and to share information on the implementation of the recommendations.'[47]

In reality, the plans for an immediate tri-national push for implementation of the Ussuri Report's recommendations came to naught. While the influence of the report would be palpable, it would be more diffuse and protracted than enthusiasts from the National Committee project hoped. Douglas Murray came to view the organization's efforts more as 'reinforcing activities' than as direct stimuli to specific results.[48] Subsequent to publication of the Ussuri Report, international institutions have promoted three major projects that reinforce and/or are reinforced by it.

The first initiative is the Wetland Biodiversity Conservation and Sustainable Use Project, whose objective is: 'To establish wetland biodiversity conservation as a routine consideration in national, provincial and local government decision making and action.' The project was approved by the Council of the Global Environmental Facility (GEF) in December 1998 and began in December 1999, administered by the United Nations Development Programme (UNDP). The six-year project was to be funded by $11.7 million from the GEF, $20.3 million from the Chinese government, and $3.4 million from the Australian Agency for International Development, though the Australians withdrew in 2004. In 2003, the project was extended through October 2007 and revised to expand its emphasis from nature reserves to broader landscape issues and to involve more civil society organizations. A project-capping workshop attracted 230 representatives from 11 countries and 24 papers that exhaustively mapped China's wetland conservation achievements and challenges.[49]

A second initiative, the Sanjiang Plains Wetland Protection Project of the Asian Development Bank (ADB), is a response to a 2002 request by the Chinese government for technical assistance. The Japan Special Fund injected 80 percent of $750,000 in technical assistance money for a feasibility study that began in December 2002, while the ADB, GEF, and Heilongjiang Province made the major contributions to the $55 million cost of the five-year project that followed completion of technical assistance in July 2004. A 2002 project technical assistance document cites the authors' concern with preserving 'the Sanjiang Plains as wetlands of international importance.' The document highlights the UNDP/GEF Wetland Biodiversity and Sustainable Use Project, on which the ADB project heavily relies. The implication is that these variously funded and administered projects are working in concert on a common environmental agenda.[50]

In November 2003, the GEF proposed a third project, which would follow through on some of the National Committee project's specific proposals. According to the approval request for a $15.25 million Integrated Management of the Amur–Heilong River Basin project:[51]

> The former [National Committee project] resulted in the proposed land-use in the Wusuli/Ussuri River basin, which will be utilised for the development of the Transboundary Diagnostic Analysis and the Regional Strategic Action Programme for the Amur/Heilong Basin [two goals of the proposed project] ...

Due to administrative changes in all three participating countries (China, Russia, and Mongolia), project preparation was halted in 2007. As of late 2011, the GEF continued to hold meetings with country representatives in hopes of reviving the project.[52]

What is the practical significance of all these studies and projects? According to Jim Harris of the International Crane Foundation:

> The Chinese certainly have protected additional areas on their side of the Ussuri basin. ... It's not purely a case of 'that [Ussuri] project is what did it,' but I think that project was one of a number of activities that was focusing attention, on the Chinese side, on wetlands.[53]

Policy influence by design: Roy Bahl's advice to the State Administration of Taxation

In contrast to the Hopkins-Nanjing Center's pursuit of autonomy and the National Committee's Ussuri project, contributing to China's policy deliberation process was an explicit goal of The 1990 Institute's sponsorship of policy papers and of monographs like Roy Bahl's *Fiscal Policy in China*. In promoting research for the Institute's first book (*China's Economic Reform*), Hang-Sheng Cheng wrote, 'While the central purpose of the study is to increase knowledge, its potential practical implications are obvious.' 'Our function,' he later said, 'is to be advisors to advisors on policy matters.'[54]

Cheng was cautious about quantifying the influence of Institute-sponsored research:

> Knowledge is essential to public policy, but the linkage between the two is clear only in concept but nebulous in reality. Knowledge developed through research is added to a public pool, from which all can draw to develop greater understanding. Hopefully, policy advisors are among them and dip into this vast pool. But, you will not be able to gauge how much understanding the policy advisors have gotten from which source.[55]

The process by which China has reformed its taxation system since the mid-1990s offers significant insights into this interplay between research and policy.

Chinese scholars in the United States and China's 1994 tax reform

For nearly three decades, from the Communist Party's consolidation of power in the early 1950s through the initiation of reforms in 1978, China's fiscal system was highly centralized. Occasional experimentation and the disorder of the Cultural Revolution notwithstanding, its primary characteristic was 'centralized revenue collection and centralized fiscal transfers' (*tongshou tongzhi*). The central government set provincial spending priorities and directly or indirectly controlled provincial revenue. The state owned most industry in the country, and its primary revenue source was the profits of these state-owned enterprises (SOEs). Additionally, the state was able to collect or reallocate revenue through its monopolistic purchase of agricultural products from farmers at suppressed prices and resale to urban residents at subsidized prices.

As Beijing began, cautiously, to divest itself of ownership and management of industry in the 1980s, tax collection progressively replaced profit allocation as the primary source of state revenue. The government attempted to improve the fiscal system through a series of reforms and experiments. Through the early 1990s, however, several destabilizing features remained constant – growing provincial and local control over in-budget and off-budget revenue, the state's dependence on negotiated tax contracts with the provinces, and vast inconsistencies in treatment within and between different classes of taxpayers.[56]

In this context, Hu Angang, research economist at the Chinese Academy of Social Sciences, went to the United States in 1991 to pursue postdoctoral studies in economics at Yale University. While at Yale, Hu met and came under the influence of fellow scholar Wang Shaoguang. Wang had come earlier to the United States, earned a doctorate from Cornell University, and become Assistant Professor of Political Science at Yale. In 1990, Wang wrote an article in Chinese, in which he developed an analysis that became the basis for his and Hu's long-term collaboration – and for their influence on China's tax policies.[57]

Wang's central thesis was that the fiscal strategy China had adopted in the early 1980s had weakened the state's capacity to pursue such important social goals as balanced economic growth, environmental protection, and income redistribution. Further, according to Wang (and, after they became collaborators, Hu), the policy of reducing the central government's restraint on economic activity by devolving economic decisions and controls to lower levels of government was, effectively, short-circuiting a more democratic, less corrupt alternative. Better, Wang and Hu argued, to withdraw the central government from micromanagement of the economy, but simultaneously to strengthen its revenue base and make its decision-making process increasingly transparent and democratic.[58]

The format in which Wang and Hu made their analysis and recommendations was an 'internal research report' to the Chinese Academy of Sciences, completed in May 1993 under the title *Report on State Capacity* (*Guoqing baogao*).[59] Hu explains the Chinese policy process that enabled the report to inspire a major tax reform the following year:

> In China, there are two major ways in which members of the leadership obtain information. One is the reporting system such as the reports localities (primarily at the provincial level) or ministries make to the Center or to the State Council. ... Normally ... reports reflect the 'good news' but do not report the 'bad news,' so as to demonstrate the political accomplishments of local or department leaders. ... The second is ... internal reference. For example, press agencies directly under the jurisdiction of the central government – such as the Xinhua News Agency or the *Renmin ribao* (*People's Daily*) publishers – may issue internal publications ... [that] report on debates

and viewpoints regarding the most important policies, including various opinions that differ from existing policies. ... These documents tend to be less affected by any particular government department or interest groups in a given locality; they are characterized by neutrality. ... [They] play an extremely important role in transmitting information to and from policy- and decision-makers, in helping to shape their policy designs, in helping them make adjustments in policies, and so on.[60]

Since 1988, Hu had published policy recommendations through internal channels at Xinhua News Agency and *Renmin ribao* and believed that his ideas had carried more influence than had he published them openly. In June and July of 1993, Xinhua News Agency and *Renmin ribao* published, for official audiences, including the top leadership, several excerpts from Hu and Wang's report. The title of these internal documents was 'Two Ph.D.s Who Have Studied in America Propose: Strengthen the Leading Role of the Central Government in the Transition Toward a Market Economy.'[61]

In June 1993, the person in charge of taxation at the Ministry of Finance told Hu and Wang he liked their report and had 'recommended it to the central leaders.' This ministry official's comments reflected a receptive attitude toward foreign advice:

As people say, 'monks from another country can recite the sutras best.' As scholars who have spent time studying in the United States, you people not only understand the experience and the theories that are current outside China, but are also conversant with actual conditions in China as well.[62]

The views of Hu and Wang coincided with and reinforced the evolving thinking of President Jiang Zemin and Vice Premier Zhu Rongji. In late July 1993, an official from the Central Policy Research Office invited Hu to discuss the 'Report on State Capacity' with a group of leaders. On 23 July, at a national work conference on fiscal policy, Vice Premier Zhu announced that China would implement Hu and Wang's key recommendations: abolish the system of negotiated tax contracts between the center and the provinces, move toward a unified national tax system, and create a formal revenue-sharing system between the center on the one hand, and provincial and local governments on the other. Subsequent reporting of the 1994 tax reform by Xinhua News Agency, Agence France-Presse, the *International Herald Tribune*, the British *Economist*, and others credited Hu and Wang's report as being a major factor in bringing the reform about.[63]

The principal architect of the 1994 reform was Xu Shanda, then head of the Reform Department of China's State Administration of Taxation (SAT). Like Wang Shaoguang and Hu Angang, Xu had studied in the West, earning an MA in public finance at the University of Bath (UK) in 1990. Xu first met C. B. Sung and other leaders of The 1990 Institute when he attended and gave a talk at the Institute's conference in December 1992 in Beijing, a presentation of preliminary research that would be published the following year as *China's Economic Reform*.

Xu's resulting friendship with Sung and respect for The 1990 Institute's work (for example, he attended the Institute's 1995 Beijing conference on foreign trade and investment law reform) complemented his prior friendship with Roy Bahl, the economist whose research the Institute sponsored for its tax reform project.[64]

American influence on post-1994 tax reform

After its implementation, the 1994 tax reform, like the centralized system of the 1950s through 1970s and the contract system of the 1980s, in turn became the subject of research and critical analysis. Bahl's *Fiscal Policy in China: Taxation and Intergovernmental Fiscal Relations* was one of the earliest results. Bahl began his research for the book in 1992 but, realizing the significance of the 1994 reform, delayed publication until 1998, in order to have time to make a preliminary assessment of that major development.

Bahl found much to commend in the 1994 reform, which he saw as heading 'clearly in the right direction,' but he identified three key areas that required continued attention if China were to develop a fiscal system adequate to the country's development goals. First, there was a need for additional policy improvements – for example, broadening the base of the new personal income tax, and rationalizing calculation of Value Added Tax (VAT), labor costs, and depreciation to bring investment incentives into line with market conditions. Second, improvements in tax administration (collection) could greatly increase revenues. Third, revenue-sharing arrangements still gave provinces, especially the wealthiest, too much leverage by allowing them to raise out-of-budget revenue.[65]

One of the central concerns that Hu and Wang had addressed and that had prompted the 1994 reform was the steady decline through the 1980s of two ratios: total tax revenue as a percent of Gross Domestic Product (GDP) and central government tax revenue as a percentage of total tax revenue. With only incomplete data from a few years available, Bahl was tentative in evaluating success in reversing the trend of these two ratios. Although they seemed to be continuing to decline from 1994 through 1996, he suspected that this might be because of transitional features the reform included to ease the shock to provinces. Using a simulated model, he predicted that at least the second ratio would steadily rise through the year 2000, though the first might not.[66]

Bahl is measured in estimating his contribution to China's policy deliberation process:

> I'd like to think I do good tax policy, and I think Xu does as well. So, the fact that people who do it right tend to reach the same conclusions is no surprise. And so, I wouldn't say that because I wrote a recommendation that most good people wouldn't come up with the same recommendation.[67]

While agreeing that 'it is very difficult to say that one policy specifically came from one person or another,' Xu, who became Vice Director of the SAT in 2000, describes Bahl as 'a very influential person in China. ... He knows many people, and his ideas influence those people, although some of those people agree with him and some may disagree.'[68] According to Xu, Bahl's role was typical of the way Chinese policy-makers welcome – even solicit – ideas from abroad and use those ideas to expand the pool of analyses and policy options on which they can draw:

> We learn from the experience of other countries and make comparative studies, to see which is good for us and which is bad. We can find scholars and experts that make suggestions to us, and we will adopt the useful ones to improve our own tax system.[69]

The active reception of Bahl's book by Xu and the SAT illustrates the policy synergy that Xu describes. It also illustrates a broader dynamic, whereby China both invites and guides foreign influences on its development. Xu not only provided Bahl with data he needed but agreed to join three American China scholars in reviewing Bahl's manuscript for The 1990 Institute in late 1997.[70] As the Institute was bringing the English edition of *China's Fiscal Policy* to press in early 1998 and began planning for a Chinese edition, Xu offered to organize a team of translators from his SAT staff. Further, the Institute accepted Xu's proposal that it appoint the SAT as the book's Chinese publisher, with a commitment to require that each of the 1,000-plus branch and sub-branch SAT offices in the country order 5–10 copies and distribute them to key staff members.[71]

As it turned out, the SAT's contribution went well beyond translation. Xu's team found several errors of fact and interpretation – some because, working in 1999, they had two additional years of data that had not been available to Bahl. They incorporated these corrections into the Chinese edition. For example, with additional data, Xu and his staff could see that the tax-revenue-to-GDP ratio began steadily increasing in 1997. Additionally, Xu wrote a 24-page introduction, in which he described and praised Bahl's achievement, summarized each chapter, explained the most significant editorial changes for the Chinese edition, and looked ahead to the continuing challenges of reforming China's fiscal system.[72] 'Outside observers see most clearly,' wrote Xu, echoing an earlier official comment on Wang Shaoguang and Hu Angang's research. 'It was a correct decision for The 1990 Institute to choose Roy Bahl for this research project.' On the other hand, Xu reminded readers of the necessary role of Chinese policy scholars: 'However, since Bahl is after all a foreigner, … it is impossible for even him to avoid some inaccuracies in understanding Chinese tax reform.'[73]

One way to evaluate the significance of Bahl's book is, where possible, to compare its recommendations and predictions to subsequent events. Bahl recommended, for example, bringing China's VAT system in line with other systems, such as Europe's, by converting it from a production to a consumption tax. In 2004, China began such an experiment in three northeastern provinces. According to Xu, the test was successful and would eventually be expanded nationwide.[74]

Another of Bahl's recommendations – equalizing the tax treatment of foreign- and Chinese-owned businesses – was implemented at the beginning of 2008, after several years of legislative gestation.[75] Bahl also recommended – contrary to the advice of some foreign and domestic economists – retaining the administrative division between provincial and central tax collectors that the 1994 reforms had created. 'Bahl explained early in his book why in China we must have separate administration. We can't say our tax reform is determined by Bahl's judgment,' says Xu, 'but his ideas solved the problem of dual loyalty and were more practical to the Chinese reality.'[76]

As Xu and Bahl realize, *Fiscal Policy in China* and its updated Chinese edition constitute but one contribution in an ongoing evaluation of China's fiscal reforms. In 2004, for example, Chinese economist Lingguang Bao proposed, as had Bahl, increasing reliance on personal income tax as a revenue-raising tool and convert- ing the VAT from a production to a consumption basis. He also advocated elimination of market-distorting tax incentives that contradict the market-oriented philosophy underpinning China's 2001 accession to the World Trade Organization (WTO).[77] American economist Christine Wong, elaborating a point also made by Bahl, has highlighted the threat to social stability of unfunded mandates for local and provincial governments. Mandates for such social services such as free primary and secondary education are a legacy of the 1994 reforms.[78]

Bahl and The 1990 Institute, thus, made a significant contribution to the ongo- ing transnational process of fiscal reform in China. In Xu's assessment, Bahl may be *primus inter pares* of foreign advisors: 'Because he has done research in this field for a very long time, knows more of China, and has many contacts with Chinese officials, therefore [Bahl's] suggestions may be more in depth.'[79] Xu also acknowledges the role of The 1990 Institute in sponsoring scholarship like Bahl's. In his introduction to the Chinese edition of *Fiscal Policy in China*, he writes:

> Through my contacts with Mr Shen Jianbai [the name Sung uses in China], the chairman of the Institute, his wife [Beulah Kwok-Sung], and Mr Cheng Hang-Sheng, the president, I have been deeply moved by their patriotic enthusiasm and professional dedication and that of The 1990 Institute, through which they are working. They tried everywhere to collect funds for their Chinese study program, while their own efforts were on a completely volunteer basis.[80]

Policy influence by design: labor law reform

Another Sino-US exchange was an exception to the indirectness of foreign influence. As part of a consortium that included Worldwide Strategies, Inc. and the Asia Foundation, the National Committee helped China's Ministry of Labor and Social Security 'develop laws and regulations based on internationally recognized workers' rights.'[81] The project represented a new departure for the National Committee, in that the goal was not so much to build relationships as to provide specific inputs into a sphere of Chinese domestic policy. The program also involved closer than usual collaboration with the US government. In this case, the US Department of Labor worked with the National Committee and its partners on project details, in addition to providing all the funding.[82]

From 2004 to 2007, the National Committee organized meetings in both China and the United States where Chinese government officials, municipal inspectors, labor lawyers, and scholars could exchange information with American experts. A centerpiece of workshop discussions was making recommendations for and reviewing drafts of a new Labor Contract Law.[83] The *Washington Post* called the new Labor Contract Law, which took effect in January 2008, 'a major victory for Chinese workers.' Features of the law prevent such abuses as unsafe working conditions, non-payment of wages, and use of subcontracting to evade legal responsibilities.[84]

The National Committee's other assignment within the consortium was helping to develop a training program for the thousands of labor inspectors that China needs, in order to enforce compliance with labor laws and regulations. Working with American and Chinese experts in the field, the National Committee developed a training manual and a program for 'training the trainers' and, in 2008, anticipated the training of 20,000 inspectors as an outgrowth of the project. Three years later, Chinese television reported that 23,000 were on the job.[85] Another key feature of the new legislation was the development of an arbitration system that migrant workers and laid-off workers could use to secure their rights. Worldwide Strategies had the US responsibility for this aspect of the program and developed a pilot project in Qingdao that reduced labor cases going to court by 20 percent at a time when cases were increasing 20–30 percent in other cities. As a result, Chinese authorities expanded the program nationwide.[86] Competent inspection strengthens workers' ability to protect their rights in arbitration over issues such as unfair layoffs and unpaid wages – and, according to one expert, 'often plays a considerable role in preventing and settling disputes.'[87]

This chapter can be seen as a response to a call by diplomatic historian Robert McMahon for the integration of policy history and diplomatic history; that is, for treating the formation of domestic policy, including the role of foreign non-state actors, as a significant dimension of foreign relations.[88] Distinct patterns of activity emerge from these case studies. The central features are: contributions by foreign actors to domestic policy formation; prominence of transnational associations in cross-border policy deliberation; encouragement of these transnational activities by governments on both sides; and pivotal roles frequently played by biculturally competent individuals.

The next two chapters depict repetitions of and variations on the last three themes. Foreigners have played a role in the growth of China's civil society and in the education of its intellectuals. The same US-based private associations have been in the forefront, often with Chinese Americans in key roles, and they have frequently worked with – or around – governments.

5 Nurturing civil society
A joint venture

One consequence of Deng Xiaoping's reforms has been the emergence, or re-emergence, of a civil society in China.[1] This chapter will explore the contributions of the Hopkins-Nanjing Center, the National Committee on US–China Relations, and The 1990 Institute to China's civil society. Chinese state, non-state, and quasi-state actors have invited this American participation, but they have also sought to retain control of the agenda.

Prologue: a brief discourse on civil society in China

Theory

As China's party-state – a totalist behemoth from the early 1950s through the late 1970s – reduced its role in managing society, other institutions arose or evolved to fill the governance vacuum. Most Western and a growing number of Chinese scholars use the term civil society to describe the sum of such non-state institutions, although there is disagreement over the scope of the term. Thomas Gold's definition is typical of contemporary social scientific thinking:

> Ideal-typical civil society includes such things as the media, religious organizations, labour unions, schools, think tanks, philanthropic and other community-oriented bodies such as foundations, and voluntary associations based on common interests or characteristics – private individuals coming together in the *public sphere* to pursue individual and group interests.[2]

For Gold and others, civil society encompasses the institutions that are distinct from the family, the state, and the economy. It may be more useful, however, to recover the classical definition of Hegel, Marx, and Weber, for whom private business organizations (and the marketplace within which they function) were not only part of civil society but the basis upon which other associative institutions could maintain their financial independence from the state.[3]

The second key concept in this chapter, non-governmental organization (NGO), denotes a large subset of civil society. 'Third sector' is often used as a collective synonym for NGOs.[4] Lester Salamon and Helmut Anheier, on the basis of extensive cross-national studies, posit five 'crucial' features that make an organization an NGO. It must be institutionalized ('to some meaningful extent'), private ('separate from government'), non-profit-distributing, self-governing, and voluntary.[5]

Practice

Initially, the emergence of new societal institutions in China was closely corre-lated with the modernization program of Deng and his colleagues, which they viewed largely in economic and scientific terms. The drive to increase agricul-tural productivity and improve rural living standards led, in the early 1980s, to the dismantling of the People's Communes, their replacement by the incentive-based Household Responsibility System, and the rise of township and village enterprises (TVEs). State support for chambers of commerce and trade associa-tions followed logically from the government's push to increase manufacturing output and encourage exports. The Party's and the State Council's need for both empirical data and strategic brainstorming to support macroeconomic planning translated into more autonomy for existing semi-official think tanks and, at times, tolerance of independent ones.[6]

While economic considerations continued to exert strong influence, both directly and indirectly, on the reorganization of Chinese society, other factors gradually made themselves felt as well – including unmet social needs, grassroots initiatives, and international and transnational organizations. Throughout the 1980s, people in the cities and the countryside formed associations ranging from hobby clubs, to professional interest groups, to social service providers, to advo-cacy groups. The latter came into sharp focus in the spring of 1989, as the Beijing Autonomous Students Union and the Beijing Autonomous Workers Federation played leading roles in confronting the Communist Party and challenging its authority. Up to that point, the government had not implemented any new laws or regulations to exert formal control over the organizations that were mushroom-ing throughout the country. Reeling from the challenge to its authority in the wake of the Tiananmen Square confrontation, the party-state required every non-governmental organization to register with the Ministry of Civil Affairs (MOCA). The applications of many associations considered politically threatening were rejected, and many additional independent-minded groups did not even try to apply. Still, most formal organizations were able to continue their activities and others simply operated informally.

Two events in 1992 gave Chinese civil society a boost. Deng's 'Southern Tour' – a visit to Shenzhen and other cities in southern China, where economic reforms were already extensive – signaled that China was still in reform mode, albeit within a context of heightened political vigilance. The following September, State Councilor Chen Junsheng, building on Liao Xun's work in Hainan Province in the late 1980s, declared at the First National Conference on the Management of Social Organizations that 'small government, big society' (*xiao zhengfu, da shehui*) was the goal of China's political reform. While it may not have been immediately clear to Chen, to his audience, or to the wider Chinese public exactly *how* society would expand, the phrase attained wide circulation and signified an ideal that has endured.[7]

Beginning in the 1980s, environmental NGOs came to constitute the first significant cluster of advocacy associations in China. They arose in response to the growing environmental degradation that was accompanying China's rapid industrialization, to the opening that the party-state had created for the formation of associations, and to rhetorical and some practical support by the state for environmentalism. The fragmented nature of political authority in China often casts the national government, or elements of it, as an ally of environmental NGOs, but development-oriented local or provincial authorities as a foe.[8]

Most activists, including environmentalists, concluded from the Tiananmen events of 1989 that they could maximize their effectiveness by pursuing a collaborative, or at least non-antagonistic, strategy vis-à-vis the government. Over time, however, some – anti-dam activists being a prominent example – were emboldened by success and more readily confronted authorities.[9] While some in the government have focused on the threat that citizen activism could get out of hand, others have lauded the advocacy role of environmental NGOs. When NGOs prodded the central government to halt Yunnan Province's dam project on the Nujiang River in 2004, some Chinese media favorably reported this 'resistance.'[10] One State Environmental Protection Administration (SEPA) official told a gathering of Chinese NGOs, 'The problem the environmental movement has in China is that there aren't enough NGOs.'[11]

The next major impetus for China's fledgling civil society was a global event, the 1995 United Nations Fourth International Women's Forum in Beijing. A series of international meetings, beginning with the First Women's Forum in Mexico City in 1975, had strengthened the global women's movement, both theoretically and organizationally.[12] The 1995 meeting continued that trend, but it also had domestic effects in China that transcended feminism. The source of these effects is the fact that, in tandem with each of the four women's forums, the UN held a companion NGO forum.

The 1995 NGO forum focused the attention of Chinese authorities on the broader issue of civil society and its relationship to government. On the one hand, in order to save face and be seen as a fully modern global citizen, Beijing made a serious investigation of international NGO standards, encouraged the formation of several grassroots women's NGOs, and supported the decision by the All-China Women's Federation (ACWF) to begin calling itself an NGO. On the other hand, the impending presence of thousands of feminist activists from around the world renewed fears within government and party circles of losing control over a restive civil society. In order to limit access by the general public to the NGO forum and by Chinese NGO representatives to foreign participants in the main forum, Beijing authorities moved the NGO forum from the Workers'

Palace in Beijing, the site of the main forum, to Huairou, a suburb 50 kilometers away.[13]

ACWF's new self-identification as an NGO was a milestone in a process that had begun in the 1980s. The Federation is one of eight 'mass organizations' (*qunzhong zuzhi*) that the Communist Party established after winning power in 1949. While these organizations theoretically represented their constituencies, in practice they served as transmission belts for the latest theories, policies, and campaigns of the Party. Only after 1979 did they begin, in varying degrees, also to represent their members' interests vis-à-vis the state. The ACWF was able to carve out much more latitude in this regard than other mass organizations such as the All-China Federation of Trade Unions, whose independence would pose a greater threat to the regime.

At the same time that the ACWF was becoming a more authentic mass organization, Chinese women sought and needed representation – in the workplace, in the community, and in the home. Deng's reforms had given women new freedom of individual choice and social mobility, but they had also created new (or revived old) social problems, such as prostitution, domestic violence, and unemployment. At its 1988 Conference, ACWF members had begun formally strategizing about new ways to represent Chinese women. In addition to refashioning itself as an interest group, albeit one still formally subordinate to the Communist Party, the ACWF became increasingly supportive of new genuine grassroots organizations such as Rural Women Knowing All. In many cases, these new groups were able to expedite the registration process by choosing the ACWF as their supervisory organization or to short-circuit the process entirely by simply affiliating as associations formally subordinate to the ACWF.[14]

In 1998, concern about the growing activism of the religious cult Falun Gong led the government to briefly put the brakes on domestic and foreign NGOs. New regulations forced all NGOs to re-register and increased their funding threshold. This episode accounts for a drop in the number of registered NGOs from 180,000 in 1995 to 130,000 in 2000.[15] The loss of momentum was only temporary, however. Also, the 1998 regulations created a new institutional category called private non-enterprise organizations. These are social service institutions, such as schools and hospitals, whereas NGOs (under Chinese regulatory definition) are membership organizations, whether based on advocacy or simply on common intellectual or recreational interests. The new category provides some financial benefits to institutions that previously had to register as commercial enterprises, but it also gives the government greater administrative control. By the end of 2003, there were approximately 142,000 traditional NGOs plus 124,000 private non-enterprise organizations.[16]

While not surrendering what control it can exert, the Chinese government has continued to affirm a legitimate role for NGOs, even as it periodically arrests NGO activists who exceed the collaborative role envisioned for them by China's leadership. A commentator in a 2007 issue of the government-run *China Daily* observed that it was no longer remarkable to hear a local official in Gansu Province say she planned 'to help catalyze the birth of NGOs' to help fight HIV/

AIDS. 'In contrast, only 10 years ago, many government officials in this country looked at grassroots NGOs suspiciously, regarding them as more hostile than cooperative.' The article cites a MOCA statistic of 345,000 Chinese NGOs by the end of 2006, a number which would apparently have to include private non-enterprise organizations.[17] The 2008 earthquake in Sichuan Province widened the opening for NGOs, who proved to be a help rather than a challenge to the Beijing government.[18] Periodic arrests of AIDS and other activists (spurred in part by Chinese governmental concern over the Color Revolutions and the Arab Spring) serve, however, as reminders of the fragile and contested nature of official affirmations.[19]

In parallel with the growth of civil society within China in the late twentieth century, foreign NGOs increasingly targeted China as an arena for their activities – in part as a function of globalizing forces that affected all spheres of social activity during this period, in part because of the importance of China's development to the rest of the world, and in part because of specific individual and institutional interests. As with native societal organizations, the party-state has had an ambivalent attitude – welcoming foreign funds and expertise but fearful of the potential for infiltration of subversive ideas and practices.

In the late 1980s, the Ford Foundation attained special operational status in China. The Foundation's director of China programs, Peter Geithner, negotiated with the State Council to put it under the jurisdiction of the prestigious Chinese Academy of Social Sciences. As had happened with the Hopkins-Nanjing Center, once Beijing was satisfied with this experiment, it gradually formalized a path for other foreign organizations to follow. In 1989, reflecting the value it placed on global economic integration, the state issued special regulations enabling foreign chambers of commerce to operate in Beijing. There were no further regulations covering foreign private institutions until 2004, however, when foreign foundations (which are not NGOs by Chinese definition or by some Western definitions) were included under new rules covering domestic foundations. Foreign NGOs are still not formally covered. They either link up with a Chinese partner – in government, academia, or civil society – or simply operate informally. In practice, the political environment became increasingly hospitable to foreign NGOs, especially after the 1995 Women's Forum.[20] By the early twenty-first century, they numbered 300–400, not counting about 700 grant-making organizations.[21]

Funds that foreigners provide to Chinese NGOs undoubtedly benefit recipients and their programs. To put funding in perspective, however, $200 million dollars in foreign funding annually 'is a relatively trifling sum compared both to the size of the population and to the level of international commercial investment in China (roughly USD 50 billion each year).'[22] Furthermore, as China has developed economically, a downward trend in foreign funding for Chinese NGOs has emerged since 1999.[23] More significant than money are less tangible influences, such as exposing Chinese citizens and officials to Western civil society ideas and practices and training NGO leaders.[24]

The China NPO Network, the Tsinghua University NGO Research Center, and the *China Development Brief* (*CDB*) are three leading examples of foreign institutions contributing to the growth of China's civil society in a broad, sustained fashion. In 1998, Professor Shang Yusheng, former head of the National Association of Natural Science Foundations, led the formation in Beijing of the China NPO [Non-Profit Organization] Network as a forum for private associations to share experiences. In 2001, the Network received substantial backing from the Ford Foundation and other foreign donors and expanded its mission to include NGO capacity building. By 2003, 90 of the most active independent Chinese NGOs had affiliated with the Network.[25]

Tsinghua University's NGO Research Center is a second example of transnational contribution to China's general education about the third sector. Founded in 1998, the Center conducts NGO research, offers a Masters in Public Administration degree, holds national and international forums and conferences, and publishes, in both Chinese and English, a quarterly journal of international scholarship (*The China Nonprofit Review*). The Center has received substantial financial support from the Ford Foundation, the Asia Foundation, the Himalaya Foundation (Taiwan), and the Sasakawa Peace Foundation (Japan).[26] The international citizen participation organization CIVICUS funded and helped guide research for a major report by the Center on the state of civil society in China. The report provides a detailed and sophisticated look at the state of civil society in China – and it does not shrink from making the same observations about heavy-handed government control that foreign scholars make.[27]

Nick Young, a British citizen, moved to China in 1996, accompanying his wife, who was the China program director for the NGO Save the Children. Attracted by the potential for associational activity in China and drawing on his background in journalism and social work, Young founded *China Development Brief* as an independent forum for Chinese and foreign NGO practitioners. The publication appeared several times a year through mid-2007, in both English and Chinese editions, online and in print. The audiences and, therefore, the content, of the two editions overlapped but also diverged. The Chinese edition served, and continues to serve, as a forum for domestic NGOs to discuss domestic and foreign experience with and ideas about civil society. The English edition mainly addressed foreign readers with a scholarly or professional interest in China's emerging civil society, a situation that led to more coverage of advocacy NGOs and of broader social development issues. The Chinese edition registered officially in its early years, while the English edition operated informally but with the knowledge of local officials in Beijing.[28] The government never interfered with *CDB*'s activities until the Beijing police abruptly shut down the English edition and expelled Young from the country in July 2007. The police made vague charges that the publication had violated a 1983 law on gathering statistics, but no clear explanation of Chinese motives has emerged.[29] In 2011, *CDB* reappeared in English, under the title *China Development Brief (English)* and the editorship of former Marist College political science professor Shawn Shieh, but this time as selected translations from the Chinese edition and in online format only.[30]

Limits

The foregoing historical overview provides a sense of the dramatic changes in state–society relations in China over the past 25 years and of the foreign role in those changes. A key point of contention among scholars and practitioners, however, is whether 'civil society' is an appropriate category for studying China. The dependence of private associations on government for personnel and funds, sharp limits on acceptable advocacy, and, especially, the dual registration system have led scholars like Anita Chan and Jonathan Unger to argue that 'corporatism' is a more accurate description of contemporary China's social reality than is 'civil society.'[31] The policy of 'dual registration,' implemented in 1989 and still in force, certainly has a corporatist character. Every association must be sponsored by a state institution, commonly referred to as a 'mother-in-law,' in addition to registering with MOCA. Further, this policy allows only one association at each level of government for each issue area. The other prominent corporatist feature of the Chinese system is that a large number of the country's NGOs are more properly designated as GONGOs (government-organized non-government organizations).

While acknowledging substantial gaps between civil society as an ideal type and Chinese reality, the majority of scholars writing from the late 1990s onward have found that term analytically useful. They note that more private associations operate informally than within the MOCA registration system. They argue that close interaction between state and civil society also exists (albeit it on a much smaller scale) in the United States and Europe and is the dominant model throughout East Asia.[32] One hopeful augur of greater NGO autonomy in China is the emergence of private foundations. Authorized in 2004 by new Regulations on Foundation Management, they have the potential to wean Chinese NGOs from substantial reliance on government funding.[33]

National Committee civil society project: environment

With the discovery that Heilongjiang and Jilin Provinces did not yet have mature environmental NGOs in the late 1990s, the National Committee had adjusted its project goal from promoting civil society to encouraging other forms of private involvement in public policy formation. The National Committee's Final Report to the project's primary funder, the Henry Luce Foundation, identified three potential areas for follow-up bilateral projects. These prospects, along with a fourth that did not make the report, provide a window onto the potential for transnational interaction to involve Chinese citizens in environmental policy-making.[34]

Several lakes in northeast China constituted one target area for follow-up activity. The National Committee project had created connections between Chinese environmentalists and the University of Michigan's Center for Great Lakes and Aquatic Sciences. The Center was represented within the American Working Group by Professor William Chang, China program manager for the

National Science Foundation. A Chinese immigrant, Chang had taught aquatic ecology at the University of Michigan in the 1980s and had studied environmental issues in China in 1984–5 and 1987–91. Chang's involvement in the project included a field trip to assess the condition of migratory birds around Lake Xianghai Nature Reserve. The credibility of the National Committee and the American experts made it possible for some of the Chinese scholars and policy experts to see Lake Xianghai firsthand for the first time. Such basic access to information is, of course, a precondition for any type of meaningful citizen involvement in policy formation.[35]

A second attempt to sustain some of the environmental project's momentum centered on Northeast Normal University (NENU) and its program for environmental education and training. One of the American members of the Working Group was Barbara Felitti of the Institute for Sustainable Communities (ISC). Founded in 1991 by former Vermont Governor Madeleine Kunin, the ISC promotes grassroots involvement in sustainable development. At the conclusion of the National Committee project, Felitti sought funding for an effort to bring Chinese university students, environmental educators, government officials, industry leaders, community groups, and nascent environmental NGOs together to establish a sustainable development center.[36] Unfortunately, Felitti could not secure funding from the US Environmental Protection Agency or the Eurasia Foundation. Nevertheless, the connections established through the National Committee project had positive impacts on the ISC and NENU.

From its initial exposure, the ISC 'determined that our experience was relevant to working in China.' Its subsequent endeavors included: a program in 2006 to help small- and medium-size businesses in southern China improve their capacity to comply with environmental regulations[37] a 2010 exchange on sustainable development, carried out in collaboration with the National Committee in the aftermath of the 2008 Sichuan Earthquake.[38] At NENU, geography professor Zhang Hongyan initially joined the National Committee Working Group as a translator. His expertise was in Geographic Information Systems (GIS), but his involvement in the project aroused his interest in environmental protection. New connections he made led to an ongoing professional relationship with the Environmental Protection Bureau (EPB) of Jilin Province. The EPB routinely contracts with Zhang's NENU group to interpret satellite data related to environmental issues. The graduate students who do much of the work have, thus, become citizen participants in environmental preservation.[39]

The third follow-up activity featured the International Crane Foundation (ICF), which was developing a grant proposal related to the protection of birds in the wetlands along the Chinese–Russian border. To earn a pre-project grant from the Global Environment Facility (GEF), ICF's Jim Harris needed to do some on-site investigation of migratory bird habitats in the Xianghai Nature Reserve.[40] So, when in 1999 Beach invited Harris to participate in the National Committee project, he welcomed the opportunity to return to the region and to expand his professional network there. While ICF would eventually have gotten to Xianghai, the National Committee connection made things easier.[41] The six-year (2003–9) ICF-initiated Siberian Crane Wetland Project yielded tangible results in four countries – China, Russia, Kazakhstan, and Iran.[42]

Whereas the National Committee's core project mission was the promotion of citizen involvement in environmental policy formation, the objective for ICF and GEF was safeguarding internationally important wetlands. There were significant areas of agenda overlap, however. 'The [ICF/GEF Siberian Crane] project takes a strong participatory approach towards site management, and stakeholder consultation procedures are an integral part of the management planning approach . . .' Training programs should include 'development of links between nature reserves and local universities or institutes.' Finally, the project also explicitly encourages '[p]articipation of NGOs, local communities and schools, scientists, and government staff.'[43]

Connections that the National Committee had established between the US Environmental Protection Agency (EPA) and the Suihua Eco-Pilot Zone were the occasion for the fourth follow-up activity. Beach invited Francesca DiCosmo of the EPA's Region III, which is headquartered in Philadelphia, to join the project's Working Group, because of EPA's experience with a Green Communities program that encourages community involvement in promoting sustainable development.[44] Environmentalists in Suihua were 'very enthusiastic' about this American approach to eliciting community involvement. Near the end of the National Committee project, they had key pages from the Green Communities website translated into Chinese.[45] Further, the working relationships established between Chinese and American environmental officials helped lay the ground-work for large-scale collaboration between the EPA and SEPA a decade later. In December 2007, the two governments signed an agreement that Liu Yanhua, Vice Minister of Science and Technology, said would 'help China tackle its growing environmental problems.'[46]

National Committee civil society project: education

While it operated under the same Luce 'civil society' grant as the environmental project and Marilyn Beach coordinated both projects, the education project diverged in two respects. Operationally, Beach learned from the environment project that working in two provinces entailed distracting competition among Chinese partners. With the education project starting several months later, she had the opportunity to restrict its geographical scope to a single province. Substantively, the National Committee contributed to China's educational civil society in very different ways. Whereas the most significant outcomes (or attempted outcomes) on the environmental front were bringing Chinese civil society actors into dialogue with both Chinese governmental institutions and foreign organizations, the education project catalyzed the formation of a lasting network among leaders of existing Chinese civil society institutions.

In 1982, 1985, and 1987, state regulations gave verbal encouragement to the establishment of private schools. In 1993, the Outline of Chinese Educational

Reform and Development provided a particularly strong endorsement: 'The state adopts a sixteen-words [*sic*] policy of *active encouragement, vigorous support, correct guidance and enhanced management* of schools established according to law by social organizations and individual citizens.'[47]

One thing the government did not do, however, was provide blueprints or training to the people who were organizing and running the new schools. In fact, by the late 1990s, government at all levels still had little insight into the conditions of existing socially strengthened schools, their potential, or the challenges they faced. In 1998, the year before the start of the National Committee project, the provincial government had conducted a 'full-scale investigation' of private education in Guizhou. As the National Committee project was getting under way in 1999, the survey results were published and presented at a provincial conference.[48]

To compound the challenge to the pioneering private vocational school administrators, there were no pre-existing networks of similarly situated professionals to which they could turn for advice and mentoring. None of this was particularly sinister. The situation was, rather, a logical extension of the extreme form of vertical, hierarchical social organization that had predominated in China from 1949 through 1978. In fact, the provincial government's investigation indicated that local officials were already favorably disposed toward the kind of horizontal interactions that the National Committee project would soon help them promote. One of the Chinese report's six recommendations read: '[W]e should establish various levels of associations of non-governmental schools, to allow social strength schools to provide services and management to themselves, organize academic research, information exchange, teacher training, and other activities.'[49]

We saw in Chapter 2 that, at the initiative of the National Committee, Principal Bi Jiangang had recruited three other principals to form a support group. In helping bring principals together in a horizontal network, the National Committee took one of many small steps that foreign NGOs and, especially, Chinese citizens have taken in a cumulative journey toward something resembling a civil society.

> Ms. Ma Ailian [Marilyn Beach], representing the United States, came to meet with the four principals. During the meetings, we discussed what we needed to investigate, and things worked quite smoothly. ... [Before this meeting,] three principals – Huang, Zhu and Wang – didn't know one another, but Principal Bi had met them all. Since that meeting, we have been in constant contact.[50]

Wang Dilun began his career as principal of a government-run public high school. When he took over as principal of the Secondary Vocational/Technical School in Liupanshui, he 'had virtually no idea about how to manage a vocational school.' To compound problems, with 74 teachers and only six students, the school was on the verge of bankruptcy. Getting connected with a network of other vocational school principals played a major role in exposing Wang to ideas he used to turn the school around. 'At my school,' he says, echoing a problem Principal Zhu Weide also cited, 'the teachers used to teach the students to "repair cars" on the blackboard, so the students only knew theories but had no practice. Now, we have many car factories where students can have their internship.'[51]

Visits to vocational colleges in the United States, organized by the National Committee, reinforced this lesson. 'In the United States,' Wang observed, 'they use the best cars for students to practice learning.' Building on the network concept developed through the National Committee project, Wang established ties with numerous schools in Guizhou. For example, the Secondary/Vocational Technical School jointly admitted students with the Guizhou Television University and shared instructional resources with other vocational schools.[52]

The Chinese visit to the United States expanded the Guizhou network across the Pacific, as well as providing the Chinese with pedagogical ideas. Principal Zhu maintained contact with Frank Kincaid, principal of Lee County Vocational School in Kentucky. That relationship reinforced for her the importance of supplementing theory with practice in vocational schools. Zhu's school has greatly improved its performance since the late 1990s, and she attributes much of the success to 'changing my old notion of management' as a result of learning from Kincaid. Her Guizhou Province Tourism School became a 'National Key Vocational School,' and graduates found it much easier than in the past to get jobs with hotels and travel agencies.[53]

As deputy director of the provincial Development Research Center, Wang Liquan represented the project's official 'champion,' Guizhou Vice Governor Guo Shuqing. Wang identified four significant benefits from the project. First, it helped promote Chinese–American friendship. Examples include ongoing contact with Marilyn Beach and Daniel Wright, an invitation from Representative Joe Pitts (who had visited Guizhou) to the Chinese principals and government officials to visit him during their trip to the United States, and the interest of an American scholar (the author of the present work) in traveling to Guiyang to meet them and study their experience. Second, the program has provided Guizhou's government with new knowledge, with a 'scientific basis for making policies concerning private education.' Third, the individual schools have benefited from the practical knowledge they gained, both from each other and from the schools and supportive institutions they visited in the United States.[54]

Finally, Guizhou's education administrators and officials were able to expand their research horizons. Marilyn Beach arranged for the six Chinese members of the Working Group to attend a 1999 international conference on private educa-tion in Beijing, at which three of them presented papers. Participation in the conference provided opportunities for these educators and officials to interact with Chinese educators from other provinces, with government officials and media representatives, and with representatives of major international institutions such as the World Bank and the United Nations.[55]

Of the project-derived benefits that Wang Liquan enumerated, the opportunity to learn from colleagues – in the United States but especially in Guizhou – is the one most highlighted by participating principals. Huang Weican, for example, reported in 2005, 'A few days ago, Principal Bi organized a trip for the graduates of their school to go to Shenzhen to find jobs. He called me from Shenzhen and asked me how I had helped our graduates find jobs there.'[56]

When visiting Lee County (Kentucky) School Superintendent Frank Kincaid tried to explain the hands-on American style of vocational instruction, his Chinese counterparts 'had a hard time visualizing it,' but the Chinese delegation's visit to the United States enabled them to see American teaching methods first-hand.[57]

The National Committee highlights the importance of such networking, as well as the principals' improved access to the policy process. 'It's very rare,' says Beach, 'that you get local-level principals sitting together with policy-makers.'[58] In Wright's retrospective:

> Because of this National Committee program, there's this ability to exchange ideas on which models are working, what kind of management styles, student recruiting – really, the operations of the school. So, rather than operating in a vacuum, through these horizontal linkages, these schools actually have a sense of comparison. ... All that has helped with the policy process of private education, because now these high school principals have a relationship with government officials.[59]

The 1990 Institute and Spring Bud

Gendered rural poverty

Assisting the emergence of a civil society in China was not an explicit motivation or a goal of The 1990 Institute when in 2001 it became a major participant in the Spring Bud program, which supports the education of girls in impoverished rural China. The program and the Institute's participation have, nonetheless, contributed to the devolution of responsibility for social services from state to society that has been a hallmark of the emergence of a Chinese version of civil society. Rosalyn Koo had a longstanding interest in the education of Chinese girls, and during the 1990s the All-China Women's Federation (ACWF) assumed an increasingly independent posture in representing the interests of Chinese women and girls. By 2001, these factors intersected with a third – economic hardship in the Chinese countryside – to elicit the Institute's involvement in Spring Bud.

A former Party cadre asserted that, despite great economic progress in rural China in the 1980s and steady increases in gross national product beyond then, the nation is experiencing a 'crisis in the countryside.' The national rural tax burden grew from 12.6 billion yuan ($1.5 billion) in 1993 to 40 billion yuan ($4.8 billion) in 1998, while the enrichment and corruption of local officials turned farmers' frustration to anger.[60] Rural protests spread and became increasingly violent. In a typical scenario, corrupt local officials provoke unrest by grossly under-compensating farmers for land seized for industrial development.[61] In response to growing unrest, after assuming the presidency in 2003, Hu Jintao aded new urgency and commitment to the 'Open Up the West' campaign that predecessor Jiang Zemin had initiated in 1999.[62] By late 2006, the incidence of rural protest had declined, but the decline may be attributable to better surveillance and more tactful policing rather than to improved conditions.[63]

Rural poverty in contemporary China is sharply gendered and significantly correlated with educational opportunities. Although a 2002 World Bank report gives China credit for 'spectacular gender equality achievements' in education since 1949 (the 1986 Law of Compulsory Education, the 1988 Regulation for Eliminating Illiteracy, and the 1995 Education Law all emphasize the goal of gender equality), it goes on to argue that 'the education gap' between Chinese men and women remains 'a major barrier to gender equality.'[64]

The two main reasons for the growth in gendered urban–rural inequality during the reform period are the decentralization and localization of funding for education (leaving poorer areas with far fewer resources) and rural families' perceived economic incentive to put daughters to work.[65] Nine years of education for all have been compulsory – without tuition fees – since 1986, but impoverished villages have had little choice but to circumvent the intentions of the law by charging a variety of miscellaneous fees for everything from books to electricity.[66]

Official statistics for 2004 tout enrollment rates in excess of 98 percent for girls as well as for boys, but that percentage is artificially inflated.[67] As Cui Linlin, Division Director of the ACWF's International Liaison Department, explains:

> Usually, [rural] people will send their children – both girls and boys – to school. First, because at that time, the girls are too young to do anything at home. So, their parents just send them to school. Then, the government will have the statistics of the enrollment rate very high – 99 or 98 percent of school-age girls are going to school. Then, they go to school – after two or three years in the school, they will jump out, gradually, because at that time, they are 10 years old, and they can do something at home. They can take care of their younger siblings.[68]

In 1999, a popular Chinese investigative television program, *Focus*, reported that school officials at a rural Anhui Province middle school forced 200 dropouts to masquerade as real students for an annual government inspection.[69]

Keeping rural kids in school

With the government's approval and encouragement, beginning in the 1990s, a number of domestic and foreign charitable organizations initiated rural education programs.[70] The largest and best publicized program is Project Hope. In 1989, the mass organization All-China Youth Federation (ACYF) established the China Youth Development Foundation (CYDF), whose main programmatic activity was administering Project Hope. The ACYF's motives were a combination of a pragmatic need to remain relevant under a changing social structure and members' genuine desire to solve one of society's most pressing problems.[71] In 1991, the CYDF ran a fundraising ad in national newspapers, radio, and television. This was the first fundraising ad that China's government-controlled media had allowed since the Communist Party took power on the mainland in 1949. Starting with $10,000 in government seed money, by 1997 Project Hope had raised $150 million, built 500 Hope schools, and helped nearly two million impoverished rural children attend school.[72] By the end of 2002, the project had helped 2.47 million students and built 9,508 Hope schools.[73]

Spring Bud's contribution

Spring Bud's mission, strategy, and place within China's socio-political configuration resemble those of Project Hope in many ways. It seeks to universalize rural education, it raises funds domestically and internationally, and it is sponsored by a mass organization that is forging a new civic identity. The ACWF established the China Children and Teenagers' Fund (CCTF) as a social welfare charity in 1981. The CCTF conducted, and continues to conduct, a variety of projects, including Spring Bud, which it launched in 1989. By the end of 2003, the program had raised over 500 million yuan (over $600,000) and had helped about 1,350,000 dropout girls return to school.[74]

Contributors to Spring Bud are as diverse as: the Ya'an Detachment of the People's Liberation Army, which began funding the education of 20 girls in that rural city in 2001; Mary Kay Cosmetics, which contributed one million yuan (over $120,000) from 2003 to 2005 toward the construction of nine Mary Kay Spring Bud Schools and raised 340,000 yuan from its Greater China sales force in 2004 to support girls attending the schools; 90-year-old Professor Hao Deyuan, who donated his savings of 100,000 yuan (about $12,000); and The 1990 Institute.[75]

Spring Bud's distinctive feature is that it targets girls only, and specifically primary school girls who have already dropped out of school. Through field research, the ACWF had discovered that the dropout problem was far more serious among girls than boys and that the dropout usually occurred in the fourth grade. Other programs could not catch all these vulnerable girls. As the ACWF's Cui Linlin explains:

Although Project Hope does not discriminate against girls, families do. If they have both boys and girls, and they have only one Project Hope contract for their family, they will prefer to send a boy back to school first. And usually, the girls will stay at home, and they will take care of their younger siblings and help their mother do chores. So, that's why we started the Spring Bud program.[76]

The 1990 Institute's contribution to Spring Bud has been substantial. When Rosalyn Koo heard from Wang Hong, ACWF Vice Chair for Shaanxi Province, that 280,000 girls in that province alone were not attending school, she realized that she and the Institute could not fully remedy the problem for even one province. She believed, though, that enabling 1,000 girls in one province to finish primary school could have a significant impact.[77] At a cost of 400 yuan per girl per year, that meant raising 1.2 million yuan (about $150,000), plus travel costs to enable Institute members to visit the girls each year. While some corporate contributions and a handful of individual donations to Spring Bud have been larger than the Institute's, those instances have typically included funds for building new schools. Taking on 1,000 girls – and then, as a follow-up, supporting them through middle school – represented a notable achievement within the Spring Bud program as a whole. Also, the Institute's maintenance of personal contact – annual visits by Koo and others, during which they talked with the girls and their families and monitored their progress – was unusual. 'Usually, people from abroad only send a check,' says Cui. 'We give them a receipt and a certificate for their donation. Sometimes we will send letters from the girls to them, and that's all.'[78]

Spring Bud and Chinese civil society

The 1990 Institute's Dragon Fund, in supporting the Spring Bud project, has had a profound impact on the lives of Chinese girls and their families, as has the project as a whole. It has also contributed to the emergence of a distinctively Chinese model of civil society and to the transnational discourse that sustains it.

A minimal goal of Spring Bud is to provide rural girls with the skills to become economically independent. In the early years, the ACWF noticed that girls would finish primary school and then return to family life with little changed. Thus the organization aims to provide such girls with basic vocational skills, so that they can become financially independent – learn 'how to use sewing machines to make clothes, hair dressing skills, computer skills, typewriting, etc.' The ACWF also noticed that some girls excelled in school and, therefore, expanded Spring Bud in a few provinces to support them through middle school.[79]

In addition to macro planning for education and skills training, Spring Bud can be tailored to specific circumstances. Cui relates the following anecdote:

> [Koo] said that once she visited some girls and she thought they did not look very healthy – undernourished. She asked if they had egg or meat, and the girls said, 'We only have grain and vegetables. We do not eat much meat.' Roz said that they may need more nutritious food, so she helped these girls' families to raise pigs.[80]

Besides helping individual girls stay healthy and get educated for independence, Koo sees Spring Bud achieving broader societal goals. She hopes the program will help 'change the mindset of the local population' about girls and education. The next step in the cycle, hopefully, will come when this generation of girls marries and teaches their own daughters to desire education and independence. 'Only in that sense,' says Koo, citing a venerable Chinese saying, 'can you eventually claim that women hold up half the sky.'[81]

In June 2002, Chinese television filmed a 12-minute segment on the Institute's project for a special series on social conditions in China's interior. In 2004, the Institute commissioned a follow-up video when the first 1,000 Dragon Fund-sponsored students graduated. The same year, students at the Ankang Primary School in Shaanxi Province wrote essays about their experience, and the local ACWF chapter published the essays.[82]

Students tell of hardship. 'Poverty was a curse,' writes one girl. 'I was destined to suffer it.'[83] Another recounts a flood that drove her family from their home and took her father's life when he went back to try to retrieve the ginger she and her mother had collected, with the expectation of selling it to pay for her school fees.[84] Different events led to the same outcome:

> I was born into a poor farming family. I have several sisters, and parents aged and weakened by years of hard work. ... Father's liver had hardened to an advanced stage. ... Older sister quit school to earn money to help pay for father's treatments. To lessen the financial strains on the family, I too left school to help out at home. The instant I stepped out of the schoolyard for what I thought was forever, tears streamed down my face.[85]

Students also speak of hope and of learning, in one girl's words, 'practical skills that will lay the foundation of the future progress of our underdeveloped villages.' As an example, this girl learned how to grow silkworms and earned 300 yuan.[86] The girls also learned about generosity and social responsibility. When one student needed hospitalization but her family could not afford the fees, her classmates went to the mountain and spent a day harvesting tea leaves, which they sold for enough to pay the hospital fees.[87]

A student essay entitled 'Father's Transformation' best illustrates the change in rural attitudes toward women that advocates like Cui Linlin and Rosalyn Koo hope will become widespread. The young author describes her father as 'a quintessential farmer' who saw no usefulness in educating girls. When her teacher came to the girl's home to explain that some Americans were paying all the school costs for girl dropouts in Ankang, her father at first refused – 'There are a lot of chores at home' – but ultimately agreed to let his daughter return to school.

> In the past, no one at home could read the scientific advice that the agricultural technology station gave us. They were just pieces of useless paper. Now, I can understand this material and explain it to father. Following such advice, our harvest last year improved greatly. Also, I read in books that our

hillside is very suitable for raising goats. ... So, I suggested that we buy some high-quality goats from outside our area. Father adopted my suggestion, and last year the money we made from goats was more than what we got from our harvest. Gradually, father recognized the importance of education.[88]

In addition to improving individual lives, contributing to local economic development, and chipping away at social bias against girls, the foregoing narrative illustrates a paradigm of civil society that has replicated itself throughout China since the 1980s. As the state has gradually shed ownership of business enterprises, it has become as much a facilitator as a provider of social services.[89] Mass organizations like the ACYF and ACWF are complementing grassroots organizations as part of an emerging third sector in China that exhibits varying degrees of control by and accountability to society. This model of Chinese civil society is further characterized by generally cooperative attitudes among the government, domestic NGOs that provide social services, and foreign NGOs and philanthropists who support them.[90]

Spring Bud and transnational civil society discourse

In addition to building institutions to improve and expand education – especially of girls – in rural China, the Chinese government, China's nascent civil society, and foreign NGOs have created a discourse through which they valorize the practices of these institutions. Scholars and artists have contributed to this effort as well. The point is not that all these actors mapped out and then implemented a propaganda program, but rather that, in seeking language and symbols to express their purposes, they have created a common vocabulary and imagery.

The initial focus here is on two movies that have been viewed widely in China and, to a lesser extent, abroad. In 1999, Zhang Yimou directed *Not One Less* (*Yige dou bu neng shao*). The film dramatizes the dire state of rural Chinese education, and Zhang donated the profits to Project Hope.[91] The protagonist is Wei Minzhi, a 13-year-old girl. Wei arrives at a dilapidated schoolhouse to substitute for one month for Teacher Gao, who has to go home to be with his dying mother. Highlighting the school's poverty, Gao counts out one piece of chalk per day. Gao and the village mayor promise Wei a 10 yuan bonus, on top of her 50 yuan salary, if all 28 students are still there when he returns at the end of the month – 'not one less.' Within a few days, though, class troublemaker Zhang Huike runs away to the city to work. Determined to keep her commitment to student retention, Wei visits Zhang's bed-ridden mother, who says she needed her son to work. Later, the mayor confirms to Wei: 'His father died young. His mother is sick. They owe people money. If he doesn't work, they can never pay their debts.'

Like the Spring Bud girls who picked tea leaves to raise money for a sick classmate, Wei and her students move bricks to pay for her bus ticket to go to the city to look for Zhang. They damage many bricks, but the brickyard owner knows Teacher Gao and is moved by the determination of Wei and her students, so he gives her 15 yuan. After further tribulations, Wei arrives in the city, only to discover that Zhang has left the temple at which he had been working. After a futile search at the train station, where Zhang was last seen – including a loudspeaker announcement and written notices – Wei follows up on a man's suggestion that she try the television station.

After she has waited outside the gate for a day and a half (spending the night on the sidewalk), the station manager learns of Wei's quest and arranges for her to be interviewed about education in the countryside on the popular program *Today in China*. When the announcer asks Wei Minzhi why so many children in the countryside are leaving school, the girl answers tersely, 'Their families are poor.' In a tearjerker ending, Zhang hears Wei's broadcast plea – 'Why don't you come back?' – from a small restaurant where the manager has taken pity on him. Donations from viewers flood the station, enough to pay Zhang's mother's debts, so that he can return to school, and to build a new school.

The closing credits reveal that Wei was played by a rural middle school student, her students by students from the countryside, the mayor by a real-life village mayor, etc. As smiling students write on the blackboard with new, colored chalk, the director's social commentary displays across the screen: 'Each year, poverty forces more than one million children in China to leave school. Through the help of donations, approximately 15 percent of these children are able to return to school.'

In *Not One Less*, the main character is a girl determined to provide education, even though it is a boy that poverty has forced from school. A low-budget but award-winning 2004 film, *The Story of Xiaoyan* (*Shang xue lu shang*) features another determined girl, this time one who herself has had to leave school because of her family's poverty.[92] Like Wei Minzhi, Wang Yan is an indomitable 13-year-old. Early in the movie, when she learns that she cannot return to school in the fall, she asks her mother, 'Why are they [her two younger brothers] going to school and I'm not?' 'Because we have no money,' her mother replies. 'As a girl, it's your future husband's family that benefits.' 'No,' replies Wang Yan, 'I'm going for myself.' 'Then don't ask others for help. You've got to learn to depend on yourself.'

Taking her mother at her word, Wang Yan resorts to an incredible array of fundraising tactics. She starts by stealing 10 eggs from the family barn and selling them, then buys and resells an ink pen and brokers the sale of a goat. Finally, she has enough money to buy a bus ticket to the reservoir, where she can pick strawberries and sell them at 4 mao (0.4 yuan) per kg. She returns home in time for a public ceremony, at which the villagers are thanking the provincial government for sending money to help educate children of families poorer than Wang Yan's. With tears of pride in her eyes, she hands her 28.8 yuan (one year's fees) to Teacher Wang.

The key elements of the civil society discourse, as it relates to rural education, are present in these two didactic commercial films: (1) underdevelopment (i.e., poverty) as the primary cause of the widespread problem of school dropouts in the Chinese countryside; (2) the gendered aspect of the problem, including the fighting spirit of Chinese girls; (3) the need for a partnership that attracts civil society and foreign support for the government's efforts to universalize education. The first two elements are most pronounced, through repeated images of material scarcity and of girls who refuse to accept the traditional role of uneducated peasant women. The presence of the third is more subtle. *Not One Less* announces at the end that the new school is called 'Shuichan Hope School,' and publicity surrounding the film's release in China made the public aware that proceeds would support Project Hope. Final credits in *Not One Less* thank the Ford Motor Company, Coca-Cola, Sony, and Sony Pictures Entertainment for their support. The ceremony at the end of *The Story of Xiaoyan* makes it clear that government is a big part of the solution, although it needs private help. The international dimension is the backstory of the film's derivation from a French translation of a Chinese girl's diary and ensuing controversy over intellectual property rights.[93]

CCTV-7's *Faces of the West* segment on The 1990 Institute's Spring Bud project and the Institute-produced follow-up DVD highlight these same themes. In *Faces of the West*, dropouts like Wu Caihong and Xie Zebei play an iconic role similar to that of Wei Minzhi and Wang Yan. As viewers see a young girl writing outdoors on a rock, the reporter explains that Wu Caihong lives in Shaanxi Province. 'She is very eager to learn, but she has been out of school for over a year because of her family's financial difficulty. Watching the students go to school with their book bags every day, Caihong is very frustrated.' Speaking to the reporter, Wu Caihong says, 'How lucky they are. I hope I can go to school again.' As the camera shows her working in the fields, the announcer elaborates: 'Just like Wu Caihong, many children in the mountains are so poor and cannot afford to go to school.' A classmate says, 'Every day when I came home from school, I saw her drawing something on a stone. She wrote on the stone, "study hard."'

Faces of the West is more explicit than the two commercial films about the role of foreign organizations and about the broader social implications of improving rural education (in effect, the need for the government's 'Open Up the West' campaign). Against a visual background of farms seen from the air, then a shot of Rosalyn Koo, the narrator explains:

> In terms of the funding for education, the government has worked hard. But because of economic conditions, still there are children who have been forced to leave school. Therefore, the help from organizations such as The 1990 Institute is just like sending coal to the needy in stormy weather. ... Just to help the children go back to school is not The 1990 Institute's ultimate goal. ... Providing funding for education and training is the only way to raise the quality of human resources. And only then can the long-term development of the western rural areas be maintained.

Figure 5.1 Teacher Gao warns Wei Minzhi not to waste precious school supplies. (*Not One Less* © 1999 Columbia Pictures Film Production Asia Limited. All rights reserved. Courtesy of Columbia Pictures. Used with permission.)

Figure 5.2 Wang Yan's mother punishes her for taking the family's eggs to sell for tuition money. (*The Story of Xiaoyan.* Used with permission of Shandong Film & TV Production Center.)

Figure 5.3 'Mister, I am begging you to sell it. ... If we close the deal, you and the other man would each pay us 1 yuan. Then we'll have 2 yuan. ... I made 80 mao stealing and selling the eggs from home. I made 5 yuan selling my pen to Mr Wang. I made another 5 yuan for raising his sheep. That's 10 yuan 80 altogether. But I paid a blind man 1 yuan for closing the deal. I spent 1 yuan buying candies for my brothers [Dagua and Ergua, to bribe them to help care for her sheep]. Now I have 8 yuan 80 [mao] left. The bus ticket to the reservoir costs 10 yuan. I am still 2 yuan short. If I get a ticket to the reservoir, I could pick some wild berries. I'll work hard, and I'll pick a lot of wild berries. I could sell the berries for 40 mao per kilo. I need to pick 62 kg. I could sell 62 kg. of wild berries for 24 yuan 80 in all. If I have 24 yuan 80, then I could pay for my tuition. Then I could go to school.' (*The Story of Xiaoyan.* Used with permission of Shandong Film & TV Production Center.)

Figure 5.4 Wu Caihong, wishing she were in school. (*Portraits of the West.* CCTV-7 newscast, 12 June 2002.)

Figure 5.5 Spring Bud girl Xie Zebei cries for joy at returning to school. (*Portraits of the West.* CCTV-7 newscast, 12 June 2002.)

Figure 5.6 'The flowers are in blossom, and your aid is arriving.' (*The Story of Xiaoyan.* Used with permission of Shandong Film & TV Production Center.)

Figure 5.7 Rosalyn Koo inspects a 1990 Institute-supported Spring Bud classroom. (*Portraits of the West.* CCTV-7 newscast, 12 June 2002.)

Figure 5.8 Narrator, at Ankang Primary School graduation: 'In this world, a little help from outsiders can change their destiny.' (*Spring Bud Project,* produced for The 1990 Institute by AFEWS & ViewAround, Inc.)

Figure 5.9 Zhang Huike is found! (*Not One Less* © 1999 Columbia Pictures Film Production Asia Limited. All rights reserved. Courtesy of Columbia Pictures. Used with permission.)

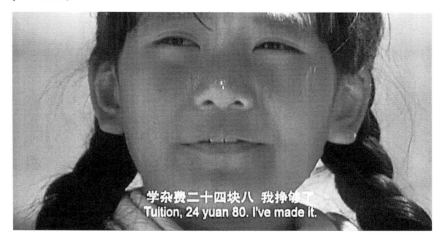

Figure 5.10 Wang Yan can return to school. (*The Story of Xiaoyan.* Used with permission of Shandong Film & TV Production Center.)

This narrative of almost seamless cooperation among government, civil society, and foreign supporters working for a noble cause has resonated with many observers. Discussion often takes Zhang Yimou's movie as a starting point. Reviewing *Not One Less* for the newsletter of the Asian Educational Media Service, for example, Kenneth Klinkner praises Zhang for 'an authenticity that is rare in cinema today' and for raising money for Project Hope, 'a truly worthy cause.'[94] A *New York Times* reviewer hails Zhang for 'enlarging the possibilities of filmmaking' and says *Not One Less* 'may be the greatest film ever made about obstinacy, which it reveals to be not only a virtue but a species of grace.'[95] Anthropologist Heidi Ross met the Spring Bud girls who appeared in the CCTV-7 newscast and the follow-up video about the project. She sees their struggle as one with Zhang's fictionalized movie heroine:

> The girls' experiences recall Zhang Yimou's affecting 1999 film, *Not One Less*. Wei Minzhi ... could easily be a Spring Bud girl ... Zhang's unsparing indictment of rural poverty and his poignant celebration of 'girl power' at the margins inspired our motto for phase two of the Spring Bud Project, to extend to 1,000 girls the opportunity to attend secondary school.[96]

Not One Less and the broader discourse of which it is a part have not been without critics and dissenters. A *Cinemaya* reviewer argues that Zhang's 'happy ending undercuts the realism he has portrayed in the film.'[97] A scholar of Chinese popular culture denounces *Not One Less* as 'an accomplice of the dominant ideology' that 'raises false hopes about China's future as an integral part of globalization by re-asserting, in a patronizing way, the proper positioning of every member of the society, including the most underprivileged.'[98] A controversy erupted over the film at the 2000 Cannes Film Festival, when some jurors charged that it was government propaganda and Zhang withdrew from the festival in protest.[99]

On balance, the rural education movement and its supportive discourse represent a constructive tendency in contemporary China. Based on largely congruent goals among central and local governments, China's emerging civil society, and foreign NGOs, these actors are contributing to improved educational opportunities for rural children, especially girls. During the decade of the 1990s, for example, China reduced the number of out-of-school girls from 1,712,900 to 554,200.[100] At the same time, these actors are facilitating the expansion of China's civil society and its interaction with both the Chinese state and international civil society institutions.

Training civil society leaders at the Hopkins-Nanjing Center

While only six to seven percent of international or Chinese alumni go on to work for NGOs, those who do so have been visible beyond their numbers in the Center's semi-annual alumni newsletter, *Centerpiece*, and on the Alumni Update page of its website.[101] In view of the expansion of civil society activity in and between the United States and China, these individuals' influence within their respective societies and on the bilateral relationship may also be disproportionate to their numbers. A 2003 issue of the Hopkins-Nanjing alumni newsletter profiled eight international students, whose post-Center careers took them to such organizations as the US–China Business Council, the Asia Foundation, and the Energy Foundation's China Sustainable Energy Program in Beijing.[102] And the National

Committee has had Hopkins-Nanjing alumni (often two or three at a time) on its staff continuously since the turn of the century.[103]

A Chinese alumna (2000), after earning a master's degree, became one of the first program staff members at Junior Achievement China, then a staff writer at *China Development Brief*. From there, she went to rural Sichuan Province to work on public health programs with Partnerships for Community Development, a Hong Kong-based community development organization. These NGO experiences reinforced her sense of 'the positive changes that can be achieved if people partake in the public life of their society and take initiative on their own to solve public problems.'[104] Another Chinese alumna (2001) also worked at Junior Achievement, which exposed her to the concept of an NGO. 'Despite the fact that many Chinese do not yet fully appreciate the role of NGOs and volunteerism,' she said, 'I believe the work I am doing will make a difference on the next generation and on Chinese society as a whole.'[105]

American alumnus Travis Tanner (2002) wanted 'to involve myself in a professional role in the field of US–China relations.' After completing the certificate program at the Center, he went on to earn an MA from SAIS and to become assistant director of Chinese Studies at the Nixon Center. Joseph Casey found that he could 'help China to better develop while concurrently developing myself' by working for the poverty-relief NGO World Vision, first in Beijing and then in Yunan.[106]

The post-Hopkins-Nanjing Center career of Yang Xuedong, a 1994 Chinese alumnus, has been particularly interesting with respect to both China's modernization and US–China relations. The Center influenced Yang's intellectual development and his professional training. His course work, especially independent study with political scientist James Thompson, gave him a solid foundation in comparative politics. This experience prepared Yang to study for six months as a visiting scholar at Harvard in 1997 and for the 2001–2 academic year at Harvard's Kennedy School of Government. It also helped prepare him to assume operational responsibility for an imaginative Ford Foundation-funded project.[107]

Since the resumption of relations between China and the United States, the Ford Foundation's approach has been well matched with China's desire to obtain foreign technical assistance with minimal foreign control. The Foundation's former country representative for China, Andrew Watson, eschewed a strategy of 'coming here to change things and to put foreign technology or foreign processes into the Chinese system.' Rather, he said, 'In terms of actually being able to help people you have to let them determine the agenda and then try to provide appropriate inputs to it.'[108]

The Ford Foundation's China representative from 1995 to 1999, Anthony Saich, had previously worked on a translation project with one of China's most creative young establishment intellectuals, Yu Keping. (As an official with the Party School's Translation Bureau, Yu was having works by Marx and Engels translated into Chinese, and Saich was supplying some of the materials.) Yu has been an avid promoter of gradual political reform. In 2007, his article for the

Central Party School entitled 'Democracy Is a Good Thing' stirred considerable debate within official circles in China. In the late 1990s, he had worked on several projects on local government reform, including participation in a couple of workshops for which the Translation Bureau had organized funding from the Ford Foundation, with which Saich had become affiliated. Yu became familiar with programs that the foundation funded on local governance innovation in several countries – Brazil, Chile, Mexico, the Philippines, South Africa, and East Africa, as well as the United States – and proposed that the foundation support a similar program in China.[109]

Saich was initially 'dubious about whether such a program could work in China and whether it would get approval.' Thus he held up funding until Yu was able to get official clearance for the program. Saich authorized some seed funding to develop the program, and Program Officer Sarah Cook provided a larger grant in 2001 (the first year of operation), followed by a ten-year grant in 2005.[110] The program, Innovations and Excellence in Chinese Local Governance (IECLG), is innovative in two respects. First, substantively, it promotes creative ways to make local government more transparent and more accountable to citizens. During odd-numbered years, dozens of local governments nominate themselves for 10 awards of 50,000 RMB. During even-numbered years, the China Center for Comparative Politics and Economics (CCCPE, the branch of the Translation Bureau charged with administering the program) coordinates and publicizes the selection of winners. Among the winners have been:

- Longhua District, Haikou City, Hainan Province for its Urban Guest Worker Centers, which mark a dramatic change from a policy toward migrant workers of 'uncover, apprehend and deport' to one of providing social services;
- Buyun Township, Shizhong District, Suining City, Sichuan Province for being the first township to hold direct elections of leaders, in 2001;
- Jialian Street Office of Siming District, Xiamen City, Fujian Province for establishing a Loving Care Supermarket (LCS). The LCS collects donated household goods from the community and distributes them free of charge to impoverished residents. Volunteer workers help full-time government employees manage operations, thus combining 'government responsibility' with 'societal participation';
- Yiwu Municipality of Zhejiang Province for integrating local government, trade unions, and volunteer lawyers to form a Center for Worker Rights Defense on behalf of rural workers.[111]

The institutional innovation of the governance program likely exceeds its substantive innovation. Because of its ultimate organizational accountability to the Party, it is hard to classify IECLG as a civil society program or its administrative body, CCCPE, as an NGO. Still, Yang Xuedong sees the program as being 'on the edge between the state and civil society. It is not an NGO, but it tries to adopt an NGO's perspective to evaluate innovations by local governments.' From a Ford Foundation perspective, Andrew Watson sees the project as linked to both sectors. '[I]t is about the only effort [in China] which involves non-governmental people evaluating and judging the quality of government performance.'[112] The premise of these statements is IECLG's organizational structure. A Steering Committee appoints a National Expert Committee (which chooses finalists) and a National Selection Committee (which chooses winners). The Expert Committee consists entirely of scholars, while a mix of government officials and scholars comprise the other two bodies.[113] As an indication of how pathbreaking its Chinese creators viewed the program, during the first round of competition, they used the term 'essay contest' rather than 'award' so as to not appear too bold as outsiders passing judgment on local governments.[114]

Julia Greenwood Bentley has posited three motivations that prompt Chinese NGOs to seek foreign support and four motivations that lead foreigners to provide that support. The Chinese seek 'recognition and legitimacy, funding of a magnitude unavailable domestically, and the opportunity to learn from international experience.' Foreigners have come to see a healthy civil society as a central component of the 'socio-economic development' they hope to assist, they seek to help those who are 'marginalized by the modernization process,' they hope to 'foster democracy,' and they simply see opportunities in 'the enormous volume of international aid currently being funneled to China.'[115]

The case studies presented in this chapter are consistent with the motives Bentley attributes to the Chinese side, although any financial incentives were secondary in the two National Committee projects. For the foreigners' motives, we need to refine Bentley's model. The four motives she lists are generally accurate as a collective portrait of advocacy organizations that operate on a global scale, but not necessarily of organizations with a sole focus on China and with as much interest in bilateral relations as in affecting Chinese society. The three organizations featured here, for example, have found funding scarce rather than plentiful. As for 'fostering democracy,' the National Committee's approach is less direct than Bentley's statement would suggest, and neither the Hopkins-Nanjing Center nor The 1990 Institute has taken positions on political issues, focusing all their energy on educational exchange and on China's social and economic reforms, respectively. Fostering socio-economic development and helping its unintended victims are motives from Bentley's list that resonate with both the National Committee's environmental and educational civil society projects and The 1990 Institute's Spring Bud project. In the case of many individuals, particularly members of The 1990 Institute, one could add to Bentley's list a feeling of 'long-distance' national solidarity on the part of some overseas Chinese.[116]

6 Impacts of educational exchange

Education, like policy and civil society, has been a fertile sphere for US–China exchanges. As soon as he solidified power, Deng Xiaoping identified access to Western – and particularly US – higher education as a key resource for China's modernization. His push to expose Chinese students to broad liberal arts, not just technical, instruction, initially took his American counterparts by surprise. Notwithstanding the fact that many Chinese students stayed abroad or brought troublesome ideas home with them, Deng and his successors have kept this door open.

Prologue: an early visiting scholar

I met with Huang Fanzhang on a sunny summer afternoon in 2006. Huang had had early contact with The 1990 Institute. After I told him I was researching the Institute, he expressed an interest in talking with me. He and his present surroundings symbolize dramatic changes in China's posture toward the outside world since 1978. Huang invited my wife and me to visit him at the office of the China Reform Forum (CRF), of which he is vice chairman. CRF's office suite, in a wooded area secluded from the surrounding bustle of Beijing, is an adjunct to the nearby Friendship Hotel. Until the mid-1980s, visiting foreigners could stay only in this and similar hotels throughout China. Today, foreigners can rent apartments, buy apartments, and (in many places) live with Chinese citizens.[1] CRF is a think tank affiliated with the Communist Party School, and its scholars have considerable independence to explore domestic and international issues, even if 'their ideas are not consistent with the current policy.'[2] CRF Chairman Zheng Bijian was the prime mover behind the recent concept of 'China's peaceful rise.'[3]

Huang joined CRF in 1998, after retiring from a career that included high-profile positions as one of China's directors at the International Monetary Fund (1986) and as Vice President of the State Planning Commission's Economic Research Center (1990–7). His early career as an economist at the Chinese Academy of Social Sciences (CASS) (1954–80) spanned the period of collectivist economics. Huang's life and career changed in 1980 when the Chinese government invited him to be among the first five social scientists to study in the United States with Ford Foundation funding.[4]

Huang fondly recalled his studies at Harvard, from 1980 to 1982. 'Before I came to Harvard, I studied at Peking University. ... Marxism was the only economics.' Learning about market economics from scholars like Martin Feldstein, who became Chairman of President Reagan's Council of Economic Advisors in 1984, gave Huang insights into how China might move toward its stated goal of a socialist market economy. On his way back to China, via San Francisco, he followed a professor's advice and stopped at the Federal Reserve Bank of San Francisco. During his tour, he met Hang-Sheng Cheng, who would later co-found The 1990 Institute. When Cheng was assigned as his tour guide, 'I was surprised! He was Chinese!' After returning to CASS for several years and then spending a year at the IMF, Huang had a second opportunity to study in the United States, this time at the University of Michigan's Center for Chinese Studies. Amazed by the number of libraries and the size of their collections, he was able to conduct extensive research on China's economy.[5]

Beginning in 1998, CRF and the American think tank RAND convened joint annual conferences – alternating between countries – on economic and security issues. At the 2003 conference, Huang presented a paper, entitled 'Analysis of China's New Path of Industrialization from a Global Perspective,' which evidenced his incorporation of market principles – and the growing globalization and informatization of the world economy – into his thinking.[6]

When I asked Huang whether he wanted to comment on anything important that I had not asked him about, he turned from markets to political culture. He recalled an American friend taking him to visit the US Congress. 'I thought I would be met by the police, but I was surprised. You can go there any time.' His friend told him, 'I can go because I am a taxpayer.' 'He was very proud,' recalled Huang. 'I saw that the government must serve the people. So, this gave me a concept of what democracy is. I got a result beyond my job, beyond my profession.'[7]

Historical background

Huang's appointment as visiting scholar at Harvard came at the beginning of the latest episode in over a century of US–China educational exchanges.[8] The story begins with Yung Wing, who, with the help of Protestant missionary Samuel Brown, went to the United States in 1846 to complete middle school. Yung eventually graduated from Yale, converted to Christianity, and became an American citizen. Of greater historical significance, he returned to China and persuaded the Qing Dynasty to send 120 Chinese young men between the ages of 12 and 16 to study in the United States for 15 years. Yung's argument was that these young men would learn skills essential to China's modernization. Americans like Mark Twain and Ulysses Grant provided financial and moral support and helped find host families. The Chinese government cancelled the China Education Mission in 1881, largely because of fears that the students were being Westernized.[9]

With the passage of Chinese Exclusion Acts in 1882 and 1892 and government opposition at home, it became difficult for individual Chinese to come to the United States to study, although a few continued to arrive under missionary sponsorship. The next organized group was comprised of college students under the Boxer Indemnity Scholarship Program. All the major powers extracted from China claims beyond actual damages they had suffered during the Boxer Rebellion of 1900–1. While others followed suit, the United States was the first to remit its excess – with strings attached. With some input from the Chinese side but the Americans having ultimate decision-making power, a fund was established to send young Chinese men and women to attend college in the United States.[10]

University of Illinois President Edmund James argued the case for the fund to President Theodore Roosevelt in terms of enlightened self-interest: 'The nation which succeeds in educating the young Chinese of the present generation will be the nation which for a given expenditure of effort will reap the largest possible returns in moral, intellectual, and commercial influence.' Between 1911 and 1930, approximately 1,800 students studied under the Boxer program, and an additional 6,000 were able to study independently. After 1930, approximately 12,000 more came, until the new Communist government stopped the practice after its victory in 1949.[11]

As promoters and participants hoped, many of the students incorporated modern, 'Western' ideas into their worldview and assumed important social, economic, and political roles upon their return to China. Among the most famous American-educated Chinese leaders of the first half of the twentieth century were rural educator James Yen, educator and diplomat Hu Shih, and politician Mayling Soong (Madame Chiang Kai-shek).[12] Additionally, American institutions helped create universities – with varying mixes of Chinese and Western methods and content – on Chinese soil. Among the most important were the Xiangya Hospital and Medical College, founded in Changsha by Yale-in-China, and missionary-founded Yenching University, which was incorporated into Peking University in the 1950s.[13]

Throughout the 1970s, individual Chinese American scientists visited China. They met with Mao Zedong and Zhou Enlai and established or re-established relationships with their Chinese counterparts that 'provided the framework for the flourishing program [of educational exchange] we see today'[14] (see Chapter 2). In July 1978, with diplomatic normalization a few months away, American and Chinese representatives met to discuss initiating formal scientific exchanges. Frank Press, President Carter's Advisor on Science and Technology, casually mentioned the possibility of exchanging students and was surprised when the Chinese side enthusiastically asked permission to send 500.[15] Deng declared that 'China has been stagnant and slow in developing for a long time. Now it is time for us to learn from advanced countries in the world.'[16]

From 1979 through 2011, over 1.4 million Chinese students studied abroad, a large percentage in the United States.[17] While only 25 to 30 percent have returned, the rate of return has been growing since 2000.[18] Far fewer American students have studied in China, and usually for shorter time periods. American figures show that 2,942 students studied in China in 2001–2, while Chinese figures show 7,359. Even the higher figure is only 12 percent of the number of Chinese students in the United States the same year.[19]

The Hopkins-Nanjing Center, the National Committee on US–China Relations, and The 1990 Institute have contributed to this US–China educational exchange in complementary ways. Education is understood broadly here. In addition to conventional semesters in classrooms in Nanjing, it includes ten-day tours of American civic institutions by Chinese scholars and graduate students. It includes three-month internships at various divisions of Time Warner for undergraduate students from Shanghai. It includes support for the research of a network of young Chinese scholars in the United States. What these forms of education have in common is the exposure of young Americans to Chinese society and, especially, of young Chinese to fundamental features of American society, such as critical inquiry and objective research, unfettered by pre-determined conclusions.

Qualitative analyses of the effects of recent educational exchanges on participants are only beginning to emerge.[20] This chapter is an attempt to understand what learning in an American intellectual environment has meant to today's Chinese students – with respect to their intellectual development, their career paths, their choices of where to live and work, and their attitudes toward US–China relations – as well as what Americans have learned.

The Hopkins-Nanjing Center for Chinese and American Studies

For both Chinese and American students, participation in the Center's one-year certificate program has provided a mix of career-building skills and cultural enlightenment. While the former is easier to quantify and has become increasingly significant, the latter is more central to the Center's mission. Since it is largely through their professional activities that alumni are able to act on cultural insights they have gained, however, we should not draw too sharp a line between these two dimensions of the Hopkins-Nanjing experience.

Where do alumni go?

A special issue of Nanjing University's newspaper, commemorating the Center's tenth anniversary, in 1996, enumerated positions of influence that Chinese alumni had attained:

> CCTV's 'Focused Interview' editor and journalist Hu Yang told us the Center's program was a turning point in his life, and that without it he would not have been able to interview foreign dignitaries such as Henry Kissinger; Wang Jianhua returned to the Shanghai Social Sciences Academy to become head of its information institute …; Xue Jinyin was appointed the Director of

the International Division of the Shanghai Far East Publishing House ... There are others who are working in diplomacy and international commerce ...[21]

Reviewing a later list of representative Chinese and American alumni, Daniel Wright concluded, 'As impressive as that possibility [of a hypothetical future meeting between a Chinese Foreign Minister and an American Secretary of State, both Hopkins-Nanjing alumni] is, however, the real difference that Hopkins-Nanjing alumni will make has already begun:'

> ... Steve Judd is chief representative for the Energy Foundation in Beijing, Chen Deming serves as mayor of Suzhou City, Peter Wonacott writes for the *Asian Wall Street Journal* from Hong Kong, Xian Weiyi works in China's Foreign Ministry, James Heller is vice consul at the U.S. Embassy in Beijing ... Multiply that group by 100, and one begins to get a sense of the impact Johns Hopkins University is having through this one-of-a-kind community in China.[22]

More recent examples include Michael (Liang) Han, a 1995 alumnus who spent several years at China's Ministry of Commerce (then called the Ministry of Trade and Economic Cooperation), where he helped negotiate China's entry in 2001 into the World Trade Organization, and Kenneth Jarrett, a 1989 alumnus who served as US Consul in Shanghai from 2006 to 2008. Chen Deming, mentioned above by Wright, went on to become China's Minister of Commerce in 2007.[23]

As business, academic, and NGO relations between China and the United States expanded, Hopkins-Nanjing alumni continued to staff institutions that helped transact them. A 2001 survey of Center alumni found that approximately 35 percent of Chinese and 47 percent of international alumni were working in the private sector. Approximately one-third of each group was in academia, 24 percent of Chinese and half as many foreigners in government, and under 10 percent of each group in the non-profit sector. Three years later, the one significant change – reflecting changes in China's economy – was a drop in government employment among Chinese alumni, offset by growth in academia and business. Data collection in recent years has been less detailed, but the trend toward increased employment in the private sector has continued for both Chinese and international alumni.[24]

For some, like former Executive Director Daniel Wright, the Hopkins-Nanjing Center itself became a career destination. Similarly, after completing his dissertation and earning his PhD, Ren Donglai became a professor at the Center and has remained there, except for occasional visiting scholar opportunities. 'I missed my life here,' he says. 'It's a wonderful environment.'[25] Kindra Tulley worked for Liz Claiborne in Shanghai for a year after she left the Center, then returned to the United States and worked at the Hopkins-Nanjing office in Washington for five years, taking charge of American student recruitment and alumni affairs.[26] Milo Manley, long-time American deputy co-director in Nanjing, had planned to go into business after his year as a student at the Center. When the position at the Center became available, he thought he would try it out 'for a couple of years,' largely to improve his oral Chinese. 'The more I did it, the more I liked it,' though, and the temporary job became a career.[27]

Morgan Alexander Jones, who completed the Hopkins-Nanjing certificate program in 2004, may have the most unusual career among the Center's alumni. Under the stage name Mojo, he has joined with a Shanghai native and a Taiwan native to form a Shanghai-based rap group that performs partly in English, partly in Chinese. He would like to return to the United States to earn an MBA, but otherwise plans to live in China, with his Shanghai wife. Host of a show on Soulfire Radio, Mojo is helping to undermine anti-black bias in China, as well as being a medium for Sino-American cross-cultural understanding.[28]

American experiences

American students enrolling for the first (1986–7) academic year at the Center could choose from 11 courses taught in Chinese by Chinese professors. Three had economic themes, six addressed Chinese history and society (e.g. 'A General Survey of Chinese History from 1911–1949,' 'Parties and Organizations in China'), and two had anachronistic titles ('International Communist Movement,' 'Mao Zedong Political Thought'). By the 1994–5 academic year, the course offering to international students had expanded to 16. There were now five dealing with economics, and a new course explored 'China–US Relations in the 20th Century.' Over the next decade, the curriculum increasingly emphasized China's ongoing economic and legal reforms. Courses added during the decade included 'Social Issues in China's Modernization,' 'China's Judicial System and Its Reform,' and 'China's Civil and Commercial Laws.'[29]

Curriculum changes, in part, simply reflected the dramatic changes in Chinese society. By the early twenty-first century, Chinese scholarship was catching up with the proliferation of everything from commercial law to an accomplished domestic film-making industry. Additionally, the changes were a response to the evolving interests of international students. 'In the early days,' recalls 2001–7 Center Co-Director Robert Daly, 'we had a lot of old-style American Sinologists, who were interested in all things Chinese, across the board. … But now, they all want to be business people, they want to be in public health. It mirrors shifts in American and Chinese education away from liberal arts and toward professional training.'[30]

Some American students have expressed disappointment with the academic component of their experience. Sara Urgate, a student in 1992–3 and later a market analyst at the World Bank's International Finance Corporation, for example, found some of her coursework shallow. 'The Chinese professors are teaching what is acceptable to the Communist Party, so it becomes rhetoric.' American criticisms were particularly pointed during the Center's early years. As the program matured, the views of James Heller, a 1992 alumnus who went on to serve as a State Department foreign affairs officer, were more representative.

Heller 'thought the classes were excellent' and felt that he had gained valuable insights into Chinese history and US–China relations.[31]

Content aside, there are differences between Chinese and foreign pedagogical styles. 'Chinese students always rely on the introduction of their professor and the professor's reading list,' notes one Chinese professor. 'But international students sometimes try to find their own way to understand some topics.'[32] Kindra Tulley (1989) was perplexed by her class in Mao Zedong Thought. 'As American students, we're taught to question and expected to question, but in a Chinese setting, you're not supposed to question.' Still, she thought the Hopkins-Nanjing program was a success as 'an agent of cross-cultural understanding. I guess it falls under [the category of] people-to-people diplomacy.' Living alone the first semester because her planned roommate cancelled at the last minute gave Tulley a unique perspective on the Center's living arrangements. 'The two semesters were very different, and it was much better to have a Chinese roommate. ... Being in the room has an intimacy in conversation.'[33]

A combination of course content, improved language skill, and cross-cultural learning has improved career prospects for the Center's international students. An annual job fair in Shanghai provides a formal job search venue, and social networks have proven valuable as well. The experience of Kathryn Gonnerman, a 2002 alumna, was not unusual. As spring semester drew to an end, with future plans uncertain, she spotted an ad on the campus bulletin board for a position as program officer at the National Committee and decided to apply. A telephone interview in Nanjing led to an invitation for a personal interview, so she returned to New York and was hired within a week. At the National Committee, Gonnerman transitioned from participant into coordinator of educational exchanges between the United States and China.[34]

For a few American students, a year at the Center supplemented previous China experiences. Daniel Wright, for example, was a Hopkins-Nanjing student in 1993–4. Having spent considerable time in China before he enrolled, Wright viewed the Center more as a 'deepening experience' than a 'milestone.'[35] Former US Consul in Shanghai Kenneth Jarrett also had had considerable exposure to China prior to the State Department sending him to the Center for the spring 1989 semester. Jarrett had lived in Hong Kong, in Taiwan, and for two years on the mainland, where he met his future wife, a Shanghai native. Still, he substantially improved his language skills at the Center and extended his cultural insight by having a Chinese roommate and the opportunity to interact with ordinary Chinese.[36]

For a growing number of American participants, study at the Hopkins-Nanjing Center has been a reinforcing experience with respect to family – rather than academic or professional – background. Chinese Americans like Diana Wang (2005) and Pen-Pen Chen (2005), American-born children of immigrants, grew up in bilingual, bicultural homes. Neither had studied Chinese formally, although Wang attended after-school classes when she was in elementary schools and Chen learned characters by watching Chinese drama series.[37] Like other American students, Wang and Chen valued their new Chinese friends. Several told Wang that it was 'easier' to relate to her because of her *Zhongguo beijing* (Chinese background), and Chen spent more time with Chinese students than did other Americans. This background could occasionally lead to awkward situations, however. Since Wang looked Chinese and spoke the language without an accent, her initial unfamiliarity with daily practices such as using the post office could elicit consternation. Chen was not sure how to react when a Chinese student, obviously not realizing that she was an American, told her, 'Wow, your English is so good.' Also, she felt discriminated against by some local organizations that preferred to hire European-looking Americans to teach English classes.[38]

For most American students, however, the Hopkins-Nanjing experience was transformative. Christi Caldwell (2000) reports that her year at the Center 'changed my life profoundly, although in ways I had never expected.' Professor Gao Hua's class on Chinese intellectual history gave her new insights, and Professor Shen Han encouraged her to do field work among China's illegal women migrant workers. Not only did she appreciate the 'academic freedom and linguistic resources' the Center provided, but she and her roommate collaborated in researching the conditions of migrant workers. Caldwell was later able to draw on her cross-cultural learning as American Assistant to the Director of the Cultural Division of Taiwan's commercial office in the United States.[39]

Roseanne Freese (1987) had had considerable prior exposure to Chinese culture, having studied for three years in a master's program at National Taiwan University. Still, she learned that mainland society is not only different from Taiwanese society – 'My preconceptions couldn't have been more wrong!' – but is highly diverse within itself.[40] Freese, who went on to specialize in US–China trade issues as an agricultural economist for the US Department of Agriculture, used a year-long incident at the Beijing Railway Station to illustrate her point. Soon after arriving in Nanjing, she began reading in *Farmer's Daily* about four carloads of watermelons that were being held up at the station. Local railway officials claimed the shippers had failed to pay appropriate 'fees' and held a farmer and his daughter captive while villagers escalated protests over the ensuing months. The national newspapers covered only the aftermath of the story, announcing that the Beijing station head had been sent to a remote depot in Xinjiang Province and his deputy had been executed. Having had access to other news sources, Freese realized that the personnel changes capped a story of official corruption and resulting rural protest.[41]

Peter Wonacott (1994) went to work writing stock market reports for Dow Jones Newswires after his year at the Center. The Hopkins-Nanjing experience helped him professionally in several ways. First, during a winter break internship at the US Embassy, he got a tip that led to the Dow Jones job. Second, developing the language skill 'to devour Chinese newspapers' greatly improved his effectiveness as a foreign journalist. Third, the connection with Dow Jones, then parent company of the *Wall Street Journal*, five years later led to a position with that paper as a foreign journalist. Finally, his former classmates provided a ready network of contacts that enables him to be 'a lot more plugged in than other journalists.'[42]

Chinese experiences

Hua Tao of Nanjing University has taught courses on China's ethnic minorities to international students at the Center since 1994. According to Professor Hua, Chinese students have become even more career-motivated than their foreign classmates. In the mid-1990s, for example, they wanted – and got – courses in law and economics. 'These changes reflect the change of Chinese society. ... People pay more and more attention to economics.'[43] In the late 1980s, the international faculty consisted of two historians, two political scientists, and one economist. By 2005, there was demand for just one historian, there were still two political scientists, and the Center had added a second economics professor and a law professor to meet the demands of Chinese students.[44]

For some Chinese students, as for American student Roseanne Freese, the library's resources constituted a major benefit of enrollment at Hopkins-Nanjing. Ren Donglai was working on his doctoral dissertation when he attended the Center during its first year of operation. The document collection at his home institution, Nankai University, was too sparse to support his research on the World War II Sino-American alliance. 'This wonderful library' was a boon to Ren's research, though not immediately. Assignments from 'very tough' American professors left little time for research. So, Ren took the unusual step of successfully applying to return to the Center for one semester as a visiting scholar, in order to fully exploit the library's materials.[45]

In the eyes of their American and other international professors, the Chinese students have been bright and eager to learn. Kenneth Louie taught economics at the Center during the 1996–7 academic year and from 2006 to 2008. 'On any given day after class,' he recalls, 'I would have more than a handful of students stay after, and they wanted to continue to ask questions or to discuss current issues in economics.'[46] At the same time, Chinese students reflected cross-national differences in classroom acculturation. William Anderson taught classes in American law at the Center from 2002 to 2006. Like many American professors, he employed a 'Socratic' teaching style that focused more on critical thinking than on 'correct' answers. His students, who had 'succeeded brilliantly over 13 years of memorizing what the professor said and repeating it back exactly as he said it,' often seemed puzzled.[47]

Despite their unfamiliar pedagogical style, the content of American professors' instruction typically expanded the intellectual horizons of their students. Professor Anderson's classes on the US Constitution and the US legal system were the favorites of one alumnus. 'Before I came here,' he says, 'I had no very clear ideas about the US legal system. Now, I know exactly what is the separation of powers and checks and balances.' He is critical of some Chinese university students who are 'too influenced by the mainstream [Chinese] media, which is wrong on many issues,' and 'can't think in an independent way.'[48]

Other Chinese students thrived on academic fresh air as well. A 2001 alumnus recalls a political science class with Moses Russell: 'His class is so amazing. It's really like, when he's in class, it's a talking show. He makes you laugh, makes you tear, makes you nervous. … But the most important thing is he lets you know there are different sides of political issues.' Similarly, Michael Latham taught history by introducing contrasting perspectives. '[He] really helped me to understand why American foreign policy became that way,' recalled the same alumnus.

> In Chinese media or propaganda, they think, 'America is crazy' or 'Bush is stupid.' But there are some reasons for that, and now I know the reasons. It doesn't mean I support or agree with them; I just understand why you think that way.[49]

Xiaoqing Wang, a 1988 Chinese alumna, reflected on the connection between the Center's cross-cultural structure and exposure to open inquiry. In 1983, she had studied American history on a one-year Fulbright at the Shanghai Language Institute. That experience 'did not change me much,' though. 'The Nanjing Center really changed my perspective. At Shanghai Language Institute, the Chinese students stayed together. There were no American students, only one American professor.' After leaving the Hopkins-Nanjing program, she taught at Hebei Normal University, where she arranged exchange programs with two American universities. In 1993, Wang got a two-year post-doctoral teaching post at Cal Tech, followed by a permanent faculty position at Cottey College, where she continues to organize Sino-US academic exchanges. Along the way, she became a US citizen.[50]

Like their American counterparts, most Chinese alumni feel they have gained both cross-cultural understanding and career-building skills. Jin Chunqing (1998), for example, is Chief Partner and Director of the Fangben Law Office in Suzhou, where most of his clients are international companies. He was the first entering Chinese student to have studied law at a Chinese university, but the Center did not yet offer law courses, so he chose a plan of study in economics. 'The courses at the Center made it easier for me to understand business models and the concept of supply and demand; I learned the business language of CEOs and CFOs.'[51]

Another Chinese alumnus, a human resource consultant with an American company in Shanghai, is typical of the hundreds of Chinese (and American) alumni whose business careers enable them to stay connected with both countries. After earning his Center certificate in 2001, he worked for two American human resource consulting firms that advise foreign and domestic companies in China. He also helped organize a Shanghai HNC alumni network that enables former Chinese and international students to maintain social and professional relationships through regular activities. Participating in the Hopkins-Nanjing program gave this alumnus the confidence to imagine more expansive career possibilities than he had previously thought were within his reach. 'As a young man, as a young graduate student in China, [people like me] have never thought about working for the World Bank or the United Nations or something like that.'[52]

An alumna (2002) who began a career at the China International and Economic Trade Arbitration Commission (CIETAC) sums up the Center's potential for long-term influence on Sino-American relations:

> I think the influence of the Center in such a big relationship is not apparent, but I would call it a latent force. … The Center has a history of 20 years, so we have over 2,000 participants – students, faculty, visiting scholars, etc. … The older students are now working in important positions, and the new generations are getting up the ladder. I think because they have this experience, when Chinese alumni think of America or American alumni think of China, there will be real experience, with memories. … They will know how [the others] look at things, how to communicate with them, how to build trust and common ground.[53]

The National Committee helps train a new generation

The National Committee on US–China Relations has placed growing emphasis over the years on exposing Chinese students and young professionals to American society and helping their American counterparts learn more about China. The organization hopes that broadening and deepening participants' mutual understanding will contribute to improved Sino-American relations and, over the long run, to a more open Chinese society. This section explores Chinese participants' impressions of two of these programs.

Scholar Orientation Program

From 1980 through 2002, the Scholar Orientation Program took visiting Chinese students and scholars on a two-week tour of important American institutions, such as the Supreme Court, the American Red Cross, and the New York Stock Exchange.[54] Weeks before the Tiananmen Square tragedy of June 1989, a writer for the *Atlantic Monthly* described the SOP in buoyant terms:

> These visitors are a tiny sample of the tens of thousands of China's future leaders who are living in this country today – and who are engaged, in complex and unprecedented ways – in what can be called the modern Chinese discovery of America. … These scholars and students … likely represent a large segment of China's next generation of intellectual leadership, and perhaps much of the economic and political leadership as well.[55]

Descending from these heights of exuberance, the author concluded by predicting that official fears of 'wholesale Westernization' would prove unfounded and that China was more likely to experience 'selective, cautious – in effect, retail Westernization.'[56]

Like the Hopkins-Nanjing Center, the SOP weathered the post-Tiananmen crisis in official US–China relations. The program was highly popular with participants. When the National Committee organized a reunion in Beijing in April 1993, 300 of 700 invitees attended. Dan Bing, well-known news anchor on national Chinese television, presumably spoke for many in reflecting on her 1983 experience:

> From the straw huts of Williamsburg to the Liberty Bell in Philadelphia, from the Washington Monument in the country's capital to the Stock Exchange in New York, we learned about the birth, struggle, growth and triumph of a great nation. ... The past years witnessed our hard work, achievements, frustration, trauma, recovery, progress, and hopes. And in the process we have become more realistic. ... We are aware of the arduous road we face, yet the dreams and ideas inspired by that summer trip along the East Coast are still with us.[57]

Participants during the program's final decade continued to view it favorably. Every respondent to a survey reported that he or she had gained a deeper under-standing of American institutions from the ten-day SOP program than from simply living in the United States for a year or more.[58] A majority said what they learned was quite different from their expectations. The following comments were typical: 'As a visiting scholar, I would have never been able to visit the State Department and VOA [Voice of America], for example, if it weren't for the SOP program.'[59]

> The National Committee on US–China Relations selects common Chinese scholars and provides them with chances to experience the US instead of talking them into believing what the US is like. This is a very different yet very efficient way to really understand something.[60]

> When I was at St Olaf as a visiting scholar, my understanding was narrow and limited. But the program enabled me to have a deeper insight into those various institutions I visited during the trip sponsored by the National Committee.[61]

Four-fifths of the respondents thought that American institutions worked unam-biguously well, using descriptions like 'efficient,' 'very well,' 'contribute to the stabilization of society.' One-third mentioned NGOs, in general or specific exam-ples, to illustrate their opinions. Four-fifths saw significant differences between American and Chinese institutions, but half of these noted similarities as well. Some comments were specific, such as one participant who noted that many American colleges and universities have a religious affiliation.[62] Some comments were pointed: 'Forms look similar, but the most different Chinese institutions don't perform as an independent unit powerfully, just an empty shell.'[63] '[Y]ou can visit any place if it doesn't say "no trespassing" in the States, while in China, you [can] visit just the place which says "Open from x to y o'clock."'[64]

Nearly three-quarters of respondents listed American institutional arrange-ments from which they thought China could benefit. The list included expanding the role of NGOs (one suggested establishing Human Rights Watch in China), voting, better protection of historical sites, and an expanded faculty role in university governance. Several respondents urged care and patience in trying to transplant institutions: '[A]daptations should consider national characteristics and changing circumstances. Gradual reform is more preferred than radical revolution.'[65] Only one-third felt that the United States could learn from China. They suggested more attention to interpersonal relations – at the individual, family, or neighborhood levels – and highlighted the bias of Chinese culture toward reaching consensus and avoiding extremes.

It is likely that ongoing ties to the United States reinforce attitudes that SOP participants acquired while in the United States, and all reported some level of continued connection. For nearly half, the connections are casual – corresponding with a few American friends, occasionally reading American newspapers, and/or occasionally receiving American visitors. For the other half, interaction with the United States is relatively intense. A 1998 participant returned in 2000 to earn a PhD at the University of Georgia, then taught at SUNY Buffalo from 2004 to 2006, planning to return to China after her husband finished his PhD in the States.[66] Another helped administer an annual exchange program with Washington State University and also organized an American Studies Conference at Yunnan University.[67] Several maintain frequent contact with American friends and regularly read popular or scholarly American publications.[68]

Interning at Time Warner

The Time Warner internship program (1998–2006) provided the most intensive American experience of the various programs that the National Committee initiated in the late 1990s and the early twenty-first century. Each year, three to six undergraduates from the prestigious Fudan University spent three months working as interns for one of the divisions of Time Warner.

When Time Warner launched the internship program, with the National Committee in charge of its development and administration, company chairman and CEO Gerald Levin outlined its two-part mission of providing technical training and enhancing mutual understanding:

> Time Warner is proud to encourage and participate in the deepening dialogue and interaction between China and the United States. In this spirit, we are pleased to establish this internship program that will enable students to gain firsthand experience in American media and entertainment as well as insights into American culture and contemporary society. We, in turn, will gain new insights from their perspectives and viewpoints.[69]

Fudan President Yang Fujia, reciprocally, hoped that:

> The program will provide our students with an in-depth understanding of American society, culture and history as well as practical work experience in

media and entertainment – all of which will better prepare them to assume leadership roles in the future.[70]

According to Peter Wolff, Senior Vice President, International at Time Warner and coordinator of the internship program, the results were 'wildly positive. ... Ninety percent of the interns have really aggressively embraced their experiences here. ... Certainly, there's nobody in the program who goes back feeling negatively about America in general. It expands their thinking.' Wolff attributes this success to a combination of a careful selection process, highly motivated participants, and careful planning. A key aspect of planning was the role played by mentors within Time Warner, who provided encouragement and were usually able to spot any adjustment problems early.[71]

Within six months of completing his or her internship, each participant wrote a report for the National Committee.[72] The reports consist of roughly half tourism memoir and half discussion of career skills acquired, with a little space devoted to suggestions to hosts, administrators, and future interns. Within each of the first two categories are embedded meaningful reflections on American and Chinese societies and their interactions.

Some of the career-related comments record memorable moments. A Warner Bros intern had the 'unforgettable' experience of meeting the famous animators, Hanna and Barbera, while the 'most exciting job' of a *Time* intern was interviewing Richard Stolley, founding editor of *People*.[73] More typically, reports relate opportunities to acquire and practice specific skills. Another Warner Bros intern reflected, 'How lucky I was to have gone through the whole production process from the creation of a rough idea to the production of a newly made movie.'[74] Work at Time Warner's Government Relations Office 'seamlessly fit into [one intern's] career goal of becoming an international relations professional.' She was able to discuss commercial issues with a Chinese trade-promotion delegation and with the Congressional-Executive Commission on China.[75]

At *Fortune*, an aspiring corporate lawyer was able to write seven articles, including one on China's powerful microwave oven manufacturer, Galanz.[76] An ecstatic CNN intern included with her report a letter to her former supervisor:

> You should be excited to learn that I am now a [CNN] World Report contributor! Believe it or not, I'm now doing a part-time job at Shanghai Broadcasting Network. I am working on stories made for CNN World Report. ... Besides, on December 18th, I gave an informal lecture at the training seminar in Shanghai Oriental Television on my impression of CNN.[77]

Each cohort of interns began their stay in the United States with the National Committee running a ten-day orientation program, similar to the one provided to SOP participants. Both the tour and subsequent everyday-life experiences provided the interns with fond memories. One was impressed by the 'natural beauty' and 'serenity' of Walden Pond.[78] Another was initially nervous around a gay host couple, but soon decided, 'I don't think they are different from others in anyway [*sic*].'[79] Two interns mentioned having formed prior impressions of New York from watching *Sex in the City*. For one, actually living in 'breathtaking' New York confirmed her advance knowledge, while the other concluded that Hollywood and other mass media give foreigners a distorted picture of American society.[80] The 9/11 attacks on the World Trade Center and the Pentagon occurred during the 2001 program, and every intern that year remarked on the courage and spontaneous bravery of the American people during that difficult period.

Many interns were struck by – and found comforting – the racial, ethnic, and cultural diversity of the United States – 'a nation of nations,' in the words of one.[81] This was especially true for those who lived at International House in New York rather than with host families in Atlanta and Washington, DC or in an apartment in Los Angeles. 'At I-House,' reported a *Fortune* intern, 'I practiced Jewish Sabbath, experienced Japanese Day, enjoyed Indian dance performance, … and organized [a] Chinese language exchange program.'[82] Several interns were pleasantly surprised to discover the number of Americans who were curious about or had significant knowledge of China – like a 'Looney Tunes' production assistant at Warner Bros, who was a big fan of Zhang Yimou's films.[83] Those who lived with host families felt, in the words of one, that they had found 'another home across the ocean.'[84]

Amid these observations on careers and tourism, the interns highlighted features of American society that differed from, and in some cases challenged, Chinese norms. Several journalistic interns noted the American penchant for checking facts, comparing it favorably to Chinese practice. A *Time* intern wrote, for example: 'The reporters and editors would write down all the contact information that would be useful to reconfirm every detail in the story, which is different in China where editors would only reconfirm the most important ones.'[85]

American society also affirmed, in the words of one CNN intern, the value of 'a more open-minded way of looking at the whole world.'[86] Others were more explicit: 'My education in China has been largely under an ideology of the Chinese Communist Party, which in a way has made me more eager than students in democratic nations to reach out for the true spirit of journalism.'[87] In a similar vein, an HBO intern reflected, 'TV stations in China are somewhat the "Voice of Government."' After attending a National Committee-sponsored lecture and discussion on US–China relations, she observed, 'Unlike people in China, these lecturers felt free to share with us their opinions on some subtle issues. I was … told some sad stories that would be restricted to be discussed in public in China.'[88]

A *Time* intern 'suffered in some degree psychological conflicts' when she encountered questions about her Communist Party membership, China's restriction of press freedom, and repression of the Falun Gong. A 'heated discussion' about press freedom with students at the Columbia School of Journalism left her appreciative of 'all the splashes of discussion.' Not feeling a need to reach a verdict on specific Chinese practices, she concluded her soliloquy, 'It is the ability to question that I cherish most from my internship – it tells me not only which way to go to Central Park, but which way to take to my life destination.'[89]

It would be wrong to conclude that most interns rejected China's present political culture and institutions as a consequence of their experiences in the United States. For some, differences in social systems paled in significance before their focus on advancing their careers. For others, exposure to the United States can best be seen as an occasion for subtle adjustments to their worldviews. The HBO intern who welcomed open discussion, for example, remained proud of China's recent economic achievements. 'But at least I am glad to know that love for my homeland is not blind.'[90] A CNN intern used a speech that President George W. Bush gave at Tsinghua University in February 2002 to make sense of a pre-emptive anti-Iraq War rally she attended in Central Park later that year. Echoing Bush's words, she wrote, 'Dissent is not disaster; diversity is not disorder. … Now my desire of being the best possible journalist and having my own show in China is even stronger.'[91] Another CNN intern, who felt 'more tolerant in different views,' further observed, 'Living on a foreign land also made me more attached to my own country and family.'[92]

A 2001 HBO intern with a flair for literary allusion may have best summed up the collective experience of the Time Warner program participants. She entitled her report 'Journey to the West,' evoking Wu Cheng'en's classic sixteenth-century novel of the same title. Familiar to every literate Chinese, the novel is a humorous fictionalized account of the adventures of a real seventh-century Chinese monk who traveled (west) to India to bring back wisdom in the form of sacred Buddhist scriptures. 'I was lucky enough,' the intern begins, 'to journey to the West, to see, to feel and to think.' Later in her report, she relates having asked Gerald Levin for his reaction to China's continued blocking of CNN and *Time* websites. She was surprised by Levin's patient reply that he was taking a long-term approach to building US–China relations.

> In the following months when I was in New York, one day, my colleagues came over to congratulate me since the AOL TW signed an agreement with the Chinese Government to open up a channel with each other. When I saw the CCTV 9 English news was showing on our office television, I suddenly realized what Jerry said in that lunch. If Jerry was the man who opened a window to China, we were lucky to be the first bevy of birds that flied [*sic*] through.[93]

With their experience at Time Warner a memorable part of their professional development, interns have headed down a variety of career paths. Of 23 for whom the National Committee had employment data as of February 2006, one was working at Warner Bros in California, three at other American media companies (including one at PBS), six at non-media companies in the United States, four at media companies in China (including one at Warner China in Beijing), eight at other jobs in China, and one in Italy. Two of the intern alumni were working in the cultural exchange field – one as a program administrator with the China Program of the Carnegie Endowment for International Peace and another as program coordinator for the Sister City Division of the Shanghai Foreign Affairs Office.[94]

The Overseas Young Chinese Forum: living and learning in two worlds

The OYCF was founded in 1998 by young Chinese who had come to the United States to study. Most have remained long enough to start professional careers, and the majority have stayed longer. Drawn together initially by a commitment to an open dialogue about China's future, the majority of members have remained engaged with their homeland in some fashion, regardless of where they were living. The OYCF has also welcomed participation in its annual meetings and contributions to its online newsletter, *Perspectives*, by earlier immigrants, by US-born Chinese Americans, by non-Chinese Americans who share their interests, and by Chinese government officials.

The 1990 Institute came to see OYCF members' scholarly interests and continued close connections to China as one answer to concerns about perpetuating its own research program. Correspondingly, the OYCF invited the Institute's two top leaders to join its advisory board and sought the Institute's financial support for members' research. This mutual interest in research led, beginning in 2002, to the Institute providing funding and peer review in support of OYCF members' research on China's economic and social reforms. The Institute is not, however, connected with the entire OYCF agenda, which also includes wide-ranging political discussions.

The articles in *Perspectives* provide a window into the intellectual development of OYCF members. This content is significant both because the organization has cultivated an expanding readership in China, including some government officials, and because many OYCF members have returned or will return to China to assume positions of leadership in government, education, law, and business. Some Chinese officials (e.g. Wu Jinglian), as well as long-resident Chinese Americans (e.g. Gregory Chow) and non-Chinese American scholars (e.g. Jeffrey Sachs), have contributed to the journal, creating a wide-ranging forum for dialogue.

When they launched *Perspectives* in 1996, Bo Li and Li-an Zhou – then an attorney and a graduate student in economics, respectively – set the tone by writing and publishing a series of articles on democratic political theory. Of 230 articles during the journal's first seven volumes, 15 (6.5 percent) were about liberalism or democracy. The lead article in the inaugural issue was 'The Limits of Irony: Rorty and the China Challenge' by Randall Peerenboom. The author, an American scholar of Chinese law, applauded philosopher Richard Rorty's attempt to make liberalism relevant to China but without Western imposition.[95]

Jiantao Ren agreed with Peerenboom that, on the one hand, 'it is a shame to a country or society if it refuses to protect basic human rights and to develop a democratic system of government,' but that, on the other hand, the 'imperial diplomacy of Western countries' was wrong.[96] In the second issue, Li critically evaluated the work of American political scientist Robert Dahl as a way to highlight the liberal and republican traditions that sustain 'modern liberal democratic states.'[97] Li moved back to China in 2004 to work at the People's Bank of China and in 2009 became director of the bank's Monetary Policy Bureau.[98] Zhou became a professor at Peking University's Guanghua School of Management,[99] and Ren returned from his studies at Harvard to teach at Zhongshan University (Sun Yat-sen University) in Guangzhou.[100]

Under present conditions in China, incremental progress toward the rule of law may be the most practical way of promoting liberal values. In any case, since 1978 the principle of the 'rule of law' has provided a common vocabulary that the Chinese and American governments, as well as intellectuals and NGOs in both countries, have used to discuss China's development path. It has also accounted for the largest number of *Perspectives* articles in a single category – 47, or 20 percent of the total. Peerenboom, in one example, distinguished between a 'thick' version of the rule of law (laden with cultural values that can accumulate only over time) and a 'thin' version (emphasizing rule-based predictability) and argued that China should emphasize the latter in the short term.[101] Li provided a summary of Western theories and highlighted the importance of individual rights and an independent judiciary. Yingyi Qian (publishing a speech he had made at a forum in Beijing) held Hong Kong up as a positive example.[102] Qian later became an economics professor at UC Berkeley, but also maintained short-term teaching relationships with Tsinghua and Peking Universities, beginning in 2002, and became an independent director of the Industrial and Commercial Bank of China in 2004.[103]

Several articles discussed the rule of law within practical commercial contexts. Dongsheng Zang's articles, for example, discussed the role of the WTO, which China joined in 2001, in enforcing transparency in commercial law.[104] Zang went on to become a professor at the University of Washington Law School, 'with a focus on the role of law in social transformation in China.'[105] Other articles approached the rule of law from a human rights perspective. A 2002 visit to Tsinghua University by American legal scholar Ronald Dworkin stimulated intense debate in *Perspectives*. Dworkin had presented a paper entitled 'Taking Human Rights Seriously.'[106] One OYCF member, a law professor in China who was spending one year as a visiting scholar at Harvard, compared Dworkin to Don Quixote and said that he failed to appreciate gains that Chinese intellectuals had made by using moderate tactics. Another OYCF member, a student at Yale Law School, was more sympathetic to Dworkin and called for less defensiveness and more bold criticism of the inadequacies of China's legal system.[107]

Another central focus of the OYCF, economic reform, accounts for 13 percent of the articles in *Perspectives*. As with the rule of law, economic reform can be a bridge between its foreign and expatriate advocates and Chinese officialdom. Some of the *Perspectives* articles on this topic have been theoretical. Li-an Zhou, for example, argued that change in people's ideology had to reach a critical mass in order for economic reform to succeed and that China's Communist Party played an important role in accomplishing these changes.[108] Other articles put China's experience into comparative perspective. Yingyi Qian argued that China's gradualist economic reform strategy was superior to Eastern Europe's more radical approach. Jianfu Yao wrote a fascinating piece on Soviet agricultural economist Alexander Chayanov, whom Stalin ordered killed for his opposition to collectivization. For Yao, a utopian novel by Chayanov prefigured the individualist socialism that China was achieving under its reform policies.[109]

As time went on, an increasing number of articles on economic reform presented empirical research on conditions and policies within China. Zhiyuan Cui and Jiquan Xiang, for example, debated the sustainability and replicability of a model of collective industry that had proven successful in a village in Henan Province.[110] Cui was an associate professor of political science at MIT at the time of his 2000 article but returned to China in 2004 to teach at Tsinghua University.[111] Xiang was an Associate Professor at the Research Center for Rural Issues in Wuhan before becoming a visiting scholar at Stanford University from 1999 to 2000, afterwards returning to his former position in Wuhan.[112]

A relatively small number of articles (four of the 230 surveyed) tried to situate China's reform process within a historical and comparative framework of modernization. Li-an Zhou and Jin Chen explored Meiji Japan's nineteenth-century modernization experience and its relevance for China, while Yu Liu's two-part article challenged a prevalent view that China's late-twentieth century modernization was superior to Russia's.[113] An MA candidate in regional studies at Harvard at the time of her *Perspectives* article, Chen went on to become editor-in-chief of the *Harvard China Review* and a reporter, based in Boston, for two Chinese business publications with reputations for aggressive reporting, *Caijing* (*Finance and Economics*) and *Caixin*.[114] After earning a PhD in political science at Columbia University, Liu returned to China to teach in Tsinghua University's Department of Political Science. In 2009, the Shanghai Joint Publishing Company (Shanghai sanlian shudian) published her *Details of Democracy* (*Minzhu de xijie*), a collections of essays about the practice of democracy in the West. The book had made it into the bestseller category by late 2010, approaching 120,000 sales and a seventeenth print run. *China Daily* reported that the book 'is one of the favorites among Party members at the [party] school.' In 2011, Stanford's Center for International Security and Cooperation selected Liu as a summer fellow.[115]

Long-term effects of educational exchange

Three sets of motivations have driven US–China educational exchanges since 1979. First, participants have worked toward varying combinations of nationalistic, humanitarian, and career development goals. The profiles presented above suggest that most Chinese and American participants were successful on this score.

Second, governments, NGOs, universities, and businesses on both sides hoped, albeit it with varying definitions, to help China modernize. For Chinese leaders from Deng Xiaoping to Hu Jintao, modernization has meant importing enough openness and dynamism into Chinese society to drive economic development, but not enough to undermine political control by the Communist Party. Making productive use of foreign-educated Chinese nationals has been a key element of President Hu's 'strategy of strengthening China through human capital (*rencai qiangguo zhanlue*).'[116] The Chinese strategy can claim many successes. The government's 2007 annual Modernization Report predicted that by 2015 'the country's social indicators will reach levels comparable to those in developed countries during the 1960s.'[117] A British think tank recently credited the increasing return rate of Chinese scientists living abroad with putting China on its way to becoming a leading scientific power.[118]

In 1997, the *Wall Street Journal* presented an upbeat synthesis of American attitudes toward the role of academic exchanges in China's modernization. 'In the long run,' the authors wrote, 'this infusion of Western ways seems certain to erode the establishment grip, leading to more shared values than anything signed at the [1997] White House summit [between President Bill Clinton and President Jiang Zemin].' The article quoted former Secretary of State Lawrence Eagleburger: 'The way it will manifest itself will be in the little decisions that people make 10 years from now. ... I'm not naïve enough to say that we can absorb China, but I am prepared to take a bet that the Chinese will absorb a lot of these Western ideas.' The article balanced such exuberance with more measured assessments from visiting Chinese students and scholars, like a PhD candidate in aerospace engineering at Princeton who said, 'I expect that China will move towards democracy ... But I don't want to see it too quickly, because I don't want to see instability in China.'[119]

The third motivation has been the hope that improved mutual understanding between people would lead to better relations between nations. Extending the hopes of the Hopkins-Nanjing Center and of the National Committee's John Holden, a Taiwanese official suggested that by 2030, China's top leader would likely be American-educated, perhaps even a classmate of the incumbent US president. Chinese American political scientist Cheng Li, however, cautions against substituting 'wishful thinking' for 'deductive analysis.' He notes that 'the two Chinese ambassadors [i.e., the Mainland and Taiwan] on opposing sides who were involved in vicious contention regarding PRC membership in the United Nations [in the 1970s] were both graduates of Yenching University in the 1930s.'[120]

While rejecting dramatic conclusions about foreign-study effects on Chinese leadership, Li sees a more gradual, diffuse process at work. He notes that by the early twenty-first century, over half the top administrators and professors at China's top universities had studied abroad. Furthermore, while foreign-educated officials have been restricted to about 10 percent of the nation's top political leadership, they play a major role, as individuals and as members of think tanks, in providing advice to policy-makers.[121] On the American side, veteran exchange leaders like Douglas Murray and David M. Lampton have spoken of the need to train the next generation of American leaders who are knowledgeable about China, as well as Chinese leaders who are knowledgeable about the United States.[122] Data presented in this and previous chapters indicate that such training has occurred. Additionally, the profiles in this chapter of Chinese scholars who have remained in the United States suggest a useful way to supplement the population of homegrown China experts – i.e., importing them from China.

Conclusion

Contemporary NGO exchanges in historical context

The end of the Cold War was a milestone in the ascendancy of the open global system envisioned by early twentieth-century American leaders like Woodrow Wilson.[1] On the one hand, the United States emerged as the world's sole super-power. On the other hand, 'development is increasingly transnational, not geocentered, in accordance with the superpower's own objectives.'[2] These developments are relevant to the present study in two respects. First, relations between the United States and China have played a leading role both in the origins of American thinking about an open global system – i.e., the Open Door Policy – and in its late twentieth-century apotheosis. Second, the global debt crisis of the 1980s and a general decline in authoritarian governments, in particular the breakup of the Soviet-led closed system, created a climate in which non-governmental organizations shouldered an increasingly important role in both national development and international relations.[3] Thus the role of non-state actors in US–China relations can potentially illuminate important patterns in contemporary world history.

Through most of the twentieth century, numerous American private associations sought to help China modernize and to draw it into a global system based on the free movement of ideas, goods, and investment (but not always people). This was true of both religious and secular organizations; of those with ties to the United States government and those without such ties; in the spheres of commerce, social reform, education, and politics; and of organizations with no Chinese American participation as well as – with increasing visibility by the end of the century – those with substantial Chinese American participation and leadership.[4]

Americans' motives have involved varying mixtures of altruism, self-interest, and nationalism – including the long-distance Chinese nationalism of some Chinese Americans. For many, contemporary China has become, in effect, a global modernization project, whose success or failure has implications for the world at large. The country's sheer size, combined with the pace of its development, means that no issue of global concern is immune from China's influence. 'China is not just another big country,' as the National Committee's Douglas

Murray wrote in discussing environmental issues, 'it represents a critical juncture in global development.'[5]

Despite often promising beginnings, pre-1949 American private initiatives in China rarely achieved their implementers' goals. Historians have sought explanations for this failure, and we might wonder whether circumstances have changed sufficiently at the turn of the twenty-first century to anticipate more salutary outcomes for today's exchanges. The major factor that ultimately undermined the earlier exchanges was a succession of political and geopolitical conflicts that engulfed China – warlord rule, civil war, and Japanese invasion. American missionaries established first-class universities in China, but – to take three pre-eminent examples – the nationalist movement led Yale to withdraw from its university and medical school in Hunan Province in 1926, while the new communist government took over and reorganized Lingnan University in Guangdong Province and Yenching University in Beijing.[6] The YMCA, having made significant contributions to education and public health, managed to survive as an indigenized institution, but much of its programming and personnel were co-opted first by the Nationalists in the 1930s and then by the Communists after 1949. The Chinese YMCA was able to re-establish links with the US-based international organization only after 1979.[7]

While such political turmoil was largely beyond the control of the Americans involved in early exchanges, another factor was less remote – the reformers' attitudes toward their Chinese partners and clients. At their best, these NGO entrepreneurs made important symbolic and practical contributions to cross-cultural understanding. The Rockefeller Foundation took steps such as using a hybrid architectural style, so that its Peking Union Medical College would be 'not something foreign to China's best ideals and aspirations.'[8] Yenching University used a similar approach to architecture and took noteworthy steps toward creating a bicultural, bilingual classroom and reducing discrimination against Chinese faculty.[9] Ultimately, though, the Americans at PUMC were 'more patronizing' than their seventeenth-century Jesuit predecessors, and Yenching was unable to fully transcend its founding as 'a Western enterprise dominated by paternalistic Western ideas of how China's needs were best served.'[10] Further, an ulterior motive shaped their perspective on such secular ventures. As was the case with most American social reform initiatives in the first half of the twentieth century, 'the eyes of missionaries had been the lens through which the [PUMC] philanthropists viewed China.'[11] Underwriting missionary activity and varying degrees of cultural arrogance was an unequal power relationship between China and Western nations. Western restriction of Chinese sovereignty, extraterritoriality in particular, simultaneously emboldened American reformers to pursue their agendas and stoked the flames of the nationalist movement that ultimately drove most Americans and other Westerners from China.[12]

An episode from the early twentieth century foreshadowed the changed contemporary relationship between China and Americans who want to help it modernize. Industrialist Zhang Jian promoted pioneering colleges, a library, and a museum as part of his effort to make Nantong, in eastern Jiangsu Province, a model for Chinese modernity. One hindrance to economic development was periodic flooding of the Huai River to the north and the Yangzi to the south. From 1911 through 1914, a group of American engineers with Panama Canal experience and American Red Cross sponsorship sought to design and implement a flood control project on the Huai River. Three factors converged to doom the project – opposition from some Chinese officials, the outbreak of World War I, and the Americans' unwillingness to cede ultimate authority to Zhang.[13]

Flood control initiatives on the Yangzi River followed a more salutary course. Zhang hired Dutch engineer Johannis de Rijke and his son Hendrik to devise and implement, with Zhang's approval, a plan that successfully strengthened the river's embankment. In a delayed sequel, I personally experienced China's new self-confidence in its dealings with foreigners. In 2005, while I was living in Nantong on a business assignment, I attended the dedication of a new city museum, commemorating the hundredth anniversary of the one built by Zhang Jian. As part of the celebration, the city invited – and funded the trip from Holland for – the great-great-nephew of Hendrik de Rijke, who died of cholera in 1919 while working on the Yangzi flood control project and was buried in Nantong. Zhang erected a graveside tablet, which includes the statement, 'With me, he, in all his dealings, seemed more like a son than an employee.'[14] What was exceptional a century ago – China inviting foreign assistance and Westerners collaborating on the basis of respect and equality – is commonplace today.

Invited influence

In the Introduction, I suggested that cultural imperialism (or its beneficent twin, soft power) is an inadequate concept for comprehending the dynamics of contemporary US–China non-governmental exchanges. The *Harper Dictionary of Modern Thought* usefully defines cultural imperialism as 'the use of political and economic power to exalt and spread the values and habits of a foreign culture at the expense of a native culture.'[15] The earliest applications of this concept to research generally focused on missionaries and media culture.[16] More recently, some scholars have explored business culture and NGOs as instruments of cultural imperialism. In differentiating the United States from traditional colonial powers through a survey of twentieth-century US–European interactions, Victoria DeGrazia argues that American empire is based on a combination of five strategies: imposition of free trade; export of 'its civil society – meaning its voluntary associations, social scientific knowledge, and civic spirit'; 'the power of norms-making'; promotion of consumption; and 'apparent peaceableness.'[17] Other scholars see the programs of unaccountable private organizations as having an 'ethical and cultural imperialist nature' that constitutes 'NGO colonialism.'[18] A recent study of US–Indonesian relations faults American foundations and universities for funding educational exchanges that complemented the US government's modernization theory-inspired policies in a way that strengthened authoritarian government in Indonesia.[19] In the 1990s, many Chinese nationalist intellectuals espoused similar ideas, highlighted by the popularity of the book *China Can Say No*.[20]

In contrast to a premise of cultural imperialism, the personal and institutional narratives presented in the preceding chapters demonstrate that many American NGO projects have found willing – often beckoning – Chinese partners. International relations scholar James Mittelman has reflected on his five visits to China – once as a government-invited observer of economic reforms and four times to teach at Chinese universities. '[China] is a case wherein hope and self-confidence are expressed in the developing world. It is a case in which indigenous cultural resources are mobilized while values worth localizing are derived from other systems.'[21] Whether at the core of the Chinese state, at its periphery, or within China's emerging civil society, Chinese actors with their own objectives have increasingly welcomed, on their own terms, the involvement of Westerners – Americans in particular – in their nation's development.

This study of the Hopkins-Nanjing Center for Chinese and American Studies, the National Committee on US–China Relations, and The 1990 Institute has depicted Chinese actively seeking American advice on and participation in the modernization of their education system; the formulation of economic, environmental, and labor policies; and the development of a civil society. Other data confirm this pattern, which began with the political ascendancy of Deng Xiaoping's reform faction. In April 1980, Deng told Robert McNamara, president of the World Bank, 'We are very poor. We have lost touch with the world. We need the World Bank to catch up. We can do it without you, but we can do it quicker and better with you.' A 1985 World Bank economic report, echoing The 1990 Institute's C. B. Sung (see Chapter 3), highlighted an example of what Deng may have meant by 'better': 'China seems wise to encourage direct foreign investment, less for the foreign capital or advanced technology it brings than for the demonstration effect of modern management techniques.'[22]

In the 1980s, China recruited American economists to help modernize the teaching of economics at Chinese universities. This effort involved the translation of a textbook by Chinese American economist Gregory Chow, numerous forums and conferences, and the training of initial Chinese faculty in American universities.[23] Marianne Bastid has explained how China's educational modernizers leveraged international advice in their policy debates with conservatives in the early 1980s.[24] Similarly, Elizabeth Economy has shown that pro-environmentalism Chinese officials have welcomed international and transnational connections, which provide them with leverage against more conservative, growth-only-oriented officials.[25] In a particularly compelling example of invited influence, in the early 1990s, China's powerful Ministry of Civil Affairs invited the Ford Foundation, the Carter Center, and the International Republican Institute to support village elections. The three American organizations would translate foreign materials, monitor elections, and train election officials. This support has continued for two decades, to the mutual satisfaction of all parties. Also, true to pattern, the Chinese evaluated proposals by foreign NGOs but retained control over the agenda.[26]

The invited influence model manifests itself in a wide range of interactions. In 2007, for example, officials from Yunnan Province who were touring the United States made a stop in Colorado. They had heard a radio commentary on teenage sexual abstinence by the organization Focus on the Family and wondered whether similar educational materials might bolster Yunnan's efforts to control population growth and sexually transmitted diseases. This random event resulted in an agreement whereby Yunnan's public schools are using an abstinence curriculum created by the US organization. Founded by Christian Evangelical James Dobson, Focus on the Family had long sought access to China. Since China strictly prohibits religious proselytizing, however, the group 'has had to make a pledge of its own: no politically sensitive material, and no religion.'[27]

Formal and informal diplomacy

Formal diplomacy refers to interactions between governments while informal diplomacy denotes the actions of private individuals and organizations. Governments augment state-to-state diplomacy with public diplomacy, whereby the government of one nation directly engages the people of another nation. For both governments and non-governmental actors, there is an additional distinction between unilateral (i.e., propaganda) and dialogic (i.e., exchange) programs. Formal diplomacy strategists have debated the respective merits of these two strategies, and policy emphasis has fluctuated. Informal policy, in the past, was predominantly unilateral – e.g. missionaries – but in recent times has mostly fallen under the dialogic heading (see Figure C.1.) Though intense scholarly interest in cultural relations is a relatively recent phenomenon, its practice by Americans reached a critical mass in the late-nineteenth century. Over the course of the twentieth century, leadership passed from missionaries to private secular institutions after World War I, then to the US government with the rise of fascism and communism and the events of World War II and the Cold War. Private organizations began reasserting influence as the Cold War ended.[28]

Historically, official and private promoters of exchange programs have found one another alternately useful and troublesome. In one widely publicized instance

Official Status

		government	private
		government	*private*
Communication Mode	*dialogic*	**A** Cultural Relations (Public Diplomacy)	**B** Cultural Relations (Informal Diplomacy)
	uni-directional	**C** Informational Programs/ Propaganda (Public Diplomacy)	**D** Informational Programs/ Propaganda (Informal Diplomacy)

Figure C.1 Cultural relations and public diplomacy.

of formal–informal negative synergy, an American private association's close-ness to the government resulted in heightened official tension and interruption of the group's activities in China. During the tumultuous spring of 1989, Perry Link of the Committee on Scholarly Communication with the People's Republic of China (CSCPRC) facilitated dissident physicist Fang Lizhi's admission to the US Embassy in Beijing, where he sought and gained asylum. In the aftermath, CSCPRC had to close its Beijing office for one year, the US government curtailed the funding on which the group heavily depended, and Link had to leave China.[29] This episode was, however, exceptional. Overall, American formal and informal roles have been both less integrated and less contentious during recent decades than during the Cold War – but without reverting to the pre-1930s pattern of a largely hands-off government posture toward non-governmental exchange.

The Hopkins-Nanjing Center

The Center's two most visible intersections with formal diplomacy are its personnel and its ability to survive crises in official relations. Many American co-directors of the Center have been veterans of the Foreign Service. Additionally, the Center's ability to survive crises in official relations has found favor with top leaders in both the United States and China and has sent a positive signal to academics and their official supporters in both countries about the potential for new partnerships.

An annual grant from American Schools and Hospitals Abroad (ASHA), a division of the US Agency for International Development, provides 14 percent of the US budget for the Hopkins-Nanjing Center. While there is no contradiction between the goals of SAIS, the American partner, (improved mutual understand-ing, academic freedom) and current US policy objectives in China, the financial connection is no doubt a potent reminder of this synergy. ASHA funding criteria include stipulations that grantee institutions 'must reflect American educational ideas and practices' and 'should not be under the control or management of a government or any of its agencies.'[30] In her April 2011 testimony on behalf of continued ASHA funding, Carla Freeman of SAIS wrote:

> Support from ASHA for our unique program strengthens our nation's foreign policy goals and serves the mission of ASHA in several ways: ASHA support of our American faculty and uncensored library helps enable the Center to provide Chinese students located in China with an American education and to open Chinese eyes to American democratic practices, values and ideals.[31]

Congress, for its part, sees the support of university programs in China as a useful complement to formal diplomacy. In 1989, a House committee report affirmed that 'the administration was correct in choosing not to suspend funding for these [three] programs [including the Hopkins-Nanjing Center] in the wake of the June 4 crackdown,' because such initiatives 'represent beacons of American thought and ideals in this troubled corner of the world.'[32] A 2011 Senate Foreign Relations Committee (Republican) Minority Staff Report criticized China for limiting American Corners (State Department-sponsored centers for promoting mutual understanding between private citizens) to five locations in China, while the United States welcomed 70 Confucius Institutes. (Beijing argued that the Institutes have non-government sponsorship but the Corners are government entities.)[33] Still, in endorsing a $100,000 grant from the State Department's Innovation Fund to Arizona State University for a cooperative program in Sichuan, the Report argues that

> the role of American universities as projectors of 'soft power' should not be underestimated, and the State Department should be encouraged to provide similar funding for other such U.S. university projects in China to serve as a dual-track PD [public diplomacy] effort.[34]

The National Committee on US–China Relations

Of the three organizations, the National Committee has had the closest relationship with the US government. It began receiving government money in 1972 and over the years government sources have accounted for 10 to 30 percent of its funding; in the past few years, the percentage has been running in the low teens.[35] Like the Hopkins-Nanjing Center, the National Committee has, in some cases, effectively used the government as a personnel service. Arthur Rosen, for example, left his position as China desk officer at the United States Information Agency in the mid-1970s to become National Committee president.[36] Jan Berris was a Foreign Service officer, serving in Washington and Hong Kong, before she joined the National Committee and became its long-time vice president. Chairs have included a former governor of Pennsylvania (Raymond Shafer), a former New York congressman and World Bank president (Barber Conable), and former HUD Secretary and US Trade Representative (Carla Hills).[37]

Coordination between the National Committee and the government was close during the 1970s, but as often involved the private organization soliciting assistance from the government as the reverse. Berris describes the dynamic during that period:

> Every fall, before [National Security Advisor Henry] Kissinger would go to China, the National Committee and CSCPRC would give him our lists of proposed exchanges and programs, and he or one of his people would have discussions in Beijing with Zhou Enlai or one of his staff. They would come back and tell us the Chinese agreed to ABC and didn't agree with XYZ. Then we would ask for X amount of money from the State Department to carry out ABC, and they would give it to us.[38]

According to Berris, 'The government has tried to influence us only two or three times in the 36 years I've been here, and we have resisted it fully on all occasions.'[39]

The financial relationship became more arm's length over time. Throughout the 1990s, Senator Jesse Helms – mostly out of antipathy toward China – led an ultimately successful campaign to require the National Committee to compete for funding from the State Department, which had previously provided non-competitive grants to several China-focused NGOs.[40] The changed financial relationship did not, however, undermine the circulation of personnel and ideas between the government and the National Committee. Barber Conable and Carla Hills have given Congressional testimony during their respective tenures as chair of the National Committee. Conable hoped that 'this Committee will continue to support the proposition that expanded trade, economic exchange, and intellectual dialogue with China (PRC) promotes not only our economic and strategic objectives, but our human rights goals as well,' and Hills expressed similar sentiments.[41]

In one sense, work with the US government has burnished the National Committee's image. 'We find it useful for the Chinese to understand that we are highly regarded by the U.S. government,' says former National Committee President John Holden. 'It adds a little bit of luster to our name and helps us with some of our other work as well.'[42] Conversely, its long-time hosting of senior Chinese officials during their US visits (from Deng Xiaoping through Hu Jintao) solidified the National Committee's image in the eyes of many Chinese.[43] A recent full-page profile of Jan Berris in *China Daily* highlighted both the non-governmental character of the National Committee and Berris's close ties to 'China hands,' in and out of government service. The paper also showcased, in a special supplement on Sino-US relations tied to Hu Jintao's early 2011 visit to the United States, an interview with National Committee President Stephen Orlins.[44]

Yet the organization has also prized and benefited from its independence. William Chang of the United States Environmental Protection Agency (EPA) observed of the civil society environmental project: 'The National Committee was seen as a neutral body, which gave them credibility with Chinese officials that representatives of the U.S. government would not have had. The EPA, for example, would not have been able to coordinate an exchange like this.'[45]

The 1990 Institute

Unlike the Hopkins-Nanjing Center and the National Committee, The 1990 Institute has neither sought nor accepted government funding. Like the Center, but in contrast to the National Committee, it has not coordinated any of its programs with the US government. Its central mission of encouraging China's modernization is, however, consistent with the China policy of the US government since the 1970s. Further, the Institute has cultivated and benefited from cordial relations with individual government officials. Because of Hang-Sheng Cheng's friendship with the president of the Federal Reserve Bank of San Francisco (a hybrid institution, with both public and private aspects[46]), for example, the bank provided helpful logistical and symbolic support during the

Institute's formative period and continues to host some of its meetings. As long as US government activities are consistent with its mission, The 1990 Institute has been willing to provide occasional assistance, as during 1996 Hearings on *China's Economic Future: Challenges to U.S. Policy* before the Joint Economic Committee of the US Congress. The Institute was the only organization outside Washington invited to participate, and its scholars contributed five research papers to the published text of the Hearing.[47]

Correspondingly, like the National Committee, the Institute has also drawn symbolic and actual support from government officials. Undersecretary of State Philip Habib and Senator Adlai Stevenson III leant their names as early honorary co-chairs, while Linda Tsao Yang served as the Institute's research chair before assuming a post as trade ambassador in the Clinton administration and has remained supportive of the Institute. When Sara Randt, wife of Ambassador Clark Randt, agreed to serve as co-chair of an Institute-sponsored children's art contest, William Lee viewed her recruitment as 'a real trump card. ... When she came, the Chinese leaders had to give face. ... [A]ll the TV, newspaper, and magazine people showed up.'[48]

On the other hand, it is also clear that the Institute's Chinese partners saw its distance from the US government as helpful in some situations. As Xu Shanda of the State Administration of Taxation put it, with reference to the Institute-sponsored book on tax reform:

> When officials from different governments exchange their ideas, there could be some limitations. But when experts – scholars, professors – are discussing issues, they could have a wider range and be more to free to talk. Therefore, third parties – I mean institutions, scholars, experts from associations – can provide an important way to communicate between the governments.[49]

Official views[50]

Career diplomats have expressed a range of views about the value of the informal diplomacy of private associations. There is a consensus that these organizations have played a constructive role in US–China educational and cultural exchange and in (at least pre-1979) commercial relations. 'While we as officials couldn't necessarily say [to the Chinese that] these are some of the pitfalls,' said one diplomat of obstacles to early exchanges, 'the non-governmental organizations would have no problems about doing that sort of thing.'[51] Prior to the formalization of relations, the non-governmental National Council for US–China Trade (later the US–China Business Council) helped lay the groundwork for commercial relations. 'We had no diplomatic relations,' recalled one Foreign Service officer, 'so this was the only way we could do these things in a non-official type relationship.'[52]

After normalization, at least one diplomat saw minuses as well as pluses in the diplomatic initiatives of NGOs. James Lilley, who became Ambassador to China shortly before the Tiananmen episode of June 1989, highlighted three potential areas of friction between formal and informal diplomacy. First, some ethnic Chinese in America tend to take sides between Taiwan and the mainland. Second, most private forays into the Chinese-Taiwan relationship fall short, because the groups involved do not fully understand the complexities of the relationship. Third, sound-bite pronouncements on US–China commercial relations can spur overheated Congressional threats, which do not advance the diplomatic process.[53]

On the other hand, Lilley saw non-governmental exchanges in such fields as medicine, education, law, and governance as 'vital to the relationship.'[54] Hitting closer to the core of diplomatic activity, a retired Foreign Service office recalls that, in 1989, private exchanges kept open channels of communication and interaction that both governments found useful, even as official Fulbright exchanges were suspended and the planned debut of the Peace Corps in China was cancelled in the wake of the events at Tiananmen Square.[55] By 2006, the non-governmental track was increasingly important because Congressional funding for government-organized exchanges had largely 'dried up.' 'We really had to pull our focus away from the mass audiences, from youth audiences,' reported a Public Affairs officer, but 'fortunately there were private institutions out there interacting with that generation.'[56]

Goal achievement

In the decades since Robert Keohane and Joseph Nye drew attention to the growing role of non-state actors in international relations, political scientists have used subsequent research to determine the conditions under which such actors achieve their goals. Thomas Risse-Kappen argued that the domestic structures of target countries, along with their governments' integration into international norms and regimes, shape the ability of transnational actors to build 'winning coalitions.'[57] Margaret Keck and Kathryn Sikkink approached the problem from the standpoint of domestic interest groups whose demands are stymied by their government. They posited a 'boomerang effect,' whereby the frustrated interest groups find non-state allies abroad, and those allies pressure *their own* government (or an intergovernmental organization), which in turn influences the originally recalcitrant government to modify its policies.[58]

Wu Fengshi has supplemented the boomerang theory with a 'double mobilization' corollary, to cover those cases in which foreign and domestic NGOs are able to build bridges to, rather than confront, a government whose policies they seek to influence.[59] The foregoing study provides support for the double mobilization theory. The three organizations studied, however, are part of what one scholar has called the 'Shanghai Coalition,' which is currently the dominant trend in American business, academic, NGO, and formal diplomacy circles. Inspired by the cooperative spirit of the 1972 Shanghai Communiqué, its adherents take US–China cooperation as a premise. A contrasting 'Tiananmen Coalition' consists of individuals and organizations that view the Chinese government as a habitually authoritarian regime that will change only when pressured.[60] A study of organizations from the latter end of the spectrum, such as Human Rights in China, would likely yield a cloudier picture.[61]

A recent exchange in the pages of the *Wall Street Journal* illustrates the clash between the 'Shanghai' and 'Tiananmen' perspectives. A column by Jamie Metzl, Executive Vice President of the Asia Society, catalogues Chinese misdeeds in the areas of computer hacking, nuclear proliferation, and abuse of intellectual property rights. Metzl calls on China to 'embrace its responsibilities' and on other countries, in the meantime, to 'band together to collectively counter some of the more harmful implications of China's rise.' National Committee President Stephen Orlins wrote a letter in response, arguing that Metzl's article 'lacks balance' and citing positive actions China has taken in several policy arenas.[62]

China's influence on the United States and the world

In the Introduction, I suggested that 'invited influence' brings into focus an important symbiotic dimension of cultural exchange, one that such concepts as 'cultural imperialism' and 'soft power' occlude. This does not mean that these alternate terms lack analytic value.[63] We might view soft power – 'getting others to want the outcomes that you want' by virtue of 'the attractiveness of one's culture and values' – as a precondition for invited influence.[64]

As a sign of how far its modernization and global integration have progressed, China has consciously built on a variety of indigenous strengths in an effort to expand its own soft power. In 2004, the Ministry of Education set up a GONGO to establish Confucius Institutes on college and university campuses around the world, with an emphasis on teaching Chinese language and culture. By August 2006, 80 Institutes had been established; by July 2011, there were 350 in 103 countries.[65] In 2011, the official newspaper *China Daily* began running promotional news stories/advertisements in US newspapers, including a full-page article on the Confucius Institutes in the *Wall Street Journal*.[66]

With China's growing importance in the world economy, Chinese is the fastest growing foreign language, though from a low starting point. In 2005, an official Chinese body estimated the current number of foreign learners at 30 million.[67] China has also celebrated and encouraged the growing global popularity of traditional Chinese medicine.[68] In 2005, the 600th anniversary of explorer Zheng He's ocean voyages to Southeast Asia, India, and Africa provided an opportunity for China to project an image of a powerful but peaceful trading nation.[69] To better integrate and guide many of these endeavors, in 2009 the Ministry of Culture launched a 'Chinese Culture Going International' strategy.[70]

Most Western observers have credited China with a sophisticated and successful campaign to expand its soft power. Some even talk of a 'Beijing Consensus' on development, reputed to offer a 'market economy + authoritarian government' alternative to the Washington Consensus of 'market economy + democratic government.' With unanimity, however, these observers highlight two limiting factors. First, impressive promotional efforts notwithstanding, China's soft power remains modest in comparison to that of the United States, Europe, and Japan.

Second, the attractiveness of the Beijing Consensus is largely limited to developing countries.[71]

Even in the developing world, Chinese soft power efforts have had mixed results. Southeast Asians have grown increasingly concerned about China's geopolitical ambitions, punctuated by competing claims in the oil-rich South China Sea.[72] In Africa, Beijing has represented its search for raw materials as a benevolent contrast to European imperialism, but local populations often resent heavy-handed Chinese business practices.[73] In reflecting on a lecture he had recently given at Peking University, Joseph Nye wrote:

> Over the past decade, China's economic and military might have grown impressively. But that has frightened its neighbors into looking for allies to balance rising Chinese hard power. The key is that if a country can also increase its power of attraction, its neighbors feel less need to balance its power. Canada and Mexico, for example, do not seek alliances with China to balance American power the way Asian countries seek an American presence to balance China.[74]

Chinese Americans and US–China relations

Over the first half of the twentieth century, many Chinese Americans promoted China's modernization – in the hope that a stronger China would raise their own social standing, as well as out of a desire to help their ancestral country. By the end of the century, the slogan 'Save China to save ourselves' had evolved into the goal of helping China become a respected member of the international community.[75] Chih-Yung Chien's indispensible role in establishing the Hopkins-Nanjing Center, the achievements of The 1990 Institute, Gregory Chow's curricular and financial contributions to economics education in China, vital contributions by Chinese American scientists to US–China relations and the reconstruction of scientific research in China – all are part of this trend.[76]

Robert Parry, former President of the Federal Reserve Bank of San Francisco, highlighted the resources that Chinese Americans bring to bilateral relations. He reflected on the role that future 1990 Institute President Hang-Sheng Cheng had played in an early American banking delegation to China:

> Hang-Sheng was literally my guide on the many trips we took to China together. His understanding of the country was invaluable both to me and to my System colleagues, including [Federal Reserve] Chairman Volcker and [Volcker's successor] Chairman Greenspan. He advised us on everything from contacts with senior officials to tips on politely declining a second serving of sea cucumbers.[77]

Chinese Americans were barely visible during the early decades of the National Committee on US–China Relations. The situation began to change, however, with the 1998 appointment of Shenyu Belsky as the National Committee's first

China-born staff member. Having married an American China scholar, in 1988 Belsky had moved to Boston, where she worked for several years in community organizations that served mostly Asian immigrants. In Boston, she became friendly with film-maker Sue Williams, who had produced a historical trilogy on China. Beginning in late 1997, Belsky worked as associate producer of Williams's next film about the reform era, *China in the Red*. That experience piqued her interest in US–China relations, and a referral by Williams led to a seven-year stint as senior program office at the National Committee. In that capacity, Belsky coordinated projects on education, labor, social safety net issues, and HIV/AIDS. Working in China, she observed that much of the real dialogue took place in informal social space, over meals and in the evening, where her cultural affinity to Chinese participants was an asset.[78]

In 2005, Belsky left the National Committee to lead the Rockefeller Brothers Fund's new program on sustainable development in southern China.[79] After her departure from the National Committee, Li Ling (a graduate of Syracuse University's Maxwell School and Columbia Law School) served as director of transnational initiatives from 2005 through 2008. In 2009, Beijing-born Yale Law School graduate Ting Wang became the National Committee's coordinator for Law and Economics Initiatives[80] – to be followed by a fellow Yale Law School graduate, Guo Haini. By 2011, there were four Chinese American program staff members (two born in China), as well as two Chinese American and two visiting Chinese interns. The growing Chinese American presence reflects the outlook of Stephen Orlins, who assumed the organization's presidency in 2005. He believes that Chinese Americans' bicultural skills will enhance the ability of the National Committee to promote exchanges.[81]

The question that Orlins's interpretation leaves unanswered, of course, is whether biculturally and bilingually competent Americans with no Chinese ancestry can be equally successful in transacting informal – or formal – relations between the United States and China. In other words, are ethnic Chinese better at mediating between the two societies because they have Chinese parents or because they are fluent in Chinese (as well as English) and can operate within both Chinese and American cultures?[82] The recent rise of Chinese Americans to prominent official positions has elicited a spectrum of reactions that complicate this discussion. In 2009, Judy Chu became the first Chinese American elected to the US Congress. The representative's 2011 visit to China drew contrasting reactions. After *China Daily* featured a front-page interview with Chu, high-lighting her advocacy of cooperation between the two nations, an American columnist castigated her 'fawning interview' while she was 'the dictatorship's guest.'[83]

In another example, a commentator in China's state-run *Global Times* expressed guarded hope about Gary Locke's appointment in 2011 as Ambassador to China:

> A Chinese-American ambassador will not necessarily be friendly to China, but with the knowledge of Chinese traditions and methods in dealing with

problems, he can recognize subtle cultural cues and have a better understanding of Chinese policies. It helps mutual communication.[84]

Some ordinary Chinese contributing to Internet forums were less subtle. One called Locke 'a foreign devil who cannot even speak Chinese.' This linguistic deficiency contrasts to the fluent Chinese of Locke's predecessor, Jon Huntsman.[85]

Chinese Americans have undoubtedly played an essential role in deepening and improving US–China relations over the past several decades, particularly in the non-governmental sphere. The Locke and Chu examples suggest, though, that as they increasingly assume roles in official relations, they will on occasion need to overcome Chinese and American nationalist suspicions.

Lasting effects of non-governmental exchange

The death of American technology entrepreneur Steve Jobs became an occasion for Chinese citizens to reflect on their nation's path into modernity. In millions of blog postings and other conversations, people addressed the question, 'Why isn't there a Steve Jobs in China?' The former head of Google China told a *Wall Street Journal* reporter the problem is that Chinese schools do not encourage critical thinking. One blogger wrote, 'If Apple is a fruit on a tree, its branches are the freedom to think and create, and its root is constitutional democracy. An authoritarian nation may be able to build huge projects collectively but will never be able to produce science and technology giants.'[86]

Will China soon move in the direction of unfettered inquiry and constitutional democracy? Signals are mixed. In the field of journalism, there are encouraging signs. According to a Hong Kong media specialist, mainland reporting on a high-speed train collision near Wenzhou in July 2011 'was on a par with what we saw in Hong Kong,' and 'even surpassed Hong Kong's [reporting] in terms of depth …' The observer attributed reporters' increasing resistance to state mandates for upbeat stories to three factors: the proliferation of media outlets; the growing professionalization of China's media by idealistic journalists; and the existence of a reform faction within the Communist Party.[87] On the other hand, just a month earlier, *China Economic Times* disbanded an investigative team that had earned accolades for its reporting on corruption scandals. The paper's Party Committee instructed reporters to focus on 'economic issues.'[88]

Anecdotal evidence about the fruits of academic exchange is similarly ambiguous. Cheng Li has shown that US-educated professionals – who presumably have, in varying degrees, internalized some of the values they learned about – are playing important roles in China's higher education, influential think tanks, and government. At universities and research institutions, for example, 60 percent of all top leaders have studied abroad. Key policy-making positions in government, however, continue to be staffed by domestically educated Party members.[89] A particularly discouraging narrative emerges from the experience 13 US scholars who collaborated on the 2004 book *Xinjiang: China's Muslim*

Borderland. Chinese officials found some of the contents politically offensive and implemented a quasi-travel ban on the authors. Several of the scholars, who have taken to calling themselves the 'Xinjiang 13,' complain that their universities have been less than aggressive in pleading their case with US and Chinese officials, presumably out of concern over jeopardizing future exchange opportunities.[90]

The confluence of several phenomena has made the southern city of Shenzhen a symbol of the possibilities that exist in contemporary China. An August 2010 speech there by Premier Wen Jiabao calling for political reform raised the hopes of many Chinese and foreign China watchers that a leadership faction would push for democratization at an upcoming Party meeting and beyond. The timing of the speech, commemorating the 30th anniversary of the establishment of a Special Economic Zone in Shenzhen, led some to hope that Wen would give political reform a decisive push in the way that Deng Xiaoping's visit to the city at the beginning of his 1992 Southern Tour reinvigorated economic reform.[91] Earlier in the year, Wen had startled many with an essay in *People's Daily* praising Hu Yaobang, the reformer whose funeral in early 1989 was one of the triggers of the pro-democracy movement in Tiananmen Square.[92] While it does not appear that Wen is a leading reformer, some level of reform sentiment exists within the Party.

Second, a university held out the promise of taking autonomy (see Chapter 4) to a new level. In 2011, innovative President Zhu Qingshi opened the doors to South University of Science and Technology of China (SUSTC), funded by the local Shenzhen government. Zhu recruited advisors from Hong Kong and vowed to create a university 'ruled by professors, not bureaucrats.' Within months, though, SUSTC was in trouble with the Ministry of Education in Beijing for admitting students outside the national examination system (*gaokao*). As of this writing, the fate of the pioneering university is uncertain.[93]

Third, Shenzhen's city government has spent several years planning reforms on two tracks. From 2004 through 2008, the city ended the NGO dual registration requirement, first for industry associations and then for social service NGOs and charities. These organizations now need register only with a local office, not additionally with a 'mother-in-law' government organization operating in the same sphere. While not extended to advocacy NGOs, this policy liberalization is a significant step in separating civil society from state control. The reform earned one of ten awards from a Ford Foundation-supported good governance project (see Chapter 5) for 2009–10.[94] More ambitiously, local Communist Party leaders in 2008 drafted a plan that would, as reported in the *Washington Post*, 'soften key aspects of China's Leninist political system, authorizing expanded powers for the local legislature, direct elections for some local officials, a more independent judiciary, and greater openness and accountability within the party.' Shenzhen's party committee published the proposals in its newspapers, and some officials suggested following Deng Xiaoping's example by making Shenzhen a 'special political zone.' While there appears to be little prospect of implementing these reforms in the near future, their formulation and publicity reflect the thinking of some Party members.[95]

As *The Role of American NGOs in China's Modernization* goes to press, China's presumptive next president, Xi Jinping, has concluded a visit to the United States. Reporting has highlighted his 1985 stop in Muscatine, Iowa, as leader of a Chinese agricultural delegation, and his return in 2012 to see 'old friends.' The 1985 visit was co-sponsored by the Iowa Sister State Friendship Committee and the Chinese People's Association for Friendship with Foreign Countries.[96] Xi was following in the footsteps of his father, Xi Zhongxun, who had led a delegation of provincial leaders on a 1980 tour of several states, including Iowa. The National Committee on United States–China Relations hosted the elder Xi's delegation and, 32 years later, presented Xi Jinping with photos from his father's visit.[97] Thus it appears that China's next leader will be someone with rich historical connections to the kinds of exchanges explored in this book.

Will Xi Jinping's ties to the United States help him establish greater trust in the bilateral relationship? Will they lead to further economic and political liberalization within China? G. W. F. Hegel famously said that 'the owl of Minerva takes flight at dusk.' For historians, even more than for philosophers, wisdom cannot appear until after the event.[98] Only in 20 or 30 or 50 years will historians know how peaceful was China's rise and whether and how long China was able to sustain an awkward marriage between a market economy and an authoritarian political system. If Beijing blocks political reform, reverses course on market reforms, or comes into serious conflict with the United States, today's Tiananmen Coalition may look prophetic. If, on the other hand, Sino-American engagement remains largely constructive and China progressively empowers its citizenry, then NGOs such as those whose stories are told herein will share some of the luster with their Chinese partners and US policy-makers.[99]

Appendix

Itinerary for June 2001 National Committee Scholar Orientation Program, summarized

Sunday, June 3 3:00 – 5:00 p.m. 8:30 p.m.	Introductions, settle at hotel in Williamsburg, VA Dinner at Ming Garden Buffet
Monday, June 4 8:30 a.m. 1:00 p.m. 3:00 p.m.	Tour of College of William and Mary Lectures: 　　Edward Crapol, 'The Roots of American Foreign 　　　　Policy' 　　Kathleen Bragdon, 'An Overview of American 　　　　Indians' 　　Ronald Hoffman, 'The Spirit of Dissension: Division and 　　　　Disorder in the American Revolution' Tour of Jamestown Settlement Tour of Yorktown Victory Center
Tuesday, June 5 8:45 a.m. Evening	Tour of Colonial Williamsburg Dinner in Washington, DC with host families
Wednesday, June 6 9:00 a.m. 10:30 a.m. 12:30 p.m. 1:30 p.m. 2:30 p.m. 4:00 p.m.	Voice of America: Tour and Briefing Library of Congress: Tour and Briefing Lunch at Library of Congress, hosted by Chinese section 　　head Tour of Capitol Building Supreme Court: Tour, Lecture, and Video Congressional Research Service: Two Briefings
Thursday, June 7 9:00 a.m. 10:30 a.m. 2:00 p.m. 4:00 p.m.	National League of Cities: Briefing The Atlantic Council of the United States: Briefing Human Rights Watch: Briefing and Discussion The Heritage Foundation: Briefing on presidential 　　election

Friday, June 8 10:00 a.m. 1:30 p.m. 3:30 p.m.	Freedom Forum: Briefing in Media's role in US Democracy United States Department of State: Briefing on foreign policy formation and on US–China relations American Enterprise Institute: Discussion of the role of public opinion in American democracy
Saturday, June 9 9:50 a.m. 1:00 p.m. 5:40 p.m.	National Air and Space Museum: Tour and IMAX Movie Tour of National Monuments Take Amtrak to Philadelphia, stay in hotel
Sunday, June 10 9:30 a.m. 1:30 p.m. 3:00 p.m.	Walking Tour of Historic Philadelphia Independence National Historical Park Philadelphia Museum of Art
Monday, June 11 10:00 a.m. 1:30 p.m. 3:30 p.m.	Balch Institute for Ethnic Studies: Tour and Briefing National Museum of Jewish History: Self-Guided Tour American Red Cross: Briefing on the ARC and Volunteerism
Tuesday, June 12 9:30 a.m. 1:00 p.m. 4:10 p.m.	Environmental Protection Agency: Briefing Quaker Information Center: Briefing Take Amtrak to New York, stay in hotel
Wednesday, June 13 9:30 a.m. 11:15 a.m. 3:00 p.m. 5:00 p.m. 8:00 p.m.	New York Police Department: Briefing National Museum of the American Indian (Smithsonian) YWCA: Briefing Sightseeing: Empire State Building, Times Square Broadway Show: 'Beauty and the Beast'
Thursday, June 14 10:00 a.m. 2:30 p.m. 5:30 p.m.	Johnson Dairy Farm: Tour of a five-generation family farm Franklin D. Roosevelt National Historic Site West Point Military Academy
Friday, June 15 9:00 a.m. 10:30 a.m. 1:30 p.m. 4:00 p.m.	New York Stock Exchange Federal Reserve Bank of New York: Tour and Lecture United Nations: Tour in Chinese City Harvest: Discussion of poverty and hunger in the US
Saturday, June 16 9:30 a.m. 11:30 a.m.	Walking Tour of Literary and Immigrant Manhattan Lunch and Wrap-Up

Notes

Preface

1. Norton Wheeler, 'Cross-lingual oral history interviewing: confronting the methodological challenges,' *Oral History*, 36: 1 (2008), pp. 82–94.

Introduction

1. See, for example, Robert G. Sutter, *U.S.–Chinese Relations: Perilous Past, Pragmatic Present* (Lanham, MD: Rowman & Littlefield, 2010); Randall E. Stross, *Bulls in the China Shop: And Other Sino-American Business Encounters* (New York: Pantheon Books, 1990); Rachel DeWoskin, *Foreign Babes in Beijing: Behind the Scenes of a New China* (New York: W. W. Norton, 2005).
2. Studies of NGOs and bilateral projects during the first half of the twentieth century are plentiful. For example: Shirley Garrett, *Social Reformers in Early China: The Chinese Y.M.C.A., 1895–1926* (Cambridge, MA: Harvard University Press, 1970); Randall E. Stross, *Stubborn Earth: American Agriculturalists on Chinese Soil, 1898–1937* (Berkeley, CA: University of California Press, 1986); James C. Thompson, *While China Faced West: American Reformers in Nationalist China, 1928–1937* (Cambridge, MA: Harvard University Press, 1969). The small number of books and edited volumes on contemporary analogues are cited at various points in the following narrative.
3. Akira Iriye, 'Culture and power: international relations as intercultural relations,' *Diplomatic History*, 3: 2 (April 1979), pp. 115–28; 'Culture,' *Journal of American History*, 77: 1 (June 1990), pp. 99–107; 'A century of NGOs,' *Diplomatic History*, 23: 3 (Summer 1999), pp. 421–35.
4. Andrew Rotter, *Comrades: The United States and India, 1947–1964* (Ithaca, NY: Cornell University Press, 2000), p. xix.
5. For a critical overview of this part of the controversy, see Volker Depkat, 'Cultural approaches to international relations: a challenge?' in Jessica C. E. Gienow-Hecht and Frank Schumacher (eds), *Culture and International History* (New York: Berghahn, 2003), pp. 175–97.
6. Andrew Rotter provides an example, from his research, in a journal issue that also includes commentators' responses. Robert Dean provides a full-throated theoretical defense of Rotter's methodology, while Robert Buzzanco says there is 'little that I find historically important' – even though there is little he disagrees with. Rotter, 'Christians, Muslims, and Hindus: religion and U.S.-South Asian relations, 1947–1954,' *Diplomatic History*, 24: 4 (Fall 2000), pp. 593–613; Dean, 'Tradition, cause, and effect, and the cultural history of international relations,' *Diplomatic History*, 24: 4 (Fall 2000), pp. 615–22; Buzzanco, 'Where's the beef? Culture without power in the study of U.S. foreign relations,' *Diplomatic History*, 24: 4 (Fall 2000), pp. 623–32.

7. For the origin of the quoted terms, see: W. T. Stead, *The Americanization of the World, or, the Trend of the Twentieth Century* (New York: H. Markley, 1902); Frank Costigliola, *Awkward Dominion: American Political, Economic and Cultural Relations with Europe, 1919–1933* (Ithaca, NY: Cornell University Press, 1984).

8. See, for example: Victoria de Grazia, *Irresistible Empire: America's Advance Through 20th-Century Europe* (Cambridge, MA: Belknap Press of Harvard University Press, 2005); Jessica Gienow-Hecht, *Transmission Impossible: American Journalism as Cultural Diplomacy in Postwar Germany, 1945–1955* (Baton Rouge, LA: Louisiana University Press, 1999); Darlene Rivas, *Missionary Capitalist: Nelson Rockefeller in Venezuela* (Chapel Hill, NC: University of North Carolina Press, 2001); Yale Richmond, *Cultural Exchange and the Cold War: Raising the Iron Curtain* (University Park, PA: Pennsylvania State University Press, 2003); Penny M. Von Eschen, *Satchmo Blows Up the World: Jazz Ambassadors Play the Cold War* (Cambridge, MA: Harvard University Press, 2004).

9. See, for example, the Roundtable on 'Cultural Transfer or Cultural Imperialism?' in the 4: 3 (Summer 2000) issue of *Diplomatic History*. The relevant articles are: Jessica C. E. Gienow-Hecht, 'Shame on *US*? Academics, cultural transfer, and the Cold War: a critical review,' p. 465–94; Richard Pells, 'Who's afraid of Steven Spielberg?' pp. 495–502; Bruce Kuklick, 'The future of cultural imperialism,' pp. 503–8; Richard Kuisel, 'Americanization for historians,' pp. 509–15; John Dower, '"Culture," theory, and practice in U.S.–Japan Relations,' pp. 517–28.

10. Ambassador Clark T. Randt Jr, commenting on the opening of a new US Embassy in Beijing. Gordon Fairclough, 'Bush's visit, new embassy highlight U.S.–China ties,' *Wall Street Journal*, 6 August 2008, p. A6. Two and a half years later, a new secretary of state echoed that the relationship is 'as important as any in the world.' Hillary Rodham Clinton, 'Inaugural Richard C. Holbrooke Lecture on a Broad Vision of U.S.–China Relations in the 21st Century,' http://www.state.gov/secretary/rm/2011/01/154653.htm (accessed 5 September 2011).

11. Throughout this book, modernization refers primarily to economic development but also, in varying degrees, to such correlated tendencies as urbanization, mass education, increasing associational activity, proliferation of informational media, legal rationalization, and improved status of women. For a fuller discussion of Chinese modernization, including its relationship to late-nineteenth/early-twentieth-century European theories and mid-twentieth century American theories, see: Norton Wheeler, 'Modernization discourse with Chinese characteristics,' *East Asia: An International Quarterly*, 22: 3 (Fall 2005), pp. 3–24.

12. My inspiration for the term 'invited influence' is Geir Lundestad, although he was writing about state-to-state rather than transnational relations. See Lundestad: 'Empire by invitation? The United States and Western Europe, 1945–1952,' *Journal of Peace Research*, 23: 3 (1986), pp. 263–77; *The United States and Western Europe Since 1945: From 'Empire' by Invitation to Transatlantic Drift* (New York: Oxford University Press, 2003).

13. Sutter, *U.S.–Chinese Relations*, pp. 65–94; Henry Kissinger, *On China* (New York: Penguin Press, 2011), pp. 202–35.

14. Zi Zhongyun, 'A multidimensional approach to Sino-U.S. relations,' in Richard H. Holton and Wang Xi (eds), *U.S.–China Economic Relations: Present and Future* (Berkeley, CA: Institute of East Asian Studies, University of California, 1989), pp. 12–16.

15. Lawrence C. Reardon, *The Reluctant Dragon: Crisis Cycles in Chinese Foreign Economic Policy* (Seattle, WA: University of Washington Press, 2002), pp. 149–209; Michael Yahuda, *Towards the End of Isolationism: China's Foreign Policy After Mao* (New York: St. Martin's Press, 1983), pp. 41–3, 54–5, 59; Jack W. Hou, Robert W. Mead, and Hiroyuki Nagahashi, 'Evolution of China's U.S. policy (1965–1972), prelude to reform?' *American Journal of China Studies*, 12: 1 (2005), pp. 1–24.

16. Chen Jian, 'Tiananmen and the fall of the Berlin Wall: China's path toward 1989 and beyond,' in Jeffrey A. Engel (ed.), *The Fall of the Berlin Wall: The Revolutionary Legacy of 1989* (New York: Oxford University Press, 2009), pp. 101–2.

17. Carl P. Parrini and Martin J. Sklar, 'New thinking about the market, 1896–1904: some American economists on investment and the theory of surplus capital,' *Journal of Economic History*, 43: 3 (September 1983), pp. 559–78; Harry Harding, *A Fragile Relationship: The United States and China since 1972* (Washington, DC: Brookings Institution Press, 1992); Robert F. Dernberger, 'Prospects for trade between China and the United States,' in Alexander Eckstein (ed.), *China Trade Prospects and U.S. Policy* (New York: Praeger, 1971), pp. 185–319. For an argument that the economic factor was far less significant than security issues in US policy calculations in the 1970s, see: Robert G. Sutter, *The China Quandary: Domestic Determinants of U.S. China Policy, 1972–1982* (Boulder, CO: Westview Press, 1983), pp. 127–40.

18. Harding, *A Fragile Relationship*, p. 95; Warren I. Cohen, 'While China faced east: Chinese-American cultural relations, 1949–71,' in Joyce K. Kallgren and Denis Fred Simon (eds), *Educational Exchanges: Essays on the Sino-American Experience* (Berkeley, CA: Institute of East Asian Studies, University of California, 1987), pp. 53–5.

19. David M. Lampton, *A Relationship Restored: Trends in U.S.–China Educational Exchanges, 1978–1984* (Washington, DC: National Academy Press, 1986); Joyce K. Kallgren, 'Public interest in Sino-American exchanges: DeTocqueville's "associations" in action,' in Kallgren and Simon, *Educational Exchange*, pp. 58–79; Jan Carol Berris, 'The evolution of Sino-American exchanges: a view from the National Committee,' in Kallgren and Simon, *Educational Exchange*, pp. 80–95.

20. L. A. Chung, 'Huge protest at S.F. Consulate: big display of grief and anger,' *San Francisco Chronicle*, 5 June 1989, p. A12. For a thoughtful discussion of cycles of American euphoria and disillusion toward China, see: Richard Madsen, *China and the American Dream: A Moral Inquiry* (Berkeley, CA: University of California Press, 1995).

21. On the pattern of protest in the United States, and worldwide, see: Winston L. Y. Yang, 'Tiananmen and its impact,' in Winston L. Y. Yang and Marsha L. Wagner (eds), *Tiananmen: China's Struggle for Democracy: Its Prelude, Development, Aftermath, and Impact* (Baltimore, MD: School of Law, University of Maryland, 1990).

22. John Eckhouse, 'China businesses tense: some U.S. firms cut staff,' *San Francisco Chronicle*, 6 June 1989, pp. C1, C6; Ken Castle, 'Bay tours to China may lose millions,' *San Francisco Chronicle*, 8 June 1989, p. A22; L. A. Chung, 'Rift in U.S.–China academic relations: California exchange programs,' *San Francisco Chronicle*, 8 June 1989, p. A22. By 1991, these unofficial dimensions of the relationship had largely recovered. Harding, *Fragile Relationship*, pp. 283–90.

23. Joseph Fewsmith, *China Since Tiananmen: The Politics of Transition* (New York: Cambridge University Press, 2001), pp. 33–4. Fewsmith traces the protracted leadership struggle over reform in Chapters 1 ('Tiananmen and the conservative critique of reform,' pp. 21–43) and 2 ('Deng moves to revive reform,' pp. 44–71).

24. David Zweig, *Internationalizing China: Domestic Interests and Global Linkages* (Ithaca, NY: Cornell University Press, 2002).

25. David M. Lampton, *Same Bed, Different Dreams: Managing U.S.–China Relations, 1989–2000* (Berkeley, CA: University of California Press, 2001), pp. 115, 380–1.

26. Lester M. Salamon, 'Globalization and the civil society sector,' in Soma Hewa and Darwin H. Stapleton (eds), *Globalization, Philanthropy, and Civil Society: Toward a New Political Culture in the Twenty-First Century* (New York: Springer, 2005), p. 137.

27. One estimate put the number of US NGOs at over two million by the late 1990s. 'The non-governmental order,' *The Economist*, 353: 8149 (11 December 1999), pp. 20–1. According to an authoritative source, just the number of internationally active NGOs worldwide increased from 1,174 in 1978 to 7,522 in 1991, 43,958 in 1999, and 54,377 in 2008. Union of International Associations, *Yearbook of International Organizations 1999/2000* (München: K. G. Saur, 1999), pp. 2356–7; *Yearbook of International Organizations 2008/2009, Volume 4* (München: K. G. Saur, 2008), p. 649.

1 The Hopkins-Nanjing Center for Chinese and American Studies

1. About the Center, http://www.nanjing.jhu.edu/about/index.htm (accessed 1 June 2010).
2. Li Shuyou, 'Nanjing University and Sino-American cultural relations,' in Priscilla Roberts (ed.), *Sino-American Relations Since 1900* (Hong Kong: Centre of Asian Studies, University of Hong Kong, 1991), pp. 53, 59–60; Jesse Gregory Lutz, *China and the Christian Colleges* (Ithaca, NY and London: Cornell University Press, 1971), pp. 255–321.
3. 'Back to the future: the Hopkins–China connection,' *The Gazette: The Newspaper of the Johns Hopkins University*, 2 September 1986, Special 10th Anniversary Supplement: 'The Johns Hopkins University in China,' p. 10; Noel Pugach, 'Embarrassed monarchist: Frank J. Goodnow and constitutional development in China, 1913–1915,' *Pacific Historical Review*, 42: 4 (1973), pp. 499–517.
4. Mary Brown Bullock, *An American Transplant: The Rockefeller Foundation & Peking Union Medical College* (Berkeley, CA: University of California Press, 1980), pp. 24–47, 93–4. The quotation is from p. 47.
5. Ningsha Zhong and Ruth Hayhoe, 'University autonomy in twentieth-century China,' in Glen Peterson, Ruth Hayhoe, and Yongling Lu (eds), *Education, Culture, and Identity in Twentieth-Century China* (Ann Arbor, MI: University of Michigan Press, 2001), pp. 272–5.
6. Chan Hoiman, 'Modernity and revolution in Chinese education: towards an analytical agenda of the Great Leap Forward and the Cultural Revolution,' in Peterson et al., *Education, Culture, and Identity in Twentieth-Century China*, pp. 73–99.
7. Shuyou Li, 'Nanjing University and Sino-American cultural relations,' in Priscilla Roberts (ed.), *Sino-American Relations Since 1900* (Hong Kong: Centre of Asian Studies, University of Hong Kong, 1991), pp. 53–62; 'The life of Comrade Kuang Yaming,' in Feng Zhiguang (chief ed.), *Kuang Yaming Memorial Collection* (Nanjing: Nanjing University Press, 1997 [in Chinese]), pp. 1–5; Chen Yongxiang, e-mail interview, Nanjing, 3–5 May 2008 (replies translated from Chinese by Ryan Ulrich).
8. Chen Yongxiang, interview; Leon M. S. Slawecki, 'Setting Up: The Johns Hopkins Center in Nanjing, China,' unpublished paper presented at ASPAC '89 [Conference of Asian Studies on the Pacific Coast], Honolulu, 30 June 1989 (copy provided to the author by Slawecki); Dale Keiger, 'Reconcilable differences,' *Johns Hopkins Magazine*, June 1996, p. 24. The Muller quote is from the Keiger article.
9. Steven Muller, interview, Washington, DC, 9 September 2005.
10. Nicholas Burns, Under Secretary for Political Affairs, US State Department, 'Remarks at the 50th Anniversary of the School of Advanced International Studies in Bologna,' 14 May 2005, http://www.sais-jhu.edu/news-and-events/fall2005.htm. See also Tammi L. Gutner, *The Story of SAIS* (Baltimore, MD: School of Advanced International Studies, 1987), pp. 125–53.
11. Muller, interview.
12. In addition to the lengthy interviews I conducted, Chien documented his recollections of the start-up phase in four pages of a Memo to George Radcliffe, Richard and Mollie Longaker, and Bill Speidel, 22 August 1984, Ferdinand Hamburger Archives, Milton S. Eisenhower Library, Johns Hopkins University, RG 07.270, sq 1, s3, b 6, 'Trip Report: Speidel.'
13. Chien, e-mail to the author, 15 May 2006.
14. Chih-Yung Chien, telephone interview, Baltimore, MD, 20 December 2005.
15. The foregoing is based primarily on the 20 December 2005 interview with Chien. The account Chien narrated to me is consistent with, but far more detailed than, discussions of his role in 'The John Hopkins University in China' and Dale Keiger, 'Reconcilable differences.' Steven Muller corroborated the key role played by Wan Li and used the word 'champion'; Muller, interview.

16. Chien, interview, 20 December 2005.
17. Ibid.
18. Muller, interview.
19. Ibid.
20. Chien, interview, 20 December 2005; Muller, interview.
21. For a discussion of the role of elite politics in the struggle over reforms to China's domestic and foreign policies during the 1980s, including Wan Li's pro-reform role, see Joseph Fewsmith, *Dilemmas of Reform: Political Conflict and Economic Debate* (Armonk, NY: M. E. Sharpe, 1994).
22. Chien, interview, 20 December 2005.
23. 'An Agreement for the Establishment of the Nanjing University-Johns Hopkins University Center for Chinese and American Studies,' 28 September 1981, Hamburger Archives, RG 07.270, sq 1, s3, b2, 'Agreements, JHU & Nanjing University, 1981–1984.'
24. Slawecki, 'Setting up.'
25. Muller, interview.
26. Jan Kiely (American Co-Director, 2007–10), e-mail to the author, 18 September 2011.
27. 'An Agreement'; Chien, interview, 20 December 2005.
28. The quotation is one of several, including Chinese and American students, in Nie Xiaoyang, 'Hopkins-Nanjing brings China, America closer,' *China Daily*, 6 November 1997, p. 9. While most early US publicity focused on the equal partnership between a Chinese and an American university, some observers picked up on the significance of cross-cultural dormitory living. One example is John Schidlovsky, 'Studies in China: Americans, Chinese learn understanding along with their lessons,' [Baltimore] *Sun Magazine*, 22 May 1988, pp. 8–9, 20–4.
29. Chih-Yung Chien, telephone interview, Baltimore, MD, 16 June 2006.
30. Chien, interview, 20 December 2005.
31. Ibid.
32. Ibid.
33. 'The Johns Hopkins University in China.'
34. Quoted in 'The Johns Hopkins University in China.' Italics in original.
35. Wang Zhigang, telephone interview, Herndon, VA, 30 September 2005.
36. Leon Slawecki, interview, Washington, Virginia, 10 September 2005.
37. Wang Zhigang, 'Respect and understanding,' *Nanda News*, 25 September 1996 (special tenth anniversary edition), p. 5.
38. Milo Manley, interview, Nanjing, 20 December 2005.
39. Manley, interview.
40. Ibid.
41. Mike Field, 'Surviving the winds of political change,' *The Gazette: The Newspaper of the Johns Hopkins University*, 26: 5 (30 September 1996), p. 1.
42. Keiger, 'Reconcilable Differences,' p. 26.
43. Harry Harding, *A Fragile Relationship: The United States and China since 1972* (Washington, DC: Brookings Institution, 1992), pp. 225–9. The anonymous State Department official is quoted in Stephens Broening, 'Hopkins decides to keep Center in China open,' *The [Baltimore] Sun*, 23 August 1989, p. 1A.
44. Steven Muller, letter to Qu Qinyue, 21 July 1989, Hamburger Archives, RG 07.270, sq 1, s 3, b 2, 'Crisis'; Qu Qinyue, letter to Muller, 26 July 1989, ibid.
45. Keiger, 'Reconcilable differences,' p. 26.
46. Chien, interview, 16 June 2006. Chien, e-mail to the author, 15 May 2006; numerous letters to and from Steven Muller, Hamburger Archives, RG 07.270, sq 1, s 3, b 2, 'Crisis.'
47. George R. Packard, e-mail to the author, 23 August 2011.

48. Robert Daly, 'The Hopkins-Nanjing Center Education: From Bilateral Exchange to International Competition,' paper presented at conference 'Bridging Minds Across the Pacific – The 25-year Sino-U.S. Educational Exchange,' Fudan University, Shanghai, 10–11 November 2003.
49. Elizabeth Knup, 'Letter from Nanjing,' *The Gazette: The Newspaper of the Johns Hopkins University*, 28: 35 (17 May 1999), p. 9.
50. Ibid.
51. Wu Baiyi, 'Chinese crisis management during the 1999 embassy bombing incident,' in Michael D. Swaine and Zhang Tuosheng (eds), *Managing Sino-American Crises: Case Studies and Analysis* (Washington, DC: Carnegie Endowment for International Peace, 2006), p. 360.
52. HNC alumna #3, interview, Nanjing, 18 July 2007.
53. Rebecca Buckman and Elizabeth Weinstein, 'Student, business trips to Asia canceled due to SARS,' *Wall Street Journal*, 4 April 2003, pp. B1, 2.
54. Hopkins-Nanjing Center Annual Report, 2002–2003, p. 4.
55. Ibid., p. 5. Parents' reactions to the early closing are from the Center's Washington, DC-based Executive Director, Daniel Wright, as reported in 'Questions and answers with …' [*sic*], *Washington Post*, 27 April 2003, p. C4.
56. Hopkins-Nanjing Center Mid-Term Report, 2003–2004, pp. 1–2.
57. Hua Tao, interview, Nanjing, 24 July 2005.
58. The following paragraphs on fundraising, unless otherwise indicated, are based on a telephone interview with Patricia Lloyd, 11 March 2006, Alexandria, VA.
59. Steven Muller, letter to Dr Kenneth Whitehead, Acting Assistant Secretary of Education, 25 October 1988, Ferdinand Hamburger Archives, Milton S. Eisenhower Library, Johns Hopkins University, RG 07.270, sq 1, s 3, b 3, 'Dept of Education Proposals'; Patricia Lloyd, Meeting Report, 7 February 1989, ibid.; Joseph F. Belmonte, Acting Director, Center for International Education, 17 January 1989, ibid.
60. Wayne Peterson (USIA), letter to William Speidel, 27 July 1987, Ferdinand Hamburger Archives, RG 07.270, sq 1, s3, b3, 'USIA Grant'; Patricia Lloyd, Meeting Report, 3 July 1991, RG 07.270, sq 1, s3, b3, 'USIA Correspondence'; [JHU Dean] George Packard, memo to Patricia Lloyd, 13 September 1991, ibid.; Packard, letter to Ambassador Stapleton Roy, 16 September 1991, Packard, letter to Roy, 7 November 1991, ibid.; Lloyd, memo to USIA File, 19 June 1992, ibid.; Lloyd, Meeting Report, 26 January 1993, ibid.
61. http://www.usaid.gov/our_work/cross-cutting_programs/asha/grant.html (accessed 8 March 2008).
62. Lloyd, interview.
63. Lloyd, interview; Mark Ward, Acting Assistant Director, USAID Asia Bureau, telephone interview, Washington, DC, 21 May 2008.
64. The foundation percentage is derived by subtracting Lloyd's estimate of 25 percent ASHA funding from her successor Timothy Brown's figure of 44 percent for government and foundation funding, combined, for the 2001–5 period. Brown, e-mail to the author, 29 November 2005.
65. For the 2001–5 period. Brown, e-mail.
66. George Packard, letter to Wang Zhigang, 30 July 1990; Patricia Lloyd, Meeting Report, 4 October 1990, Ferdinand Hamburger Archives, RG 07.270, sq 1, s 3, b 3, 'Wang Zhigang'; Robert Benjamin, 'Hopkins Backs Nanjing Center, broadens scope,' *The* [Baltimore] *Sun*, 8 January 1991, p. 1B.
67. On the 1992 dinner the Sungs hosted for Hummel, see Rosalyn Koo, 'Johns Hopkins-Nanjing Chairman honored,' *Newsletter: The 1990 Institute*, February 1992, p. 7.
68. Sheryl WuDunn, 'Cultural links with Chinese are eroding,' *New York Times*, 6 November 1991, p. A6. Leaders in both countries had celebrated the Dalian campus

as a model for cooperative university management and transfer of business management skills from the United States to China. Richard W. H. Lee, 'Training ground for a new breed of professionals,' *China Business Review*, May–June 1985, pp. 39–42.

69. Hopkins-Nanjing Center Annual Report, 2002–2003, p. 4.

70. Daly, 'The Hopkins-Nanjing Center education.'

71. Baltimore's *Sun Magazine* reported that the Chinese side had been responsible for the technical mistake. John Schidlovsky, 'Studies in China: Americans, Chinese learn understanding along with their lessons,' 22 May 1988, p. 22. In a letter to the editor that apparently was not published, Center Co-Directors Wang and Slawecki corrected this factual error as well as refuting the article's allegation that the Chinese government was constantly spying on the Center's students. Wang Zhigang and Leon Slawecki, letter to the Editor, *Sun Magazine*, 22 June 1988, Hamburger Archives, RG 07.720, sq 1, s 3, b 3, 'Wang Zhigang.'

72. Slawecki, 'Setting up.' On the language proficiency problem, see also: Wang Zhigang and Leon Slawecki, letter to JHU President William Richardson, 3 November 1990, Hamburger Archives, RG 07.270, sq 1, s 3, b 3, 'Wang Zhigang'; George L. Crowell, memorandum to George Packard, 16 April 1991, Hamburger Archives, RG 07.270, sq 1, s 3, b 2, 'Chinese Language Program.'

73. Newman, e-mail to the author, 1 March 2006. In 2009, SAIS began accepting up to four classes at the Center for full credit toward a degree with a China Studies concentration. As a result, more SAIS students began spending a year at the Center. Carla Freeman (Associate Director, China Studies, Johns Hopkins-SAIS), e-mail to the author, 29 January 2012.

74. Keiger, 'Reconcilable differences,' p. 27.

75. Daly, 'The Hopkins-Nanjing Center education.'

76. Ibid.; Manley, interview; Newman, e-mail, 1 March 2006; Bill Speidel, Memorandum to Dean George Packard, Hamburger Archives, RG 07.270, sq 1, s 3, b 2, 'Chinese Language Program.'

77. Sharon Newman, telephone interview, Washington, DC, 6 October 2005.

78. Ren Donglai, interview, Nanjing, 24 July 2005.

79. William Anderson, Albert Yee, James Riedel, Wilton Fowler, and Martin Overby had all appeared on previous faculty rosters.

80. Robert Daly, interview, Nanjing, 6 June 2005.

81. Daly, 'The Hopkins-Nanjing Center education.'

82. Ren, interview.

83. Daly, interview; Pen-Pen Chen, interview, Nanjing, 10 June 2005; Diana Wang, interview.

84. Slawecki, interview; Ren, interview; Daly, interview.

85. Daly, interview.

86. Hua, interview.

87. Kathryn Mohrman, 'Hopkins-Nanjing Center Mid-Year Report,' 2003–2004, p. 4.

88. 'Memorandum of Understanding Between the Johns Hopkins University and Nanjing University for Design and Administration of a Joint Master's Degree in International Studies,' July 2005, pp. 2–3 (HNC files).

89. 'Memorandum of Understanding,' pp. 4–5.

90. The Paul H. Nitze School of Advanced International Studies Catalog, 2007–2008, p. 141, http://www.sais-jhu.edu/pressroom/publications/catalog/2007/catalog2007.pdf (accessed 17 September 2011); 'CAE [Committee on Architecture for Education] Honors 11 Projects with 2008 Design Awards,' http://info.aia.org/aiarchitect/thisweek08/0411/0411d_edawards.cfm (accessed 14 August 2011). The building earned one of four Awards of Merit.

91. Chih-Yung Chien, letter to Steven Muller, 24 September 1986, Hamburger Archives RG 07.270 sq 1, s 3, b 2, 'Trip Report: Chien.'

92. Kathryn Mohrman, 'Hopkins-Nanjing Center,' *SAISPHERE* 2004, p. 64; Bill Speidel, 'Report on First Semester (Fall 1987) Evaluation,' 26 January 1988, Hamburger Archives, RG 07.270, sq 1, s 3, b 2, 'Chinese Language Program'; Wang Zhigang, interview; Daniel Wright, telephone interview, Washington, DC, 1 October 2005; Huang Chengfeng, interview, Nanjing, 10 June 2005; Kathryn Mohrman, interview, Nanjing, 24 March 2005.

93. Carolyn Townsley (Director of Washington Support Office), e-mail to the author, 22 September 2011.

94. Carolyn Townsley, telephone interview, Washington, DC, 15 August 2011.

95. Jan Kiely (American co-director from fall 2007 through spring 2010), telephone interview, Hong Kong, 15 August 2011.

96. Shen Dingli, 'Joint Master's Degree in International Studies Program Review,' p. 29 April 2011; Ralph Litzinger, 'Master's Degree in International Studies Program Review, undated (based on 27–28 March 2011 visit). (Both documents from HNC files.)

97. This and the following two paragraphs are based on Townsley, interview; Carla Freeman, e-mail to the author, 31 January 2012.

98. Townsley, interview; Carla Freeman, 'Written testimony submitted by the Hopkins-Nanjing Center, Johns Hopkins University, Fiscal Year 2012,' *State, Foreign Operations, and Related Programs Appropriations for 2012: Hearings before a Subcommittee of the Committee on Appropriations on State Foreign Operations, and Related Programs*, 112th Congress, 1st sess., 14 April 2011, 601–605. The percentages are based on the most recent publicly available data, 'Budget for Fiscal Year 2008,' Hopkins-Nanjing Center for Chinese and American Studies Annual Report 2008, p. 18, http://nanjing.jhu.edu/pdf/Home/publications/2008AnnualReport. pdf (accessed 17 September 2011).

99. Fei-Ling Wang, 'Balancing the cross-Pacific exchange: American study-abroad programs in the PRC,' in Cheng Li (ed.), *Bridging Minds Across the Pacific: U.S.–China Educational Exchanges, 1978–2003* (Lanham, MD: Lexington Books, 2005), pp. 177–200.

100. See Chapter 4.

101. 'Yale and Peking university students to live and learn together in new exchange program,' *Yale Bulletin & Calendar*, 34: 13 (2 December 2005), http://www.yale.edu/ opa/arc-ybc/v34.n13/story1.html (accessed 7 August 2008); 'University presidents delve into co-operative, educational issues,' *China Daily*, 6 October 2005, p. 7.

102. Paul Mooney, 'In a rural Chinese province, an American educational outpost,' *Chronicle of Higher Education*, 52: 24 (17 February 2006), p. A49; Don Lee, 'Chinese school is rah-rah for U.S.-style campus,' *Los Angeles Times*, 4 December 2007, p. C.1; SIAS website, http://en.sias.edu.cn/index.php (accessed 16 October 2011); Fort Hays State University website, http://www.fhsu.edu/departments.aspx?id=1288 4905750&terms=china+sias (accessed 16 October 2011).

2   The National Committee on United States–China Relations

1. Near the opening of episode 1701 ('National Committee on United States–China Relations') of the Sam Waterston-produced series *Visionaries*, due to be broadcast on public television sometime in 2012.

2. J. William Fulbright, 'Foreign Policy – Old Myths and New Realities,' 88th Cong., 2d sess., 25 March 1964, *Congressional Record*, 110, Part 5, 6228. A representative of Fulbright's office told journalist A. T. Steele that the response was more than two-thirds favorable. The Associated Press reported a four-to-one favorable reaction. A. T. Steele, *The American People and China* (New York: McGraw-Hill, 1966),

p. 214; Gordon Brown, 'Quiet, intellectual Sen. Fulbright has knack of infuriating critics,' *Reading Eagle*, 12 July 1964, p. 47, http://news.google.com/newspapers?nid=1955 &dat=19640712&id=MrYhAAAAIBAJ&sjid=MJ0FAAAAIBAJ&pg=5844,5223182 (accessed 31 January 2012).

3. 'Let's open the door to China,' *Saturday Evening Post*, 237: 27 (25 July 1964), p. 84.

4. Robert A. Mang and Pamela Mang, 'A History of the Origins of the National Committee on United States–China Relations' (unpublished document, written 'at the request of the Christopher Reynolds Foundation, Inc.'), 1–2 January 1976 (NCUSCR files),' pp. 9–14. This early history is also summarized in Robert A. Scalapino, 'What we wanted to do,' *Notes from the National Committee*, 30: 2 (Fall/Winter 2001), p. 6.

5. Mang and Mang, 'History of the Origins,' pp. 20–4, 31–5.

6. 'A brief history of the National Committee,' *Annual Report 1991*, National Committee on United States–China Relations, p. 6.

7. Guoqi Xu, 'The sport of ping-pong diplomacy,' in *Olympic Dreams: China and Sports 1895–2008* (Cambridge, MA: Harvard University Press, 2008), pp. 117–63, provides a detailed narrative of the ping-pong matches. The quotation is from Jan Berris, 'The evolution of Sino-American exchanges: a view from the National Committee,' in Joyce K. Kallgren and Denis Fred Simon, *Educational Exchanges: Essays on the Sino-American Experience* (Berkeley, CA: Institute of East Asian Studies, University of California, 1987), p. 81.

8. Kallgren, 'Public interest and private interest,' in Kallgren and Simon, *Educational Exchanges*, p. 67. CSCPRC was established in 1966, the same year as the National Committee. By an informal initial division of labor, the National Committee conducted public education while the CSCPRC tried to initiate scientific and academic exchanges. The 1971 ping-pong matches and Nixon's 1972 visit to China quickened these efforts. Also, between those two events, Chinese American Nobel Laureate physicist Chen-Ning Yang met with Chinese scientists and with Mao Zedong and Zhou Enlai. This meeting and subsequent visits by other Chinese American scientists throughout the 1970s helped pave the way for the CSCPRC's scientific and scholarly exchanges, as well as, more indirectly, the National Committee's policy exchanges. See: Kathlin Smith, 'The role of scientists in normalizing U.S.–China relations: 1965–1979,' *Annals of the New York Academy of Social Scientists*, 866 (December 1998), pp. 122, 124; Zuoyue Wang, 'Chinese American scientists and U.S.–China scientific relations,' in Peter H. Koehn and Xiao-huang Yin (eds), *The Expanding Roles of Chinese Americans in U.S.–China Relations: Transnational Networks and Trans-Pacific Interactions* (Armonk, NY: M. E. Sharpe, 2002), pp. 207–34; Yuegen Yu, 'The Bond of an Enduring Relationship: United States–China Scientific Relations, 1949–1989' (PhD dissertation, West Virginia University, 1999), pp. 255–63. In the 1990s, the CSCPRC changed its name to Committee on Scholarly Communication with China (reflecting exchanges with Taiwan as well as the PRC). It also dramatically downsized, reflecting both the maturation and decentralization of US–China educational exchange and decreased government funding. See Mary Brown Bullock, 'Mission accomplished: the influence of the CSCPRC on educational relations with China,' in Cheng Li (ed.), *Bridging Minds Across the Pacific: US–China Educational Exchanges, 1978–2003* (Lanham, MD: Lexington Books, 2005), pp. 49–68, especially pp. 61–2.

9. David M. Lampton, interview, Washington, DC, 9 September 2005.

10. Ibid.

11. Berris, 'Evolution of Sino-American exchanges,' p. 87.

12. Jan Berris, telephone interview, New York, 28 January 2012.

13. Rosalind Daly, National Committee Vice-President for Administration and Development, e-mail to the author, 9 April 2007.

14. Berris, 'Evolution of Sino-American exchanges,' p. 87.

15. During the hiatus, the National Committee turned its public education activities, along with grant money and a program staff member, over to the Asia Society's China Council. Berris, e-mail, 27 December 2011.

16. Berris, interview, 12 July 2004; 'Program,' *Annual Report 1989*, National Committee on United States–China Relations, p. 4.
17. Jan Berris, telephone interview, New York, 30 December 2011.
18. The Office of Education was at the time a division of the Department of Health, Education, and Welfare. In 1980, it evolved into the Department of Education. David Adams (Senior Program Officer, Council for International Exchange of Scholars), interview, Washington, DC, 8 September 2005; Jan Berris, telephone interview, New York, 7 April 2007.
19. Berris, interview, 7 April 2007; *Annual Reports*, National Committee on US–China Relations (each report contains a brief discussion of the Fulbright-Hayes exchanges).
20. *Annual Report 2001*, National Committee on US–China Relations, p. 10.
21. Berris, interview, 4 April 2007; *Annual Reports*, National Committee on US–China Relations.
22. 'Legal programs in conjunction with the Ford Foundation,' *Notes from the National Committee*, 20: 1 (Winter 1990/1), p. 5.
23. 'Legal delegation studies American criminal code,' *Notes from the National Committee*, 20: 2 (Spring/Summer 1991), pp. 6, 13; 'Chinese administrative law group studies bureaucratic control in the United States,' *Notes from the National Committee*, 21: 1 (Winter/Spring 1992), pp. 8, 13; 'Judicial workshops offer occasion for professional training … [*sic*],' *Notes from the National Committee*, 29: 1 (Spring/Summer 2000), p. 4; 'American and Chinese judges share interest in rule of law development,' *Notes from the National Committee*, 29: 2 (Fall/Winter 2000), p. 4.
24. 'Supreme Court justice travels to China,' *Notes from the National Committee*, 24: 1 (Fall 1995), pp. 8, 14; Helen Ginger Berrigan (United States District Judge, Eastern District of Louisiana), 'I think this is the start of a beautiful friendship,' *Notes from the National Committee*, 30: 1 (Spring/Summer 2001), pp. 4–5. The latter report includes of photo of a beaming Judge Berrigan embracing Judge Zhang Jun, Vice President of the Supreme People's Court.
25. Thomas Carothers, 'The rule of law revival,' *Foreign Affairs*, 77: 2 (March/April 1998), pp. 96, 99; reprinted in Carothers, *Critical Mission: Essays on Democracy* (Washington, DC: Carnegie Endowment for International Peace, 2004), pp. 122, 124.
26. Richard H. Holton and Xia Yuan Lin, 'China and the World Trade Organization,' *Asian Survey*, 38: 8 (August 1998), pp. 745–62; Randall Peerenboom, *China's Long March toward Rule of Law* (New York: Cambridge University Press, 2002).
27. For a collection of thoughtful essays by Chinese and American authors, see *China Rights Forum*, 1 (2009), Special Issue: 'Rule of Law?'
28. 'Jiang's stark warning over corruption,' *CNN*, 8 November 2002, http://archives.cnn.com/2002/WORLD/asiapcf/east/11/08/chn.congress/index.html (accessed 18 March 2008).
29. See, for example, an article by the director of the China Center for Comparative Politics & Economics: Yu Keping, 'Toward an incremental democracy and governance: Chinese theories and assessment criteria,' *New Political Science*, 24: 2 (2002), pp. 181–99.
30. Margaret McKeown, '… [*sic*] and personal reflection,' *Notes from the National Committee*, 29: 1 (Spring/Summer 2000), p. 5; 'American and Chinese judges share,' p. 4.
31. 'Deng Pufang Visits the U.S.,' *Notes from the National Committee*, 17: 1 (Spring 1988), p. 3; Sam Howe Verhovek, 'Chinese visitor admires home built for disabled,' *New York Times*, 5 October 1987, p. B2.
32. Berris, 'Evolution of Sino-American exchanges,' pp. 87–90; Berris, interview, 12 July 2004. The quotation is from the interview.
33. Raymond P. Shafer (Chairman) and David M. Lampton (President), 'Chairman's and President's Introduction,' *Annual Report 1989*, National Committee on United States–China Relations, p. 2.
34. 'Program,' *Annual Report 1989*, pp. 4, 9.

35. Berris, interview, 12 July 2004. The number 13 is derived from the fact that the vans the NCUSCR rented could hold this many students, in addition to a driver and an escort. See the Appendix for a typical itinerary.
36. 'Scholar program reunion a big hit in Beijing,' *Notes from the National Committee*, 22: 2 (Summer 1993), p. 8.
37. Jan Berris, telephone interview, New York, 30 January 2006. For details on participant reactions to SOP, see Chapter 6.
38. 'Policy leaders orientation program,' *Notes from the National Committee*, 35: 1 (Winter/Spring 2008), pp. 19–20; 'Chinese policy leaders orientation program,' *Notes from the National Committee*, 35: 2 (Winter 2008–9), pp. 11–12.
39. 'Fourth binational dialogue held in Beijing,' *Notes from the National Committee*, 19: 1 (Winter 1989/90), p. 1.
40. Ibid.; '11th United States–China Dialogue,' *Notes from the National Committee*, 31: 2 (Fall/Winter 2002), p. 5.
41. Barber B. Conable, Jr (Chairman) and John L. Holden (President), 'Letter from the Chairman and President,' *Annual Report 1999*, National Committee on United States–China Relations, p. 3.
42. John Holden, interview, New York, 12 July 2004.
43. 'Continuity and change at the National Committee,' *Notes from the National Committee*, 17: 1 (Spring 1988), p. 1 (NCUSCR files).
44. Lampton, interview.
45. Berris, interview, 28 January 2012.
46. John Holden, telephone interview, New York, 12 August 2000.
47. '1993 exchanges and conferences,' *Annual Report 1993*, National Committee on United States–China Relations, p. 8.
48. Lampton, interview.
49. Elizabeth Knup, interview, Beijing, 28 July 2005.
50. Lampton, interview.
51. 'Leaders of Chinese non-profit organizations visit the United States,' *Notes from the National Committee*, 24: 1 (Fall 1995), p. 16.
52. Ibid.
53. 'Study group examines evolving non-governmental sectors in greater China,' *Notes from the National Committee*, 25: 2 (Fall 1996), pp. 5–6, 12.
54. Knup, interview, 2005.
55. Peter Riggs, memo to Mike [David M.] Lampton and Elizabeth Knup of NCUSCR on his recent visit to China, 24 August 1993 (NCUSCR files); '1993 exchanges and conferences,' p. 18. Additional funding was provided by the John D. and Catherine T. MacArthur Foundation, the Frank Weeden Foundation, and the Trust for Mutual Understanding.
56. Douglas Murray, telephone interview, New York, 16 August 2005.
57. Knup, interview, 2005; Murray, interview; Gerald Stryker, 'A Report: Ussuri Watershed Land Use Planning Project, American Team Visit, May 26 – June 20, 1993' (NCUSCR files).
58. Stryker, 'A Report.'
59. Knup, interview, 2005; Murray, interview.
60. Stryker, 'A Report.'
61. Peter Riggs, letter to Douglas Murray, 16 April 1993 (NCUSCR files); Zhang Xue, 'Summary of talks [held in Beijing 18 June 1993],' translated by Gerard Stryker, 23 June 1993 (NCUSCR files).
62. Stryker, 'A Report.'
63. Ibid.
64. 'The Chinese-Russian pas-de-deux continues,' *Notes from the National Committee*, 23: 2 (Winter 1995), p. 14.
65. Bob G.[lennon of ESD?], 'Notes on Steering Committee Meeting, April 4–10,' Vladivostok, 23 May 1996.

66. *A Sustainable Land Use and Allocation Program for the Ussuri/Wusuli River Watershed and Adjacent Territories (Northeastern China and the Russian Far East)* (Elizabethtown, NY: Ecologically Sustainable Development, 1996); [Douglas] Murray, e-mail to Anita Davis and George Davis, 4 February 1997; Anita Davis, e-mail to [Douglas] Murray, Mike [David M.] Lampton, and Elizabeth Knup, 9 February 1997 (NCUSCR files); 'Ussuri Project completed,' *Notes from the National Committee*, 26: 1 (Spring 1997), p. 8.
67. Terrill Lautz, Vice-President, Henry Luce Foundation, telephone interview with the author, New York, 10 March 2006.
68. 'The Three Revolutions Project' [grant proposal by the National Committee on United States–China Relations to the Henry Luce Foundation], 31 October 1997 (NCUSCR files).
69. Marilyn Beach, telephone interview, Houston, 7 February 2005.
70. Ibid.
71. Ibid.; Marilyn Beach, fax to John Holden, Jan Berris, and Doug[las] Murray, 22 September 1998 (NCUSCR files).
72. Daniel A. Viederman [identified in a misprint as Gordon Claridge], 'Wetlands conservation in China: action planning,' *China Review: Magazine of the Great Britain-China Centre*, 7 (Summer 1997), pp. 34–7. [*China Review* archivist Laura Rivkin clarified the author's identity in an 18 April 2006 e-mail to the author.]
73. National Committee on United States–China Relations, 'Report to the Henry Luce Foundation – The Civil Society Project: 1999 activities,' January 2000; Zhang Hong-yan, interview, Changchun,16 June 2008. The Chinese side recruited Zhang as a translator, but because of his expertise in Geographic Information Systems (GIS), he was eventually drawn into a substantive role in the exchange.
74. Beach, interview; William Chang, telephone interview, Beijing, 14 January 2006.
75. 'Report to the Henry Luce Foundation,' January 2000.
76. Marilyn Beach, e-mail to Doug[las] Murray, John Holden and Jan Berris, 25 September 1998 (NCUSCR files); Liu Fengkai (Heilongjiang Environmental Protection Bureau) and Douglas P. Murray (National Committee on United States–China Relations), 'Summary of Sino-US Academic Symposium on Ecosystem Recovery and Restoration in Disaster Areas in Heilongjiang Province,' 15 May 1999 (NCUSCR files).
77. Marilyn Beach, 'Agenda for the [29 March 1999] Conference Call' (NCUSCR files).
78. Marilyn Beach, e-mail to Jan Berris, 21 May 1999 (NCUSCR files).
79. 'Local initiatives in environmental protection,' *Notes from the National Committee*, 29: 1 (Spring/Summer 2000), p. 6.
80. '2000 exchanges and conferences,' *Annual Report 2000*, National Committee on United States–China Relations, pp. 14–15.
81. National Committee on United States–China Relations, 'Final Report to the Henry Luce Foundation: The Civil Society Project, undated [some time after June 2001, based on internal evidence] (NCUSCR files).
82. Marilyn Beach, e-mail to Professor Shang Jingcheng (of Northeast Normal University) and Professor Deng Wei (of the Changchun Institute of Geography), 14 April 1999 (NCUSCR files); Beach, interview; NCUSCR, 'Final Report.'
83. Daniel Wright, telephone interview, Washington, DC, 1 October 2005.
84. Marilyn Beach, e-mail to Dan[iel] Wright, 3 August 1998 (NCUSCR files); Dan[iel] Wright, e-mail to Marilyn Beach, 5 August 1998 (NCUSCR files).
85. Marilyn Beach, e-mail to Doug[las] Murray, Jan Berris, and John Holden, 21 September 1998 (NCUSCR files).
86. Beach, interview; Daniel B. Wright, *The Promise of Revolution: Stories of Fulfillment and Struggle in China's Hinterland* (Lanham, MD: Rowman & Littlefield, 2003), pp. 131–7. Chapter 14 is entitled 'Sprouts in a hard place: Principal Bi and the "p"-word'.
87. Huang Weican, interview, Guiyang, 29 October 2005 (translated by Yi Honggen).
88. Daniel Wright, e-mail to Marilyn Beach, 23 September 1998 (NCUSCR files).

89. Daniel Wright, e-mail to Marilyn Beach, 22 March 1999 (NCUSCR files). According to Beach, the fact that Guo 'was a real strong supporter of our project ... was one of the reasons we succeeded.' Beach, interview.
90. Daniel Wright, e-mail to Marilyn Beach, 9 April 1999 (NCUSCR files).
91. 'Report to the Henry Luce Foundation,' January 2000.
92. 'Meeting the challenge of private education in Guizhou,' *Notes from the National Committee*, 28: 2 (Fall/Winter 1999), p. 5.
93. Frank Kincaid, telephone interview, Beattyville, Kentucky, 21 May 2008.
94. Daniel B. Wright, '"Real China": U.S. Congress Visits Guizhou,' ICWA Letters, DBW-23 East Asia, August 1999 (provided to the author by Daniel Wright).
95. '[Secretary of the Provincial Committee] Liu Fangren Meets with Mr. Pitts, a Member of the U.S. Congress,' *Guizhou Ribao*, 15 August 1999, p. 1 [in Chinese] (translated by Liu Lina).
96. Marilyn Beach, letter to Henry R. Luce III, 12 May 2000 (NCUSCR files); Leslie Change, 'In China, private schools spring up to fill the gap: colleges are few, and society's need for skills is strong,' *Wall Street Journal*, 9 May 2000, p. A21.
97. '1999 exchanges and conferences,' p. 16; '15–31 May U.S. Itinerary for Vocational Education Delegation Study Tour from Guizhou' (NCUSCR files).
98. '2000 Exchanges and Conferences,' *Annual Report 2000*, National Committee on United States–China Relations, p. 9.
99. Berris, interview, 30 December 2011; 'Promoting Constructive Engagement' (National Committee brochure), undated but post-2005 since it lists Stephen Orlins as president (provided to the author by Jan Berris).
100. Jan Berris, telephone interview, New York, 25 July 2011; National Committee website, http://www.ncuscr.org/programs/barnett-oksenberg (accessed 15 October 2011). While the emphasis on public education in China was new, there were precedents to build on. The National Committee had previously sent historian Daniel Boorstein and political analyst David Gergen on lecture tours in China.
101. 'Journalism internship at Time Warner: Committee facilitates innovative program,' *Notes from the National Committee*, 28: 1 (Winter/Spring 1999), pp. 5, 16; Berris, interview, 12 July 2004; Holden, interview, 12 July 2004; Kathryn Gonnerman, interview, New York, 13 July 2004.
102. Holden, interview, 12 July 2004; Time Warner Internship, http://www.ncuscr.org/?q=programs/time-warner-internship (accessed 31 May 2010).
103. Holden, interview, 12 July 2004.
104. Ibid.
105. 'Young leaders forum,' *Notes from the National Committee*, 32: 2 (Winter/Spring 2004), p. 5. Giffords gained wide publicity in 2011, when she became the victim of an attempted assassination.
106. Berris, interview, 12 July 2004; Holden, interview, 12 July 2004. Wang is a common Chinese surname. *Lao* literally means old. Chinese, who rarely address adults other than relatives or very close friends by their personal names, often use *Lao* as a casual form of address for people over 40 (or *Xiao* – meaning small – for people under 40).
107. Holden, interview, 12 July 2004; Gonnerman, interview.
108. 'U.S. foreign policy colloquium meets in Washington,' *Notes from the National Committee*, 32: 1 (Spring/Summer 2003), pp. 1, 3.
109. Jeff Tao, '2004 foreign policy colloquium: a participant's perspective,' *Notes from the National Committee*, 33: 1 (Winter/Spring 2005), p. 12.
110. 'U.S.–China student leaders exchange,' *Notes from the National Committee*, 33: 1 (Winter/Spring 2005), p. 5.
111. 'Student leaders exchange to China,' *Notes from the National Committee*, 35: 2 (Winter 2008–9), pp. 20–1.
112. 'Round one of the public intellectuals program ends; round two to begin,' *Notes from the National Committee*, 35: 1 (Winter/Spring 2008), pp. 17–18.

113. Preventive Defense is a concept for US defense strategy in the post-Cold War era, premised on the belief that the US defense establishment's highest priority is to forestall developments that could directly threaten the vital interests and survival of American citizens. PDP is a research collaboration between Stanford University and Harvard University's Kennedy School of Government. See its website: http://www. preventivedefenseproject.org/ (accessed 28 January 2012).

114. Berris, interview, 28 January 2012. On the McNamara-led delegation, see: 'Sino-American military relations,' *Notes from the National Committee*, 23: 2 (Winter 1995), pp. 12–13. On the Schlesinger-led delegation, see: 'Committee releases report on strategic security issues,' *Notes from the National Committee*, 25: 2 (Fall 1996), pp. 1–2, 4, 13. On Perry's role in early exchanges, see: 'Perry leads Committee delegation to China for second year,' *Notes from the National Committee*, 28: 1 (Winter/Spring 1999), pp. 1, 16.

115. 'Rule of law and human rights dialogue,' *Notes from the National Committee*, 38: 1 (Spring 2011), p. 6.

116. 'U.S.–China Track II economic dialogue,' *Notes from the National Committee*, 38: 1 (Spring 2011), p. 4.

117. 'American and Chinese experts share ideas on natural disaster relief,' *Notes from the National Committee*, 30: 1 (Spring/Summer 2001), p. 8.

118. 'Sichuan-Gulf Coast redevelopment exchange,' *Notes from the National Committee* 36: 1 (Spring 2011), pp. 10–11.

119. Berris, interview, 28 January 2012.

120. '2003 exchanges and conferences,' *Annual Report 2003*, National Committee on United States–China Relations, pp. 15–16.

121. Lampton, interview.

3 The 1990 Institute: Chinese Americans bridge the Pacific

1. Sung is an unusually dynamic individual. His personal energy – in personal, business, and civic spheres – is on full display in a 40-minute interview broadcast on Chinese television on 8 January 2007, on the program *Up Close*, http://www.cctv.com/program/upclose/20070108/104379_1.shtml (accessed 31 January 2012).

2. C. B. Sung, interview, San Mateo, California, 10 July 1999; Sung, interview, San Mateo, California, 30 April 2005.

3. Sung, interview, April 2005.

4. C. B. Sung, letter to Neil L. Rudenstine, President, Harvard University, 15 May 1998 (Institute files).

5. Sung, interview, 10 July 1999; 'A new generation of China trade,' *Harvard Business School Bulletin*, May/June 1980, pp. 5–6.

6. Julia Xue, 'Enabling China to enter the 21st century: Chinese-American scholar and entrepreneur C. B. Sung,' in *Chinese in the World: Brief Biographies of the Chinese Entrepreneurs*, Vol. 2 (Beijing: Editorial Committee of the Chinese Entrepreneurs All Over the World, 1994), pp. 159–76 at p. 162; Sung, interview, April 2005.

7. Sung, interview, July 1999. For a detailed narrative of the indispensable role that both Sungs, C. B. in particular, played as both business executives and cultural mediators, see Jim Mann, *Beijing Jeep: A Case Study of Western Business in China* (Boulder, CO: Westview Press, 1997), pp. 38–48.

8. Julia Xue, 'Enabling China,' p. 167.

9. Soon after the economic dialogue, Vasey retired and the Pacific Forum merged with the Atlantic-oriented Center for Strategic and International Studies, where its Asia focus waned. Sung, interview, April 2005; L. R. Vasey, e-mails to the author, 8 and 10 July 2005.

10. See Chapter 1 on HNC. For Sung's involvement with HNC: Patricia Lloyd, telephone interview, Alexandria, Virginia, 11 March 2006; Sung, résumé (Institute files).

11. Xiao-huang Yin and Zhiyong Lan, 'Chinese Americans: a rising factor in U.S.–China relations,' *Journal of American–East Asian Relations*, 6: 1 (1997), pp. 35–7; Norton Wheeler, 'Improving mainland society and U.S.–China relations: a case study of four Chinese American-led transnational associations,' in Peter H. Koehn and Xiao-huang Yin (eds), *The Expanding Roles of Chinese Americans in U.S.–China Relations: Transnational Networks and Trans-Pacific Interactions* (Armonk, NY: M. E. Sharpe, 2002), pp. 185–206.
12. Hang-Sheng Cheng, Curriculum Vitae, 1996 (1990 Institute files); Cheng, e-mail to the author, 12 February 2002.
13. Hang-Sheng Cheng (ed.), *Financial Policy and Reform in Pacific Basin Countries* (Lexington, MA: Lexington Books, 1986); Cheng (ed.), *Monetary Policy in Pacific Basin Countries* (Dordrecht: Kluwer, 1988); Cheng, 'Historical factors affecting China's economic development,' in Hung-chao Tai (ed.), *Confucianism and Economic Development: An Oriental Alternative?* (Washington, DC: Washington Institute Press, 1989), pp. 55–69.
14. Cheng, 'Great Leap Outward?' *FRBSF Weekly Letter*, 5 January 1979, http://www.frbsf.org/publications/economics/letter/1979/el79-01.pdf (accessed 5 August 2008).
15. Cheng, 'China: nation in transition,' *FRBSF Weekly Letter*, 24 October 1980, http://www.frbsf.org/publications/economics/letter/1979/el79-01.pdf (accessed 5 May August 2008).
16. Cheng, 'China: a visitor's report,' *FRBSF Weekly Letter*, 18 January 1985, http://www.frbsf.org/publications/economics/letter/1985/el85-03.pdf (accessed 5 August 2008).
17. Cheng, 'Inflation in China,' *FRBSF Weekly Letter*, 4 November 1988, http://www.frbsf.org/publications/economics/letter/1988/el88-45.pdf (accessed 5 August 2008).
18. Cheng, 'Whither China?' *FRBSF Weekly Letter*, 23 June 1989, http://www.frbsf.org/publications/economics/letter/1989/el89-25.pdf (accessed 5 August 2008).
19. See Chapter 6 for a fuller discussion of the Boxer Indemnity Scholarships.
20. Rosalyn Koo, interview, San Mateo, California, 30 April 2005.
21. Ibid.; Heidi Ross, 'Historical memory, community, hope: reclaiming the social purposes of education for Shanghai McTyeire School for Girls,' in Glenn Peterson, Ruth Hayhoe, and Yongling Lu (eds), *Education, Culture, and Identity in Twentieth-Century China* (Ann Arbor, MI: University of Michigan Press, 2001), pp. 375–402.
22. Rosalyn Koo, e-mail to the author, 26 December 2011. The characterization of the reception is from another attendee: Ezra F. Vogel, *Deng Xiaoping and the Transformation of China* (Cambridge, MA: Harvard University Press, 2011), p. xii.
23. See Chapter 5 for further discussion of Chinese mass organizations and Project Hope.
24. Koo, interview, April 2005; Ross, 'Historical memory.'
25. See Ping-Tsang Chen, 'Chinese fraternities in America,' in Richard Butrick (ed.), *American University Men in China* (Shanghai: American University Club of Shanghai, 1936), pp. 153–64.
26. William M. S. Lee, interview, 30 April 2005, San Mateo, California; e-mail to the author, 6 May 2006. Lee also gave architectural lectures at American universities and in Rome, Italy.
27. B. A. Garside, *One Increasing Purpose: The Life of Henry Winters Luce* (New York: Fleming H. Revell, 1948), pp. 86, 135–6, 173–88.
28. James Luce, interview, San Francisco, 11 July 1999; James Luce, e-mail to the author, 7 May 2006.
29. Luce, interview; Luce, e-mail.
30. Matilda Young, telephone interview, San Francisco, 2 May 2005.
31. Wei-Tai Kwok, telephone interview, San Francisco, 1 May 2005; Kwok, e-mail to the author, 14 July 2006.
32. Wei-Tai Kwok, telephone interview, San Francisco, 1 May 2005; Kwok, e-mail, 14 July 2006.
33. On the relationship between Chinese American history and the history of US–China relations, see: Sucheng Chan, 'Public policy, U.S.–China relations, and the

Chinese American experience: an interpretive essay,' in Edwin G. Clausen and Jack Bermingham (eds), *Pluralism, Racism, and Public Policy: The Search for Equality* (Boston: G. K. Hall, 1981), pp. 5–38; Michael Hunt, *The Making of a Special Relationship: The United States and China to 1914* (New York: Columbia University Press, 1983); Norton Wheeler, 'A civic trend within ethnic transnationalism? Some insights from classical social theory and the Chinese American experience,' *Global Networks*, 4: 4 (October 2004), pp. 391–408.

34. Charles McClain, interview, San Mateo, California, 29 April 2005; McClain, curriculum vitae, http://www.law.berkeley.edu/faculty/profiles/facultyCVPDF.php?facID=76 (accessed 7 May 2006). Among McClain's published writings are: 'In Re Lee Sing: the first residential segregation case,' *Western Legal History*, 3: 2 (1990), pp. 179–96; (with Laurene Wu McClain), 'The Chinese contribution to the development of American law,' in Sucheng Chan (ed.), *Entry Denied: Exclusion and the Chinese Community in America, 1882–1943* (Philadelphia, PA: Temple University Press, 1991), pp. 3–24; *In Search of Equality: The Chinese Struggle Against Discrimination in Nineteenth-Century America* (Berkeley, CA: University of California Press, 1994).

35. 'The birth of the Institute,' *Newsletter: The 1990 Institute*, December 1990, p. 1.

36. Ibid., pp. 1, 4, 5; Sung, interview, 10 July 1999; Hang-Sheng Cheng, interview, San Mateo, California, 10 July 1999. For a more detailed rendition of the formative period of the Institute, see Norton Wheeler, 'Bridging the Pacific: The 1990 Institute and Transnationalism in late-20th Century U.S.–China relations' (MA thesis, University of Kansas, May 2002), pp. 34–112.

37. 'The birth of the Institute'; Sung, interview, 10 July 1999; Cheng, interview, 10 July 1999.

38. For the list of founding honorary co-chairs and the additions of Kennedy and Stevenson, see June 1990 (page 4), September 1990 (page 2), and July 1993 (page 2) issues of *Newsletter: The 1990 Institute*. For Parry's dinner speeches, see: 'Record attendance at First Anniversary Dinner,' *Newsletter*, July 1991, 1; Robert Parry, 'Reflections on China,' *Newsletter*, July 1995, pp. 2, 4–5, 10; Parry, 'Globalization: threat or opportunity?' *Newsletter*, December 2004, pp. 1, 8–10. For Scalapino's dinner speches, see: Robert Scalapino, 'China's foreign relations: perspective for the future,' *Newsletter*, June 1990, pp. 4–7; '"U.S.–China relations": an address by Dr. Robert Scalapino to attendees of The 1990 Institute Sixth Anniversary Dinner,' *Newsletter*, October 1996, pp. 3–4, 8–10. For Stevenson's dinner speeches, see: Senator Adlai E. Stevenson, 'U.S.–China relations: the challenge of a third way,' *Newsletter*, July 1993, pp. 1, 4–6, 11.

39. Luce, interview.

40. Charles McClain, interview, Berkeley, California, 12 July 1999; Minutes of the Meeting of the Executive Committee, 7 February 1994; Minutes, 11 November 1999; *Newsletter: The 1990 Institute*, March 2000, p. 2.

41. For a thoughtful discussion of these problems by a prominent social scientist who was in Beijing in the spring of 1989, see: Craig Calhoun, *Neither Gods Nor Emperors: Students and the Struggle for Democracy in China* (Berkeley, CA: University of California Press, 1994).

42. Wei-Tai Kwok, interview, San Fransisco, 11 July 1999; Rosalyn Koo, interview, South San Francisco, 11 July 1999; Cheng, interview, 10 July 1999. In a partial dissent, Luce saw a silver lining in an otherwise very dark cloud: the fact that the government – perhaps uniquely in Chinese history – 'pondered, contemplated, agonized over whether to use force.' Luce, interview, 11 July 1999.

43. Koo, interview, 11 July 1999. For a detailed analysis of media reporting, see: Wheeler, 'Bridging the Pacific,' pp. 74–7.

44. Koo, interview, 11 July 1999; McClain, interview, 12 July 1999.

45. For a more detailed discussion, see Wheeler, 'Bridging the Pacific,' pp. 114–35.

46. Hang-Sheng Cheng, 'Project 1990: Phase I & Phase II,' *Preliminary Summary Reports on China's Economic Reform*, Issue Paper No. 4, The 1990 Institute, June 1992, pp. 3–6.

47. John Hamilton, 'What is the status of Phase I research?' *Newsletter: The 1990 Institute*, February 1992, p. 2; Matilda Young, 'Publication of the Book for Phase I,' memo to Executive Committee, 5 January 1993 (Institute files).

48. Hang-Sheng Cheng, memo to The 1990 Institute Executive Committee, The 1990 Institute Research Management Committee, and the Asia Pacific Committee, 21 December 1990 (Institute files).

49. Hang-Sheng Cheng, memo to C. B. Sung, 17 May 1992 (Institute files). For further details on the Institute's campaign to win Chinese clearance, see Wheeler, 'Bridging the Pacific,' pp. 97–105.

50. Stephen T. Lee, 'Shanghai and Beijing Conferences: great success,' *Newsletter: The 1990 Institute*, July 1993, p. 8; 'Institute's First Book Presented to President Jiang Zemin and Vice Premier Zou Jia Hua [photo caption],' *Newsletter: The 1990 Institute*, March 1994, p.1.

51. Stacey Bieler, *'Patriots' or 'Traitors'? A History of American-Educated Chinese Students* (Armonk, NY: M. E. Sharpe, 2004), pp. 276–7, 316–22, 357.

52. Hang-Sheng Cheng, memo to Linda Yang, Chairman of Research Management Committee, 'Project 1990 Budget Planning: Phase I and Phase II,' 5 April 1991 (Institute files). Hang-Sheng Cheng, 'All about Project 1990,' in Issue Paper No. 1, The 1990 Institute, August 1991, pp. 7–9 at p. 8.

53. Cheng, 'Project 1990: Phase I and Phase II,' pp. 3–6.

54. Cheng, 'Project 1990 Budget Planning'; Cheng, e-mail to the author, 12 April 2001.

55. Pitman Potter, e-mail to the author, 17 September 2001; James V. Feinerman, fax to Matilda Young, 11 November 1994 (Institute files). Among the works citing Potter are Stanley Lubman, 'The study of Chinese law in the United States: reflections on the past and concerns about the future,' *Washington University Global Studies Law Review*, 2: 1 (2003), pp. 1–35.

56. Charles McClain and Hang-Sheng Cheng, *Chinese Foreign Trade and Foreign Investment Law*, Issue Paper No. 11, 1990 Institute, December 1995; McClain, interview, 12 July 1999.

57. Minutes of the Executive Committee Meeting, 18 August 1993; Minutes of the Executive Committee Meeting, 24 June 1994.

58. Hang-Sheng Cheng, 'Report on my China Trip, October 15 – November 3,' memo to Executive Committee, 10 November 1993 (Institute files).

59. Thomas Mayer, *Should China Tolerate High Inflation?* Issue Paper No. 11, November 1994, 1990 Institute; Wu Jinglian, letter to Hang-Sheng Cheng, reprinted under 'Letters to the Institute,' *Newsletter: 1990 Institute*, December 1994, p. 16.

60. Hang-Sheng Cheng, 'Meeting with Mr. Yao Xitang, September 15,' memo to C. B. Sung, 18 September 1995 (Institute files); Colin Carter, Funing Zhong, and Fang Cai, *China's Ongoing Agricultural Reform* (San Francisco: 1990 Institute, 1996), p. 7.

61. Roy Bahl, telephone interview, Atlanta, 8 December 2005; Xu Shanda, interview, 11 May 2006, Beijing.

62. Hang-Sheng Cheng, letter to Julia Xue, 22 July 1992; Roy Bahl, letter to Hang-Sheng Cheng, 3 September 1992; Chen, letter to Bahl, 30 September 1992 (Institute files).

63. Bahl, letter to Cheng, 9 November 1995 (Institute files).

64. Xu Shanda, fax to Hang-Sheng Cheng, 13 February 1998 (Institute files). See Chapter 4 for a detailed discussion.

65. The foregoing is based on correspondence from the Institute's files, fully documented in Wheeler, 'Bridging the Pacific,' pp. 160–3.

66. Hang-Sheng Cheng, telephone interview, Walnut Creek, California, 30 April 2005.

67. Hang-Sheng Cheng, 'Pension reform,' *Newsletter: The 1990 Institute*, September 2001, pp. 2, 6; Cheng, 'Pension reform in China,' *Newsletter*, May 2002, pp. 2, 6, 8; Keran and Cheng, *International Experience and Pension Reform in China*, Issue Paper No. 16, 1990 Institute, April 2002.

68. The early phase is documented in Wheeler, 'Bridging the Pacific,' pp. 163–7; the collapse of the original plan, in 'Minutes of the Executive Committee,' 1990 Institute, 19 July 2000 and 12 July 2002 (Institute files).
69. Hang-Sheng Cheng, 'Successful conference on state-owned enterprise reform,' *Newsletter: The 1990 Institute*, December 2004, p. 1.
70. Wei-Tai Kwok, interview, 11 July 1999; Kwok, interview, 1 May 2005; Matilda Young, interview, South San Francisco, 11 July 1999.
71. Koo, interview, 11 July 1999; William M.S. Lee, interview, San Francisco, 11 July 1999.
72. Sung, interview, 10 July 1999; '9th Annual Dinner: Speech by 1990 Institute President Hang-Sheng Cheng,' *Newsletter: The 1990 Institute*, March 2000, p. 6; Sung, 'Ultimate volunteerism,' *Newsletter*, March 2004, p. 3.
73. McClain, interview, 12 July 1999.
74. Deng's observation has embedded itself in popular and scholarly discourse about China. 'There are those who say we should not open our windows, because open windows let in flies and other insects. They want the windows to stay closed, so we all expire from lack of air. But we say, "Open the windows, breathe the fresh air and at the same time fight the flies and insects."' Quoted in George J. Church, 'Deng Xiaoping leads a far-reaching, audacious but risky second revolution,' *Time*, 127: 1 (6 January 1986) ['Man of the Year' issue], p. 32.
75. Stephen Lee, 'Protecting China's culture and environment: a crisis in value,' *Newsletter: The 1990 Institute*, December 1994, pp. 4–5.
76. 'Institute to sponsor social ethics contest in China,' *Newsletter*, February 1996, p. 4; Hang-Sheng Cheng, 'Institute to focus on environment, social ethics in newly launched phase of research,' *Newsletter*, October 1996, pp. 1, 10; Matilda Young, 'Social ethics contest in China: a great success,' *Newsletter*, March 1997, pp. 1, 6; *'Social Ethics in China': An Essay Contest Sponsored by The 1990 Institute and the Shanghai Academy of Social Sciences*, Issue Paper No. 13, 1990 Institute, December 1997 [translated into English for The 1990 Institute by Ted Chiao].
77. William M. S. Lee, 'Environmental protection initiative,' *Newsletter: The 1990 Institute*, March 1997, p. 6.
78. Wei-Tai Kwok, 'Institute's environmental initiative gains momentum in China,' *Newsletter*, December 1997, p. 6.
79. Lee, interview, 11 July 1999.
80. '9th Annual Dinner: Speech by 1990 Institute President Hang-Sheng Cheng,' p. 5.
81. Bill Lee, 'The Women, Leadership, and Sustainability Forum story,' *Newsletter: The 1990 Institute*, April 2001, p. 4; Cui Linlin (Director, Foreign Affairs Department, ACWF), interview, Beijing, 12 May 2006.
82. Rosalyn Koo, 'Women, Leadership, and Sustainability: a conference summary,' *Newsletter: The 1990 Institute*, p. 6.
83. Lee, 'The Women, Leadership, and Sustainability Forum Story,' pp. 12–13.
84. Koo, 'Women, Leadership, and Sustainability,' p. 14.
85. Wei-Tai Kwok, 'All-China Women's Federation initiates dialogue with Institute to promote environmental education,' *Newsletter: The 1990 Institute*, December 1997, pp. 1, 6; Lee, interview, 30 April 2005. The formal Chinese sponsor of the ensuing exchanges was the State Environmental Protection Administration (SEPA), but by mutual agreement CNCC did the work for the Chinese side.
86. Lee, interview, 30 April 2005; Lee, e-mail, 17 January 2006; Chen Ying, interview, Beijing, 11 May 2006.
87. Bill Lee, 'US–China Children's Environmental Drawing Project: first phase art competition has begun,' *Newsletter: The 1990 Institute*, May 2002, pp. 3, 11; Billy Lee, 'Winners selected in Children's Environmental Drawing Competition in Beijing,' *Newsletter*, January 2003, pp. 1, 5; Billy Lee, 'Letter to CAEP advisors and contributors,' *Newsletter*, March 2004, pp. 1, 4–5.

88. Billy Lee, 'Letter to CAEP advisors and supporters,' *Newsletter: The 1990 Institute*, December 2004, p. 3, 17; Chen Ying, interview; Marjorie Mader, 'Connecting to China – artists from Hillview Middle School create colorful mural for Beijing Wall,' *The Almanac*, 7 April 2004, http://www.almanacnews.com/morgue/204/204_04_07. china.shtml (accessed 22 June 2005).

89. Chen Ying, interview; Billy Lee, 'The 1990 Institute's C2C-C2C Project: a long-term vision,' *Newsletter: The 1990 Institute*, September 2005, pp. 1, 10.

90. Li Changping, 'The crisis in the countryside,' in Chaohua Wang (ed.), *One China, Many Paths* (London: Verso, 2003), pp. 198–218.

91. Koo, interview, 30 April 2005; Rosalyn Koo and Matilda Young, 'The Dragon Fund: educating for the future,' *Newsletter: The 1990 Institute*, September 2001, pp. 1, 9.

92. Koo and Young, 'The Dragon Fund'; *2000–2001 Annual Report*, The Women's Foundation (San Francisco), p. 21, http://www.womensfoundca.org/atf/cf/%7BF4E8B0D2-94CD-4B29-B9F4-FEE4BA76EAE1%7D/2001_ar.pdf (accessed 19 June 2006).

93. Marsha Vande Berg, 'ACWF hosts Institute delegation in China,' *Newsletter: The 1990 Institute*, May 2002, p. 1, 4–5.

94. *Faces of the West*, CCTV-7 national telecast, 12 June 2002. [Special segment on The 1990 Institute's Dragon Fund project, reproduced by the Institute. Translation by Sonia Ng; voiceover by Johnny Wong, Joanna Lowe, and Rosanna Kwok.]

95. Heidi Ross, 'Providing school for one thousand girls, not one less,' *Newsletter: The 1990 Institute*, March 2004, pp. 7–11; Ross, 'Narrowing China's great divide, one thousand girls at a time,' *Newsletter*, December 2004, pp. 1, 10–15.

96. Ross, 'Narrowing China's great divide.'

97. Matilda Young, 'Dragon Fund Provides new computers for Gansu Province school,' *Newsletter: The 1990 Institute*, January 2003, p. 14. On the history of the school, see: 'Shandan Bailie School,' http://nzchinasociety.org.nz/shandan-bailie-school/ (accessed 2 February 2011).

98. Young, interview, 2 May 2005.

99. Dan Chao, 'The Institute begins a microcredit program in China,' *Newsletter: The 1990 Institute*, March 2008, pp. 2, 11, 17; Chao, 'The Pucheng microfinance program exhibits early success,' *Newsletter: The 1990 Institute*, November 2008, pp. 1, 10; Chao, 'Microfinance program moving along despite global economic recession,' *Newsletter: The 1990 Institute*, September 2009, pp. 6, 16; 'From poverty to Hope' (video), http://1990institute.org/microfinance/intro. The $450,000 figure comes from Wei-Tai Kwok, e-mail to the author, 14 January 2012.

100. Lucille Lee, 'Microfinance program expands and improves more borrowers' lives,' *Newsletter: The 1990 Institute*, September 2010, pp. 1, 14, 21. The quotation is from p. 14.

101. Hang-Sheng Cheng, memo to Research Committee, 5 November 2000 (Institute files); Richard H. Holton, memo to Hang-Sheng Cheng, 1 December 2000 (Institute files); Wei-Tai Kwok, 'Institute convenes high-level symposium to discuss China WTO entry,' *Newsletter: The 1990 Institute*, May 2002, pp. 1, 7.

102. Cheng, interview, 30 April 2005.

103. Charlie Schlangen, 'Wei-Tai Kwok succeeds retiring president, Hang-Sheng Cheng,' *Newsletter: The 1990 Institute*, March 2008, pp. 1, 15.

104. Minutes of the Board of Directors Meeting, The 1990 Institute, 18 February 2011 (Institute files); Wei-Tai Kwok, e-mail to the author, 8 September 2011.

105. On the founding of OYCF, see also Wheeler, 'Improving mainland society.'

106. Overseas Young Chinese Forum, 'Official brochure,' December 2004 (copy provided by C. B. Sung).

107. Bo Li, telephone interview, New York, 16 December 2001.

108. Hao Zou, telephone interview, San Francisco, 22 July 2005. Zou was a founder of OYCF and the only member to attend every annual meeting from 1999 through 2005.

109. 'The 1990 Institute welcomes five new board members,' *Newsletter: The 1990 Institute*, September 2005, pp. 3–4; Wei-Tai Kwok, e-mail to the author, 16 July 2010; Lei Guang, 'The OYCF way,' *Newsletter: The 1990 Institute*, December 2006, pp. 1, 7–11.
110. Zou, interview.
111. Executive Committee Meeting Minutes, The 1990 Institute, 17 November 2001 (Institute files); Cheng, interview, 30 April 2005; Lee, interview, 30 April 2005.
112. 'Announcement of Joint OYCF – The 1990 Institute Research Fellowships,' 15 October 2002 (Institute files).
113. Katherine Xu and Hang-Sheng Cheng, 'A new initiative: the Joint OYCF – The 1990 Institute Research Fellowship Program,' *Newsletter: The 1990 Institute*, January 2003, pp. 2, 5.
114. Katherine Xu and Hao Zou, 'Update on the Institute's collaboration with OYCF,' *Newsletter: The 1990 Institute*, September 2005, pp. 1, 11; 'Research fellowships granted,' *Newsletter*, September 2005, p. 4.
115. C. B. Sung, 'Three-dimensional growth,' *Newsletter: The 1990 Institute*, September 2005, pp. 1, 13.
116. James T. Lorence, 'Organized business and the myth of the China market: the American Asiatic Association, 1898–1937,' *Transactions of the American Philosophical Society*, Vol. 71, Part 4, pp. 88–9.

4 Invited influence in the policy sphere

1. James K. Galbraith, telephone interview, Fort Worth, 6 April 2006. Joseph Stiglitz, *Globalization and Its Discontents* (New York: W. W. Norton, 2002), pp. 66–7, 125–6. Galbraith refers to the advice Jeffrey Sachs and others gave to Russia in the early 1990s to administer the controversial 'shock therapy' of rapid marketization. See Anders Aslund, *How Russia Became a Market Economy* (Washington, DC: Brookings Institution Press, 1995), p. 16–20.
2. Roy Bahl, telephone interview, Atlanta, 8 December 2005.
3. Caroline Haiyan Tong and Hongying Wang, 'Sino-American educational exchanges and public administration reforms in China: a study of norm diffusion,' in Cheng Li (ed.), *Bridging Minds Across the Pacific: U.S.–China Educational Exchanges, 1978–2003* (Lanham, MD: Lexington Books, 2005), pp. 155–75.
4. Ningsha Zhong and Ruth Hayhoe, 'University autonomy in twentieth-century China,' in Glen Peterson, Ruth Hayhoe, and Yongling Lu (eds), *Education, Culture, and Identity in Twentieth-Century China* (Ann Arbor, MI: University of Michigan Press, 2001), pp. 265–75; Ruth Hayhoe, *China's Universities, 1895–1995: A Century of Cultural Conflict* (New York: Garland, 1996), p. 117; Hayhoe, 'Cultural tradition and educational modernization: lessons from the republican era,' in Hayhoe (ed.), *Education and Modernization: The Chinese Experience* (Oxford: Pergamon Press, 1992), pp. 47–72 at p. 57.
5. Chan Hoiman, 'Modernity and revolution in Chinese education: towards an analytical agenda of the Great Leap Forward and the Cultural Revolution,' in Peterson et al. (eds), *Education, Culture, and Identity in Twentieth-Century China*, pp. 73–99; Marianne Bastid, 'Chinese educational policies in the 1980s and economic development,' *China Quarterly*, 98 (June 1984), p. 189; Ruth Hayhoe and Qiang Zha, 'Becoming world-class: Chinese universities facing globalization and internationalization,' *Harvard China Review*, Spring (2004), p. 88.
6. Ka-Ho Mok, 'Policy of decentralization and changing governance of higher education in post-Mao China,' *Public Administration and Development*, 22 (2002), pp. 261–73.
7. Ibid.; Zhong and Hayhoe, 'University autonomy,' pp. 275–88; Wan-hua Ma, *Economic Reform and Higher Education in China*, CIDE Higher Education Occasional Paper No. 2, Center for International and Development Education (CIDE), UCLA Graduate School of Education and Information Studies, July 2003; Terrill

Lautz, 'Higher education in China and Hong Kong,' *Notes from the National Committee*, 25: 1 (Summer 1996), pp. 4, 12–13; Yeguo Qi and Yukun Chen, 'Diversification of sources of funding and innovation in management methods in Chinese universities,' *Current Issues in Chinese Higher Education* (Paris: OECD, 2000), pp. 55–66.

8. Li Wang, 'Higher education governance and university autonomy in China,' *Globalization, Societies and Education*, 8: 4 (November 2010), pp. 477–95.

9. The Hong Kong Museum of History reported 700,200 from 1978 through 2003, as cited in Cheng Li, 'Coming home to teach: status and mobility of returnees in China's higher education,' in Li, *Bridging Minds*, p. 72. Data from the Institute of International Education reflect 719,141 from 2003/4 through 2010/11, 'Open Doors Fact Sheet: China,' http://www.iie.org/en/Research-and-Publications/Open-Doors/Data/Fact-Sheets-by-Country/~/media/Files/Corporate/Open-Doors/Fact-Sheets-2011/Country/China%20Fact%20Sheet%20-%20Open%20Doors%202011.ashx (accessed 12 January 2012). By all (Chinese and American) accounts, roughly one-quarter of the students have returned to China.

10. Kathryn Mohrman, 'Sino-American educational exchanges and the drive to create world-class universities,' in Li, *Bridging Minds*, pp. 219–35 at p. 221.

11. Bastid, 'Chinese educational policies,' pp. 189–92.

12. Ibid., p. 191; Tong and Wang, 'Sino-American educational exchanges,' p. 158.

13. Zhen Tan, 'Internationalization of higher education in China: Chinese-foreign cooperation in running schools and the introduction of high-quality foreign educational resources,' *International Education Studies*, 2: 3 (August 2009), pp. 166–71.

14. Chih-Yung Chien, telephone interview, Baltimore, 16 June 2006.

15. *First Ten Years, First in Asia* (Shanghai: CEIBS, 2004).

16. Quoted in Keith Goodall, M. Warner, and V. Lang, 'HRD in the People's Republic: the MBA "with Chinese characteristics"?' *Journal of World Business*, 39: 4 (2004), p. 319.

17. David B. Southworth, 'Building a business school in China: the case of China Europe International Business School (CEIBS),' *Education and Training*, 41: 6/7 (1999), pp. 325–30.

18. Paul Mooney, 'In a rural Chinese province, an American educational outpost,' *Chronicle of Higher Education*, 52: 24 (17 February 2006), p. A49; Don Lee, 'Chinese school is rah-rah for U.S.-style campus,' *Los Angeles Times*, 4 December 2007, p. C1.

19. Lee, 'Chinese school is rah-rah.'

20. Ian Gow, 'Removing the rose-tinted spectacles,' in Anna Fazackerley (ed.), *British Universities in China: The Reality Beyond the Rhetoric* (London: Agora: Forum for Culture and Education, 2007), pp. 7–9, http://academiccouncil.duke.edu/wp-content/uploads/2008/05/Agora-China-Report1.pdf (accessed 21 March 2008). 'Bridge from China to the world: official opening by Deputy PM,' *Nottingham Alumni Online*, 28 February 2006, http://www.alumni.nottingham.ac.uk/News/news.aspx?newsId=370 (accessed 21 March 2008); Paul Mooney, 'The wild, wild East: foreign universities flock to China, but are there riches to be made, or just fool's gold?' *Chronicle of Higher Education*, 52: 24 (17 February 2006), pp. A46–A49. Xu Jitao, 'Chinese, UK universities team up,' *China Daily, Shanghai & Delta Supplement*, 30 May 2006, p. 2.

21. 'Kean University to open the first American university in China,' Kean University Administrative Report, http://www.kean.edu/publications/2006/AdminReportChina.pdf (accessed 5 June 2010); Eugene McCormack, 'Kean University, based in New Jersey, to open full-scale campus in China,' *Chronicle of Higher Education*, 52: 37 (19 May 2006), p. A46.

22. Nic Corbett, 'Kean plan to branch out with satellite campus in China,' *Star-Ledger*, 22 December 2011, p. 70.

23. Neil Offen, 'Duke breaks ground on new China campus,' *Herald-Sun*, 29 January 2010; Offen, 'Duke's China campus delayed,' *Herald-Sun*, 5 December 2010, p. A1; Lauren Carroll, 'Kunshan campus opening delayed,' *Duke Chronicle*, 16 September 2011, pp. 1, 8; Ian Wilhelm, 'Duke faculty question the University's global ambitions,' *Chronicle of Higher Education*, 4 November 2011, p. A8.

24. Joseph Berger, 'N.Y.U. to establish a degree-granting campus in Shanghai,' *New York Times*, 28 March 2011, p. A19.
25. 'NYU and Shanghai partner to create NYU Shanghai,' 'About NYU,' 27 March 2011, http://www.nyu.edu/about/news-publications/news/2011/03/27/nyu-and-shanghai-partner-to-create-nyu-shanghai.html (accessed 18 Decembeer 2011).
26. 'John Sexton on NYU Shanghai' (interview with Bo Hershey), *zaiShanghai* [in Shanghai], http://www.nyuzaishanghai.org/features/john-sexton-on-nyu-shanghai-in-and-of-the-city-with-a-global-character/ (accessed 18 December 2011).
27. Li Zheng, 'Official opening of New York University, Shanghai,' *China News*, 3 November 2011, http://www.cnreports.info/official-opening-of-new-york-university-shanghai-microblogging-worldwide-admissions-2013/ (accessed 18 December 2011).
28. Gow, quoted in Elizabeth Redden, 'The phantom campus in China,' *Inside Higher Ed*, 12 February 2008, http://www.insidehighered.com/news/2008/02/12/china (accessed 30 December 2011).
29. Oliver Staley and Daniel Golden, 'China halts U.S. college freedom at class door,' *Bloomberg News*, 28 November 2011, http://mobile.bloomberg.com/news/2011-11-28/china-halts-u-s-college-freedom-at-class-door (accessed 30 December 2011). For a collection of thoughtful, nuanced articles on the prospects for American university presence in authoritarian countries, including China, see the forum 'American campuses abroad: promises and perils,' *Chronicle of Higher Education*, 9 December 2011, pp. B6–B14.
30. Blumenthal is quoted in Scott Jaschik, 'Rose-colored glasses on China?' *Inside Higher Ed*, 7 December 2007, http://www.insidehighered.com/news/2007/12/07/china (accessed 30 December 2011).
31. Ian Wilhelm, 'China's new guidelines seek to recharge outmoded and ill-equipped colleges,' *New York Times*, 21 May 2010, p. A23; Wang Yiqing, 'Open up education for reform,' *China Daily*, 25 March 2010, p. 9. The 'transformation' quotation is Wang's summary of Zhang's ideas.
32. Shen Hong, 'Academic freedom and academic duty in Chinese universities,' in *Current Issues in Chinese Higher Education* (Paris: OECD, 2000), p. 28; Li Xiaoping, 'University autonomy in China: history, present situation and perspective,' in *Current Issues in Chinese Higher Education*, pp. 40, 38.
33. Rui Yang, Lesley Vidovich, and Jan Currie, '"Dancing in a cage": changing autonomy in Chinese higher education,' *Higher Education*, 54: 4 (2007), p. 587.
34. Staley and Golden, 'China halts U.S. college freedom at class door.'
35. Elizabeth Knup, interview, Beijing, 28 July 2005.
36. Asian Development Bank (ADB), 'Report and Recommendation of the President to the Board of Directors on a Proposed Loan and Global Environment Facility Grant to the People's Republic of China for the Sanjiang Plain Wetlands Protection Project' (Document RRP: PRC35289), February 2005, http://www.adb.org/Documents/RRPs/PRC/rrp-prc-35289.pdf (accessed 21 March 2008); ADB, 'Technical Assistance (Financed by the Japan Special Fund) to the People's Republic of China for Preparing the Sanjiang Plains Wetland Protection Project' (Document TAR: PRC 35289), November 2002, http://www.adb.org/Documents/TARs/PRC/tar_prc_35289.pdf (accessed 21 March 2008); Bruce G. Marcot, Sergei S. Ganzei, Tiefu Zhang, and Boris A. Voronov, 'A sustainable plan for conserving forest biodiversity in Far East Russia and Northeast China,' *Forestry Chronicle*, 73: 5 (October 1997), pp. 565–71.
37. ADB, 'Technical Assistance,' p. 1.
38. ADB, 'Report and Recommendation,' pp. 2–3; 'Wetland Biodiversity Conservation and Sustainable Use in China – Project Revision,' Government of China United Nations Development Programme (Document CPR/98/G32), April 2005, http://www.wetland-gef-cpr98.org/wetland_english/pro_document_03/R_Document.htm (accessed 21 March 2008).
39. ADB, 'Report and Recommendation,' pp. 4–5.

40. Jin Xiangcan (Chinese Research Academy of Environmental Sciences, Beijing) and Zhai Pingyang (Heilongjiang Environmental Safeguard Science Academy, Harbin), 'Lake Xingkai/Khanka: experience and lessons learned brief,' International Lake Development Committee (Japan, 2006), p. 457, http://www.ilec.or.jp/eg/lbmi/pdf/28_Lake_Xingkai_Khanka_27February2006.pdf (accessed 26 December 2011).

41. Elizabeth Knup, memo to National Committee Staff, re: 'Discussion with Jim Harris, International Crane Foundation,' 9 July 1993 (NCUSCR files).

42. Wanxin Li, 'Looking at the Songhua River incident from an environmental regulatory governance perspective: a long standing issue in China,' *Perspectives* (English edition), Overseas Young Chinese Forum, 7: 1 (March 2006), http://www.oycf.org (accessed 21 March 2008).

43. David M. Lampton, letter to Russell A. Phillips, Jr of Rockefeller Brothers Fund, 7 February 1997 (NCUSCR files).

44. Richard Stone, 'Trans-Pacific alliance draws up ecology plan,' *Science*, 272 (31 May 1996), p. 1260.

45. Peter Riggs, letter to David M. Lampton, 7 March 1999 (NCUSCR files).

46. Marcot et al., 'A sustainable plan,' pp. 565, 569–70.

47. Douglas Murray, telephone interview, New York, 16 August 2005.

48. Ibid.

49. 'UNDP Request [to GEF] for Amendment to GEF Project ["Wetland Biodiversity Conservation and Sustainable Use in China"]' and approval letter by GEF CEO and Chairman, Leonard Good, 7 March, 2005, http://www.thegef.org/gef/sites/thegef.org/files/repository/China_-_Wetland_BD_Conservation___Sust_Use-AMEND-MENT.pdf (accessed 27 July 2006); 'Wetland Biodiversity Conservation and Sustainable Use in China (CPR/98/G32): Project Revision,' http://www.wetland-gef-cpr98.org/wetland_english/pro_document_03/R_Document.htm (accessed 27 July 2006); 'Mainstreaming Wetland Biodiversity Conservation: experience and lessons learned in practical applications of mainstreaming,' http://www.un.org.cn/public/resource/e7774bcdceb9ed784eb221dc624455a7.pdf (accessed 5June 2010).

50. ADB, 'Technical Assistance'; ADB, Report and Recommendation.'

51. The Heilongjiang, or Heilong River, is called the Amur River in Russia. The Ussuri River is one of its major tributaries.

52. 'Request for PDF Block B Approval,' GEF, 14 July 2005, http://www.gefonline.org/ProjectDocs/International%20Waters/Regional%20-%20Integrated%20Manageme nt%20of%20the%20Amur-Heilong%20River%20Basin/07-15-05%20Amur_PDF-B%20for%20review.doc (accessed 19 August 2006). Ampai Harakunarak, Task Manager, GEF-International Waters, Asia and the Pacific Region, GEF, e-mail to the author, 29 December 2011.

53. Jim Harris, telephone interview, Baraboo, Winsconsin, 2 November 2005.

54. Hang-Sheng Cheng, 'China's Economic Reform, 1979–89,' 22 September 1989 (Institute files); Cheng, interview, San Mateo, California, 10 July 1999.

55. Cheng, e-mail to the author, 25 July 2002. For a concurring scholarly interpretation, see: Evert Lindquist, 'Think tanks and the ecology of policy inquiry,' in Diane Stone (ed.), *Banking on Knowledge: The Genesis of the Global Development Network* (London: Routledge, 2000), p. 29.

56. *Chinese Law & Government*, 37: 2 (March–April 2004) [special issue on 'China's Fiscal System in Transition,' edited by Vivian Zhan]; Wang Shaoguang and Hu Angang, *The Chinese Economy in Crisis: State Capacity and Tax Reform* (Armonk, NY: M. E. Sharpe, 2001), pp. 40–50 [this section originally published in *Chinese Economic Studies*, 28: 3 (May–June 1995), pp. 44–53].

57. Hu Angang, 'Background to writing the report on state capacity,' in Wang and Hu, *The Chinese Economy in Crisis*, pp. 185–211[originally written for and published under the same title in *The Chinese Economy*, 31: 4 (July–August 1998), pp. 3–29]. Wang's 1990 article was 'Jianli yige qiangyouli de minzhu guojia: Jianlun "zhengquanxingxi"

yu "guojia nengli" de quibie' ('On establishing a powerful democratic state: on the difference between "governmental form" and "state capacity"').

58. Ibid.
59. The English version comprises the first six chapters of *The Chinese Economy in Crisis*, reprinted from *Chinese Economic Studies*, 28: 3 (May/June 1995) and 28: 4 (July/August 1995).
60. Hu, 'Background,' pp. 194–5.
61. Ibid., pp. 196–7.
62. Ibid., p. 198.
63. Ibid., pp. 198–200. See also Joseph Fewsmith, 'Editor's introduction,' *Chinese Economic Studies*, 28: 3 (May/June 1995), p. 4; State Council, 'Decision concerning the implementation of the tax sharing system,' reprinted in *Chinese Law & Government*, 37:2 (March–April 2004), pp. 41–8.
64. C. B. Sung, interview, San Mateo, California, 30 April 2005; Xu Shanda, interview, Beijing, 11 May 2006; Roy Bahl, interview. Bahl emphasized the term 'principal architect' in describing Xu's role in the 1994 tax reform.
65. Bahl discusses fiscal policy in Chapter 3 (pp. 20–46, with problems summarized on p. 46), tax administration in Chapter 4 (pp. 47–69), and revenue sharing in Chapters 5 and 6 (pp. 70–136 and 137–73).
66. Wang and Hu, *The Chinese Economy in Crisis*, pp. 50–61; Roy Bahl, *Fiscal Policy in China: Taxation and Intergovernmental Fiscal Relations* (South San Francisco: 1990 Institute, 1999), pp. 108–11.
67. Bahl, interview.
68. Xu, interview.
69. Ibid.
70. Hang-Sheng Cheng, letters to Charles McClure, Jr, Christine Wong, Bert Hofman, and Xu Shanda, 31 October 1997; Cheng, memo to [Institute administrative assistant] Jean Crehan, 12 May 1998 (Institute files).
71. Xu Shanda, fax to Hang-Sheng Cheng, 13 February 1998; Xu, fax to Cheng, 22 March 1999; Cheng, memo to Executive Committee, 1 April 1999; Cheng, fax to Xu, 13 April 1999 (Institute files); Cheng, e-mail to the author, 6 February 2002.
72. Hang-Sheng Cheng, memo to Executive Committee, attached to Minutes of 11 January 2000 Executive Committee (Institute files); Sung, interview, 30 April 2005; Xu Shanda, 'Preface of the translator,' in Roy Bahl, *Zhongguo de shuizheng zhengce: shuizhi yu zhongyang ji difang de shuizheng guanxi*, translated by Xu et al. (Beijing: State Administration of Taxation, May 2000), pp. 1–24.
73. Xu, 'Preface of the translator' (translated into English for the author by Zhai Li).
74. Sue Bei, 'Tax reforms target social and economic development,' *China* Daily, 9 January 2006, 2; Xu, interview. In fact, the conversion was complicated. Because it meant ending exemptions for investment, there were short-term implications for economic growth. After nationwide extension of the conversion was postponed in 2005, the reform was restarted in 2007 on a more limited scale. Christine P. W. Wong and Richard M. Bird, 'China's fiscal system: a work in progress,' in Loren Brandt and Thomas G. Rawski (eds), *China's Great Economic Transformation* (New York: Cambridge University Press, 2008), p. 441.
75. Sun Min, '"Honeymoon" tax period for foreign companies may soon be over,' *China Daily*, 13 June 2006, 10; Matthew Mui and Raymond Wong, 'Tax regime change,' *China Business Review*, 35: 2 (March/April 2008), pp. 32–5.
76. Xu, interview.
77. Lingguang Bao, 'China: the characteristics and trend of the new tax system reform,' *Intertax*, 32: 10 (2004), pp. 519–23.
78. Christine Wong, *Can China Change Development Paradigm for the 21ˢᵗ Century? Fiscal Policy Options for Hu Jintao and Wen Jiabao After Two Decades of Muddling Through*, Working Paper FG 7, Research Unit Asia, German Institute for International

and Security Affairs, April 2005, http://www.swp-berlin.org/common/get_document. php?id=1248 (accessed 5 September 2005); Wong and Bird, 'China's fiscal system.'
79. Xu, interview.
80. Xu, 'Preface of the translator.'
81. 'U.S.–China labor law cooperation project,' *Notes from the National Committee*, 33: 1 (Winter/Spring 2005), p. 6.
82. Jan Berris, interview, New York, 12 July 2004.
83. 'U.S.–China labor law cooperation project,' pp. 6–7; Berris, interview, 12 July 2004; Ling Li, (NCUSCR program officer), e-mail to the author, 19 August 2008.
84. Ariana Eunjung Cha, 'New law gives Chinese workers power, gives businesses nightmares,' *Washington Post*, 14 April 2008, pp. A1, 12.
85. 'U.S.–China labor law cooperation project,' p. 7; 'CCTV insight: how will new system change labor inspection?' 3 June 2001, http://english.cntv.cn/program/ china24/20110603/102922.shtml (accessed 16 October 2011).
86. Worldwide Strategies, Asia Foundation, National Committee on U.S.–China Relations, *U.S.–China Labor Law Cooperation Project Final Report, 2002–2007*, 30 September 2007, pp. 26–7; Zhan Lisheng, 'Labor arbitration cases soaring,' *China Daily*, 11 December 2008, p. 5.
87. Masayuki Kobayashi, 'The labor inspection system in China: its role in the labor dispute settlement framework' [summary of research in Japanese], *Annual Report 2008*, Institute of Developing Economies, p. 33, http://www.ide.go.jp/English/Info/ Profile/Nenpo/pdf/2008_all.pdf (accessed 15 October 2011).
88. Robert J. McMahon, 'Diplomatic history and policy history: finding common ground,' *Journal of Policy History*, 17: 1 (2005), pp. 93–109.

5 Nurturing civil society: A joint venture

1. Gordon White, Jude Howell, and Shang Xiaoyuan, *In Search of Civil Society: Market Reform and Social Change in Contemporary China* (Oxford: Clarendon Press, 1996); Qiusha Ma, *Non-Governmental Organizations in Contemporary China: Paving the Way to Civil Society?* (Abingdon: Routledge, 2006); Andrew Watson, 'Civil society in a transitional state: the rise of associations in China,' in Jonathan Unger (ed.), *Associations and the Chinese State: Contested Spaces* (Armonk, NY: M. E. Sharpe, 2008), pp. 14–47.
2. Thomas Gold, 'Bases for civil society in reform China,' in Kjeld Erik Brødsgaard and David Strand (eds), *Reconstructing Twentieth-Century China: State Control, Civil Society, and National Identity* (Oxford: Clarendon Press, 1998), p. 165. Emphasis in original.
3. For a helpful intellectual history of theories of civil society, see Jean L. Cohen and Andrew Arato, *Civil Society and Political Theory* (Cambridge, MA: MIT Press, 1992). The authors summarize the plethora of definitions on p. 75. Dialogue with Martin Sklar has persuaded me of the contemporary scholarly value of the classical definition.
4. Lester Salamon, 'The rise of the nonprofit sector,' *Foreign Affairs*, 73: 4 (July/August 1994), pp. 109–22.
5. Lester M. Salamon and Helmut K. Anheier, 'Social origins of civil society: explaining the nonprofit sector cross-nationally,' *Voluntas: International Journal of Voluntary and Nonprofit Organizations*, 9: 3 (September 1998), p. 216.
6. On trade associations, see: White et al., *In Search of Civil Society*, pp. 184–207. On think tanks, see Barry Naughton, 'China's economic think tanks: their changing roles in the 1990s,' *China Quarterly*, 171 (September 2002), pp. 625–35.
7. Kjeld Erik Brødsgaard, 'State and society in Hainan: Liao Xun's ideas on "small government, big society,"' in Brødsgaard and Strand, *Reconstructing Twentieth-Century China*, pp. 189–215; Chan Kin-man, Qiu Haixong and Zhu Jiangang, 'Chinese NGOs strive to survive,' *Social Transformations in Chinese Societies*, 1 (2005), p. 155; Kin-man Chan and Haixiong Qiu, 'Small government, big society,' *Social*

Organizations and Civil Society in China, China Area Studies Series No. 8 (Tokyo University, 1998), p. 34. As a source for Chen's speech, Chan and his co-authors cite 'Collection of Documents in Registration and Administration of Social Organizations' (in Chinese, unpublished). For an indication that some Chinese intellectuals have a sophisticated understanding of the relationship between statism and social welfare, see an article in English by Tsinghua University historian Hui Qin: 'Small government, big society? What role for the state in the Chinese transition process?' *Social Research*, 73: 1 (Spring 2006), pp. 29–52.

8. Matt Forney, 'Voice of the people,' *Far Eastern Economic Review*, 161: 19 (7 May 1998), p. 12.

9. Elizabeth Economy, 'Interview with Elizabeth Economy: China's development and the environment,' *Harvard Asia Quarterly*, 7: 1 (Winter 2003), pp. 6–8; Jennifer L. Turner, 'Small government, big and green society: emerging partnerships to solve China's environmental problems,' *Harvard Asia Quarterly*, 8: 2 (Spring 2004), pp. 4–13; Elizabeth Knup, *Environmental NGOs in China: An Overview*, China Environment Series 1 (Princeton, NJ: Woodrow Wilson Center, 1997), pp. 9–15; Jonathan Schwartz, 'Environmental NGOs in China: roles and limits,' *Pacific Affairs*, 77: 1 (Spring 2004), pp. 28–49; Fengshi Wu, 'Environmental GONGO autonomy: unintended consequences of state strategies in China,' *Good Society*, 12: 1 (2003), pp. 35–45.

10. Li Fei, 'NGOs getting more prominence,' *China Daily*, 12 April 2005, p. 6. The article quoted Wang Ming, Director of Tsinghua University's NGO Research Center (see below), who called this NGO influence on official policy-making a 'turning point.'

11. 'Chinese environmentalist Liang Congjie on NGO life,' report from the American Embassy in Beijing, February 2000, http://www.usembassy-china.org.cn/sandt/liangNGO.htm (accessed 24 March 2008).

12. Elisabeth Jay Friedman, 'Gendering the agenda: the impact of the transnational women's rights movement at the UN Conferences of the 1990s,' *Women's Studies International Forum*, 26: 4 (2003), pp. 313–31.

13. Jude Howell, 'Post-Beijing reflections: creating ripples, but not waves in China,' *Women's Studies International Forum*, 20: 2 (1997), pp. 235–52.

14. Jude Howell, 'The struggle for survival: prospects for the Women's Federation in post-Mao China,' *World Development*, 24: 1 (1996), pp. 129–43.

15. Shaoguang Wang and Jianyu He, 'Associational revolution in China: mapping the landscapes,' *Korea Observer*, 35: 3 (Autumn 2004), pp. 498–500; Zhang Ye, *China's Emerging Civil Society*, Brookings Institution, Center for Northeast Asian Policy Studies, June 2003.

16. Wang and He, 'Association revolution,' pp. 498–502. Chinese statistics on the number of NGOs in existence are notoriously unreliable, largely because of associations that operate informally or register as enterprises. For other estimates, both higher and lower, see Julia Greenwood Bentley, 'The role of international support for civil society organizations in China,' *Harvard Asia Quarterly*, 7: 1 (Winter 2003), pp. 13–14.

17. Xiong Lei, 'NGOs finally accepted as valuable partners,' *China Daily*, 13 April 2007, p. 10. The author is identified as 'a council member of the China Society for Human Rights Studies,' a government research institution established in 1993.

18. Maureen Fan, 'Citizens' groups step up in China: wary rulers allow role in quake aid,' *Washington Post*, 29 May 2008, pp. A1, 10.

19. See, for example, Keith B. Richburg, 'China reins in nonprofit groups, sparking fears,' *Washington Post*, 11 May 2010, p. A9.

20. Qiusha Ma, *Non-Governmental Organizations in Contemporary China*, pp. 167–200, especially p. 189; Renee Yuen-Jan Hsia and Lynn T. White III, 'Working amid corporatism and confusion: foreign NGOs in China,' *Non-Profit and Voluntary Sector Quarterly*, 31: 3 (September 2002), pp. 329–51; Sun Xiaohua, 'NGO management comes under review,' *China Daily*, 15 December, 2005, p. A2. For a recap of

the evolving legal and regulatory framework for NGOs in China, see Watson, 'Civil society in a transitional state,' pp. 39–41.

21. Nick Young, 'Introduction: NGOs: the diverse origins, changing nature and growing internationalisation of the Species,' in *200 International NGOs in China* (Beijing: China Development Brief, January 2005), pp. 9–39; Nancy Yuan, 'Prepared statement,' in *To Serve the People: NGOs and the Development of Civil Society in China*, Roundtable Before the Congressional-Executive Commission on China, 108th Congress, First Session, 24 March 2003 (Washington, DC: US Government Printing Office, 2003), pp. 38–42.

22. Young, 'Introduction,' p. 36.

23. 'Bilateral donors trim budgets, advance governance, policy agendas,' *China Development Brief*, 7: 1 (Spring 2004), pp. 13–18, http://www.chinadevelopmentbrief.com/node/122/print (accessed 14 January 2007).

24. Howell, 'Post-Beijing reflections'; Ma, *Non-Governmental Organizations*, pp. 180–95; Katherine Morton, 'The emergence of NGOs in China and their transnational linkages: implications for domestic reform,' *Australian Journal of International Affairs*, 59: 4 (December 2005), pp. 519–32.

25. Ma, *Non-Governmental Organizations*, pp. 186–7; Nick Young (ed.), 'Civil society in the making: 250 Chinese NGOs,' *China Development Brief* (August 2001), p. 89.

26. Young, *Civil Society in the Making*, p. 105; Zhao Liqing, *An Historical First Step: The International Conference on Non-Profit Sector (NPO) and Development, July 26–28, 1999 Beijing, China*, Conference Summary, NGO Research Center, Tsinghua University, http://unpan1.un.org/intradoc/groups/public/documents/APCITY/UN-PAN005475.pdf (accessed 24 March 2008); Wang Ming, 'Foreword,' *China Nonprofit Review*, 1: 1 (2009), pp. 1–3.

27. *CIVICUS Civil Society Index Report: China (Mainland)* (Beijing: NGO Research Center, Tsinghua University, April 2006), http://www.civicus.org/new/media/CSI_China_Country_Report.pdf (accessed 24 March 2008). See also CIVICUS's website: http://www.civicus.org/new/default.asp?skip2=yes.

28. Interview with a Chinese editor of *China Development Brief*, 29 July 2005, Beijing; 'About China Development Brief,' 7 October 2005, http://www.chinadevelopment-brief.com/node/260/print (accessed 5 September 2011).

29. Joseph Kahn, 'China orders Western newsletter to halt operations, editor says,' *New York Times*, 12 July 2007, p. A3; Nick Young, 'Message from the Editor,' *China Development Brief*, 10 October 2007, http://www.chinadevelopmentbrief.com/node/508 (accessed 24 March 2008).

30. Shawn Shieh, 'Good news for 2011: starting up China Development Brief (English),' http://ngochina.blogspot.com/2011/01/good-news-for-2011-starting-up-china.html (accessed 5 September 2011); Shawn Shieh, e-mail to the author, 6 August 2011; *China Development Brief (English)* website, http://www.chinadevelopmentbrief.cn.

31. Jonathan Unger and Anita Chan, 'Associations in a bind: the emergence of political corporatism,' in Unger, *Associations and the Chinese State*, pp. 48–68; Yijiang Ding, 'Corporatism and civil society in China: an overview of the debate in recent years,' *China Information*, 12: 4 (Spring 1998), pp. 44–67. For an example of an advocacy association persisting and thriving in the face of government surveillance, see Ngai-Ming Yip and Yihong Jiang, 'Homeowners united: the attempt to create lateral networks of homeowners' associations in urban China,' *Journal of Contemporary China*, 20 (November 2011), pp. 735–50.

32. Tadashi Yamamoto, 'Integrative report,' in Yamamoto (ed.), *Emerging Civil Society in the Asia Pacific Community: Nongovernmental Underpinnings of the Emerging Asia Pacific Regional Community* (Singapore and Tokyo: Institute of Southeast Asian Studies and Japan Center for International Exchange, 1995), pp. 3–5, 26–7; S. Jayasankaran, Margot Cohen, Ben Dolven, Shim Jae Hoon, and Julian Baum, 'Thorns in the flesh: across Asia, grassroots groups test state control,' *Far Eastern Economic Review*, 161: 19 (7 May 1998), p. 15.

33. Liu Haiying, 'The impact of private foundations on domestic NGOs,' *China Development Brief (English)*, Summer 2011 [special issue: 'Philanthropy and Civil Society in China'], http://www.chinadevelopmentbrief.cn/?p=333#more-333 (accessed 10 August 2011); Wang Hui, 'Changes in the development of private foundations,' ibid. For a sophisticated analysis of the pros and cons of the close relationship between Chinese NGOs and the Chinese state, see Yiyi Lu, *Non-Governmental Organizations in China: The Rise of Dependent Autonomy* (London: Routledge, 2009).

34. Marilyn Beach, telephone interview, Houston, 7 February 2005; NCUSCR, 'Final Report to the Henry Luce Foundation: The Civil Society Project,' undated [written in the latter half of 2001 based on internal evidence in the report] (NCUSCR files).

35. William Chang, telephone interview, Beijing, 14 January 2006; Chang, e-mail to the author, 31 December 2006. Chang participated in the Working Group in an unofficial capacity, working on his own time. Late in 2005, the NSF sent him to Beijing on a two-year renewable assignment to head its new office in Beijing which opened in May 2006. See NSF Press Release #06-091, http://www.nsf.gov/news/news_summ.jsp?cntn_id=107006 (accessed 24 December 2006).

36. http://www.iscvt.org; NCUSCR, 'Final Report'; Barbara Felitti, e-mail to the author, 8 November 2005.

37. Felitti, e-mail.

38. Jan Berris, e-mail to the author, 29 December 2011.

39. Zhang Hongyan, interview, Changchun, 16 June 2008.

40. The technical term for the pre-project grant is PDF-B, or Project Development Facility, Block B.

41. Beach, interview; Harris, interview.

42. Harris, interview; 'Saving Wetlands across Eurasia: Inspired by the Siberian Crane,' http://www.scwp.info/documents/Saving%20Wetlands%20Across%20Eurasia.pdf (accessed 29 July 2010); 'Managing Water Wisely to Save Wetlands and Waterbirds,' http://www.thegef.org/gef/node/3052 (accessed 29 July 2010).

43. 'Development of a Wetland Site,' pp. 14–15, 17, 18.

44. Beach, interview. Francesco DiCosmo, telephone interview, Philadelphia, 9 January 2007; Green Communities website: http://www.epa.gov/greenkit/index.htm.

45. DiCosmo, interview.

46. DiCosmo, interview; Wang Shanshan, 'China, US to work together on green issues,' *China Daily*, 2 April 2008, p. 3.

47. Quoted in Jing Lin, 'Private education in China: its development and dynamics,' *Harvard China Review*, 3: 2 (2002), pp. 24–5 (emphasis in the original). On the background of private education in the post-Mao era, see also Jing Lin, Yu Zhang, Lan Gao, and Yan Liu, 'Trust, ownership, and autonomy: challenges facing private higher education China,' *China Review*, 5: 1 (Spring 2005), pp. 61–81.

48. Wang Lanshan, interview, Guiyang, 29 October 2005 (interpreted and translated by Yi Honggen); Wang Liquan, interview, Guiyang, 29 October 2005 (interpreted and translated by Yi Honggen); Wang Liquan and Wang Lanshan, 'Investigation and Research Report on Social Strength Schools in Guizhou Province,' October 1999 (NCUSCR files).

49. Wang and Wang, 'Investigation and Research Report.'

50. Huang Weican, interview, Guiyang, 29 October 2005 (interpreted and translated by Yi Honggen).

51. Wang Dilun, interview, Guiyang, 29 October 2005 (interpreted and translated by Yi Honggen).

52. Ibid.

53. Zhu Weide, interview, Guiyang, 29 October 2005i (interpreted and translated by Yi Honggen).

54. Wang Liquan, interview.

55. Wang Liquan, interview; NCUSCR, 'Report to the Henry Luce Foundation: The Civil Society Project: 1999 Activities,' January 2000 (NCUSCR files).

56. Huang Weican, interview.
57. Frank Kincaid, telephone interview, Beattyville, Kentucky, 21 May 2008.
58. Beach, interview.
59. Daniel Wright, telephone interview, Washington, DC, 1 October 2005.
60. Li Changping, 'The crisis in the countryside,' in Chaohua Wang (ed.), *One China, Many Paths* (London: Verso, 2003), pp. 198–212 at pp. 210–11.
61. Yu Jianrong, 'Let farmers speak for themselves,' *China Development Brief*, 1 July 2003 (translated by Jim Weldon), http://www.chinadevelopmentbrief.com/node/142 (accessed 28 December 2006); Edward Cody, 'For Chinese, peasant revolt is rare victory,' *Washington Post*, 13 June 2005, p. A1; Philip P. Pan, 'Chinese officials retreat in farmland dispute,' *Washington Post*, 22 July 2005, p. A20; Edward Cody, 'In China, crossing the line into activism: seizure of farmland turns peasant woman into protest leader,' *Washington Post*, 12 November 2005, p. A1.
62. Heike Holbig, 'The emergence of the campaign to Open Up the West: ideological formation, central decision-making and the role of the provinces,' *China Quarterly*, 178 (June 2004), pp. 335–57; Xing Zhigang, 'Premier pledges prosperity for all: building of new countryside set to help narrow widening wealth gap,' *China Daily*, 6 March 2006, p. 1; Fu Jing, 'Development focus shifts to rural areas,' *China Daily*, 6 March 2006, p. 1.
63. Edward Cody, 'China reins in rural protests, but not resentment,' *Washington Post*, 19 November 2006, p. A24.
64. Wang Chaogang (ed.), *China: Country Gender Review* (New York: East Asia Environment & Social Development Unit, World Bank, June 2002). For an argument that the gender gap began narrowing again in the 1990s, see: Emily Hannum, 'Market transition, educational disparities, and family strategies in rural China: new evidence on gender stratification and development,' *Demography*, 42: 2 (May 2005), pp. 275–99. For a broader discussion of gender disparities in reform-era China, see Carolyn Cartier, 'Engendered industrialization in China under reform,' in Chia-min Hsieh and Max Lu (eds), *Changing China: A Geographical Appraisal* (Boulder, CO: Westview Press, 2003), pp. 268–90.
65. Suzanne Pepper, 'China's rural education reform: consequences, remedies, prospects,' http://www.usc.cuhk.edu.hk/wk_wzdetails.asp?id=1599 (accessed 22 June 2005).
66. 'China pledges elimination of rural compulsory education charges in two years,' *People's Daily Online* (English Edition), 5 March 2006, http://english.peopledaily.com.cn/200603/05/eng20060305_248042.html (accessed 28 December 2006).
67. 'China pledges elimination.'
68. Cui Linlin, interview, Beijing, 12 May 2006.
69. Elisabeth Rosenthal, 'School a rare luxury for rural Chinese girls,' *New York Times*, 1 November 1999, pp. A1, 10.
70. On NFE, see Liu Jun, 'Rural girls dream the impossible,' *China Daily*, 8 September 2005, p. 14. On the Candlelight Project, see Antoaneta Bezlova, 'Community comes to rural teachers' rescue,' *Asia Times*, 16 November 1999, http://www.atimes.com/china/AK16Ad01.html (accessed 18 June 2006). On RECF and SVRS, see http://www.ruralchina.org (accessed 10 January 2006); Diane Geng, 'Students set out to alleviate "poverty of spirit,"' *China Development Brief*, 7: 2 (Winter 2004/5), pp. 30–3, http://www.chinadevelopmentbrief.com/node/97 (accessed 31 December 2006). On several smaller, all-domestic programs, see Geng, 'Citizen idealists go to school,' *China Development Brief* (July/August 2005), pp. 12–17, http://us.fulbrightonline.org/documents/dgeng.pdf (accessed 31 December 2006).
71. B. Michael Frolic, 'State-led civil society,' in Timothy Brook and B. Michael Frolic (eds), *Civil Society in China* (Armonk, NY: M. E. Sharpe, 1997), pp. 60–1. In 1999, CYDF began to shift some of its organizational resources to environmental issues, launching a forest preservation project. 'Education tops corporate giving list,'

China Development Brief,' 1 April 2000, http://www.chinadevelopmentbrief.com/node/227 (accessed 31 December 2006).

72. Daniel B. Wright, *The Promise of Revolution: Stories of Fulfillment and Struggle in China's Hinterland* (Lanham, MD: Rowman & Littlefield, 2003), pp. 61–7 (Chapter 6, 'Reason to hope: the China Youth Development Foundation').

73. China Youth Development Foundation English-language website, http://www.cydf.org.cn/gb/english/project.htm (accessed 31 December 2006).

74. 'Spring Bud Plan: a helpful hand for rural girls,' *China Daily*, 24 December 2003, http://www.china.org.cn/english/2003/Dec/83214.htm (accessed 31 December 2006). The CCTF website – http://en.cctf.org.cn/-q=node-23.asp – contains minimal information about Spring Bud (as of June 2010), reflecting the fact that this is but one of several of the fund's projects.

75. 'Story of the Spring Bud Girl Class of the Armed Force,' *PLA Daily*, 26 April 2004, http://211.166.76.6/english/pladaily/2004/04/26/20040426001038_China-MilitaryNews.html (accessed 31 December 2006); Yang Cheng, 'Mary Kay enriches women's lives in China,' *China Daily*, 19–20 November 2005, p. S5 (supplement on 'Sino-US Friendship'); 'Spring Bud Plan.'

76. Cui Linlin, interview. See also Emily Hannum and Albert Park, 'Educating China's rural children in the 21st century,' *Harvard China Review*, 3: 2 (Spring 2002), pp. 8–14 (especially pp. 10–11).

77. Rosalyn Koo, interview, San Mateo, California, 30 April 2005.

78. Cui, interview. Cui notes that individuals within China support girls in the Spring Bud program, as they can afford to – she supports two, for example – but rarely does one individual support more than ten.

79. Ibid.

80. Ibid.

81. Koo, interview, April 2005.

82. *Faces of the West* (*Xibu xiezhen*), CCTV-7 newscast, 12 June 2002 (DVD with English voice-over commissioned by The 1990 Institute); *Spring Bud Project: 2004* (produced by AFEWS and ViewAround Inc. for The 1990 Institute, 2004); *Collection of Essays by Students Sponsored under The 1990 Institute's Spring Bud Program*, edited by the Ankang Chapter of the All-China Women's Federation (Ankang: ACWF, 2004).

83. 'I Love My Spring Bud Class,' from *Collection of Essays*.

84. 'My Story,' from *Collection of Essays*.

85. 'Love Enabled Me to Return to School,' from *Collection of Essays*.

86. Ibid.

87. 'Our Warm, Loving Family,' from *Collection of Essays*.

88. 'Father's Transformation,' from *Collection of Essays*.

89. Nick Young and Pia MacRae, 'Three "C"s: civil society, corporate responsibility, and China,' *China Business Review*, 29: 1 (January–February 2002), pp. 34–8. Based on research she conducted in the early twenty-first century, Vivienne Shue says this trend may be reversing, with the state increasingly having both the fiscal and administrative capacity and the political need to provide for social welfare. 'The political economy of compassion: China's "charity supermarket" sage,' *Journal of Contemporary China*, 20 (November 2011), pp. 751–72.

90. Xing Zhigang, 'NGOs can become key social "partner,"' *China Daily*, 13–14 March 2004, p. 3; Fu Jing, 'Institutions take on public services,' *China Daily*, 24 March 2004, p. 1; Qin Chuan, 'Government turns up NGO volume,' *China Daily*, 26 April 2005, p. 5; Wang Zhenghua, 'NGOs win bid for poverty relief: gesture changes governmental role in developing relations with NGOs,' *China Daily*, 22 February 2006, p. 2.

91. *Yige dou bu neng shao* (*Not One Less*), directed by Zhang Yimou (Sony Pictures Entertainment, 1999).

92. *Shang Xue Lu Shang* (literally *On the Road to School*, but distributed with the English title *The Story of Xiaoyan*, meaning *The Story of Young Yan*), directed by Fang Gangliang (Shandong Film Studio, 2004).

93. Alan Riding, 'A Chinese girl's diary builds a bridge out of rural poverty,' *New York Times*, 24 March 2004, p. E3; Guy Dixon, 'The diary of a young girl, a film and a festival fight,' *Globe and Mail*, 24 April 2006, p. R1.

94. Kenneth K. Klinkner, 'Learning one's sums: *Not One Less*,' *News and Reviews* (Asian Educational Media Service, Center for East Asian and Pacific Studies, University of Illinois Urbana-Champaign), 4: 4 (Summer 2001), pp. 6–7, www.aems.uiuc.edu/downloads/Summer2001.pdf (accessed 3 January 2007).

95. A. O. Scott, 'A substitute teacher is put to the test,' *New York Times*, 18 February 2000, p. E24.

96. Heidi Ross, 'Providing school for one thousand girls, not one less,' *Newsletter: The 1990 Institute*, March 2004, p. 7.

97. Valerie Wang, 'Not One Less (Yige dou bu neng shao),' *Cinemaya*, 45 (1999), pp. 20–1.

98. Gang Gary Xu, 'The pedagogical as the political: ideology of globalization and Zhang Yimou's *Not One Less*,' *Communication Review*, 6: 4 (2003), pp. 331, 333.

99. Lan Da, 'After Zhang Yimou's withdrawal from Cannes,' *Chinese Sociology and Anthropology*, 32: 2 (1999–2000), pp. 47–50.

100. Heidi Ross, 'China Country Study,' background paper for the Education for All Global Monitoring Report 2006, *Literacy for Life* (UNESCO, 2005), p. 37. Ross cites the following Chinese government source: Ministry of Education, *2002 Statistical Report on Education* (*2002 nian jiao yu tong ji bao gao*) (Beijing, 2003).

101. Surveys conducted in 2003 and 2007 yielded figures of 7 and 6 percent, respectively. 'The Hopkins-Nanjing Center for Chinese and American Studies Alumni Employment Report for 2004'; 'Employment trends,' *Centerpiece*, Spring 2008, p. 5 (HNC files).

102. 'HNC alumni in the world of NGOs: non-governmental organizations lure,' *Centerpiece*, Winter 2003, 1 (HNC files).

103. Jan Berris, e-mail to the author, 29 December 2011.

104. Chinese alumna #1, e-mail to the author, 14 August 2005.

105. Ying (Isa) Luo, 'Chinese alumni profile,' *Centerpiece*, Spring 2005, p. 4 (HNC files).

106. 'Hopkins-Nanjing Center Annual Report, 2003–2004,' pp. 3–4 (HNC files).

107. Yang Xuedong, interview, Beijing, 16 July 2008.

108. Andrew Watson, interview with Nick Young, *China Development Brief*, 5: 3 (Winter 2002–3), p. 25.

109. Kathleen Hartford and Sarah Cook, interview, Beijing, 26 July 2008; Anthony Saich, e-mail to the author, 31 July 2008; Joseph Fewsmith, 'Democracy is a good thing,' *China Leadership Monitor*, 22, http://media.hoover.org/documents/CLM22JF.pdf (accessed 14 August 2008); Yu Keping, *Democracy Is a Good Thing: Essays on Politics, Society, and Culture in Contemporary China* (Washington, DC: Brookings Institution Press, 2008).

110. Hartford and Cook, interview; Saich, e-mail.

111. The project descriptions are drawn from longer descriptions in the project's biennial, bilingual reports: *Innovations and Excellence in Chinese Local Governance, 2004* (Beijing: IECLG, 2004), pp. 28–9, 32–3; *Innovations and Excellence in Chinese Local Governance, 2005–2006* (Beijing: IECLG, 2006), pp. 42–3; *Innovations and Excellence in Chinese Local Governance, 2007–2008* (Beijing: IECLG, 2008), pp. 20–2.

112. Yang Xuedong, interview; Andrew Watson, e-mail to the author, 28 July 2008.

113. *Innovations and Excellence in Chinese Local Governance, 2007–2008* (Beijing: IECLG, 2008), pp. 4–12.

114. Yang Xuedong, e-mail to the author, 27 July 2008.
115. Bentley, 'The role of international support,' pp. 16, 15.
116. See Nina Glick Schiller, 'Long-distance nationalism,' in Melvin Ember, Carol R. Ember, and Ian Skoggard (eds), *Encyclopedia of Diasporas: Immigrant and Refugee Cultures Around the World.* Vol. I: *Overviews and Topics* (New York: Kluwer, 2004), pp. 570–9.

6 Impacts of educational exchange

1. Anne-Marie Brady, *Making the Foreign Serve China: Managing Foreigners in the People's Republic* (Lanham, MD: Rowman & Littlefield, 2003), pp. 131, 203–4.
2. Huang Fanzhang, interview, Beijing, 28 July 2006.
3. Zheng Bijian, 'China's "Peaceful Rise" to great power status,' *Foreign Affairs*, 84: 5 (September–October 2005), pp. 18–24; Bonnie S. Glaser and Evan S. Medeiros, 'The changing ecology of foreign policy-making in China: the ascension and demise of the theory of "peaceful rise,"' *China Quarterly*, 190 (June 2007), pp. 291–310.
4. Huang, interview.
5. This and the next paragraph are based on my interview with Huang.
6. Huang Fanzhang, 'Analysis of China's New Path of Industrialization from a Global Perspective.' See also a commentary: John Despres, 'Remarks on Huang Fanzhang's Paper.' Both are posted at http://www.rand.org/pubs/conf_proceedings/CF195/ (accessed 10 January 2007).
7. Huang, interview.
8. For a good overview, in addition to the works cited below, see T. K. Chu, '150 years of Chinese students in America,' *Harvard China Review*, 5: 1 (Spring 2004), pp. 7–21, 26.
9. Edward J. M. Rhoads, *Stepping Forth into the World: The Chinese Educational Mission to the United States, 1872–1881* (Hong Kong: Hong Kong University Press, 2011).
10. Michael H. Hunt, 'The American remission of the Boxer Indemnity: a reappraisal,' *Journal of Asian Studies*, 31: 3 (May 1972), pp. 539–59.
11. Stacey Bieler, *'Patriots' or 'Traitors'? A History of American-Educated Chinese Students* (Armonk, NY: M. E. Sharpe, 2004), pp. 17–89, 315–27. The James quotation is from p. 43. The statistics are presented, somewhat obliquely, on pp. 88 and 327. Cheng Li gives the same figure of 1,800 Boxer students in 'Coming home to teach: status and mobility of returnees in China's higher education,' in Cheng Li (ed.), *Bridging Minds across the Pacific: U.S.–China Educational Exchanges, 1978–2003* (Lanham, MD: Lexington Books, 2005), p. 73. See also Weili Ye, *Seeking Modernity in China's Name: Chinese Students in the United States, 1900–1927* (Stanford, CA: Stanford University Press, 2001); Chu, '150 years,' pp. 7–22.
12. See Charles W. Hayford, *To the People: James Yen and Village China* (New York: Columbia University Press, 1990); Barry Keenan, *The Dewey Experiment in China: Educational Reform and Political Power in the Early Republic* (Cambridge, MA: Harvard University Press, 1977), pp. 129–52; Ceferina G. Hess, 'Reflections on America's "love affair" with Madame Chiang Kai-Shek from 1927 to 1950,' *National Social Science Journal*, 23: 1 (2004), pp. 43–55. For the careers of other important, if less famous, returnees of the Republican period, see Zhang Yufa, 'Returned Chinese students from America and the Chinese leadership (1846–1949),' *Chinese Studies in History*, 35: 3 (Spring 2002), pp. 52–86.
13. Xiao Hong Shen, 'Yale's China and China's Yale'; He Di, 'Yenching University and educational modernization in China,' in Priscilla Roberts (ed.), *Sino-American Relations Since 1900* (Hong Kong: Centre of Asian Studies, University of Hong Kong, 1991), pp. 82–93.

14. Mary Brown Bullock (former director of CSCPRC), 'Mission accomplished: the influence of the CSCPRC on educational relations with China,' in Li, *Bridging Minds*, pp. 53–4.
15. Chu, '150 years,' p. 7.
16. Deng Xiaoping, *Deng Xiaoping wenxuan* (*Selected Works of Deng Xiaoping*), Vol. 2, 2nd edn (Beijing: Renmin chubanshe, 1994), p. 132, cited in Caroline Haiyan Tong and Hongying Wang, 'Sino-American educational exchanges and public administration reforms in China: a study of norm diffusion,' in Li, *Bridging Minds*, p. 157.
17. For the calculation, see note 9, Chapter 4.
18. Cheng Li, 'Bringing China's best and brightest back home: regional disparities and political tensions,' *China Leadership Monitor*, 11 (September 2004), http://www.hoover.org/publications/clm/issues/2904206.html (accessed 23 February 2007).
19. Fei-Ling Wang, 'Balancing the cross-Pacific exchange: American study-abroad programs in the PRC,' in Li, *Bridging Minds*, pp. 177–200 at pp. 181–2.
20. See, for example, Guangqiu Xu, 'The ideological and political impact of U.S. Fulbrighters on Chinese students: 1979–1989,' *Asian Affairs: An American Quarterly*, 26: 3 (Fall 1999), pp. 139–57; Ning Qian, *Chinese Students Encounter America* (Seattle, WA: University of Washington Press, 2002); David Zweig and Stanley Rosen, *China's Brain Drain to the United States: Views of Overseas Chinese Students and Scholars in the 1990s* (Berkeley, CA: Institute of East Asian Studies, University of California Press, 1995); Stanley Rosen and David Zweig, 'Transnational capital: valuing academic returnees in a globalizing China,' in Li, *Bridging Minds*, pp. 111–32; seven special issues of *Chinese Education & Society* – 31: 2 (March–April 1993), 33: 5 (September–October 2000), 34: 3 (May–June 2001), 36: 2 (March–April 2003), 36: 4 (July–August 2003), 37: 2 (March–April 2004), and 38: 3 (May–June 2005).
21. Wang Anhu, 'The ferry,' *Nanda News*, 25 September 1996, p. 2.
22. Daniel B. Wright, 'Hopkins-Nanjing alumni in a globalizing China: grand vision, one student at a time,' *SAISPHERE*, 2000, pp. 32–3.
23. Han told a US Congressional committee that the Center experience helped prepare him for work in an international environment. 'Testimony from Hopkins-Nanjing Center Alumni,' appended to Carla Freeman, 'Written Testimony Submitted by the Hopkins-Nanjing Center, Johns Hopkins University, Fiscal Year 2012,' *State, Foreign Operations, and Related Programs Appropriations for 2012: Hearings before a Subcommittee of the Committee on Appropriations on State Foreign Operation, and Related Programs*, 112th Congress, 1st sess, 14 April 2011, pp. 602–3. According to Wang Zhigang, the Center's first Chinese co-director, Chen 'audited a course or two at the Center in its first academicyear but was never a regular student.' Wang, e-mail to the author, 13 November 2011.
24. 'Alumni Employment Report 1986–2001' and 'Alumni Employment Report 2004,' Hopkins-Nanjing Center for Chinese and American Studies (HNC files); Carolyn Townsley, telephone interview, Baltimore, 15 August 2011.
25. Ren Donglai, interview, Nanjing, 24 July 2005.
26. Kindra Tulley, telephone interview, Washington, DC, 22 January 2006.
27. Milo Manley, interview, Nanjing, 20 December 2005.
28. Ida Relsted, 'With rhyme and reason,' *China Daily*, 11 January 2008, p. 19.
29. 'Catalog for 1986–1987'; 'Catalog 1994–95'; '2005–2006 Annual Report' (HNC files).
30. Robert Daly, interview, Nanjing, 10 June 2005.
31. The quotations are from Dale Krieger, 'Reconcilable differences,' *Johns Hopkins Magazine*, June 1996, p. 25. For several detailed American critiques from the first two years, see Hamburger Archives, RG 07.270, sq 1, s 3, b 2, 'Critiques.'
32. Hua Tao, interview, Nanjing, 24 July 2005.

33. Tulley, interview.
34. Kathryn Gonnerman, telephone interview, Brattleboro, Vermont, 3 April 2007. Dan Murphey, 2007 alumnus, became a program officer at the National Committee. 'Alumni Class Notes,' *Centerpiece*, Fall 2009, p. 8 (HNC files).
35. Daniel Wright, telephone interview, Washington, DC, 1 October 2005.
36. Kenneth Jarrett, interview, Shanghai, 13 January 2006.
37. Diana Wang, interview, Nanjing, 10 June 2005; Pen-Pen Chen, interview, Nanjing, 10 June 2005.
38. Diana Wang, interview; Pen-Pen Chen, interview.
39. Christi Caldwell, 'International alumni profile,' *Centerpiece*, Winter 2004, p. 4. When the United States switched diplomatic recognition from Taipei to Beijing in 1979, the island government established the Taipei Economic and Cultural Office to represent its interests in Washington.
40. Roseanne Freese, interview, Washington, DC, 9 September 2005.
41. Freese, interview.
42. Peter Wonacott, telephone interview, Delhi, 17 January 2008.
43. Hua Tao, interview.
44. Ren Donglai, interview.
45. Ren Donglai, interview. Later, during the 1992–3 academic year, Ren was a visiting scholar at the University of North Carolina, where he had the opportunity to work closely with Michael Hunt, a specialist in US–China diplomatic history.
46. Kenneth Louie, telephone interview, Erie, Pennsylvania, 18 January 2006.
47. William Anderson, interview, Nanjing, 25 September 2005. See also Vincent A. Auger and L. Marvin Overby, 'Teaching and learning in Nanjing: community, communities, and politics in an overseas program,' *Journal of Political Science Education*, 1: 2 (May–August 2005), pp. 233–47.
48. Chinese alumnus #1, interview, Nanjing, 10 June 2005.
49. Chinese alumnus #2, interview, Shanghai, 12 November 2005.
50. Xiaoqing Wang, telephone interview, Ontario, California, 4 August 2011.
51. Jin Chunqing, 'Chinese alumni profile,' *Centerpiece*, Fall 2004, p. 3 (HNC files).
52. Chinese alumnus #2, interview.
53. Chinese alumna #2, telephone interview, Beijing, 15 May 2006.
54. For a sample itinerary, see Appendix.
55. Fred Strebeigh, 'Training China's new elite,' *Atlantic Monthly*, 263: 4 (April 1989), pp. 72, 74.
56. Ibid., p. 80.
57. 'Scholar program reunion a big hit in Beijing,' *Notes from the National Committee*, 22: 2 (Summer 1993), p. 8.
58. In 2006, the author conducted a mail survey of SOP participants for 1997–2001. Twenty-one of 61 responded (China's post office returned six surveys as undeliverable).
59. SOP participant #6.
60. SOP participant #8.
61. SOP participant #13.
62. SOP participant #6.
63. SOP participant #14.
64. TEP participant #2.
65. SOP participant #5.
66. SOP participant #6.
67. SOP participant #7.
68. SOP participant #8 became a close friend when we studied together at the University of Kansas and we have maintained contact.
69. 'Time Warner establishes internship program for students at China's Fudan University,' Time Warner press release, 14 September 1998, http://www.timewarner.com/newsroom/press-releases/1998/09/Time_Warner_Establishes_Internship_Program_for_Students_09-14-1998.php (accessed 18 May 2011).

70. Ibid.
71. Peter Wolff, telephone interview, New York, 3 April 2007.
72. The National Committee provided me with 26 reports, from 1998 through 2003. In the discussion that follows, I assign numbers to the interns I cite, using the lower numbers for the earlier years.
73. Time Warner interns #1 and #8.
74. Time Warner intern #10.
75. Time Warner intern #21. The CECC is a watchdog agency, co-commissioned by the executive and congressional branches of the US government, that conducts research and hearings and issues reports on all aspects of China's foreign and domestic policies.
76. Time Warner intern #24.
77. Time Warner intern #13.
78. Time Warner intern #8.
79. Time Warner intern #10.
80. Time Warner interns #26 and #23.
81. Time Warner intern #23.
82. Time Warner intern #19.
83. Time Warner intern #20.
84. Time Warner intern #21.
85. Time Warner intern #15.
86. Time Warner intern #6.
87. Time Warner intern #13.
88. Time Warner intern #17.
89. Time Warner intern #7.
90. Time Warner intern #17.
91. Time Warner intern #18. Bush had said, 'Life in America shows that liberty, paired with law is not to be feared. In a free society, liberty is not disorder. Debate is not strife. And dissent is not revolution.' http://georgewbush-whitehouse.archives.gov/news/releases/2002/02/20020222.html (accessed 31 May 2011). Intern #19 also used Bush's speech as a way of reflecting on this demonstration.
92. Time Warner intern #22.
93. Time Warner intern #14.
94. 'Time Warner Internship Program – Contact List,' National Committee on US–China Relations, 21 February 2006 (NCUSCR files).
95. *Perspectives*, 1: 1 (August 1999).
96. Ibid.
97. Bo Li, 'Republicanism and democracy,' *Perspectives*, 1: 2 (October 1999).
98. 'Yanghang queding chengli huobi zheng ce er si' ('Central bank decides to establish second monetary policy bureau'), *Caijing* (*Finance and Economics*), 30 October 2009, http://www.caijing.com.cn/2009-10-30/110299012.html (accessed 6 July 2010).
99. See Zhou's faculty page: http://www.gsb.pku.edu.cn/content.asp?id=90 (accessed 24 April 2008).
100. Although his article in issue 1: 1 does not list his Harvard affiliation, the announcement of his earlier participation at the first annual retreat in April 1999 does: http://www.oycf.org/Retreats/1999.htm (accessed 11 March 2007). For his subsequent return to his former position at Zhongshan University, see Zhan Lisheng, 'Local gov't tries to curb commercial bribery,' *China Daily*, 19 July 2006, p. 3.
101. Randall Peerenboom, 'China and the Rule of Law: Part 1,' *Perspectives*, 1: 5 (April 2000); Peerenboom, 'China and the Rule of Law: Part 2,' *Perspectives*, 1: 6 (June 2000).
102. Bo Li, 'What is the rule of law?' *Perspectives*, 1: 5 (April 2000); Li, 'What is constitutionalism?' *Perspectives*, 1: 6 (June 2000); Li, 'Constitutionalism and the rule of law,'

Perspectives, 2: 1 (August 2000); Li, 'What is law?' *Perspectives*, 2: 4 (February 2001); Yingyi Qian, 'The modern market economy and the rule of law,' *Perspectives*, 2: 4 (February 2001).

103. See Qian's faculty profile: http://elsa.berkeley.edu/~yqian/cvqian.pdf (accessed 25 April 2008).

104. Dongsheng Zang, 'Seeking transparency in antidumping actions through procedural review: the GATT/WTO jurisprudence and its implications for China (Part 1),' *Perspectives*, 2: 5 (April 2001); Zang, 'Seeking transparency … (Part 2),' *Perspectives*, 2: 6 (June 2001). See also Xiaowen Qiu, 'How Chinese laws regulate tender offers for the stock of public companies,' *Perspectives*, 3: 1 (August 2001); Yee Sze Thian, 'Independence of the board of directors and globalization of China's corporations: lessons in effective corporate governance,' *Perspectives*, 6: 2 (June 2005).

105. University of Washington faculty profile: http://www.law.washington.edu/Directory/Profile.aspx?ID=189 (accessed 25 April 2008).

106. Richard Dworkin, 'Taking rights seriously in Beijing,' *Perspectives*, 3: 7 (December 2002) [originally published in *The New York Review of Books*, 26 September 2002].

107. Liufang Fang, 'Taking academic games seriously,' *Perspectives*, 3: 7 (December 2002); Yanan Peng, 'Taking Dworkin seriously,' *Perspectives*, 4: 1 (March 2003).

108. Li-an Zhou, 'The role of ideology in China's economic reform,' *Perspectives*, 1: 1 (August 1999).

109. Yingyi Qian, 'Goal and process,' *Perspectives*, 2: 2 (October 2000); Jianfu Yao, 'Dogmatism + remnant feudalism = catastrophe: thoughts on the tragedy of Chayanov,' *Perspectives*, 1: 2 (October 1999).

110. Zhiyuan Cui, 'How did Nanjie Village overcome the free-rider problem?' *Perspectives*, 2: 1 (August 2000); Jiquan Xiang, 'The Nanjie model and its vitality,' *Perspectives*, 2: 1 (August 2000).

111. Zhiyuan Cui, faculty page, http://www.cui-zy.cn/ (accessed 26 July 2011).

112. Jiquan Xiang, telephone interview (conducted for the author by Yi Honggen), Wuhan, 9 June 2010.

113. Li-an Zhou, 'Grabbing hand vs. enabling hand: a comparison of China and Japan in response to the West in late 19th century,' *Perspectives*, 1: 3 (December 1999); Jin Chen, 'Japan: the thinking of the early Meiji leaders,' *Perspectives*, 1: 1 (August 1999); Yu Liu, 'Russia's fall, China's rise? – comparing transitions of Russia and China (Part 1),' *Perspectives*, 2: 5 (April 2001); Liu, 'Russia's fall, China's rise? … (Part 2),' *Perspectives*, 2: 6 (June 2001).

114. Author information, Jin Chen, 'China's financial system: an evaluation and some recommendations,' *Perspectives*, 7: 4 (December 2006); speaker information, panel announcement, '13th Overseas Young Chinese Forum Annual Conference, St Lawrence University: Debating the China Model, May 13–15, 2001,' http://www.oycf.org/oycf_annual_2011.pdf (accessed 27 July 2011).

115. Tsinghua University faculty profile: http://www.tsinghua.edu.cn/publish/psen/2597/2010/20101224143723906872056/20101224143723906872056_.html (accessed 27 July 2011). Book information: Didi Kirsten Tatlow, 'Writing odes to America, flaws and all,' *International Herald Tribune*, 1 October 2010, p. 2 [also published in *New York Times*, online edition, under title 'Chinese writers give a warmer take on U.S. democracy,' *New York Times*, 30 September 2010, http://www.nytimes.com/2010/10/01/world/asia/01iht-letter.html (accessed 27 July 2011)]; Han Bingbin, 'Reading on the way up,' *China Daily*, 16 June. Summer fellow announcement: http://cisac.stanford.edu/docs/AB40F2870ccbb19595kJU194C067-556 (accessed 27 July 2011).

116. Cheng Li, 'The status and characteristics of foreign-educated returnees in the Chinese leadership,' *China Leadership Monitor*, 16 (Fall 2005), p. 1, http://www.hoover.org/publications/clm/issues/2898976.html (accessed 5 June 2010).

117. 'Industrialization on track: report,' *China Daily*, 29 January 2007, p. 3. The quotation is from the article and is probably a summary of the report's conclusions.
118. Cited in Fu Jing, 'China may become scientific superpower: returnee scientists, more funds helping development, report says,' *China Daily*, 18 January 2007, p. 4.
119. Robert S. Greenberger and Ian Johnson, 'Chinese who studied in U.S. undercut dogmas at home,' *Wall Street Journal*, 3 November 1997, p. A24. See also Elizabeth Bukowski, 'A Western virus among China's leaders,' *Wall Street Journal*, 19 June 1997, p. A18.
120. Cheng Li, 'Introduction: open doors and open minds,' in Li, *Bridging Minds*, pp. 1–24.
121. Li, 'Bringing China's best and brightest back home,' p. 2; Li, 'The status and characteristics,' pp. 15–18.
122. Douglas Murray, telephone interview, New York, 15 August 2005; David M. Lampton, interview, Washington, DC, 9 September 2005.

Conclusion

1. Tony Smith and Richard C. Leone, *America's Mission: The United States and the Worldwide Struggle for Democracy in the Twentieth Century* (Princeton, NJ: Princeton University Press, 1994), especially pp. 84–110.
2. Martin J. Sklar, 'The open door, imperialism, and postimperialism: origins of U.S. twentieth-century foreign relations, circa 1900,' in David G. Becker and Richard L. Sklar (eds), *Postimperialism and World Politics* (Westport, CT: Praeger, 1999), pp. 317–36. Pages 331–6 develop this argument, and the quotation is from p. 333.
3. Kendall W. Stiles, 'Grassroots empowerment: states, non-state actors and global policy formation,' in Richard A. Higgott, Geoffrey R.D. Underhill and Andreas Bieler (eds), *Non-State Actors and Authority in the Global System* (New York: Routledge, 2000), pp. 32–4; Kim D. Reimann, 'A view from the top: international politics, norms and the worldwide growth of NGOs,' *International Studies Quarterly*, 50: 1 (2006), pp. 45–67.
4. See, for example, Shirley Garrett, *Social Reformers in Urban China: The Chinese Y.M.C.A., 1895–1926* (Cambridge, MA: Harvard University Press, 1970); Ernest R. May and John K. Fairbank (eds), *America's China Trade in Historical Perspective: The Chinese and American Performance* (Cambridge, MA: Harvard University Press, 1986); James C. Thomson, Jr, *While China Faced West: American Reformers in Nationalist China, 1928–1937* (Cambridge, MA: Harvard University Press, 1969); Renqiu Yu, *To Save China, To Save Ourselves: The Chinese Hand Laundry Alliance of New York* (Philadelphia, PA: Temple University Press, 1992).
5. Douglas P. Murray, *America's Interests in China's Environment*, China Policy Series No. Six, National Committee on US–China Relations, 1993, p. 1.
6. Xiao Hong Shen, 'Yale's China and China's Yale: Americanizing Higher Education in China, 1900–1927' (PhD dissertation, Yale University, 1993), pp. 320–6, 337; Dong Wang, *Managing God's Higher Learning: U.S.–China Cultural Encounter and Canton Christian College (Lingnan University), 1888–1952* (Lanham, MD: Lexington Books, 2007); Philip West, *Yenching University and Sino-Western Relations, 1916–1952* (Cambridge, MA: Harvard University Press, 1976), pp. 195–214.
7. Garrett, *Social Reformers in Urban China*, p. 164–80; Thomson, *When China Faced West*, pp. 160–9, 242–4; Daniel H. Bays, *A New History of Christianity in China* (New York: Wiley-Blackwell, 2011), pp. 160–6; 'History of YMCA Work in China,' Kautz Family YMCA Archives, http://special.lib.umn.edu/findaid/html/ymca/yusa0009x2x4.phtml#a2h (accessed 12 August 2011).
8. Mary Brown Bullock, *An American Transplant: The Rockefeller Foundation & Peking Union Medical College* (Berkeley, CA: University of California Press, 1980), p. 8.

9. Arthur Rosenbaum, 'Yenching University and Sino-American interactions, 1919–1952,' *Journal of American-East Asian Relations*, 14, Issues 1–4 (2007), pp. 11–60.

10. Bullock, *An American Transplant*, p. 8; Rosenbaum, 'Yenching University,' p. 14.

11. Bullock, *An American Transplant*, p. 37.

12. Thomson, *While China Faced West* pp. 4–5, 14–15; Bullock, *An American Transplant*, p. 139.

13. Randall E. Stross, *Stubborn Earth: American Agriculturalists on Chinese Soil, 1898–1937* (Berkeley, CA: University of California Press, 1986), pp. 59–65; Samuel C. Chu, *Reformer in Modern China: Chang Chien, 1853–1926* (New York: Columbia University Press, 1965), pp. 144–61.

14. Zhang Tingxi, 'Zhang Jian and the Dutch engineer, Hendrik De Rijke' (article in Chinese, abstract in English), Zhang Jian Research Institute of Nantong University, http://zjyjnt.com.cn/show.asp?id=154 (accessed 5 September 2011); Zhang Xuwu, 'Cherish the memory of Hendrik Christian de Rejke [*sic*] forever' (*Yongyuan huainian Henglike telai Ke xiansheng*) (Nantong: Zhang Jian Foundation Management Committee, 2005). Peer De Rijke provided me with a copy of the latter, a 29-page bilingual pamphlet written by Zhang Jian's grandson. The document most likely is available at the Zhang Jian Research Institute in Nantong.

15. Alan Bullock and Oliver Stallybrass (eds), *The Harper Dictionary of Modern Thought* (New York: Harper & Row, 1977), p. 303.

16. For surveys of the scholarly career of 'cultural imperialism' and analyses that accord, in terms of critique, with much that is said here, see Ryan Dunch, 'Beyond cultural imperialism: cultural theory, Christian missions, and global modernity,' *History and Theory*, 41: 3 (October 2002), pp. 301–25; Jessica C. E. Gienow-Hecht, 'Cultural imperialism,' *Encyclopedia of American Foreign Policy*, 2nd edn, Vol. 1 (New York: Charles Scribner's Sons, 2001), pp. 397–408.

17. Victoria de Grazia, *Irresistible Empire: America's Advance Through 20th Century Europe* (Cambridge, MA: Belknap Press of Harvard University Press, 2005), pp. 6–9.

18. D. Parthasarathy, 'From white man's burden to good governance: economic liberalization and the commodification of law and ethics,' in Bernd Hamm and Russell Smandych (eds), *Cultural Imperialism: Essays on the Political Economy of Cultural Domination* (Ontario, Canada: Broadview Press, 2005), p. 198; Susantha Goonatilake, 'Cultural imperialism: a short history, future, and a postscript from the present,' ibid., p. 47.

19. Bradley R. Simpson, *Economists with Guns: Authoritarian Development and U.S.–Indonesian Relations, 1960–1968* (Stanford, CA: Stanford University Press, 2008), pp. 18–23, 256–9.

20. Guangqiu Xu, 'Anti-Western nationalism in China, 1989–99,' *World Affairs*, 163: 4 (Spring 2001), pp. 151–62; [Our Commentator,] 'Should or should we not guard against and resist cultural colonialism?' *Chinese Sociology and Anthropology*, 31: 4 (Summer 1999) [Special Issue: 'The Contention in China over "Cultural Colonialism"'], pp. 23–35.

21. James H. Mittelman, 'Globalization and development: learning from debates in China,' *Globalizations*, 3: 3 (September 2006), p. 388.

22. Pieter Bottelier, 'China and the World Bank: how a partnership was built,' *Journal of Contemporary China*, 16 (May 2007), pp. 242, 247.

23. Gregory Chow, 'The teaching of modern economics in China,' *Comparative Economic Studies*, 42: 2 (Summer 2000), pp. 51–60.

24. Marianne Bastid, 'Chinese educational policies in the 1980s and economic development,' *China Quarterly*, 98 (June 1984), pp. 189–219.

25. Elizabeth Economy, 'Chinese policy-making and global climate change: two-front diplomacy and the international community,' in Miranda A. Schreurs and Elizabeth Economy (eds), *The Internationalization of Environmental Protection* (Cambridge, UK: Cambridge University Press, 1997), pp. 19–41.

26. Qingshan Tan, 'Foreign NGOs' role in local governance in China,' in Zheng Yongnian and Joseph Fewsmith (eds), *China's Opening Society: The Non-State Sector and Governance* (London: Routledge, 2008), pp. 196–222.

27. William Wan, 'Abstinence program in China a milestone for U.S. evangelicals,' *Washington Post*, 3 September 2010, p. A1.

28. John King Fairbank (ed.), *The Missionary Enterprise in China and America* (Cambridge, CA: Harvard University Press, 1974); Frank Ninkovich, *U.S. Information Policy and Cultural Diplomacy*, Headline Series No. 308 (New York: Foreign Policy Association, 1996); Liping Bu, *Making the World Like Us: Education, Cultural Expansion and the American Century* (Westport, CT: Praeger, 2003); Frank Ninkovich and Liping Bu (eds), *The Cultural Turn: Essays in the History of U.S. Foreign Relations* (Chicago: Imprint Publications, 2001).

29. Mary Brown Bullock, 'Mission accomplished: the influence of the CSCPRC on educational relations with China,' in Cheng Li (ed.), *Bridging Minds Across the Pacific: US–China Educational Exchanges, 1978–2003* (Lanham, MD: Lexington Books, 2005), pp. 49–68 at pp. 60–1.

30. Agency for International Development, American Schools and Hospitals Abroad, Program Criteria, *Federal Register*, 44: 228 (26 November 1979), reproduced (as of 17 October 2011) at http://www.usaid.gov/our_work/cross-cutting_programs/asha/criteria.html.

31. Carla Freeman, 'Written Testimony Submitted by the Hopkins-Nanjing Center, Johns Hopkins University, Fiscal Year 2012,' *State, Foreign Operations and Related Programs Appropriations for 2012: Hearings before a Subcommittee of the Committee on Appropriations on State Foreign Operations, and Related Programs*, 112th Congress, 1st sess, 14 April 2011, p. 601.

32. Report [To accompany H.R. 2939], Foreign Operations, Export Financing, and Related Programs Appropriations Bill, 1990, Committee on Appropriations, United States House of Representatives, One Hundred First Congress, First Session, 14 September 1989 (Washington, DC: US Government Printing Office, 1989), pp. 119–20 (brackets in original).

33. 'Another U.S. Deficit – China and America – Public Diplomacy in the Age of the Internet,' A Minority Staff Report, prepared for the Use of the Committee on Foreign Relations, United States Senate, One Hundred Twelfth Congress, First Session, 15 February 2011 (Washington, DC: US Government Printing Office, 2011), pp. 5, 13.

34. Ibid., 15.

35. For 2010, the most recent data available, US government grants accounted for $521,215, 13 percent of the organization's $4,020,415 in 'support and revenue.' 'Statement of Financial Position,' *Annual Report 2009*, National Committee on United States–China Relations, p. 23.

36. Interview by Robert Amerson with Robert L. Nichols, Association for Diplomatic Studies and Training Foreign Affairs Oral History Project, 13 September 1996, http://memory.loc.gov/ammem/collections/diplomacy/diploquery.html (accessed 5 April 2007).

37. Jan Berris, interview, New York, 12 July 2004.

38. Jan Berris, telephone interview, New York, 7 April 2007.

39. Berris, interview, 12 July 2004.

40. Berris, interview, 12 July 2004; Steven Mufson, 'Abroad at home: China relations group feels Helms's pull,' *Washington Post*, 19 October 2000, p. A29.

41. Barber B. Conable, Testimony, 'United States–China Trade Relations,' Hearing before the Subcommittee on Trade of the Committee on Ways and Means, House of Representatives, One Hundred Third Congress, Second Session, 24 February 1994 (Washington, DC: US Government Printing Office, 1994); Carla A. Hills, Testimony, 'Finding Common Ground with a Rising China,' Hearing before the Committee on Foreign Relations, United States Senate, One Hundred Eleventh Congress, Second

Session, 23 June 2010 (Washington, DC: US Government Printing Office, 2010). The Conable quotation is from p. 54.

42. John Holden, telephone interview, New York, 21 August 2000.

43. Berris, e-mail, 29 December 2011.

44. Chen Weihua, 'China at her fingertips: veteran US–China relations expert says bilateral ties have withstood the test of time,' *China Daily USA Weekly*, 2–8 September 2011, p. 24; 'Orlins: US–China ties deeper, wider,' *China Daily USA, Special Edition on President Hu Jintao's Visit*, 21 January 2011, p. 3.

45. William Chang, telephone interview, Beijing, 14 January 2005.

46. See the Fed's website, http://www.federalreserve.gov/generalinfo/faq/faqfrs.htm.

47. Joint Economic Committee, Congress of the United States, *China's Economic Future: Challenges to U.S. Policy*, 104th Congress, 2d sess., August 1996. The essays by Institute scholars are: Hang-Sheng Cheng, 'A mid-course assessment of China's economic reform,' pp. 24–33; Colin Carter A. Carter and Scott Rozelle, 'How far along is China in developing its food markets?' pp. 139–61; Hang-Sheng Cheng, H. Gifford Fong, and Thomas Mayer, 'China's financial reform and monetary policy: issues and strategies,' pp. 203–20; Pitman Potter, 'Law reform and China's emerging market economy,' pp. 221–42; Anthony Y. C. Koo and K. C. Yeh, 'The impact of township, village and private enterprises' growth on state enterprises reform: three regional case studies,' pp. 381–402.

48. 'Speech by Linda Tsao Yang [at the Institute's 20th Annual Dinner],' *Newsletter: The 1990*, 21: 1 (August 2010), pp. 1, 15, 19, 23; William Lee, interview, San Mateo, California, 30 April 2005.

49. Xu Shanda, interview, Beijing, 11 May 2005. Xu also stressed that private groups, unlike governments, have the time, resources, and requisite specialization to conduct sustained research.

50. The following range of official views on US–China non-governmental relations is similar to results of a survey that was global in scope. See Cynthia J. Chataway, 'Track II Diplomacy: from a Track I perspective,' *Negotiation Journal*, 14: 3 (July 1998), pp. 269–87.

51. Interview by Charles Stuart Kennedy with Ambassador H. Holdridge, Association for Diplomatic Studies and Training Foreign Affairs Oral History Project, 20 July 1995, http://memory.loc.gov/ammem/collections/diplomacy/diploquery.html (accessed 5 April 2007).

52. Interview by Charles Stuart Kennedy with Donald M. Anderson, Association for Diplomatic Studies and Training Foreign Affairs Oral History Project, 8 July 1992, http://memory.loc.gov/ammem/collections/diplomacy/diploquery.html (accessed 5 April 2007).

53. James R. Lilley, telephone interviews, Washington, DC, 31 January and 16 April 2007. Lilley, who passed away in November 2009, recorded his China experiences in an autobiography, co-authored with his son Jeffrey Lilley, *China Hands: Nine Decades of Adventure, Espionage, and Diplomacy in Asia* (New York: Public Affairs Books, 2005, new edition).

54. Lilley, interviews.

55. McKinney Russell, telephone interview, Washington, DC, 7 February 2008.

56. Fred Whitaker, telephone interview, 18 October 2006, Beijing.

57. *International Organization*, XXV: 3 (1971) [Special Issue, Robert O. Keohane and Joseph S. Nye, Jr (eds), on 'Transnational Relations and World Politics']; Thomas Risse-Kappen, 'Bringing transnational relations back in: introduction,' in Risse-Kappen (ed.), *Bringing Transnational Relations Back In: Non-State Actors, Domestic Structures and International Institutions* (New York: Cambridge University Press, 1995), pp. 3–33.

58. Margaret E. Keck and Kathryn Sikkink, *Activists Beyond Borders: Advocacy Networks in International Politics* (Ithaca, NY: Cornell University Press, 1998), pp. 12–13.

59. Fengshi Wu, 'Double Mobilization: Transnational Advocacy Networks for China's Environment and Public Health' (PhD dissertation, University of Maryland, 2005), pp. 60–78, 357–64.

60. Mark P. Lagon, 'The "Shanghai Coalition": the chattering classes and China,' *Perspectives on Political Science*, 29: 1 (Winter 2000), pp. 7–16. For a recent example of the 'Tiananmen Coalition' argument, see Aaron L. Friedberg, *A Contest for Supremacy: China, America, and the Struggle for Mastery in Asia* (New York: W. W. Norton, 2011). On p. 197, Friedberg endorses Lagon's critique of the Shanghai coalition.

61. On human rights in China, see http://www.hrichina.org; Norton Wheeler, 'Improving mainland society and U.S.–China relations: a case study of four Chinese American-led transnational associations,' in Peter H. Koehn and Xiao-huang Yin (eds), *The Expanding Roles of Chinese Americans in U.S.–China Relations: Transnational Networks and Trans-Pacific Interactions* (Armonk, NY: M. E. Sharpe, 2002), pp. 196–8.

62. Jamie F. Metzl, 'China's threat to world order,' *Wall Street Journal*, 17 August 2011, p. A13; Stephen Orlins, 'China is doing a lot of good, too' [letter to the editor, with the title presumably provided by the paper], *Wall Street Journal*, 22 August 2011, p. A12. My focus here is on the ideas expressed by the two individuals, which may or may not be fully representative of the organizations with which they are affiliated. The Asia Foundation, for example, would not normally be found in the ranks of the Tiananmen Coalition.

63. On the intellectual career of cultural imperialism, see Dunch, 'Beyond Cultural Imperialism,' Jessica Gienow-Hecht, *'Shame on US?* Academics, cultural transfer, and the Cold War – a critical review,' *Diplomatic History*, 24: 3 (Summer 2000), pp. 465–94.

64. Joseph Nye, Jr, *Soft Power: The Means to Success in World Politics* (New York: Public Affairs, 2004), pp. 5, 7.

65. The 2006 figure is from '"China threat" countered by culture,' *China Daily*, 29 May 2006, p. 2. The 2011 figure is from Mike Peters and Zhang Chunyan, 'Confucius lives,' *Wall Street Journal*, 26 October 2011, p. A10. See also Sheng Ding and Robert A. Saunders, 'Talking up China: an analysis of China's rising cultural power and global promotion of the Chinese language,' *East Asia*, 23: 2 (Summer 2006), pp. 3–33; James F. Paradise, 'China and international harmony: the role of Confucius Institutes in bolstering Beijing's soft power,' *Asian Survey*, 49: 4 (July/August 2009), 647–69.

66. Peters and Zhang, 'Confucius lives.' The stories run under the 'China Watch' heading. A note at the top reads, 'PAID ADVERTISEMENT,' and one at the bottom reads, 'CHINA WATCH, prepared by China Daily, did not involve the news or editorial departments of The Wall Street Journal.'

67. Wang Ying, 'Economic growth spurs language learning,' *China Daily*, 16 July 2005, p. 2. The article attributes the estimate to the National Office for Teaching Chinese as a Foreign Language.

68. Jia Hepeng, 'TCM remedies are making a healthy impact in the West,' *China Daily*, 12 January 2007, p. 12.

69. For example, 'Chinese maritime hero commemorated,' *China Daily*, 30 August 2005, p. 13. For a contrasting realpolitik interpretation of the voyages, see Edward L. Dreyer, *Zheng He: China and the Oceans in the Early Ming Dynasty, 1405–1433* (New York: Longman, 2006).

70. Chen Jie and Liu Wei, 'World's a stage for culture,' *China Daily USA*, 20–22 August 2010, pp. 1–2.

71. Bates Gill and Yanzhong Huang, 'Sources and limits of Chinese "soft power,"' *Survival*, 48: 2 (Summer 2006), pp. 17–36; Andrew Nathan and Andrew Scobell, 'Human rights and China's soft power expansion,' *China Rights Forum*, 4 (2009), pp. 4, 10–23; Michael Wines, 'China tries to add cultural clout to economic muscle,' *New York Times*, 8 November 2011, p. A8; Ding and Saunders, 'Talking up China';

Peter Ford, 'What does China want?' *Christian Science Monitor*, 103: 50 (7 November 2011), pp. 26–32.

72. Robert Sutter, 'A research note: China's rise and US leadership in Asia – growing maturity and balance,' *Journal of Contemporary China*, 19 (June 2010), pp. 601–3; Laura Meckler and Patrick Barta, 'Myanmar shifts gaze toward West: U.S., Suu Kyi bestow pivotal backing as regime looks to ease China's grasp,' *Wall Street Journal*, 19–20 November 2011, p. A9; James Hookway, 'Old U.S. foe proves useful in Asia: Vietnam emerges in a central role in Washington's full-court press to counter China,' *Wall Street Journal*, 18 November 2011, p. A12; Craig Whitlock, 'U.S. seeks to expand presence in Philippines: nations discussing a bigger military footprint to help counter China,' *Washington Post*, 26 January 2012, pp. A1, A12.

73. 'We are forces for peace, Hu tells Africa,' *China Daily*, 8 February 2007, p. 2; He Wenping, 'China's aid to Africa: with respect and friendship,' *Renmin Ribao [People's Daily]*, 8 August 2011, p. A22 [English version in *Current Digest of the Chinese Press* 1: 0 (8–14 August 2011), pp. 22–4]; Yaroslav Trofimov, 'In Africa, China's expansion begins to stir resentment,' *Wall Street Journal*, 2 February 2007, pp. A1, 16.

74. Jospeh S. Nye, Jr, 'China undoes its charm offensive,' *Washington Post*, 27 March 2011, p. A17.

75. Xiao-huang Yin, comments at a workshop on transnational philanthropy, Peter F. Geithner, Paula D. Johnson, and Lincoln C. Chen (eds), *Diaspora Philanthropy and Equitable Development in China and India* (Cambridge, MA: Global Equity Initiative, Asia Center, Harvard University, 2005), p. 359. See also Norton Wheeler, 'A civic trend within ethnic transnationalism? Some insights from classical social theory and the Chinese American experience,' *Global Networks*, 4: 4 (October 2004), pp. 391–408.

76. For some highlights of Chinese American scientists' contribution to scientific research in China in the 1980s, see Marjorie Sun, 'U.S.-Chinese scientists see dreams imperiled,' *Science*, 244 (9 June 1989), pp. 1131–2.

77. Robert Parry, 'Globalization: threat or opportunity for the U.S. economy?' *Newsletter: The 1990 Institute*, December 2004, p. 8.

78. Shenyu Belsky, interview, Beijing, 29 July 2006. For a description of *China in the Red* and associated teaching materials, see http://www.pbs.org/wgbh/pages/frontline/shows/red/. The earlier well-received trilogy was *China: A Century of Revolution*.

79. Belsky, interview.

80. http://www.ncuscr.org/ting-wang (accessed 22 August 2010).

81. Jan Berris, telephone interview, New York, 25 July 2011.

82. Philip C. C. Huang has developed a useful profile of individuals who are able to function effectively within both Chinese and American societies: 'Biculturality in modern China and in Chinese studies,' *Modern China*, 26: 1 (January 2000), pp. 3–31.

83. Alexis Hooi, 'Congresswoman: nations can learn from each other,' *China Daily USA*, 5 September 2011, p. 1; Charles C. Johnson, 'Chu chooses silence on China,' *National Review*, 15 September 2011 [published online only], http://www.nationalreview.com/articles/277174/chu-chooses-silence-china-charles-c-johnson.

84. Ding Gang, 'Locke's China ties no guarantee of easy ride,' *Global Times*, 10 March 2011, http://www.globaltimes.cn/opinion/commentary/2011-03/631925.html. A *China Daily* commentator expressed the same ambivalence: Tao Wenzhao, 'New ambassador new hope,' *China Daily USA*, 15 August 2011, p. 11.

85. Barbara Demick, 'Ambassador raises strong emotions in China,' *Los Angeles Times*, 10 March 2011, p. A6.

86. Li Yuan, 'China frets: innovators stymied here,' *Wall Street Journal*, 8–9 October 2011, p. B3.

87. Qian Gang, 'China's reporters push the boundaries,' *Wall Street Journal*, 3 August 2011, p. A11. See also James T. Areddy and Josh Chin, 'Chinese media resist curbs on coverage of train crash,' *Wall Street Journal*, 1 August 2011, p. A7.

88. Josh Chin, 'Beijing state newspaper closes its investigative team,' *Wall Street Journal*, 19 July 2011, p. A8.
89. Cheng Li, 'The status and characteristics of foreign-educated returnees in the Chinese leadership,' *China Leadership Monitor*, 16 (Fall 2005), http://media.hoover.org/sites/default/files/documents/clm16_lc.pdf (accessed 18 October 2011); Cheng Li, 'China's new think tanks: where officials, entrepreneurs, and scholars interact,' *China Leadership Monitor*, 29 (Summer 2009), http://media.hoover.org/sites/default/files/documents/CLM29CL.pdf (accessed 18 August 2011).
90. Daniel de Vise, 'The plight of the Xinjiang 13: U.S. scholars say their book on restive western region led to China travel ban,' *Washington Post*, 21 August 2011, p. A2; Daniel Golden and Oliver Staley, 'China banning U.S. professors elicits silence from colleges employing them,' *Bloomberg*, 10 August 2011, http://www.bloomberg.com/news/2011-08-11/china-banning-u-s-professors-elicits-silence-from-colleges.html (accessed 18 October 2011).
91. Ian Johnson, 'Talk of reform to enliven leaders' meeting in China,' *New York Times*, 30 September 2010, p. A14; Jeremy Page, 'Chinese elders blast censorship: unprecedented letter inspired by premier's call for political reform stokes debate ahead of Communist Party Congress,' *Wall Street Journal*, 14 October 2010, p. A10; Alice Miller, 'Splits in the Politburo leadership?' *China Leadership Monitor*, 34 (Winter 2011), http://media.hoover.org/sites/default/files/documents/CLM34AM.pdf (accessed 18 October 2011); Joseph Fewsmith, 'Political reform was never on the agenda,' *China Leadership Monitor*, 34, http://media.hoover.org/sites/default/files/documents/CLM34JF.pdf (accessed 18 October 2011).
92. Sharon LaFraniere, 'Chinese premier offers a tribute to a reformer,' *New York Times*, 16 April 2010, p. A14.
93. 'Linda Yeung, 'Setback for reforms at new university,' *University World News*, 173 (29 May 2011), http://www.universityworldnews.com/article.php?story=20110527211710595 (accessed 18 September 2011); Mimi Leung, 'Compromises for new "autonomous" university,' *University World News*, 186 (28 August 2011), http://www.universityworldnews.com/article.php?story=2011082619493164 (accessed 18 September 2011).
94. 'Shenzhen (Guangdong): reforming registration of social organizations,' *Innovations and Excellence in Chinese Local Governance, 2009–2010* (Beijing: IECLG, 2010), p. 28.
95. Edward Cody, 'Pioneering Chinese city offers a peek at political ferment,' *Washington Post*, 30 June 2008, p. A1. In late 2011, one of the leading Guangdong liberalizers, Party Secretary Wang Yang, faced a challenge to his political reputation. Farmers in Guangdong's Wukan village staged a massive protest against a typical local government takeover of their land for commercial development. Wang tried to resolve the problem through negotiations and concessions – with apparent success, as of this writing (January 2012). Jeremy Page and Brian Spegele, 'Land dispute in China Town sparks revolt,' *Wall Street Journal*, 15 December 2011, p. A12; Brian Spegele and Angela Yeoh, 'Officials offer rare concession to Chinese protestors,' *Wall Street Journal*, 22 December 2011, p. A13; Keith B. Richburg, 'Uprising challenges a rising star in China,' *Washington Post*, 24 December 2011, p. 8.
96. Jeremy Page and Mark Peters, 'Heartland return for Chinese leader,' *Wall Street Journal*, 31 January 2012, pp. A1, A12. A series of political and human interest stories on the visit dominated the *Muscatine Journal* on 15 February 2012 (the day of Xi's visit) and 16 February 2012. The 15 February issue reprinted the paper's front page of 8 May 1985, which included the story 'Chinese Visitors Receive Warm Welcome' by Helen Weiershauser (reprinted on p. 3A). An editorial welcomed Xi: 'From our perspective, only good can come from the *diplomacy* practiced today in Roger and Sarah Lande's historic home on Muscatine's West Hill' [emphasis added]. '"Only good can come" from today,' *Muscatine Journal*, 15 February 2012, p. 4A.

97. Jeremy Page, 'Like father like son: Xi Jinping not first in family to visit Iowa,' *Wall Street Journal*, 6 February 2012 (web-only publication), http://blogs.wsj.com/china-realtime/2012/02/06/like-father-like-son-chinese-leaderxi-jinping-not-first-in-family-to-visit-iowa-photos/?KEYWORDS=jeremy+page (accessed 25 February 2012).
98. For a thoughtful discussion of these issues, see Adam Schaff, 'Why history is constantly rewritten,' *Diogenes*, 8 (June 1960), pp. 62–74.
99. For an optimistic outlook, based on the combined strength and attractiveness of the web of intergovernmental institutions and norms that the United States has orchestrated since the end of World War II, see G. John Inkenberry, 'The rise of China: power, institutions, and the Western order,' in Robert S. Ross and Zhu Feng, *China's Ascent: Power, Security, and the Future of International Relations* (Ithaca, NY: Cornell University Press, 2008), pp. 89–114.

Bibliography

Aslund, Anders, *How Russia Became a Market Economy* (Washington, DC: Brookings Institution Press, 1995).

Auger, Vincent A. and Overby, L. Marvin, 'Teaching and learning in Nanjing: community, communities, and politics in an overseas program,' *Journal of Political Science Education*, 1: 2 (May–August 2005), pp. 233–247.

Bahl, Roy, *Fiscal Policy in China: Taxation and Intergovernmental Fiscal Relations* (South San Francisco: The 1990 Institute, 1999).

Bao, Lingguang, 'China: the characteristics and trend of the new tax system reform,' *Intertax*, 32: 10 (2004), pp. 519–23.

Bastid, Marianne, 'Chinese educational policies in the 1980s and economic development,' *China Quarterly*, 98 (June 1984), pp. 189–219.

Bays, Daniel H., *A New History of Christianity in China* (New York: Wiley-Blackwell, 2011).

Bentley, Julia Greenwood, 'The role of international support for civil society organizations in China,' *Harvard Asia Quarterly*, 7: 1 (Winter 2003), pp. 11–20.

Berris, Jan Carol, 'The evolution of Sino-American exchanges: a view from the National Committee,' in Joyce K. Kallgren and Denis Fred Simon (eds), *Educational Exchanges: Essays on the Sino-American Experience* (Berkeley, CA: Institute of East Asian Studies, University of California, 1987), pp. 80–95.

Bieler, Stacey, *'Patriots' or 'Traitors'? A History of American-Educated Chinese Students* (Armonk, NY: M. E. Sharpe, 2004).

Bottelier, Pieter, 'China and the World Bank: how a partnership was built,' *Journal of Contemporary China*, 16 (May 2007), pp. 239–58.

Brady, Anne-Marie, *Making the Foreign Serve China: Managing Foreigners in the People's Republic* (Oxford: Rowman & Littlefield, 2003).

Brødsgaard, Kjeld Erik, 'State and society in Hainan: Liao Xun's ideas on "small government, big society,"' in Kjeld Erik Brødsgaard and David Strand (eds), *Reconstructing Twentieth-Century China: State Control, Civil Society, and National Identity* (New York: Oxford University Press, 1998), pp. 189–215.

Bu, Liping, *Making the World Like Us: Education, Cultural Expansion and the American Century* (Westport, CT: Praeger, 2003).

Bullock, Alan and Stallybrass, Oliver (eds), *The Harper Dictionary of Modern Thought* (New York: Harper & Row, 1977).

Bullock, Mary Brown, 'Mission accomplished: the influence of the CSCPRC on educational relations with China, in Cheng Li (ed.), *Bridging Minds Across the Pacific: U.S.–China Educational Exchanges, 1978–2003*, (Lanham, MD: Lexington Books, 2005), pp. 49–68.

Bullock, Mary Brown, *An American Transplant: The Rockefeller Foundation & Peking Union Medical College* (Berkeley, CA: University of California Press, 1980).

Buzzanco, Robert, 'Where's the beef? Culture without power in the study of U.S. foreign relations,' *Diplomatic History*, 24: 4 (Fall 2000), pp. 623–32.

Calhoun, Craig, *Neither Gods Nor Emperors: Students and the Struggle for Democracy in China* (Berkeley, CA: University of California Press, 1994).

Carothers, Thomas, 'The rule of law revival,' *Foreign Affairs*, 77: 2 (March/April 1998), pp. 95–106. Reprinted in Carothers, *Critical Mission: Essays on Democracy* (Washington, DC: Carnegie Endowment for International Peace, 2004).

Carter, Colin, Zhong, Funing, and Cai, Fang, *China's Ongoing Agricultural Reform* (San Francisco: The 1990 Institute, 1996).

Cartier, Carolyn, 'Engendered industrialization in China under Reform,' in Chia-min Hsieh and Max Lu (eds), *Changing China: A Geographical Appraisal* (Boulder, CO: Westview Press, 2003), pp. 268–90.

Chan, Hoiman, 'Modernity and revolution in Chinese education: towards an analytical agenda of the Great Leap Forward and the Cultural Revolution,' in Glenn Peterson, Ruth Hayhoe, and Yongling Lu (eds), *Education, Culture, and Identity in Twentieth-Century China* (Ann Arbor, MI: University of Michigan Press, 2001), pp. 73–99.

Chan, Kin-man and Qiu, Haixiong, 'Small government, big society,' *Social Organizations and Civil Society in China*, China Area Studies Series No. 8 (Tokyo University, 1998), pp. 34–47.

Chan, Kin-man, Qiu, Haixong and Zhu, Jiangang, 'Chinese NGOs strive to survive,' *Social Transformations in Chinese Societies*, 1 (2005), pp. 131–59.

Chan, Sucheng, 'Public policy, U.S.–China relations, and the Chinese American experience: an interpretive essay,' in Edwin G. Clausen and Jack Bermingham (eds), *Pluralism, Racism, and Public Policy: The Search for Equality* (Boston: G. K. Hall, 1981), pp. 5–38.

Chataway, Cynthia J., 'Track II Diplomacy: from a Track I perspective,' *Negotiation Journal*, 14: 3 (July 1998), pp. 269–87.

Chen, Hang-Sheng, 'Historical factors affecting China's economic development,' in Hung-chao Tai (ed.), *Confucianism and Economic Development: An Oriental Alternative?* (Washington, DC: Washington Institute Press, 1989), pp. 55–69.

Chen, Hang-Sheng (ed.), *Financial Policy and Reform in Pacific Basin Countries* (Lexington, MA: Lexington Books, 1986).

Chen, Hang-Sheng (ed.), *Monetary Policy in Pacific Basin Countries* (Dordrecht: Kluwer, 1988).

Chen, Jian, 'Tiananmen and the fall of the Berlin Wall: China's path toward 1989 and beyond,' in Jeffrey A. Engel (ed.), *The Fall of the Berlin Wall: The Revolutionary Legacy of 1989* (New York: Oxford University Press, 2009), pp. 96–131.

Chen, Ping-Tsang, 'Chinese fraternities in America,' in Richard Butrick (ed.), *American University Men in China* (Shanghai: American University Club of Shanghai, 1936), pp. 153–64.

China Rights Forum, 1 (2009) [special issue, 'Rule of Law?'].

Chinese Law and Government, 37: 2 (March–April 2004) [special issue, Vivian Zhan (ed.), on 'China's Fiscal System in Transition'].

Chow, Gregory, 'The teaching of modern economics in China,' *Comparative Economic Studies*, 42: 2 (Summer 2000), pp. 51–60.

Chu, Samuel C., *Reformer in Modern China: Chang Chien, 1853–1926* (New York: Columbia University Press, 1965).

Chu, T. K., '150 years of Chinese students in America,' *Harvard China Review*, 5: 1 (Spring 2004), pp. 7–21, 26.

Cohen, Jean L. and Arato, Andrew, *Civil Society and Political Theory* (Cambridge, MA: MIT Press, 1992).

Cohen, Warren I., 'While China faced East: Chinese-American cultural relations, 1949–71,' in Joyce K. Kallgren and Denis Fred Simon (eds), *Educational Exchanges: Essays on the Sino-American Experience* (Berkeley, CA: Institute of East Asian Studies, University of California, 1987), pp. 44–57.

Costigliola, Frank, *Awkward Dominion: American Political, Economic and Cultural Relations with Europe, 1919–1933* (Ithaca, NY: Cornell University Press, 1984).

de Grazia, Victoria, *Irresistible Empire: America's Advance Through 20th-Century Europe* (Cambridge, MA: Belknap Press of Harvard University Press, 2005).

Dean, Robert, 'Tradition, cause, and effect, and the cultural history of international relations,' *Diplomatic History*, 24: 4 (Fall 2000), pp. 615–22.

Depkat, Volker, 'Cultural approaches to international relations: a challenge?' in Jessica C.E. Gienow-Hecht and Frank Schumacher (eds), *Culture and International History* (New York: Berghahn, 2003), pp. 175–97.

Dernberger, Robert F., 'Prospects for trade between China and the United States,' in Alexander Eckstein (ed.), *China Trade Prospects and U.S. Policy* (New York: Praeger, 1971), pp. 185–319.

DeWoskin, Rachel, *Foreign Babes in Beijing: Behind the Scenes of a New China* (New York: W. W. Norton, 2005).

Ding, Sheng and Saunders, Robert A., 'Talking up China: an analysis of China's rising cultural power and global promotion of the Chinese language,' *East Asia*, 23: 2 (Summer 2006), pp. 3–33.

Ding, Yijiang, 'Corporatism and civil society in China: an overview of the debate in recent years,' *China Information*, 12: 4 (Spring 1998), pp. 44–67.

Dower, John, '"Culture," theory, and practice in U.S.–Japan relations,' *Diplomatic History*, 4: 3 (summer 2000), pp. 517–28.

Dreyer, Edward L., *Zheng He: China and the Oceans in the Early Ming Dynasty, 1405–1433* (New York: Longman, 2006).

Dunch, Ryan, 'Beyond cultural imperialism: cultural theory, Christian missions, and global modernity,' *History and Theory*, 41: 3 (October 2002), pp. 301–25.

Economy, Elizabeth, 'Chinese policy-making and global climate change: two-front diplomacy and the international community,' in Miranda A. Schreurs and Elizabeth Economy (eds), *The Internationalization of Environmental Protection* (Cambridge, UK: Cambridge University Press, 1997), pp. 19–41.

Economy, Elizabeth, 'Interview with Elizabeth Economy: China's development and the environment,' *Harvard Asia Quarterly*, 7: 1 (Winter 2003), pp. 4–10.

Fairbank, John King (ed.) *The Missionary Enterprise in China and America* (Cambridge, MA: Harvard University Press, 1974).

Fewsmith, Joseph, 'Editor's introduction,' *Chinese Economic Studies*, 28: 3 (May/June 1995), pp. 3–4.

Fewsmith, Joseph, *China Since Tiananmen: The Politics of Transition* (New York: Cambridge University Press, 2001).

Fewsmith, Joseph, *Dilemmas of Reform: Political Conflict and Economic Debate* (Armonk, NY: M. E. Sharpe, 1994).

First Ten Years, First in Asia (Shanghai: CEIBS, 2004).

Forney, Matt, 'Voice of the people,' *Far Eastern Economic Review*, 161: 19 (7 May 1998), pp. 10–12.

Friedberg, Aaron L., *A Contest for Supremacy: China, America, and the Struggle for Mastery in Asia* (New York: W. W. Norton, 2011).

Friedman, Elisabeth Jay, 'Gendering the agenda: the impact of the transnational women's rights movement at the UN conferences of the 1990s,' *Women's Studies International Forum*, 26: 4 (2003), pp. 313–31.

Frolic, B. Michael, 'State-led civil society,' in Timothy Brook and B. Michael Frolic (eds), *Civil Society in China* (Armonk, NY: M. E. Sharpe, 1997), pp. 46–67.

Galenson, Walter (ed) *China's Economic Reform* (San Francisco: The 1990 Institute, 1993).

Garrett, Shirley, *Social Reformers in Urban China: The Chinese Y.M.C.A., 1895–1926* (Cambridge, MA: Harvard University Press, 1970).

Garside, B. A., *One Increasing Purpose: The Life of Henry Winters Luce* (New York: Fleming H. Revell, 1948).

Gienow-Hecht, Jessica, 'Cultural imperialism,' *Encyclopedia of American Foreign Policy*, 2nd edn, Vol. 1 (New York: Charles Scribner's Sons, 2001), pp. 397–408.

Gienow-Hecht, Jessica, *Transmission Impossible: American Journalism as Cultural Diplomacy in Postwar Germany, 1945–1955* (Baton Rouge, LA: Louisiana University Press, 1999).

Gienow-Hecht, Jessica, '*Shame on US?* Academics, cultural transfer, and the Cold War – a critical review,' *Diplomatic History*, 24: 3 (Summer 2000), pp. 465–94.

Gill, Bates and Huang, Yanzhong, 'Sources and limits of Chinese "soft power,"' *Survival*, 48: 2 (Summer 2006), pp. 17–36.

Gold, Thomas, 'Bases for civil society in reform China,' in Kjeld Erik Brødsgaard and David Strand (eds), *Reconstructing Twentieth-Century China: State Control, Civil Society, and National Identity* (Oxford: Clarendon Press, 1998), pp. 163–88.

Goodall, Keith, Warner, M., and Lang, V., 'HRD in the People's Republic: the MBA "with Chinese characteristics"?' *Journal of World Business*, 39: 4 (2004), pp. 311–23.

Goonatilake, Susantha, 'Cultural imperialism: a short history, future, and a postscript from the present,' in Bernd Hamm and Russell Smandych (eds), *Cultural Imperialism: Essays on the Political Economy of Cultural Domination* (Ontario, Canada: Broadview Press, 2005), pp. 33–51.

Gow, Ian, 'Removing the rose-tinted spectacles,' in Anna Fazackerley (ed.), *British Universities in China: The Reality Beyond the Rhetoric* (London: December 2007, Agora: Forum for Culture and Education), pp. 7–9, http://www.agora-education.org/pubs/docs/Agora_China_Report.pdf (accessed 21 March 2008).

Gutner, Tammi L., *The Story of SAIS* (Baltimore, MD: School of Advanced International Studies, 1987).

Hannum, Emily, 'Market transition, educational disparities, and family strategies in rural China: new evidence on gender stratification and development,' *Demography*, 42: 2 (May 2005), pp. 275–99.

Hannum, Emily and Park, Albert, 'Educating China's rural children in the 21st century,' *Harvard China Review*, 3: 2 (Spring 2002), pp. 8–14.

Harding, Harry, *A Fragile Relationship: The United States and China since 1972* (Washington, DC: Brookings Institution, 1992).

Hayford, Charles W., *To the People: James Yen and Village China* (New York: Columbia University Press, 1990).

Hayhoe, Ruth, 'Cultural tradition and educational modernization: lessons from the republican era,' in Ruth Hayhoe (ed.), *Education and Modernization: The Chinese Experience* (Oxford: Pergamon Press, 1992), pp. 47–72.

Hayhoe, Ruth, *China's Universities, 1895–1995: A Century of Cultural Conflict* (New York: Garland, 1996).

Hayhoe, Ruth and Zha, Qiang, 'Becoming world-class: Chinese universities facing globalization and internationalization,' *Harvard China Review* (Spring 2004), pp. 87–92.

He, Di, 'Yenching University and educational modernization in China,' in Priscilla Roberts (ed.), *Sino-American Relations Since 1900* (Hong Kong: Centre of Asian Studies, University of Hong Kong, 1991), pp. 82–93.

Hess, Ceferina G., 'Reflections on America's "love affair" with Madame Chiang Kai-Shek from 1927 to 1950,' *National Social Science Journal*, 23: 1 (2004), pp. 43–55.

Holbig, Heike, 'The emergence of the campaign to Open Up the West: ideological formation, central decision-making and the role of the provinces,' *China Quarterly*, 178 (June 2004), pp. 335–57.

Holton, Richard H. and Lin, Xia Yuan, 'China and the World Trade Organization,' *Asian Survey*, 38: 8 (August 1998), pp. 745–62.

Hou, Jack W., Mead, Robert W., and Nagahashi, Hiroyuki, 'Evolution of China's U.S. policy (1965–1972): prelude to reform?' *American Journal of China Studies*, 12: 1 (2005), 1–24.

Howell, Jude, 'Post-Beijing reflections: creating ripples, but not waves in China,' *Women's Studies International Forum*, 20: 2 (1997), pp. 235–52.

Howell, Jude, 'The struggle for survival: prospects for the Women's Federation in post-Mao China,' *World Development*, 24: 1 (1996), pp. 129–43.

Hsia, Renee Yuen-Jan and White, Lynn T. III, 'Working amid corporatism and confusion: foreign NGOs in China,' *Non-Profit and Voluntary Sector Quarterly*, 31: 3 (September 2002), pp. 329–51.

Hu, Angang, 'Background to writing the report on state capacity,' in Wang Shaoguang and Hu Angang, *The Chinese Economy in Crisis: State Capacity and Tax Reform* (Armonk, NY: M. E. Sharpe, 2001), pp. 185–211.

Huang, Philip C. C., 'Biculturality in modern China and in Chinese studies,' *Modern China*, 26: 1 (January 2000), pp. 3–31.

Hunt, Michael H., 'The American remission of the Boxer Indemnity: a reappraisal,' *Journal of Asian Studies*, 31: 3 (May 1972), pp. 539–59.

Hunt, Michael, *The Making of a Special Relationship: The United States and China to 1914* (New York: Columbia University Press, 1983).

Inkenberry, G. John, 'The rise of China: power, institutions, and the Western order,' in Robert S. Ross and Zhu Feng (eds), *China's Ascent: Power, Security, and the Future of International Politics* (Ithaca, NY: Cornell University Press, 2008), pp. 89–114.

International Organization, XXV: 3 (1971) [Special Issue, Robert O. Keohane and Joseph S. Nye, Jr (eds), on 'Transnational Relations and World Politics'].

Iriye, Akira, 'A century of NGOs,' *Diplomatic History*, 23: 3 (Summer 1999), pp. 421–35.

Iriye, Akira, 'Culture,' *Journal of American History*, 77: 1 (June 1990), pp. 99–107.

Iriye, Akira, 'Culture and power: international relations as intercultural relations,' *Diplomatic History*, 3: 2 (April 1979), pp. 115–28.

Jayasankaran, S., Cohen, Margot, Dolven, Ben, Hoon, Shim Jae, and Baum, Julian, 'Thorns in the flesh: across Asia, grassroots groups test state control,' *Far Eastern Economic Review*, 161: 19 (7 May 1998), p. 15.

Kallgren, Joyce K., 'Public interest in Sino-American exchanges: De Tocqueville's "associations" in action,' in Joyce K. Kallgren and Denis Fred Simon (eds), *Educational Exchanges: Essays on the Sino-American Experience* (Berkeley, CA: Institute of East Asian Studies, University of California, 1987), pp. 58–79.

Keck, Margaret E. and Sikkink, Kathryn, *Activists Beyond Borders: Advocacy Networks in International Politics* (Ithaca, NY: Cornell University Press, 1998).

Keenan, Barry, *The Dewey Experiment in China: Educational Reform and Political Power in the Early Republic* (Cambridge, MA: Harvard University Press, 1977).

Kissinger, Henry, *On China* (New York: Penguin Press, 2011).

Knup, Elizabeth, *Environmental NGOs in China: An Overview*, China Environment Series No. 1 (Princeton, NJ: Woodrow Wilson Center, 1997), pp. 9–15.

Kucklik, Bruce, 'The future of cultural imperialism,' *Diplomatic History*, 24: 4 (Fall 2000), pp. 503–8.

Kuisel, Richard, 'Americanization for historians,' *Diplomatic History*, 24: 4 (Fall 2000), pp. 509–15.

Lagon, Mark P., 'The "Shanghai Coalition": the chattering classes and China,' *Perspectives on Political Science*, 29: 1 (Winter 2000), pp. 7–16.

Lampton, David M., *A Relationship Restored: Trends in U.S.–China Educational Exchanges, 1978–1984* (Washington, DC: National Academy Press, 1986).

Lampton, David M., *Same Bed, Different Dreams: Managing U.S.–China Relations, 1989–2000* (Berkeley, CA: University of California Press, 2001).

Lan, Da, 'After Zhang Yimou's withdrawal from Cannes,' *Chinese Sociology and Anthropology*, 32: 2 (1999–2000), pp. 47–50.

Lee, Richard W. H., 'Training ground for a new breed of professionals,' *China Business Review* (May–June 1985), pp. 39–42.

Li, Changping, 'The crisis in the countryside,' in Chaohua Wang (ed.), *One China, Many Paths* (London: Verso, 2003), pp. 198–218.

Li, Cheng, 'Coming home to teach: status and mobility of returnees in China's higher education,' in Cheng Li (ed.), *Bridging Minds Across the Pacific: U.S.–China Educational Exchanges, 1978–2003* (Lanham, MD: Lexington Books, 2005), pp. 69–109.

Li, Cheng, 'Introduction: open doors and open minds,' in Cheng Li (ed.), *Bridging Minds Across the Pacific: U.S.–China Educational Exchanges, 1978–2003* (Lanham, MD: Lexington Books, 2005), pp. 1–24.

Li, Cheng, 'The status and characteristics of foreign-educated returnees in the Chinese leadership,' *China Leadership Monitor*, 16 (Fall 2005), http://www.hoover.org/publications/clm/issues/2898976.html (accessed 5 June 2010).

Li, Shuyou, 'Nanjing University and Sino-American cultural relations,' in Priscilla Roberts (ed.), *Sino-American Relations Since 1900* (Hong Kong: Centre of Asian Studies, University of Hong Kong, 1991), pp. 53–62.

Li, Xiaoping, 'University autonomy in China: history, present situation and perspective,' in *Current Issues in Chinese Higher Education* (Paris: OECD, 2000), pp. 37–44.

'The life of Comrade Kuang Yaming,' in Feng Zhiguang (chief ed.), *Kuang Yaming Memorial Collection* (Nanjing: Nanjing University Press, 1997) [in Chinese], pp. 1–5.

Lilley, James R. and Lilley, Jeffrey, *China Hands: Nine Decades of Adventure, Espionage, and Diplomacy in Asia* (New York: Public Affairs Books, 2005, new edition).

Lin, Jing, 'Private education in China: its development and dynamics,' *Harvard China Review*, 3: 2 (2002), pp. 21–6.

Lin, Jing, Zhang, Yu, Gao, Lan, and Liu, Yan, 'Trust, ownership, and autonomy: challenges facing private higher education in China,' *China Review*, 5: 1 (Spring 2005), pp. 61–81.

Lindquist, Evert, 'Think tanks and the ecology of policy inquiry,' in Diane Stone (ed.), *Banking on Knowledge: The Genesis of the Global Development Network* (London: Routledge, 2000), pp. 221–38.

Lorence, James T., 'Organized business and the myth of the China market: the American Asiatic Association, 1898–1937,' *Transactions of the American Philosophical Society*, Vol. 71, Part 4, 1981.

Lu, Yiyi, *Non-Governmental Organizations in China: The Rise of Dependent Autonomy* (London: Routledge, 2009).

Lubman, Stanley, 'The study of Chinese law in the United States: reflections on the past and concerns about the future,' *Washington University Global Studies Law Review*, 2: 1 (2003), pp. 1–35.

Lundestad, Geir, 'Empire by invitation? The United States and Western Europe, 1945–1952,' *Journal of Peace Research*, 23: 3 (1986), pp. 263–77.

Lundestad, Geir, *The United States and Western Europe Since 1945: From 'Empire' by Invitation to Transatlantic Drift* (New York: Oxford University Press, 2003).

Lutz, Jesse Gregory, *China and the Christian Colleges* (Ithaca, NY and London: Cornell University Press, 1971).

Ma, Qiusha, *Non-Governmental Organizations in Contemporary China: Paving the Way to Civil Society?* (Abingdon: Routledge, 2006).

Ma, Wan-hua, *Economic Reform and Higher Education in China*, CIDE Higher Education Occasional Paper No. 2, Center for International and Development Education (CIDE), UCLA Graduate School of Education and Information Studies, July 2003, http://www. gseis.ucla.edu/cide/reports/Download%20Ma%20Occasional%20Paper,%20July%202003.pdf (accessed 10 May 2006).

McClain, Charles, 'The Chinese contribution to the development of American law,' in Sucheng Chan (ed.), *Entry Denied: Exclusion and the Chinese Community in America, 1882–1943* (Philadelphia, PA: Temple University Press, 1991), pp. 3–24.

McClain, Charles, *In Search of Equality: The Chinese Struggle Against Discrimination in Nineteenth-Century America* (Berkeley, CA: University of California Press, 1994).

McClain, Charles and McClain, Laurene Wu, 'In Re Lee Sing: the first residential segregation case,' *Western Legal History*, 3: 2 (1990), pp. 179–96.

McMahon, Robert J., 'Diplomatic history and policy history: finding common ground,' *Journal of Policy History*, 17: 1 (2005), pp. 93–109.

Madsen, Richard, *China and the American Dream: A Moral Inquiry* (Berkeley, CA: University of California Press, 1995).

Mann, Jim, *Beijing Jeep: A Case Study of Western Business in China* (Boulder, CO: Westview Press, 1997).

Marcot, Bruce G., Ganzei, Sergei S., Zhang, Tiefu, and Voronov, Boris A., 'A sustainable plan for conserving forest biodiversity in Far East Russia and Northeast China,' *Forestry Chronicle*, 73: 5 (October 1997) pp. 565–71.

May, Ernest R. and Fairbank, John K. (eds), *America's China Trade in Historical Perspective: The Chinese and American Performance* (Cambridge, MA: Harvard University Press, 1986).

Mittelman, James H., 'Globalization and development: learning from debates in China,' *Globalizations*, 3: 3 (September 2006).

Mohrman, Kathryn, 'Sino-American educational exchanges and the drive to create world-class universities,' in Cheng Li (ed.), *Bridging Minds Across the Pacific: U.S.–China Educational Exchanges, 1978–2003* (Lanham, MD: Lexington Books, 2005), pp. 219–35.

Mok, Ka-Ho, 'Policy of decentralization and changing governance of higher education in post-Mao China,' *Public Administration and Development*, 22 (2002), pp. 261–73.

Morton, Katherine, 'The emergence of NGOs in China and their transnational linkages: implications for domestic reform,' *Australian Journal of International Affairs*, 59: 4 (December 2005), pp. 519–32.

Mui, Matthew and Wong, Raymond, 'Tax regime change,' *China Business Review*, 35: 2 (March/April 2008), pp. 32–5.

Nathan, Andrew and Scobell, Andrew, 'Human rights and China's soft power expansion,' *China Rights Forum*, 4 (2009), pp. 10–23.

Naughton, Barry, 'China's economic think tanks: their changing roles in the 1990s,' *China Quarterly*, 171 (September 2002), pp. 625–35.

Ninkovich, Frank, *U.S. Information Policy and Cultural Diplomacy*, Headline Series No. 308 (New York: Foreign Policy Association, 1996).

Ninkovich, Frank and Bu, Liping (eds), *The Cultural Turn: Essays in the History of U.S. Foreign Relations* (Chicago: Imprint Publications, 2001).

Nye, Joseph Jr, *Soft Power: The Means to Success in World Politics* (New York: Public Affairs, 2004).

Paradise, James F., 'China and international harmony: the role of Confucius Institutes in bolstering Beijing's soft power,' *Asian Survey*, 49: 4 (July/August 2009), pp. 647–69.

Parrini, Carl P. and Sklar, Martin J., 'New thinking about the market, 1896–1904: some American economists on investment and the theory of surplus capital,' *Journal of Economic History*, 43: 3 (September 1983), pp. 559–78.

Parthasarathy, D., 'From white man's burden to good governance: economic liberalization and the commodification of law and ethics,' in Bernd Hamm and Russell Smandych (eds), *Cultural Imperialism: Essays on the Political Economy of Cultural Domination* (Ontario, Canada: Broadview Press, 2005), pp. 191–210.

Peerenboom, Randall, *China's Long March Toward Rule of Law* (New York: Cambridge University Press, 2002).

Pells, Richard, 'Who's afraid of Steven Spielberg?' *Diplomatic History*, 4: 3 (Summer 2000), pp. 495–502.

Potter, Pitman, *Foreign Business Law in China: Past Progress, Future Challenges* (San Francisco: The 1990 Institute, 1995).

Pugach, Noel, 'Embarrassed monarchist: Frank J. Goodnow and constitutional development in China, 1913–1915,' *Pacific Historical Review*, 42: 4 (1973), pp. 499–517.

Qi, Yeguo and Chen, Yukun, 'Diversification of sources of funding and innovation in management methods in Chinese universities,' in *Current Issues in Chinese Higher Education* (Paris: OECD, 2000), pp. 55–66.

Qian, Ning, *Chinese Students Encounter America* (Seattle, WA: University of Washington Press, 2002).

Qin, Hui, 'Small government, big society? What role for the state in the Chinese transition process?' *Social Research*, 73: 1 (Spring 2006), pp. 29–52.

Reardon, Lawrence C., *The Reluctant Dragon: Crisis Cycles in Chinese Foreign Economic Policy* (Seattle, WA: University of Washington Press, 2002).

Reimann, Kim D., 'A view from the top: international politics, norms, and the worldwide growth of NGOs,' *International Studies Quarterly*, 50: 1 (2006), pp. 45–67.

Rhoads, Edward J. M., *Stepping Forth into the World: The Chinese Educational Mission to the United States, 1872–1881* (Hong Kong: Hong Kong University Press, 2011).

Richmond, Yale, *Cultural Exchange and the Cold War: Raising the Iron Curtain* (University Park, PA: Pennsylvania State University Press, 2003).

Risse-Kappen, Thomas, 'Bringing transnational relations back in: introduction,' in Thomas Risse-Kappen (ed.), *Bringing Transnational Relations Back In: Non-State Actors, Domestic Structures and International Institutions* (New York: Cambridge University Press, 1995), pp. 3–33.

Rivas, Darlene, *Missionary Capitalist: Nelson Rockefeller in Venezuela* (Chapel Hill, NC: University of North Carolina Press, 2001).

Rosen, Stanley and Zweig, David, 'Transnational capital: valuing academic returnees in a globalizing China,' in Cheng Li (ed.), *Bridging Minds Across the Pacific: U.S.–China Educational Exchanges, 1978–2003* (Lanham, MD: Lexington Books, 2005), pp. 111–32.

Rosenbaum, Arthur, 'Yenching University and Sino-American interactions, 1919–1952,' *Journal of American-East Asian Relations*, 14, Issues 1–4 (2007), pp. 11–60.

Ross, Heidi, 'China country study,' background paper for the Education for All Global Monitoring Report 2006, *Literacy for Life* (UNESCO, 2005).

Ross, Heidi, 'Historical memory, community, hope: reclaiming the social purposes of education for Shanghai McTyeire School for Girls,' in Glenn Peterson, Ruth Hayhoe, and Yongling Lu (eds), *Education, Culture, and Identity in Twentieth-Century China* (Ann Arbor, MI: University of Michigan Press, 2001), pp. 375–402.

Rotter, Andrew, 'Christians, Muslims, and Hindus: religion and U.S.–South Asian relations, 1947–1954,' *Diplomatic History*, 24: 4 (Fall 2000), pp. 593–613.

Rotter, Andrew, *Comrades: The United States and India, 1947–1964* (Ithaca, NY: Cornell University Press, 2000).

Salamon, Lester M., 'Globalization and the civil society sector,' in Soma Hewa and Darwin H. Stapleton (eds), *Globalization, Philanthropy, and Civil Society: Toward a New Political Culture in the Twenty-First Century* (New York: Springer, 2005), pp. 137–52.

Salamon, Lester M., 'The rise of the nonprofit sector,' *Foreign Affairs*, 73: 4 (July/August 1994), pp. 109–22.

Salamon, Lester M. and Anheier, Helmut K., 'Social origins of civil society: explaining the nonprofit sector cross-nationally,' *Voluntas: International Journal of Voluntary and Nonprofit Organizations*, 9: 3 (September 1998), pp. 213–48.

Schaff, Adam, 'Why history is constantly rewritten,' *Diogenes*, 8 (June 1960), pp. 62–74.

Schiller, Nina Glick, 'Long-distance nationalism,' in Melvin Ember, Carol R. Ember, and Ian Skoggard (eds), *Encyclopedia of Diasporas: Immigrant and Refugee Cultures Around the World.* Vol. I: *Overviews and Topics* (New York: Kluwer, 2004), pp. 570–9.

Schwartz, Jonathan, 'Environmental NGOs in China: roles and limits,' *Pacific Affairs*, 77: 1 (Spring 2004), pp. 28–49.

Shen, Hong, 'Academic freedom and academic duty in Chinese universities,' in *Current Issues in Chinese Higher Education* (Paris: OECD, 2000), pp. 11–36.

Shen, Xiao Hong, 'Yale's China and China's Yale: Americanizing Higher Education in China, 1900–1927' (PhD dissertation, Yale University, 1993).

[Our Commentator,] 'Should or should we not guard against and resist cultural colonialism?' *Chinese Sociology and Anthropology*, 31: 4 (Summer 1999) [Special Issue, 'The Contention in China over "Cultural Colonialism"'], pp. 23–35.

Shue, Vivienne, 'The political economy of compassion: China's "charity supermarket" sage,' *Journal of Contemporary China*, 20 (November 2011), pp. 751–72.

Simpson, Bradley R., *Economists with Guns: Authoritarian Development and U.S.–Indonesian Relations, 1960–1968* (Stanford, CA: Stanford University Press, 2008).

Sklar, Martin J., 'The open door, imperialism, and postimperialism: origins of U.S. twentieth-century foreign relations, circa 1900,' in David G. Becker and Richard L. Sklar (eds), *Postimperialism and World Politics* (Westport, CT: Praeger, 1999), pp. 317–36.

Smith, Kathlin, 'The role of scientists in normalizing U.S.–China relations: 1965–1979,' *Annals of the New York Academy of Social Scientists*, 866 (December 1998), pp. 114–36.

Smith, Tony and Leone, Richard C., *America's Mission: The United States and the Worldwide Struggle for Democracy in the Twentieth Century* (Princeton, NJ: Princeton University Press, 1994).

Southworth, David B., 'Building a business school in China: the case of China Europe International Business School (CEIBS),' *Education and Training*, 41: 6/7 (1999), pp. 325–30.

Stead, W. T., *The Americanization of the World, or, the Trend of the Twentieth Century* (New York: H. Markley, 1902).

Steele, A. T., *The American People and China* (New York: McGraw-Hill, 1966).

Stiglitz, Joseph, *Globalization and Its Discontents* (New York: W. W. Norton, 2002).

Stiles, Kendall W., 'Grassroots empowerment: states, non-state actors and global policy formation,' in Richard A. Higgott, Geoffrey R.D. Underhill and Andreas Bieler (eds), *Non-State Actors and Authority in the Global System* (New York: Routledge, 2000), pp. 32–47.

Stone, Richard, 'Trans-Pacific alliance draws up ecology plan,' *Science*, 272 (31 May 1996), p. 1260.

Strebeigh, Fred, 'Training China's new elite,' *Atlantic Monthly*, 263: 4 (April 1989), pp. 72, 74.

Stross, Randall E., *Bulls in the China Shop: And Other Sino-American Business Encounters* (New York: Pantheon Books, 1990).

Stross, Randall E., *Stubborn Earth: American Agriculturalists on Chinese Soil, 1898–1937* (Berkeley, CA: University of California Press, 1986).

Sun, Marjorie, 'U.S.-Chinese scientists see dreams imperiled,' *Science*, 244 (9 June 1989), pp. 1131–2.

A Sustainable Land Use and Allocation Program for the Ussuri/Wusuli River Watershed and Adjacent Territories (Northeastern China and the Russian Far East) (Elizabethtown, NY: Ecologically Sustainable Development, 1996).

Sutter, Robert, 'A research note: China's Rise and US leadership in Asia – growing maturity and balance,' *Journal of Contemporary China*, 19 (June 2010), pp. 591–604.

Sutter, Robert G., *The China Quandary: Domestic Determinants of U.S. China Policy, 1972–1982* (Boulder, CO: Westview Press, 1983).

Sutter, Robert G., *U.S.–Chinese Relations: Perilous Past, Pragmatic Present* (Lanham, MD: Rowman & Littlefield, 2010).

Tan, Qingshan, 'Foreign NGOs' role in local governance in China,' in Zheng Yongnian and Joseph Fewsmith (eds), *China's Opening Society: The Non-State Sector and Governance* (London: Routledge, 2008), pp. 196–222.

Tan, Zhen, 'Internationalization of higher education in China: Chinese–foreign cooperation in running schools and the introduction of high-quality foreign educational resources,' *International Education Studies*, 2: 3 (August 2009), pp. 166–71.

Thomson, James C. Jr, *While China Faced West: American Reformers in Nationalist China, 1928–1937* (Cambridge, MA: Harvard University Press, 1969).

Tong, Caroline Haiyan and Wang, Hongying, 'Sino-American educational exchanges and public administration reforms in China: a study of norm diffusion,' in Cheng Li (ed.), *Bridging Minds Across the Pacific: U.S.–China Educational Exchanges, 1978–2003* (Lanham, MD: Lexington Books, 2005), pp. 155–75.

Turner, Jennifer L., 'Small government, big and green society: emerging partnerships to solve China's environmental problems,' *Harvard Asia Quarterly*, 8: 2 (Spring 2004), pp. 4–13.

Unger, Jonathan and Chan, Anita, 'Associations in a bind: the emergence of political corporatism,' in Jonathan Unger (ed.), *Associations and the Chinese State: Contested Spaces* (Armonk, NY: M. E. Sharpe, 2008), pp. 48–68.

Union of International Associations, *Yearbook of International Organizations 1999/2000* (Munich: K. G. Saur, 1999).

Union of International Associations, *Yearbook of International Organizations 2008/2009*, Vol. 4 (Munich: K. G. Saur, 2008).

Viederman, Daniel A. [identified in a misprint as Gordon Claridge], 'Wetlands conservation in China: action planning,' *China Review: Magazine of the Great Britain-China Centre* #7 (Summer 1997).

Vogel, Ezra F., *Deng Xiaoping and the Transformation of China* (Cambridge, MA: Harvard University Press, 2011).

Von Eschen, Penny M., *Satchmo Blows Up the World: Jazz Ambassadors Play the Cold War* (Cambridge, MA: Harvard University Press, 2004).

Wang, Chaogang (ed.), *China: Country Gender Review* (New York: East Asia Environment & Social Development Unit, World Bank, June 2002).

Wang, Dong, *Managing God's Higher Learning: U.S.–China Cultural Encounter and Canton Christian College (*Lingnan University), 1888–1952 (Lanham, MD: Lexington Books, 2007).

Wang, Fei-Ling, 'Balancing the cross-Pacific exchange: American study-abroad programs in the PRC,' in Cheng Li (ed.), *Bridging Minds Across the Pacific: U.S.–China Educational Exchanges, 1978–2003* (Lanham, MD: Lexington Books, 2005), pp. 177–200.

Wang, Li, 'Higher education governance and university autonomy in China,' *Globalization, Societies and Education*, 8: 4 (November 2010), pp. 477–95.

Wang, Ming, 'Foreword,' *China Nonprofit Review*, 1: 1 (2009), pp. 1–3.

Wang, Shaoguang and He, Jianyu, 'Associational revolution in China: mapping the landscapes,' *Korea Observer*, 35: 3 (Autumn 2004), pp. 485–533.

Wang, Shaoguang and Hu, Angang, *The Chinese Economy in Crisis: State Capacity and Tax Reform* (Armonk, NY: M. E. Sharpe, 2001).

Wang, Valerie, 'Not one less (*Yige dou bu neng shao*),' *Cinemaya*, 45 (1999), pp. 20–1.

Wang, Zuoyue, 'Chinese American scientists and U.S.–China scientific relations,' in Peter H. Koehn and Xiao-huang Yin (eds), *The Expanding Roles of Chinese Americans in U.S.–China Relations: Transnational Networks and Trans-Pacific Interactions* (Armonk, NY: M. E. Sharpe, 2002), pp. 207–34.

Watson, Andrew, 'Civil society in a transitional state: the rise of associations in China,' in Jonathan Unger (ed.), *Associations and the Chinese State: Contested Spaces* (Armonk, NY: M. E. Sharpe, 2008), pp. 14–47.

West, Philip, *Yenching University and Sino-Western Relations, 1916–1952* (Cambridge: Harvard University Press, 1976), pp. 195–214.

Wheeler, Norton, 'A civic trend within ethnic transnationalism? Some insights from classical social theory and the Chinese American experience,' *Global Networks*, 4: 4 (October 2004), pp. 391–408.

Wheeler, Norton, 'Bridging the Pacific: The 1990 Institute and Transnationalism in Late-20th Century U.S.–China Relations' (MA thesis, University of Kansas, May 2002).

Wheeler, Norton, 'Cross-lingual oral history interviewing: confronting the methodological challenges,' *Oral History*, 36: 1 (2008), pp. 82–94.

Wheeler, Norton, 'Improving mainland society and U.S.–China relations: a case study of four Chinese American-led transnational associations,' in Peter H. Koehn and Xiao-huang Yin (eds), *The Expanding Roles of Chinese Americans in U.S.–China Relations: Transnational Networks and Trans-Pacific Interactions* (Armonk, NY: M. E. Sharpe, 2002), pp. 185–206.

Wheeler, Norton, 'Modernization discourse with Chinese characteristics,' *East Asia: An International Quarterly*, 22: 3 (Winter 2005), pp. 3–24.

White, Gordon, Howell, Jude, and Shang, Xiaoyuan, *In Search of Civil Society: Market Reform and Social Change in Contemporary China* (Oxford: Clarendon Press, 1996).

Wong, Christine, *Can China Change Development Paradigm for the 21st Century? Fiscal Policy Options for Hu Jintao and Wen Jiabao After Two Decades of Muddling Through*, Working Paper FG 7, Research Unit Asia, German Institute for International and Security Affairs, April 2005, http://www.swp-berlin.org/common/get_document.php?id=1248 (accessed 5 September 2005).

Wong, Christine P. W. and Bird, Richard M., 'China's fiscal system: a work in progress,' in Loren Brandt and Thomas G. Rawski (eds), *China's Great Economic Transformation* (New York: Cambridge University Press, 2008), pp. 429–66.

Wright, Daniel B., *The Promise of Revolution: Stories of Fulfillment and Struggle in China's Hinterland* (Lanham, MD: Rowman & Littlefield, 2003).

Wu, Baiyi, 'Chinese crisis management during the 1999 Embassy bombing incident,' in Michael D. Swaine and Zhang Tuosheng (eds), *Managing Sino-American Crises: Case Studies and Analysis* (Washington, DC: Carnegie Endowment for International Peace, 2006), pp. 351–75.

Wu, Fengshi, 'Double Mobilization: Transnational Advocacy Networks for China's Environment and Public Health' (PhD dissertation, University of Maryland, 2005).

Wu, Fengshi, 'Environmental GONGO autonomy: unintended consequences of state strategies in China,' *Good Society*, 12: 1 (2003), pp. 35–45.

Xu, Gang Gary, 'The pedagogical as the political: ideology of globalization and Zhang Yimou's *Not One Less*,' *Communication Review*, 6: 4 (2003), pp. 327–39.

Xu, Guangqiu, 'Anti-Western nationalism in China, 1989–99,' *World Affairs*, 163: 4 (Spring 2001), pp. 151–62.

Xu, Guangqiu, 'The ideological and political impact of U.S. Fulbrighters on Chinese students: 1979–1989,' *Asian Affairs: An American Quarterly*, 26: 3 (Fall 1999), pp. 139–57.

Xu, Guoqi, *Olympic Dreams: China and Sports 1895–2008* (Cambridge, MA: Harvard University Press, 2008).

Xue, Julia, 'Enabling China to enter the 21st century: Chinese-American scholar and entrepreneur C. B. Sung,' in *Chinese in the World: Brief Biographies of the Chinese Entrepreneurs*, Vol. 2 (Beijing: Editorial Committee of the Chinese Entrepreneurs All Over the World, 1994), pp. 159–76.

Yahuda, Michael, *Towards the End of Isolationism: China's Foreign Policy After Mao* (New York: St. Martin's Press, 1983).

Yamamoto, Tadashi, 'Integrative report,' in Yamamoto (ed.), *Emerging Civil Society in the Asia Pacific Community: Nongovernmental Underpinnings of the Emerging Asia Pacific Regional Community* (Singapore and Tokyo: Institute of Southeast Asian Studies and Japan Center for International Exchange, 1995), pp. 1–40.

Yang, Rui, Vidovich, Lesley, and Currie, Jan, '"Dancing in a cage": changing autonomy in Chinese higher education,' *Higher Education*, 54: 4 (2007), pp. 575–92.

Yang, Winston L. Y., 'Tiananmen and its impact,', in Winston L. Y. Yang and Marsha L. Wagner (eds), *Tiananmen: China's Struggle for Democracy: Its Prelude, Development, Aftermath, and Impact* (Baltimore, MD: School of Law, University of Maryland, 1990), pp. 263–90.

Ye, Weili, *Seeking Modernity in China's Name: Chinese Students in the United States, 1900–1927* (Stanford, CA: Stanford University Press, 2001).

Ye, Zhang, *China's Emerging Civil Society*, Brookings Institution, Center for Northeast Asian Policy Studies, June 2003.

Yin, Xiao-huang and Lan, Zhiyong, 'Chinese Americans: a rising factor in U.S.–China relations,' *Journal of American–East Asian Relations*, 6: 1 (1997), pp. 35–57.

Yip, Ngai-Ming and Jiang, Yihong, 'Homeowners united: the attempt to create lateral networks of homeowners' associations in urban China,' *Journal of Contemporary China*, 20 (November 2011), pp. 735–50.

Young, Nick, 'Introduction: NGOs: the diverse origins, changing nature and growing internationalisation of the species,' in *200 International NGOs in China* (Beijing: China Development Brief, January 2005), pp. 9–39.

Young, Nick (ed.), *Civil Society in the Making: 250 Chinese NGOs* (Beijing: China Development Brief, August 2001).

Young, Nick and MacRae, Pia, 'Three "C"s: civil society, corporate responsibility, and China,' *China Business Review*, 29: 1 (January–February 2002), pp. 34–8.

Yu, Keping, *Democracy Is a Good Thing: Essays on Politics, Society, and Culture in Contemporary China* (Washington, DC: Brookings Institution Press, 2008).

Yu, Renqiu, *To Save China, To Save Ourselves: The Chinese Hand Laundry Alliance of New York* (Philadelphia, PA: Temple University Press, 1992).

Yu, Yuegen, 'The Bond of An Enduring Relationship: United States–China Scientific Relations, 1949–1989' (PhD dissertation, West Virginia University, 1999), pp. 255–63.

Zhang, Yufa, 'Returned Chinese students from America and the Chinese leadership (1846–1949),' *Chinese Studies in History*, 35: 3 (Spring 2002), pp. 52–86.

Zheng, Bijian, 'China's "peaceful rise" to great power status,' *Foreign Affairs*, 84: 5 (September–October 2005), pp. 18–24.

Zhong, Ningsha and Hayhoe, Ruth, 'University autonomy in twentieth-century China,' in Glen Peterson, Ruth Hayhoe, and Yongling Lu (eds), *Education, Culture, and Identity in Twentieth-Century China* (Ann Arbor, MI: University of Michigan Press, 2001), pp. 265–96.

Zi, Zhongyun, 'A multidimensional approach to Sino-U.S. relations,' in Richard H. Holton and Wang Xi (eds), *U.S.-China Economic Relations: Present and Future* (Berkeley, CA: Institute of East Asian Studies, University of California, 1989), pp. 12–16.

Zweig, David, *Internationalizing China: Domestic Interests and Global Linkages* (Ithaca, NY: Cornell University Press, 2002).

Zweig, David and Rosen, Stanley, *China's Brain Drain to the United States: Views of Overseas Chinese Students and Scholars in the 1990s* (Berkeley, CA: Institute of East Asian Studies, University of California Press, 1995).

Index

Printed in the USA/Agawam, MA
April 16, 2014

588038.063